Hoover's FBI

....

The Inside Story by
Hoover's Trusted Lieutenant

Hoover's FBI

The Inside Story by Hoover's Trusted Lieutenant

Cartha "Deke" DeLoach

Regnery Publishing, Inc.
Washington, D.C.

Library of Congress Cataloging-in-Publication Data

DeLoach, Cartha, 1920-
    Hoover's FBI / Cartha "Deke" DeLoach.
        p.   cm.
    Includes index.
    ISBN 0-89526-479-X
    1. United States. Federal Bureau of Investigation. 2. Hoover, J.
Edgar (John Edgar), 1895-1972.   I. Title
HV8138.D34 1995
353.0074--dc20   95-16230
                                                                CIP

Published in the United States by
Regnery Publishing, Inc.
An Eagle Publishing Company
422 First Street, SE, Suite 300
Washington, DC 20003

Distributed to the trade by
National Book Network
4720-A Boston Way
Lanham, MD 20706

Printed on acid-free paper.
Manufactured in the United States of America

10 9 8 7 6 5 4 3 2

Books are available in quantity for promotional or premium use. Write to Director of Special Sales, Regnery Publishing, Inc., 422 First Street, SE, Suite 300, Washington, DC 20003, for information on discounts and terms or call (202) 546-5005.

To the Eight: my wife, Barbara, and children, Barbie, Deke Jr., Tom, Theresa, Greg, Sharon, and Mark.

Their love, affection, and many sacrifices have made the years spent in writing this book all worthwhile.

Contents

Hoover's FBI

1

....

Hoover's FBI

SHORTLY AFTER THE DEATH of President John Kennedy, I became the official FBI liaison to President Lyndon Johnson. I was given this assignment because of my position as third in command in the FBI, second only to Hoover's old friend, Clyde Tolson. Within a few months I began to realize just how far LBJ was willing to go to use the FBI for his own political purposes.

The 1964 Democratic Convention was to be held in Atlantic City, New Jersey, late in August of that year. Everyone knew that Lyndon Johnson would be the party's nominee and that he would probably win the general election. As a consequence, the bureau's prevailing philosophy was to please the president by helping him in every way possible within the legal limits of our mission. This was not unusual. Virtually every president since the founding of the bureau has been able to count on a courteous and friendly hand from an agency that is, after all, under his command—through the attorney general—and dependent on his favor. But Johnson, a man I admired then and now, wanted more.

On August 1st, I was on the telephone when my secretary, Fran

Lurz, interrupted to tell me that the White House was on the line. It was Walter Jenkins, the President's Chief of Staff.

"Deke," he said, "the president is very concerned about his personal safety and that of his staff while they're at the convention. Would you head a team to keep us advised of any potential threats? We want to make sure the president is safe and... *that there aren't any disruptions at the convention.*"

The emphasis is mine. Jenkins spoke as neutrally as possible, as if to suggest that the last portion of the request was just an afterthought, a natural extension of his concern for the president's safety. But I knew Jenkins, and I knew Lyndon Johnson, and I knew that was not what the phone call was about.

There is an entire federal service dedicated almost exclusively to the protection of the president—the Secret Service. We have always cooperated with them in helping to identify potential threats to the president. But until after the assassination of JFK a few months before, murdering a president had not even been a federal crime and so was not under our jurisdiction. Only with the greatest difficulty had the FBI been able to take charge of that investigation.

The law was then changed, and conceivably that change authorized us to take a more active role in guarding the president, though that would be stretching it a bit. Under its charter, the FBI is an investigative, not an operational agency. We are not a national police force. Ninety percent of what police do is outside our charter. We do not do crowd control, we are not available for guard duty, we do not make decisions to prosecute nor, in most cases, to arrest. In fact, we make few arrests compared to our volume of investigations. We are investigators.

Protection, of course, was not what Johnson wanted. He wanted a showcase convention, no "incidents," no angry demonstrators on TV, no pictures of police cracking the heads of civil rights protestors, pictures that could upset LBJ's liberal and black supporters and persuade Southern conservatives that the country was falling apart. In other words, he didn't want what happened to Hubert Humphrey and the Democrats in Chicago four years later. He wanted us to prevent such a political disaster.

I didn't like the sound of it.

"Let me check with the director and get back to you," I said.

First—as always—I went to Tolson. He passed me along to Hoover without comment. Those were dangerous waters, and Tolson wasn't about to wet his big toe, much less dive in head first. When I told Hoover what Jenkins wanted, he blinked, then wagged his head in disapproval.

"Lyndon is way out of line," he grunted.

"Should I just tell him we can't do it, that it's beyond the limits of our mission?"

Hoover sat for a moment, brooding. A master bureaucrat, he had often been able to circumvent what had been his biggest headache over the years—politicians who wanted to turn the FBI into their personal political goon squad. That was exactly what the department had been on its way to becoming when Hoover had been appointed to reform it decades before. But the same bureaucratic instincts also told him when he was trapped. Jenkins had been careful to phrase the request under the cover of a legal and imperative duty: to protect the president. Only a few months before, Hoover's beloved agency had been bitterly criticized for failing to stop Lee Harvey Oswald, a man whose bizarre history the bureau had in its files, from assassinating JFK. If Hoover did not cooperate now, and, heaven forbid, anything happened, the bureau could be destroyed in the crossfire. Certainly it would be the end of Hoover's career. LBJ wasn't a bad bureaucratic infighter himself.

"No, I guess not," Hoover replied. "Tell Walter we'll give him whatever help he wants."

We selected a team of seasoned agents who could handle an assignment involving masses of people, agents level-headed enough to remain calm in a crowd, whatever the provocation. The hours would be long and pressure-packed. Most of the agents—based in Washington, Newark, and Atlantic City—were familiar with the dissident groups most likely to cause trouble and were trained to detect hot spots before a fire broke out.

Because the White House had called for our involvement at the last minute, we had to work day and night to plan our strategy, leaving many heavy case loads in abeyance. First, we compiled all available background data on the organizations most likely to cause disruptions and developed profiles of their leadership. We then prepared blind memoranda so that prompt reports could be sent to the White House staff should any of these groups or leaders begin to stir up trouble.

The group that most concerned the White House staff was a black civil rights group, the militant wing of the Mississippi Freedom Democratic Party (MFDP), composed largely of black political activists. The MFDP as a group had challenged the right of the regular Mississippi delegation to represent Mississippi at the convention, arguing that the MFDP group should be recognized instead. There may have been some substance to their claim, but the credentials committee had ruled in favor of the regulars. The White House suspected that this militant group would try to occupy the convention seats of the regular Mississippi delegation, causing at best a scuffle and at worst a riot on the convention floor. Jenkins wanted full reports on the MFDP chairman, Dr. Aron Henry, and an emerging leader, Robert Moses, as well as on the MFDP as a group.

In addition to gathering background data on the MFDP, we also compiled thumbnail sketches of Communist party groups, known hoodlums who frequented the area, compulsive thieves, and others who could be counted on to show up at the convention and make trouble.

By the time the convention was scheduled to open, we were ready. On Sunday afternoon, August 23rd, our advance party left for Atlantic City, with the remainder to report by 5:00 P.M. that afternoon. When we got to Atlantic City, we established liaison with the Secret Service, the Atlantic City Police Department, the New Jersey Highway Patrol, and the White House staff members managing the convention. Our headquarters was in one small wing of a building that formerly housed the Atlantic City Post Office.

In talking to White House staff members, I realized they were expecting a glitch-free convention, largely because of our presence. It was Lyndon Johnson's absolute faith in the FBI that generated such expectations, and that worried me.

The president's right-hand men in Atlantic City were Walter
Jenkins, Cliff Carter, and Bill Moyers, later of PBS fame. One of our
first tasks was to coach them on effective measures to prevent a
"stall-in" demonstration planned by Dick Gregory, the black come-
dian, who had a bone to pick with the Democrats. We also recommended major improvements in procedures for controlling admission to the convention hall. Carter and Moyers were particularly
concerned that we gather all possible intelligence on the Mississippi Freedom Democratic Party and their plans.

In 1964, the networks featured gavel-to-gavel coverage of the
national political conventions; and during the daytime, when little
of significance was occurring in the center ring, reporters were
always interested in controversial sideshows. They often gave air
time to all sorts of marginal groups that would be ignored in convention coverage today. Any activist with the price of a ticket to
Atlantic City had a good chance of getting on the tube and airing
his complaints to the huge television audience watching the convention. And several groups had laid careful plans to assure coverage of their respective agendas.

With this scenario in mind, our assignment—which came directly
from Walter Jenkins, Bill Moyers, and Cliff Carter—was to keep up
with the activities of these people around the clock. Given the
growing militancy, particularly among the black civil rights organizations, it was a tall order. Messrs. Jenkins, Moyers, and Carter
were particularly interested in suppressing dissent from black
groups, since the Democrats were counting on a large voter turnout
in the black community to defeat Senator Barry Goldwater, the
expected Republican nominee.

To keep abreast of all serious disruptive plans and activities, we
carefully disbursed our contingent of FBI operatives: ten informants
(who operated under code numbers) from two nearby bureau
offices, two agents working in an undercover capacity, four black
informants associated with our Newark office, eighteen established
information sources in the Atlantic City area, one Nation of Islam
informant, and two Atlantic City security informants.

The late Julius Hobson—then a leader of the black community

in the District of Columbia and a paid FBI informant—traveled to Atlantic City to offer his help and was accepted immediately into the inner planning circle of the militants. Another informant was actually the leader of the Progressive Labor Movement in Atlantic City. And a third informant succeeded in getting an assignment as a chauffeur for leaders of SNCC (Student Nonviolent Coordinating Committee) and CORE (Congress of Racial Equality).

Our team met every morning at 8:30 for strategy sessions. After one of those sessions, a black agent came to me with a problem.

"There's a leader in this group, a woman, and she's willing to tell me everything. But... well... she says she'll only do her talking in bed. What should I do?"

"You're on your own," I said. "I'm not about to give you any advice."

The next morning he gave us a detailed account of the group's plans. At the conclusion of his briefing, he said to me privately, "Believe me, it's not always wise to place duty over discretion."

Our black agents were particularly challenged. Highly trained, they successfully penetrated the headquarters of the MFDP at the Gem Hotel and infiltrated the group's strategy meetings, held in the basement of the Union Baptist Temple. One agent developed such a close relationship with Dick Gregory that the entertainer-turned-activist revealed to him in advance all his plans for inciting various groups to racial violence.

With Justice Department authorization, we tapped the phones at CORE/SNCC headquarters, and learned that CORE and SNCC leaders were making plans to acquire uniforms of Young Citizens for Johnson and use them to gain entrance to the convention hall. Tipped off beforehand, we were able to thwart their plan and avoid a disturbance on the convention floor during prime time.

We also picked up a number of orders to disrupt the convention, and in some instances they explicitly called for violence. One CORE leader said, for instance, "While I don't want any killing, I don't mind if some people get a little scorched or roughed up."

We issued walkie-talkies to Jenkins and Moyers so they could keep in constant touch with the 250-watt transmitter and receiver at our command post. One evening, a group from the MFDP successfully infiltrated the convention hall and seated themselves in the section assigned to the Mississippi delegation. When valid members of the delegation asked the interlopers to leave, they refused. Moyers, frantic, called me on his two-way radio:

"Deke," he shouted, "get some agents in here fast and move these intruders out!"

"I'm sorry, Bill," I said, "but that's going too far. The FBI simply can't haul people out of the convention—whether or not they belong here."

Moyers was furious, but he finally got the message that we were not to be turned into a glorified goon squad for the Democratic party. At that point I was convinced that we were wrong to have accepted the assignment in the first place. Moyers and the rest of the president's staff had come to regard us as their own private security force, which they felt free to deploy in a partisan political struggle. At best, it was demeaning; at worst, it was a serious breach of the law.

Yes, there were arguments on the other side as well. Some unruly demonstrations and confrontations broke out at or outside the convention and these led to legitimate arrests and federal indictments. Emotions were running high, and any incident, however trivial, could have escalated into a bloody riot, endangering the president and his cabinet. At the beginning of his administration, the president had ordered us to assist the Secret Service in protecting him. In this case, we were carrying out that order. But, in the end, the line between national security and political activism had been blurred. We felt we had been compromised. At that point I resolved never to be used again in that fashion. But I found it was a resolution I could not keep.

We didn't give in every time, however. Whenever Hoover thought he could win a game of chicken with LBJ—on any matter affecting the honor and reputation of the bureau—he'd press the pedal to the floor. In the late summer of 1964, shortly after Barry Goldwater had won the Republican presidential nomination, Walter Jenkins asked me to come to the White House and talk over a matter he didn't want to discuss on the telephone. When I heard what he had to say, I understood why.

"We want whatever information you have in your files on Barry Goldwater's staff. Not just his senatorial staff, but his campaign staff as well."

"Why?" I asked him, as innocently as I knew how.

He shrugged his shoulders and smiled.

"The Boss wants to know who he's up against."

I raised my eyebrows.

"I'll see what we've got and let you know."

I went back over to FBI headquarters and asked to see the director. When I told him about Jenkins's request, he was clearly upset.

"This is going too far," he said. "The operation in Atlantic City involved a potential national security matter, even though we knew what the White House wanted from us. But this is pure politics."

"No doubt about it," I said.

Hoover shook his head.

"We can't do it."

I nodded in agreement.

"Why don't we just tell them we don't have any of Goldwater's staff in our files?" I suggested.

Hoover agreed, and after a day or two I called Walter and told him we'd drawn a blank. He thanked me for checking and said he'd pass the information along to the president. I waited for a call from Johnson himself, but it never came. Maybe he believed me, or maybe with the election all but in the bag he just didn't want to push Hoover too far.

The popular myth, fostered of late by would-be historians and sensationalists with their eyes on the bestseller list, has it that in his day J. Edgar Hoover all but ran Washington, using dirty tricks to intimidate congressmen and presidents, and phone taps, bugs, and informants to build secret files with which to blackmail lawmakers. This is the picture most often drawn today of Hoover's FBI. That was not the FBI I knew.

As assistant to the director—the number three man at the bureau—it was my job to deal with Congress and with the president.

Far from telling them what to do, I had to struggle constantly to keep them from abusing the powers of the FBI. And Hoover made my life easier; he was jealous of the bureau's powers and reputation and did not easily acquiesce to the political machinations suggested by even the most powerful of leaders. If one great story about the FBI in Hoover's day remains untold, it is that a titanic war was being waged over whether the FBI would be turned into a partisan national police department. And in almost every case the man defending the Constitution and trying to limit the powers of the bureau was J. Edgar Hoover, and the people trying to politicize the bureau were the politicians—from moderate conservatives such as Richard Nixon to liberal icons such as Bobby Kennedy (who as attorney general never saw a wiretap he didn't like), and of course LBJ.

Hoover and the bureau often lost these struggles. When the president of the United States gives the FBI a direct order, and defines the task at hand as a matter of national security, there is not much to do but obey. But that the bureau was as insulated as possible from politics was due largely to one man—Hoover himself. Hoover's virtues kept the FBI clean—and so did his vices. He was for most of his life personally incorruptible, though in later years his confidence in his own incorruptibility led him occasionally into ethical compromises; and he was an old-fashioned political conservative who truly believed in limited government.

He was also a man of monstrous ego. And because his own identity had so merged with the agency he had created, that ego served to protect his beloved bureau from anything he perceived as a threat—including any expansion of its powers that might ultimately endanger the bureau's reputation or, for most of his reign, its enormous popularity. Like MacArthur in Japan during the occupation, Hoover made himself a demigod. But he used his semidivine status not for personal gain but to protect the bureau the only way he knew how—by keeping his personal power over the FBI unquestioned and unquestionable.

During the Hoover years, the FBI was headquartered with the rest of the Justice Department in a grim granite building on Constitution Avenue. Our offices were crowded, the larger rooms subdivided into cubicles by glass or steel partitions. Some cubicles were occupied by as many as four agents and four secretaries. There were no luxuries and little privacy.

Even Mr. Hoover's office was unpretentious. To see him, you walked down the hallway through a large conference room and then into his modest office. Furnished with a couple of old over-stuffed chairs and a sofa, the office reflected the austerity of his life—its narrow limits, its stern rejection of frivolity. Over the door hung a sailfish he'd caught on one of his brief outings.

When you entered the door, the ritual was always the same. He would leap up from his desk and come to meet you at the center of the room. He would shake hands, offer you a seat to the right, and then return to his desk. On that desk, about a foot from his left elbow, lay a worn, black Bible—a gift from his mother. The Bible was more than a prop. It was a modest but deliberate statement—one that few people who knew him failed to recognize and honor.

The desk stood on a dais, and when you sat in your chair, he stared down at you like Louis XIV on the throne of France. With a tall window behind him, the sunlight would often slant through the blinds and dazzle you as you stared up at his solemn, bulldog face. The arrangement was intimidating, and no doubt he planned it that way.

Even when I was assistant to the director, I never just strolled into Mr. Hoover's office uninvited. Either he would summon me or I would make an appointment through his secretary, Helen Gandy. During that period, he would call and send me memos daily; but response to these memos didn't usually require a face-to-face meeting. He kept his distance and expected his subordinates to do likewise. Calls and memos were familiarity enough.

But he was by no means thoughtless or unfeeling. In some ways he was like a father to me, though an old-fashioned father, the kind who kept his feelings to himself. He didn't go in for pats on the arm or back, nor was he quick to praise accomplishment. He expected everyone to perform well, and when they met those expectations, he did little more than nod in silent approval—and more often than not he didn't even nod. When he went out of his way to congratulate you for a job well-done, your world lit up.

On the other hand, he was capable of genuine thoughtfulness.

He often asked about my wife and children, and always listened carefully as I reported on progress in school or repeated some anecdote. He was also solicitous of my health and would notice when I was tired or under great strain. Not that he would lighten my load, but he would at least let me know that he was aware of the burden.

And though slow to praise, he was generous in awarding cash bonuses for good work. When I was a young agent raising a growing family on barely adequate wages, an extra $200 check in my envelope meant being able to pay off a worrisome bill or indulge in some small but rare luxury. I realized eventually that Mr. Hoover was really a shy man who found some words difficult to say and could better communicate with cash. But if you tried to thank him for the commendatory bonus, he would wave your thanks aside and proceed to the business at hand. And he preferred a curt telephone call to a visit.

When the calls and memos stopped for two or three days, you knew you were in trouble. I recognized the signs immediately, but always hesitated to ask why. Then his secretary, Helen Gandy, would prod me.

"Don't you think you should apologize to Mr. Hoover?" she'd say.

"For what?" I'd ask.

"I don't know, but obviously for something."

I'd nod and sigh.

"All right. Make an appointment for me."

Then I'd go back to my office, stare at the wall, and try to figure out what I'd done to make him mad. Was it something I'd said to a newspaper reporter? Did the press give me too much credit for a recent operation? Had I neglected to keep him sufficiently informed about an ongoing investigation?

When the time came for my appointment, I'd enter the room like Dorothy confronting the Great and Powerful Oz. Mr. Hoover would come around the desk, shake hands in the same cordial way, and then sit down behind his desk, an expectant look on his face.

"I want to apologize," I'd say. "If I've offended you in any way, I can assure you it was unintentional."

"What makes you think you've offended me?" he'd say, eyebrows arched in surprise.

"Well, Miss Gandy..."

"That old biddy," he'd say. "Don't pay any attention to her."

And that would be the end of it. He'd change the subject and we'd talk about the business of the bureau. I was never quite sure why I'd been disciplined, but the punishment was certainly effective. I could always think of half a dozen things I'd done wrong, and I made every effort to amend my life by staying out of the limelight and making my reports more frequent and detailed. When I walked out of the office, as light-headed as a boy after his first confession, Miss Gandy would smile and nod approvingly.

In Hoover's office there were no pictures of presidents with fading inscriptions that read "to Edgar, with affection," no posed shots in the Oval Office, no White House mementos. Hoover had seen presidents come and go, and he knew their worst secrets. The closest thing to the standard Washington trophy photo was the proclamation, signed by Lyndon Johnson, waiving mandatory retirement age and allowing Hoover to continue as director after he turned seventy. But even that proclamation was hung in the conference room *outside* his door. The only official portrait space inside the office was reserved for Harlan Fiske Stone, whose picture hung in Hoover's inner sanctum. It was Stone who, as attorney general, had recommended him to be director of the FBI. Hoover owed Stone, and he never forgot it.

When Stone became attorney general in April of 1924, it could have been bad news for the young Hoover's career. A Justice Department lawyer since 1917, Hoover had been appointed head of the department's General Intelligence Division (GID) when it was established in 1919 by Attorney General A. Mitchell Palmer. The Red Raids, as they were called, led by Palmer's Justice Department against communists, anarchists, and agitators, had been justified in large part after the fact by relying on the comprehensive files—listing seditious individuals and their activities—that had been compiled by Hoover and his GID. Palmer was severely criticized for the raids by many who complained that the roundups had violated the civil rights of hundreds if not thousands of people. And Harlan Fiske Stone—once dean of the Columbia Law School—was one of Palmer's most vocal detractors. The locus of many of the department's abuses had been the smallish Bureau of Investigation—started in 1908, but not yet called the FBI. Stone complained that the bureau had an "exceedingly bad odor" and within a month forced its chief, William J. Burns, to resign. The GID was part of the bureau, and many believed that Hoover virtually ran the bureau for Burns.

Stone, however, did not toss Hoover out with Burns. Hoover had earned a number of recommendations that were forwarded to the new attorney general, including the support of then-Commerce Secretary Herbert Hoover (no relation—the future president had an assistant who was a friend of J. Edgar's). Stone wanted to reform the bureau—which had been a dumping ground for political hacks who used their patronage jobs as investigators to harass and intimidate political enemies—and he came to see in Hoover a man of like mind.

"There is always the possibility that a secret police may become a menace to free governments and free institutions because it carries with it the possibility of abuses of power that are not always quickly apprehended or understood," Stone announced on the day he ousted Burns. The Bureau of Investigation is "a necessary instrument of law enforcement. But it is important that its activities be strictly limited to the performance of those functions for which it was created and that its agents themselves be not above the law or beyond its reach." Stone concluded that the "Bureau of Investigation is not concerned with political or other opinions of individuals. It is concerned only with their conduct and then only with such conduct as is forbidden by the laws of the United States. When a police system passes beyond these limits, it is dangerous to the proper administration of justice and to human liberty, which it should be our first concern to cherish."

Hoover assured Stone that he shared the new attorney general's worries, and that he would only take the job—an interim appointment to replace Burns—if he could professionalize the outfit, get rid of the hacks, and grant promotions only on the basis of "proven ability." Hoover moved quickly to carry out the detailed instructions Stone gave him to reorder the bureau. He fired the political hacks, known as "dollar-a-year men,"an action later referred to in the bureau as the "great purge." Hoover's quick action convinced

Stone that Hoover was serious about reforming the bureau, and he kept him on the job. Hoover stuck to Stone's principles throughout his career, and in many ways the bureau that Hoover remade was a product of Stone.

The emphasis on strict demarcations of the bureau's authority was key to Hoover's vision of the bureau, but it somehow led to perpetual confusion over the role of the FBI, a confusion that caused problems for me when I dealt with politicians as assistant director of the FBI, and a confusion that persists to this day.

Late in July of 1966, for example, Congressman John Dingell, a Michigan Democrat, called me at my office. From the moment he began to talk, I knew he was highly agitated. He spoke in staccato sentences and repeated himself. The story he told was disturbing. Someone had called him several times and threatened his life, apparently because he had supported civil rights legislation. He told me that his wife and children were back in Dearborn, waiting to hear that they were being placed under FBI protection.

"I want you to get there," he said, "and goddamned quick."

I understood his concern. I would have felt the same way myself. But I had to tell him that despite the seriousness of the situation the FBI had no authority to provide either him or his family with guards.

"We'll be happy to investigate this matter," I told him, "but we can't protect you and your family."

In deliberately measured words he said, "Would you repeat that?"

I told him once again that we would investigate the threats but that we had no authority to offer protection to members of Congress or their families.

"If something happens to my wife and family, I'll hold you personally responsible. And if you won't assign some protection, I'll call Hoover and get it!"

"You're certainly free to call the director if you want," I told him, "but I'm sure he'll tell you the same thing."

I didn't mention that if he tried to contact J. Edgar Hoover, his call would be transferred right back to me.

"Then I'll call the attorney general," he shouted.

"Believe me, I understand," I said. "But the Department of Justice established this policy in the first place. We're all bound by it. Look, why don't you call the local police?"

"I don't have any confidence in them," he said, a little calmer now. "I want the FBI."

"I'm sorry that we can't offer you the kind of help you want, but I will call our Detroit office as soon as we hang up and ask the special agent in charge to look into the matter immediately."

He seemed less angry when he hung up, but he was still an unhappy man. I immediately called Paul Stoddard, our special agent in charge (SAC) at the Detroit Office.

"He ought to contact the Dearborn police," Stoddard said. "They're very effective—for their size, as good as any police force in the country."

I told him to launch an investigation, though neither one of us had high hopes that we would find the caller. Then I dictated a report to Hoover, informing him of Dingell's call. The memo came back in due course with one of Hoover's characteristic blue ink messages: "He acts like an adult beatnik." It was a curious comment, and I never understood precisely what he meant by it.

Needless to say, neither John Dingell nor his family was murdered. He remains in Congress to this day.

His mistake, however, was a common one—he believed that the FBI could provide him with protection. And he was not the first to make such an assumption. From Martin Luther King to Lyndon Baines Johnson to Estes Kefauver, people have assumed we had the power to offer protective services—and to do just about anything else we (or they) wanted. Washington bigwigs have asked us to perform every unlikely task from babysitting their children to repairing their television sets. And daily we received calls from ordinary citizens reporting the worst crimes imaginable—axe murders, rapes, child molestations—and we've had to tell them the same thing I told Congressman Dingell: "Sorry, but what you've described doesn't fall under our jurisdiction. This is the Federal Bureau of Investigation."

Had everyone understood precisely what our mission and limitations were, as envisioned by Stone, determined by Congress, and defined by our name, many of the controversies surrounding the FBI would never have developed.

The FBI's jurisdiction is limited to federal crimes. As I noted above, one of the great ironies of the Kennedy assassination was that Lee Harvey Oswald broke no federal law when he killed the president of the United States. For this reason, a good deal of confusion surrounded the investigation of Kennedy's death; and some of the subsequent conspiracy theories grew out of that confusion. For example, Dallas County Coroner Earl Rose was acting properly when he refused to surrender Kennedy's body to the presidential party. The crime had been committed in his jurisdiction. It was his responsibility to gather forensic evidence. He was prevented from doing so through enormous political pressure. As a direct consequence, more than thirty years later critics are still raising questions about the nature of the president's wounds and the number of bullets fired.

At the time, the FBI had no legal authority to interject itself into that particular murder investigation, no matter that the victim was the highest official in the federal government. But we were ordered to do so by President Johnson, and since we were on the scene, we took over the investigation and began gathering evidence. Still, we had to fight the Dallas Police Department every step of the way, and they had the law on their side. Today, it's a federal crime to kill the president of the United States; and should such a tragedy ever recur the FBI will have primary jurisdiction.

Most crimes committed in the United States are violations of state law rather than federal law. Ordinarily, robbery, rape, murder, and other such acts aren't covered under federal statutes but fall under state penal codes and are tried in state courts. There are exceptions, of course. For example, if any of these crimes is committed on federal property, or if other federal crimes are involved, then the FBI can immediately move into the case.

Most people believe that the bureau has jurisdiction over all kidnappings. This is not so. The FBI becomes involved only if the kidnapper transports the victim across state lines. For this reason, the bureau waits twenty-four hours before entering many kidnapping cases. When this period has elapsed, the courts presume that the kidnapper and victim have had time to leave the state, and the FBI enters the picture with all its resources, since transporting a kidnap victim across state lines is a federal offense. Much as the FBI was given the authority to investigate presidential assassinations because of the bungling of the local police, so too jurisdiction over kidnapping grew out of a notorious national case mishandled by local authorities—the kidnapping of the Lindbergh baby in 1932.

Kidnapping remains one of the few common crimes not committed against the federal government that the FBI is permitted to investigate. As horrible as the crimes of multimurderers John Wayne Gacy and Jeffrey Dahmer were, they were still beyond the purview of the FBI. On the other hand, the bureau is called in frequently on cases of mere larceny, when what is stolen is government property. And our agents are continually used to investigate applicants for positions in the federal government.

The bureau is not a free-standing agency with the option to do whatever pops into the director's head. The director and every single agent work under the authority of the attorney general of the United States, who is a political appointee of the president. So in a sense, the FBI belongs to the administration in power. When the attorney general calls and gives the director an order, ordinarily the director has to obey, even when the order is outrageous and demeaning. And by the same token, any time the attorney general wants to restrict the activities of the bureau, he is empowered to do so.

Although assassinations and kidnappings are high profile cases that forge the public's perception of the agency, the primary responsibility of the FBI is to investigate violations of federal law. If FBI agents come knocking at your door, they are probably looking for information rather than coming to arrest you. Even if you've committed a federal crime, you're more likely to receive a subpoena than be hauled off to prison by the bureau, though in many cases agents track down and arrest criminals just as police officers do.

Because the FBI is strictly an investigative agency, it cannot perform many functions that Americans expect from a more conventional police force. During the peak of the civil rights movement, liberals demanded that the FBI protect civil rights marchers and demonstrators from angry mobs and bushwhackers, and conservatives insisted that we arrest New Left demonstrators and throw them in the darkest federal dungeon. We received angry phone calls and letters from senators as well as from private citizens on both sides of the issue. At times the pressure was almost unbearable. Yet we neither had the authority to provide protection to anyone, nor the power to arrest demonstrators who were not violating federal law. Such authority would have carried additional power, and many of the same people who called for us to protect civil rights demonstrators were also charging us with being repressive. You can't have it both ways. Either the FBI is limited in its mission and in the power it wields, or else it can perform numerous functions and assume new and more awesome authority. When J. Edgar Hoover was telling the American people that he would not assign agents to protect or arrest civil rights demonstrators nor arrest militant demonstrators, he was also saying that he wanted no more power than he already had.

Of course, during those years we were sometimes forced to perform tasks beyond our purview. We did provide protection for at least one attorney general's wife—Martha Mitchell, who, we theorized, badgered her husband into assigning agents to follow her around the Washington social scene, much to Hoover's displeasure. It was not a duty they enjoyed. She would introduce them at cocktail parties, pinching them on the cheeks as if they were five-year-old boys. Agents were also assigned to babysit their little girl, Marnie, who was easier to handle than her mother.

During J. Edgar Hoover's tenure, presidents and attorneys general ordered the director and his agents to intimidate corporate executives, to conduct illegal surveillance of private citizens, and even to engage in political espionage. In such cases, the director usually protested and used every means in his power to avoid carrying out such orders, especially if illegal. But in the end he and the bureau have often been forced to comply. In these cases everyone involved understood precisely what was going on. The chief law enforcement officer of the nation knew that he was ordering subordinates to violate the law. So did the president. And in most cases, these were the same politicians who championed civil liberties in the political arena. Today their admirers are the first to talk about FBI abuses of civil liberties and the tyranny of J. Edgar Hoover. It is safe to say that without the liberal administrations of the 1960s, the FBI would have stayed more often within the legal limits of its mission and not become embroiled in the dirty tricks of partisan politics.

I'm not suggesting that Hoover was without fault—and I should know. I dealt with him constantly, was in and out of his office frequently, and talked to him on the phone. He was proud and vain, perpetually concerned with covering his own rear, and not above abusing his powers. He could be petty and vindictive. He stayed in office too long, and in so doing, he helped damage the reputation of the FBI he had virtually invented and almost perfected. In this respect he almost ruined the great achievement of his life.

On the other hand, while he was in charge, the bureau was the best law enforcement agency in the world. Today, the point may be debatable. In recent years, an FBI agent was arrested for burglary. Another was seduced by a Russian spy and became an agent for the Soviet Union. Still another stole drugs with intent to sell them on the streets. To those of us who served under J. Edgar Hoover, such crimes are surprising and sickening. We don't believe they could have happened under his leadership. One thing is certain—they didn't. The high caliber of personnel the FBI enjoyed during those years is directly attributable to the standards he maintained.

During the Hoover years, FBI agents were recruited with the same care and attention given the screening of medical students or an NFL draft. (At one time we could have fielded an All-American football team.) We brought in the brightest and best from all over the country. Someone once found that we had agents in the FBI from 625 colleges and universities, many of them with law or accounting degrees.

We checked their backgrounds, made certain that they had lived clean and responsible lives, and continued to monitor their behavior even after they had become experienced agents. We were interested in whether they could hold their liquor, or slept with other men's wives, or, and mainly, performed their duties within the regulations and guidelines set by the bureau.

I remember being called in by the director and told to investigate a complaint from a man in Puerto Rico who charged that one of our agents had used martial arts in an effort to extract information.

"The charges sound like they might be legitimate," he said. "Fly down there and find out. Stay as long as it takes."

I flew to Puerto Rico. When I arrived, I sent one of our San Juan agents into the mountains to bring the man back so I could hear his story. Several hours later I got a telephone call. It was our San Juan bureau chief.

"Deke," he said, "we've got a problem."

"You can't find the guy?"

"Oh, no," he said, "I've found him. He's standing right here. But he says he won't come in."

"Tell him he's got nothing to worry about. Nobody's going to hurt him. He can bring a lawyer along if he wants to. We're here to investigate his charges."

"He's not afraid," the agent told me. "He's embarrassed. He says he doesn't want to come into town because he doesn't have any shoes."

"Tell him I don't care if he doesn't have shoes. It won't bother me."

The agent told me to hold, and I heard some conversation in the background. Then the agent came back on the line.

"He says it may not bother you, but it bothers him."

I'd flown all the way out to Puerto Rico, and the charges this man had made were serious. The director became very unhappy when anyone suggested that agents had misbehaved, and use of physical force, except in cases of extreme provocation, was grounds for immediate dismissal.

"Tell him I'll buy him a pair of shoes," I said. "Ask him what size he wears."

I went out, bought the man a pair of shoes, and sent them to him by messenger. A few hours later, he walked into bureau headquarters, a smile on his face, the new shoes on his feet. Then he told me his story. After a few questions and answers, I began to believe that he was telling the truth. The agent had apparently tossed him around in an effort to extract information. After more investigation, I determined beyond reasonable doubt that the charges were true, and the agent was severely disciplined. When I got back to Washington, I thought about putting the shoes on my expense account, but decided against it. Mr. Hoover always looked over such reports with a cold eye, and I didn't want to explain the purchase. Besides, they were cheap shoes.

I tell this story to illustrate the care the FBI took to keep its ranks free from the abuse of power so often associated with law enforcement agencies. At the time I was a high-ranking official in the bureau, yet I was sent all the way from Washington to a tiny Caribbean island to investigate the complaint of a man who lived in the mountains and was too poor to buy a pair of shoes. And it wasn't simply that Mr. Hoover wanted the bureau to be above criticism. Just as important was the director's insistence that every agent obey orders and operate strictly within regulations. If an agent used unauthorized tactics in Puerto Rico, then he was untrustworthy no matter where he was stationed or what his assignment. J. Edgar Hoover didn't want him.

This stress on discipline derived in part from the fact that the FBI under Hoover was a semimilitary organization. Strict obedience to regulations and commands was just one of several significant ways in which the FBI resembled a military unit.

The mission of the FBI is similar to that of the armed forces— and the dangers are comparable. Recruits are taught to react quickly and obediently because their lives and the lives of others may well hang in the balance. Like military personnel, they are being trained for combat with a hostile and sometimes deadly enemy. The criminal element in society is accustomed to using any means whatsoever to achieve its purposes. To counter this, FBI agents must lead careful and disciplined lives. Agents are also often called to testify in federal court concerning cases they have investigated, and they must be credible witnesses whose character and behavior stand up to the most rigorous cross-examination. For these reasons it is essential that prospective FBI agents be investigated thoroughly in order to uncover any vices—drunkenness, drug use, sexual indiscretion—that might compromise their effectiveness in the field or on the witness stand.

Local police forces abound with examples of corrupt officers who have received payoffs or threatened physical abuse. The FBI, which deals with crime on a grand scale, must maintain a higher standard. During the Hoover years, we did. After Hoover, the bureau's reputation was tarnished by a number of scandals.

Perhaps these recent incidents are simply a sign of changing times, part of a general breakdown in public morality. Perhaps they are the result of a laxity in the bureau, which is far more democratic—and far less militaristic—than it used to be. Today's FBI has better technology at its disposal, and in some respects its agents are better trained and more sophisticated than we were, but there is a marked change in morale and spirit.

This change is particularly obvious in the attitude of agents toward the director. When Hoover was in charge, he was a five-star general. When he walked down the hallways, agents viewed him with a mixture of awe and terror. Though small in stature, he exuded strength and authority. In the rare moments when his eyes met the eyes of a mere agent, he was ten feet tall. And even those of us who saw him every day never quite felt at ease in his presence.

In part, his authority came from the sharp focus of his personality. He was always completely absorbed with the business of the bureau—every second of every day. Most of the time when you were in his presence, you were not so much an individual or a personality as a cog in the vast machinery of the universe he'd created and was controlling. You existed at his whim, and if he chose to he could snap his fingers and you'd disappear.

The military discipline did not make the FBI some sort of American gestapo as has been suggested by several recent books. There is just enough truth to this to keep it alive, but in many ways the reverse was true. Hoover, though by no means a plaster saint, fought just as hard to limit the powers of the FBI as he did to protect them. The strict discipline of the FBI was a way of keeping agents in line, of making sure they wouldn't overstep their authority and abuse the rights of citizens, nor abuse even those who, like the Puerto Rican man I interviewed, didn't enjoy the full rights and privileges of American citizenship.

Hoover understood, as had Stone, the dangers of a national police department. He had seen what had happened to his predecessor, Burns, and knew that if the FBI ever became such an abusive force, the American people would eventually turn on the agency. This was why Hoover fought every attempt on the part of well-meaning members of Congress to separate the bureau from the Justice Department and allow it to operate independently. Although Hoover often found it difficult to work with superiors like Bobby Kennedy and Ramsey Clark, he wanted the FBI to remain an arm of the Department of Justice—and a purely investigative arm at that. Had he been the power-hungry monster of recent accounts, he could have allowed his many friends on Capitol Hill to legislate a private fiefdom for him and run it without interference from the president or his appointees. That he chose otherwise was not so much a lack of ego on his part as his firm grasp of the concept that the FBI was better as a "bureau" than as an autonomous federal agency. That it continues to be so is more a tribute to J. Edgar Hoover than to several generations of civil libertarians.

2

·····················

The Secret Files That Weren't

SEVERAL RECENT BOOKS on Mr. Hoover and the FBI maintain that the director kept "secret files" and used them to intimidate high government officials. Of these alleged files, Ronald Kessler, in *The FBI: Inside the World's Most Powerful Law Enforcement Agency,* writes

> Hoover's defenders have tried to obfuscate the issue through semantics—quibbling about whether or not the files were blackmail files or secret files. Most of them were contained in Hoover's Official and Confidential files maintained in his suite. But what they were called and whether they were kept in Hoover's suite or in the general files is irrelevant. Reading those files that survived makes it clear they could have been gathered for no other purpose than for blackmail material.

Anthony Summers, in a book that would have made Kitty Kelley blush, *Official and Confidential: The Secret Life of J. Edgar*

Hoover, makes the same charges in terms even more extravagant and outrageous. To explain the absence of such files, Summers spins a tale of furtive figures clandestinely hauling a large object across J. Edgar Hoover's lawn after his death:

> Early that morning two of Edgar's neighbors had seen something mysterious. "It was early in the morning," Andrew Calomaris recalled in 1992. "I was seventeen then, and I was getting ready for school. And my mother called me into her room, onto the balcony we had then. There were two men carrying something out of Mr. Hoover's kitchen door, and Annie the housekeeper was at the door. What they were carrying was long and obviously heavy, wrapped in something like a quilt. They heaved it into a station wagon parked in the alley and drove away."
>
> Because of the shape of the bundle, Calomaris and his mother assumed at the time that it contained a body—that Edgar had died in the night and that these were undertakers, working early to avoid the press. The documented record, however, is that Edgar's body was not removed until much later, around lunchtime. At the hour the neighbors saw the men with a bundle, the body had not, according to all available testimony, even been discovered.
>
> Yet Calomaris and his mother are adamant that they saw something being removed before Andrew left for school. The men were surely not interlopers—had they been, the housekeeper would not have been calmly seeing them to the door. Given the known desire of others to get at Edgar's secrets, were allies removing something before the death became generally known, to thwart later searchers?

This passage is typical of recent biographies that claim to reveal dark and sinister secrets but are nothing more than distortions of well-known facts. Summers himself states that Hoover's body hadn't even been discovered when the Calomaris family claimed to have witnessed this titillating scene; it is absurd to suggest that someone intuited his death and thereupon removed his files.

In any event, the files in question were not even kept at Hoover's house, neither in a sealed vault, nor in some sliding panel in his office. They were kept in two standard metal file cabinets behind the desk of Helen Gandy, Hoover's secretary, and they were available to any official in the bureau who had good reason to see them.

The truth is, the FBI kept no "secret files" during the Hoover years. And certainly no files were squirreled away for purposes of blackmail. Virtually all of the FBI's records were closed to the general public, since they contained sensitive and personal information about federal employees, as well as persons suspected of crimes but not convicted. I can't imagine that anyone would want the results of clearance investigations made available to any reporter or busybody who walked in off the street. It was precisely to avoid the possibility of blackmail or intimidation that such files were open only to authorized personnel. Indeed, the Privacy Act of 1974 mandated just such handling of personnel files throughout the government.

In rereading the testimony before the House Subcommittee of the Committee on Government Operations, I was struck by the inability of members to understand the FBI's filing system, which to me always seemed logical and simple in concept. I suspect that at least some of the blackmail charges stem from a genuine confusion concerning this system, though others stem from a willful disregard of the obvious.

The largest and most common files were the "Central Files," which held most correspondence and information. This file contained reports of investigations, letters of complaint, general correspondence directed to the agency, most of the intelligence collected from various kinds of surveillance, memos and directives from other government agencies, personnel files, and miscellaneous communications and information. The Central Files were in an area open to virtually the entire bureau staff and were used many times every day by a variety of people, many of them filing clerks.

Needless to say, the Central Files were enormous, as in any federal agency. Numerous people fed information into those files over the years, and they were too large for any one person to master. We tried to purge these records periodically, but with the growth of the bureau's activities, it was a losing battle.

Because some materials were too sensitive to file in such an open marketplace, the FBI maintained two small cabinets of "Official-and-Confidential Files." These files, located in Hoover's suite behind Helen Gandy's desk, contained information about well-known people both in and out of government. The purpose of keeping the O&C Files in an area of limited access was to protect the privacy of those about whom information had been gathered, not to maintain secret records for the purpose of blackmail.

The same kind of information was stored both in the Central Files and the O&C Files. In fact, when someone became famous enough to warrant special treatment, his or her file was transferred from the more accessible area to Hoover's suite. Thus when John F. Kennedy won the Democratic nomination for the presidency, the files concerning his affair with an alleged German espionage agent were transferred from the Central Files to the O&C Files.

In marked contrast to the Central Files, the O&C Files were relatively small. Helen Gandy, testifying under oath, said they amounted to "[a]bout a drawer and a half." This was the file that contained information on political figures. Gathering information about these figures was never initiated by the FBI for the purpose of influencing either Congress or the White House.

It is important to note here that these were not "secret" in the sense that no one but Hoover could look at them, as several commentators have suggested. As to who else had access, Miss Gandy testified as follows when questioned by Congressman Frank McCloskey:

> *Mr. McCloskey:* Did you have the right to determine who looked at these files and who did not?
> *Miss Gandy:* With Mr. Hoover's approval. From time to time there would be inquiries about something that might be in those files, but Mr. Hoover had to give his

personal approval before an assistant director was
allowed to read them.

Actually, in some cases access was not monitored quite so closely.
As assistant to the director, I sometimes took O&C Files from the
Hoover suite to my office, where I could examine them at my leisure.
The point is important. Hoover did not keep these files secret, as he
would have had they contained information for blackmail purposes.
I consulted them from time to time for the general background mate-
rial they contained rather than for anything scandalous.

In fact, most of these folders did not contain information that
was demeaning or derogatory. They were standard background
files that gave addresses, phone numbers, family information—the
kind of data that people in high places ordinarily hide from the general public to avoid being the target of the curious. We certainly
didn't want someone to be arrested for stalking a high official or
the relative of a high official, only to have the stalker say, "Oh, I
got the information from where I work—at the FBI."

The third kind of file maintained in Mr. Hoover's suite was the
Bureau File. Again, Miss Gandy says this segment consisted of no
more than a drawer and a half of materials. The information here
was strictly internal, having to do largely with personnel matters—
staff evaluations, disciplinary actions, financial records. Nothing in
this file pertained to anyone outside the FBI.

A fourth file contained Hoover's correspondence—that is, letters
written to him by friends and admirers. These "personal" files were
clearly for Hoover's eyes only, since they had no relevance to FBI
business. In some cases, however—when Hoover was expecting a
visit and needed to be briefed concerning his visitor—his personal
files were consulted for relevant information; that is, they were not
"secret."

The speculation about Hoover's "secret files" derived in part
from the guilty conscience of some members of Congress, those
who were engaged in shady financial dealings and sexual adventures. Unfortunately, since a good many were indulging in such conduct, they thought every click on their telephone line was a wiretap,
every bellboy an FBI agent in disguise.

Others were ideologically predisposed to think that Hoover was the devil incarnate. If he had personal files then he must have used them for the most monstrous right-wing purposes. No one could admit that, like every other successful man, he received numerous letters from friends and admirers and was predisposed to keep them on file, if only to refer to when he heard from the correspondent again. It was much more satisfying to think that hidden in those steel cabinets was evidence of his hypocrisy and malevolence.

Still others believed such a story because they didn't understand how the federal government operates. In keeping certain files, Hoover was doing nothing more than officials of other agencies were doing. Consider what former FBI agent William C. Sullivan, no friend of Hoover's, told a congressional subcommittee investigating the possibility that the director used files to intimidate lawmakers:

> The general rule was that when a man was elected to the House of Representatives or he was elected to the U.S. Senate, a man or woman, immediately the bureau indexes, the indexes were reviewed on that officeholder, that new officeholder, to see what we had on him, good or bad. Could he be looked upon as a person to cultivate and to use and to draw in the stable on Capitol Hill, or should he be looked upon as one that would be unfriendly to the bureau? If so, then he would be treated accordingly.

There's nothing particularly sinister about this practice, and certainly nothing illegal. No need to initiate a wiretap or to go through a congressman's garbage for this kind of information. All we had to do was look at newspaper articles, interviews, and campaign literature to see how he or she stood on law-and-order issues. In our official liaison with Congress, it was always useful to know if people were predisposed to dislike the bureau or inclined to support it. Other government agencies collected similar information about people on Capitol Hill. When the Department of Agriculture shows interest in such matters, members of Congress are unperturbed.

When the FBI does the same thing, cold sweat forms on their brows.

You could almost see the beads of perspiration on Congressman Fink's forehead as he continued this line of questioning:

> *Mr. Fink*: Did any of these files contain [a] collection of derogatory information? Were efforts ever made to go out and seek derogatory information about not only congressmen but people prominent in life? People who were influential?

Sullivan, who in the final stages of his life was bitter toward Mr. Hoover and the bureau, could not bring himself to answer yes, knowing full well that the FBI did not seek out such information and that he was testifying under oath. Instead, he talked vaguely about gathering information on authors critical of the FBI.

> *Mr. Sullivan*: Well, anyone who wrote a book or was writing a book or we knew was going to be critical of Mr. Hoover and the FBI, we made efforts right then and there to find out anything that we could use against him.

By "use against him" he meant use to refute charges against the bureau in public debate. Again, this practice was by no means restricted to the FBI. The strategy was adopted by other government agencies (to say nothing of private corporations) when confronted by a critic. You found out all you could about the troublemaker and passed that information along to the person authorized to deal with the press. Then, when the attack came, you were in a position to offer the strongest possible rebuttal. Sullivan didn't allege that the FBI engaged in illegal surveillance to get such information—nor could he have, since we never considered such tactics for so trivial a purpose.

The line of questioning pursued at this hearing indicates the degree to which the vague and insubstantial rumor about Hoover's secret files took on flesh and blood for so many people in Washington. I have personally read quotations attributed to otherwise responsible people to the effect that such files existed and that Hoover used them in a high-handed way. Richard Helms, former CIA director, is quoted by Summers as saying:

> I learned a lot from fellows who had worked in Hoover's office before joining us. I used to hear how certain senators and congressmen would get caught in cathouses over in Virginia. When the report came in, Hoover would put it in his personal safe. If there was any problem with that senator, he would say, "Don't worry. I've got those papers right in my safe. You don't have a thing to worry about..." He played a very skillful game.

I knew Helms, helped to get him his job, and have always respected his intelligence and integrity; so I have to question the authenticity of such a quotation. FBI involvement in such cases is highly unlikely and the details too vague. It sounds like a story concocted by someone who didn't understand the limits of the FBI's jurisdiction or how the bureau operated. As for Hoover making such a statement to underlings, I was closer to him than anyone except Tolson and Gandy, and he never said any such thing to me. Whatever one might think of him, he was no loose-tongued fool.

Summers also quotes Walter Trohan, a *Chicago Tribune* reporter, as saying: "Some of Hoover's overwhelming support on the Hill was due to what I can only call blackmail, quiet blackmail." Ronald Kessler even cites me to corroborate the story that the FBI used information to blackmail members of Congress during the Hoover years. In this particular example, I begin to see how rumors of this nature could gain credibility among a general public that doesn't understand how the federal government in general or the FBI in particular works. Kessler quotes testimony by a former agent that I made the following statement during a speech for agents receiving in-service training:

> The other night, we picked up a situation where this
> senator was seen drunk, in a hit-and-run accident, and
> some good-looking broad was with him. We got the
> information, reported it in a memorandum, and by
> noon the next day, the senator was aware we had the
> information, and we never had any trouble with him on
> appropriations since.

No one who would say anything so irresponsible could have remained in government as long as I did, much less risen to the level I reached. Such a statement, repeated outside the walls of the room in which it was uttered, could have meant the end of my career. To begin with, the entire Washington press corps would have descended on the bureau. Next, the entire U.S. Senate would have raged against the FBI (a dozen or so members would have been certain they were the senator in question). And finally, J. Edgar Hoover would have booted me out the door before the day was out.

And, in fact, I said no such thing, because it was untrue—and had I wished to tell an untruth, I certainly would not have been so rash as to do so to a roomful of agents.

The former agent who made that claim—Arthur Murtagh—was a man we called "the crying agent," because he was forever making emotional proclamations that the bureau had engaged in illegal activities and that the truth must out. Whenever a hearing, any hearing, was held on the FBI or the intelligence-gathering community, he would come forward and beg to be heard. If the hearing was being held by an enemy of the agency, Murtagh would be called as a witness and allowed to repeat these old and largely discredited charges. I am not quite sure why he told such outlandish stories. He may have thought that he was ill-treated while at the bureau. He may have enjoyed the spotlight. He may have had other problems.

A careful reading of statements by other ex-agents, including William C. Sullivan, indicates that neither Hoover nor the FBI sought to uncover misdeeds by political figures, though we sometimes came across such information in the course of investigating other people's activities.

Thus, in attempting to prove that Hoover was a blackmailer, Summers quotes a statement by G. Gordon Liddy in which he describes precisely how such information fell into our hands:

> Say there was a bank robbery someplace. An informant might tell us the man to look for was holed up in the Skyline Motel, about six blocks south of the Capitol in Washington. Agents search the motel, and in the process they come across Senator X in bed with Miss Lucy Schwartzkopf, age fifteen and a half. They make their apologies and withdraw. But everything has to go into the record. The supervisor who gets the report may think there's no need to keep stuff on the peccadilloes of Senator X, but he has no authority to destroy it. The report has to go up to the director's office.

Liddy explained the use of such information as follows:

> Say the director was expecting to meet Senator X or if the senator's name had come up in some way, I would have to prepare a memorandum. I would check out the card held by Miss Gandy, and if there was something noteworthy I would write a note—perhaps a blind memorandum, "For the Director Only." It would say something like, "The director may wish to recall that Senator X was involved in such-and-such an incident, and is not very discreet."

You couldn't ask for a more accurate account of how such intelligence came into the bureau's hands and how Hoover would use it. Note first that the information in Liddy's example came to the attention of the FBI accidentally, while agents were pursuing a case unrelated to Senator X. This kind of intelligence fell into our laps constantly. After all, the federal government is no larger in population than a single city; and the Washington elite, the nation's real power brokers, number no more than a few thousand. They are constantly stumbling across each other in the dark.

Liddy is perfectly correct in saying that all information gathered in an investigation was routinely reported and entered into the individual's file. And when the individual visited Hoover or had dealings with the director, Hoover got the file—regardless of what was in it. But there is absolutely no proof that Hoover ever used such information for blackmail purposes. For this there is a simple explanation—until the late 1960s and early 1970s, when Hoover and the FBI were under attack by liberals on Capitol Hill, the bureau got most of what it wanted from Congress. And that was because the agency enjoyed the almost unanimous support of the American people.

The information on John F. Kennedy mentioned earlier, for example, found its way into our files just as Liddy has described. During World War II, while a young naval officer stationed at Charleston—and a figure of little political import—Kennedy allegedly had slept with Inga Arvid, a woman suspected of being a German espionage agent. When the FBI verified that he had indeed consorted with this woman, Kennedy was immediately transferred, though she was later cleared of any espionage charges. There were five other files involving sexual misconduct by Kennedy. Again, it seemed prudent to withhold these files from the wider scrutiny of bureau personnel.

When Kennedy was being considered as the Democratic vice presidential nominee in 1956, Hoover asked for a name check. Clyde Tolson called me from New York to say, "The boss and I want you to check Senator Kennedy's files. Handle it personally." I did so and reported back by telephone. When he heard what I had to report, Tolson called back. "Deke," he said, "you've got the wrong Kennedy. That must be the older brother you're talking about."

I said, "No, I've got the right one."

"Check again," Tolson said, and hung up. Hoover was a close friend of Ambassador Kennedy and probably did not want to be responsible for a report that would damage the political career of old Joe's promising son. When I called back to report there had been no mistake, he was shocked.

At lunch one day, a retired agent told this story about Kennedy, which also came to the bureau's attention quite by accident. I taped the story with his permission. I still have the transcription and have edited it only slightly:

> I had an informant by the name of Gloria. Gloria was a cute character. She had a circular bed in her apartment with her initials carved in the headboard, if that's a clue. Gloria got a call from a lumberman in Pennsylvania who was a good friend of Jack Kennedy's.
>
> He said, "Gloria, you still in business?"
>
> She said, "Sure."
>
> So he said, "O.K. I want you to go to the Waldorf Towers and identify yourself as Mildred. Somebody will tell you what to do."
>
> So she went to the Waldorf Towers, and as soon as she got out of the elevator a matron frisked her, and she was taken up the second elevator to the very top. There she was escorted into a darkened room.
>
> After she'd gotten used to the light, she realized there was a second girl there. They sat for a minute or two, saying nothing. Then the second girl says, "Well, I guess we ought to get ready." Gloria says, "Sure. I guess so. But for what?"
>
> So who comes in but the president of the United States, and he takes both of them on.
>
> We have no reason to doubt the authenticity of this story, because she told me about it two years later. She was a pretty good informer. As a matter of fact, she got one of the Russian diplomats in the sack and was willing to give him up with pictures, the whole bit, if that's what we wanted.

Again, it's important to remember that this information on Kennedy came to the FBI in the course of its investigation into other matters and from an informant who was dealing with agents specializing in espionage. In the first instance, we were watching Inga Arvid, not a naval officer named Kennedy. Nor were we checking on the president of the United States in using this particular prostitute as an informant. In addition, there was nothing unusual about J. Edgar Hoover requesting a background check on John Kennedy. At the request of the White House or the attorney general, the FBI routinely checks the background of potential top level federal officeholders—as the general public well knows. It is for this purpose that such information is usually gathered.

Another charge frequently made in connection with FBI files was that they contained information on a wide number of people, including entertainers, newspaper columnists, and artists. One woman, Natalie Robins, has written a book on the subject, *Alien Ink: The FBI's War on Freedom of Expression*. The dust jacket describes the work as "[d]rawing on nearly 150 files released to the author under the Freedom of Information Act..."

Robins's thesis rests on the fact that a number of writers had files at the FBI and that somehow or other gathering such information amounted to "hounding and intimidation." I'm listed as one of her sources. She did visit me, but when I tried to explain to her why these files were in existence, she chose not to believe me, because if she had there would have been no book. And she wanted to write a book.

It was our practice, in compiling files, to cross-reference information. We maintained what we called "main files," that is, files on a primary subject begun as the result of an investigation. But when we opened a main file, we also cross-referenced anyone whose name cropped up in the course of an investigation. In other words, if a criminal under investigation was known to have dined with a particular person, we would start a secondary file, merely noting the date and circumstances of the meal. Sometimes, the same name would turn up again in another investigation. This was one of the ways we used to identify members of the mob and to map their criminal associations.

In most cases, however, the secondary file would remain dormant, with only that one contact listed. This accounts for the number of entertainers and writers that found their way into our files. They had casual associations with people under investigation for some reason or another.

Particularly galling is the idea that Hoover maintained secret files on members of Congress. Those who make such statements are either ignorant of the facts or malicious gossips. I suspect you'd find more of the former than the latter. Unfortunately, this rumor persisted, especially during Hoover's latter years, when he had stayed too long and stepped on too many toes.

I can say categorically that during all the years I served at FBI headquarters, I never saw a main file on a legislator—except on those that had been charged with a criminal act within the FBI's jurisdiction.

Sadly, there were a good many of these. Because Congress exempts itself from many of the laws it passes, its members often get the idea that they are so powerful they don't have to obey the rest of the laws. Over the past twenty-five years alone, more than thirty members of Congress have been convicted of felonies or else have pleaded guilty to such charges. Their crimes have included defrauding the government, lying under oath, misappropriation of funds, and malfeasance in office. The FBI has investigated such charges when ordered to do so by the Department of Justice and has supplied evidence later used in federal court. But neither the director nor any one else in the bureau would have authorized such gratuitous snooping, not only because it would have undermined our crucial relationship with Congress, but also because we never had the manpower to waste on fishing trips.

Of course, some members of Congress have themselves leveled these charges, and for more than one reason. Summers writes of the late House Majority Leader Hale Boggs:

> Boggs accused Edgar of using the tactics of the Soviet Union and Hitler's Gestapo. Edgar issued a flat denial and circulated information on Boggs, typed on the usual untraceable paper, to influential people. The row blew over.

According to Boggs' son Thomas, however, the congressman had proof of his charge—transcripts of bugged conversations, supplied to him by bureau officials with uneasy consciences. An investigator for the Chesapeake and Potomac Telephone Company, moreover, told Boggs that his own home telephone had been tapped by the FBI.

First, it is important to note the claim, unproven and unprovable, that Hoover had "circulated information on Boggs, typed on the usual untraceable paper..." If it was untraceable, how does anyone know it came from Hoover? Such speculations—as nasty as they are flimsy—fill Summers' book. In addition, I happen to know more about this incident than either Summers or Thomas Boggs, even though it occurred after I left the bureau.

When Boggs made these charges, I was vice president of Pepsico and living in New York City. My secretary, somewhat excited, told me that J. Edgar Hoover was on the line. After a few terse words of greeting he got right to the point. He remembered that I had worked closely with Boggs during the period when I was liaison between the bureau and Capitol Hill. And now Boggs had made these wild charges. Would I fly down to Washington as his personal emissary to Boggs and demand that the congressman corroborate the charges or back off? I agreed to make the trip.

The next day I found myself in the majority leader's office, sitting with Boggs, an extremely likeable man. We talked about things in general for a few minutes, but we both understood the purpose of my visit. When I finally brought the matter up, he immediately admitted that he'd made a mistake.

"Facts?" he said, shaking his head. "I don't have any. I'd had a few too many drinks and was on my way to a baseball game when I said those things. It grew out of something that happened to me earlier. A group of young people down in Florida came up to me and challenged me to take on Hoover and the FBI—you know, New Left types. I figured that once I'd made the charge, other members of Congress would come forward with some facts."

He shook his head sadly.

"I shouldn't have criticized the Old Man like that. Tell him I'm sorry."

I nodded, and that was the end of our discussion of the charges. Hale and I talked about other things for a while, and then, after a few minutes, I said goodbye. Before I went back to the airport, I dropped by the bureau and reported to Hoover, who nodded, grim-lipped. He said he was happy the matter was resolved. One brush fire extinguished—but only one of many. Members of Congress had made such charges before. They would make them again. We both knew it. He thanked me, and we shook hands. I was pleased he'd called on me and was glad to be of service, particularly since I'd always believed he'd been hurt by my early retirement.

Hale Boggs had an excuse for making his charge—a couple of drinks too many, a hurried interview, a gut feeling that the rumors about FBI files on members of Congress were true. Had anyone come forward with concrete evidence, he would have been a hero. In the absence of such evidence, he admitted his mistake and made an honest apology.

One practice during the Hoover years provided more legitimate cause for alarm—a folder on a figure from an investigation ordered by the attorney general or the president of the United States. Occasionally, we would receive such orders, usually with some barely plausible excuse for the investigation. At times we resisted. At other times, it was impossible to do so, particularly when the White House would say it was "a matter of national security." In many instances, the subjects of such investigations were famous people, and, as usual, the folders would be kept behind Miss Gandy's desk.

It seems that during his presidency, Franklin Roosevelt asked the bureau to investigate rumors that his wife, Eleanor, had been sexually involved with other men. Shortly after I arrived at the Washington office, someone mentioned these investigations to me. The file was there in the cabinet behind Miss Gandy's desk, but I never bothered to look at the report, so I didn't know the outcome of the investigations. It never occurred to me that Mrs. Roosevelt could have had a lover other than her husband. Years later I was told that she'd apparently possessed charms I didn't fully appreciate.

After I'd left the bureau I invited a group of ex-agents living in the New York area to have lunch with me. I told them I wanted this to be a time for reminiscing, and when we'd finished lunch, I turned on a tape recorder with their permission. We started telling war stories, one of which was the Kennedy anecdote mentioned above.

Afterward, I had my secretary transcribe the tape, and I have the transcription to this day. For the most part, it's unintelligible to outsiders. It's full of bureau jargon and shorthand references to cases and people we all knew. But two separate agents—one the case agent and both older than I—told tales about investigating Mrs. Roosevelt.

"Tolson asked Agent Tom Spencer to establish whether or not Joseph P. Lash, the perennial youth leader and later Mrs. Roosevelt's biographer, was spending too much sack time with Eleanor at her apartment down in Washington Square [in New York City]," one agent recounted. "She also had a townhouse on 65th Street, but Franklin's mother [Sarah Delano Roosevelt], lived in the townhouse right next door, so Eleanor couldn't rendezvous with anybody, because the old lady sat at the bay window twenty hours a day.

"I draw the assignment, so I go down discreetly to look over the building that faces Washington Square—Washington Square West, as I recall. I finally enter the building under some pretext, and there's this nice Irish doorman in there. Well, we talk and it turns out we've got about thirty common relatives in the same county in Ireland.

"At this point, I say, 'By the way, doesn't Mrs. Roosevelt live in here?'

"He says, 'Well, she's supposed to live here, but that goddamned boyfriend is here most of the time. That's why we have the place for her, you know. He's such a crud. There's two baths in that apartment, and I don't think he uses either. You can smell him in the elevator. I spray something in there every time he comes out.'

"She flew halfway across the Pacific to visit Joe [Lash]. She was interested in his career, and he was the head of the youth movement in America. I guess Franklin found out she was playing with him, because all of a sudden his job with the New York Youth Administration wasn't that important for national security any more; so Joe's deferment was withdrawn, and he wound up in the army air corps, out on some island in the Pacific.

"The next thing we know, Eleanor flies out. And it's not just that she's going to visit. She's bringing Joe his dog for a visit. I know there was an army plane that had to go halfway across the Pacific so she could visit Joe Lash on this island."

The other agent had a similar, if less glamorous tale to tell.

"I got a call from the bureau and they said, 'You have to find out whether or not Eleanor Roosevelt is spending the weekends up in Loudenville with her old lover—that state trooper she's been having an affair with. You can't tell anybody, but we have to know one way or the other.'

"I thought about it and remembered I was well wired with a guy in the New York State government. He was an election commissioner, a real great guy—and something of a con man. I told him what I needed and he said, 'Don't worry. I'll handle it for you, Jack.'

"So he went to the dairy that delivers milk in Loudenville, and they let him take over the truck. He put on a uniform. He learned the route. And he delivered the milk on Saturday and Sunday.

"He was talkative, brash, and he walked right in the kitchen. He saw Eleanor standing there in her housecoat, cooking eggs for the guy, and she chatted away with him while he was bringing in the milk. He did that for two days and came back to report to me. And I reported back to the bureau."

These stories concerning Mrs. Roosevelt may or may not still be in the bureau files. There was, in the same cabinet behind Miss Gandy's desk, a folder with information on Sumner Welles, undersecretary of state, who had propositioned a pullman porter while on his way to the funeral of Tennessee's Senator McKeller. When this information was given to President Roosevelt, he requested Welles's resignation.

There was also an investigation of Richard Nixon, who—after graduating from Duke University Law School—applied for the position of special agent. He was offered an appointment, but chose instead to practice law.

No one tried to blackmail anyone with any of this information, least of all Hoover or the FBI. President Roosevelt may have violated the law by using the bureau for a private matter, but it is arguable that in such dire times the sexual misconduct of a First Lady has national and even international implications.

Roosevelt requested the information on Sumner Welles, and Hoover provided it only on request. Arguably, in the climate of the 1940s, homosexuals, particularly those in the State Department, were subject to blackmail. There were those who maintained (then, as now) that national security might have been compromised. Apparently President Roosevelt thought something of the sort was involved.

In the final analysis, no one can prove that potential "secret blackmail" files did not exist. You can't prove that leprechauns don't exist either. With no Irish blood in me, I'm more willing to believe in the Little People than the idea that J. Edgar Hoover kept clandestine records. Unlike Mr. Kessler and Mr. Summers, I was there during those years and—I know what I didn't see.

3

....

Bobby Kennedy's Bugs

THE CHARGE THAT THE FBI routinely tapped the telephone lines of thousands of Americans is absurd. We barely had the manpower to tap the lines of mob kingpins and espionage agents. And we certainly had no reason to set up such an elaborate and costly surveillance, just on the off chance that some senator or congressman would make a remark we could use in budget negotiations. Besides, until 1970, we were required to get authorization from the attorney general himself to tap a telephone line, though we did have a standing order that allowed us to use other electronic surveillance equipment. And we always stuck by that rule—whatever statements to the contrary.

I suspect that much of the suspicion about our wiretapping practices stems from a single event—Bobby Kennedy's famous statement that he never authorized a wiretap that wasn't a national security case—a statement that raised a number of eyebrows and resulted in a heated controversy. Here's what happened.

In 1966, the question of wiretapping arose in the midst of political squabbling within the Democratic party. Bobby Kennedy, by then a U.S. senator from New York, was generally regarded as a potential challenger for the Democratic presidential nomination, although incumbent Lyndon Johnson was eligible to run for reelection. But to win the nomination, Bobby had to win the heart of the liberal wing of his party, a formidable task in view of the aggressive tactics he had used as attorney general in his war against organized crime.

Civil libertarians, for their part, were skeptical of his candidacy, and on June 26, 1966, two newsmen pursued this question on ABC's "Issues and Answers." One asked him directly: "Did you ever authorize any wiretaps as attorney general except in national security cases?" Kennedy replied unequivocally: "I did not." This initial question and answer led to the following exchange:

> *Reporter*: Would this mean that wiretaps were made by someone at the Justice Department without your knowledge?
> *Kennedy*: Well, if there were any wiretaps that took place outside of national security cases, then they were.
> Reporter: Do you think this might mean the FBI was doing some wiretapping that you didn't know about?
> *Kennedy*: Well, I expect maybe some of those facts are going to be developed. The only time I authorized or was ever requested to authorize wiretapping was in connection with national security cases under an arrangement that originally had been made by President Roosevelt and Attorney General Biddle.

This exchange is what got the controversy going. Here was the former attorney general, and potential presidential candidate, suggesting that the FBI was running its own rogue wiretapping operation. It wasn't exactly specific—"I expect maybe some of those facts are going to be developed"—but it was a bombshell nonetheless. Kennedy had succeeded in making news. And more news was yet to be made—not all of it favorable to Bobby.

It would have been too ugly and damaging to the bureau for the director to leap into a direct confrontation with Bobby Kennedy.

Instead, Hoover talked to a friend, Congressman H. R. Gross, who was more than happy to give Hoover a pretext for responding to Kennedy by writing this letter requesting information:

> It has been my impression in the past that the FBI engaged in "eavesdropping" and wiretapping only upon authority from the attorney general. It was my understanding that the FBI had adhered to this policy, and that there exists "full documentation" of the fact that the FBI actions were authorized by the attorney general.

Gross asked if this was not still the case. Hoover took full advantage of Gross's request. Not only did he use the opportunity to state for the record that he had proof that every wiretap had formal authorization, he also weighed in against Kennedy in a manner calculated to hurt him with the liberals he was courting. Bobby not only approved a number of bugs and wiretaps, he was enthusiastic about them and occasionally listened in himself. Hoover wrote:

> Your impression that the FBI engaged in the usage of wiretaps only upon the authority of the attorney general of the United States is absolutely correct. You are also correct when you state that it is your understanding that "full documentation" exists as proof of such authorizations.
> All wiretaps utilized by the FBI have always been approved in writing, in advance, by the attorney general. As examples of authorization covering the period in which you were specifically interested, you will find attached to this letter a communication dated August 17, 1961, signed by former Attorney General Robert F. Kennedy, in which he approved policy for the usage of microphones covering both security and major criminal cases. Mr. Kennedy, during his term of office, exhibited great interest in pursuing such matters and, while in different metropolitan areas, not only listened to the

results of microphone surveillances but raised questions relative to obtaining better equipment. He was briefed frequently by an FBI official regarding such matters. FBI usage of such devices, while always handled in a sparing, carefully controlled manner and, as indicated, only with the specific authority of the attorney general, was previously increased at Mr. Kennedy's insistence while he was in office.

In fact, in both Chicago and New York, while listening to tapes from microphone coverage, Kennedy was surrounded by FBI agents. For this reason alone, it was almost inconceivable that he could deny knowledge of such surveillance.

The Hoover letter did give Kennedy an out—an opportunity to call what might have been a bluff on the director's part. Kennedy's initial comments had only involved wiretaps, that is, listening into private phone lines. That practice has always been held to a different standard of authorization than mere bugging, that is, placing microphones to pick up nontelephonic conversations. Kennedy said he had approved no telephone wiretaps for any surveillance not tied to national security. Hoover had responded that he had proof Bobby had signed off on bugs. In that sense Hoover had failed to refute Kennedy's allegations, a fact Bobby could make much of.

Kennedy fired back in a press release that was guaranteed to keep the issue alive, and it unintentionally gave Hoover the opportunity for a free shot. But Bobby thought he was on firm ground, having contacted former Assistant Director Courtney Evans, who had acted as liaison between the FBI and the Department of Justice. Evans must have had a flawed memory, and Bobby made the mistake of releasing the following statement:

For Immediate Release December 10, 1966

Apparently Mr. Hoover has been misinformed. He should have consulted Mr. Courtney Evans before issuing his statement. Mr. Evans, now in private practice in Washington, served with the FBI for 21 years and served as assistant director while I was attorney general. He was appointed by Mr. Hoover, and in that capacity was present on each occasion when any matter was discussed with any representative of the FBI, including matters referred to in Mr. Hoover's statement. Mr. Evans wrote me this year, and a copy of his letter is attached.

The Evans letter, dated February 17, 1966, said, among other things:

Since prior attorneys general had informed the FBI that the use of microphones, as contrasted to telephone taps, need not be specifically approved by the attorney general, I did not discuss the use of these devices with you in national security or other cases, nor do I know of any written material that was sent to you at any time concerning this procedure, or concerning the use, specific location or other details as to installation of any such devices in Las Vegas, Nevada, or elsewhere.

So now, instead of claiming that he had never given authorization for *wiretaps* (that is, telephone taps), Kennedy submitted Evans's statement to show that he had not signed off on *any* sort of electronic surveillance. He must have assumed that with Evans backing him up, no actual paper trail existed. If so, Kennedy was very wrong. He might also have figured that Hoover had tried to shift the ground of the argument because he would have lost a debate fought on the original terrain. One thing sure: as matters stood, Hoover had Kennedy's tail in a crack. Kennedy, could hardly woo the liberal supporters he needed by saying, "Sure, I authorized bugs, just not wiretaps." So he had to respond to Hoover's insinuation that Kennedy was an electronic surveillance enthusiast. (Which he was; Kennedy loved using bugs—couldn't get enough of them.)

For whatever reason, Kennedy did not leave it just to Evans to assert that he had had nothing to do with electronic surveillance in nonsecurity cases. Instead, Bobby upped the ante with a detailed December 11, 1966, press release in which he took Hoover's bait. It was a bad move:

> Although Mr. Hoover says this activity was "intensi-
> fied" while I was attorney general, and implies that we
> discussed it, the fact is that he never discussed this
> highly important matter with me, and no evidence
> exists supporting his recollections that we did. Indeed,
> there is no indication that Mr. Hoover ever asked me
> for authorization of any single bugging device, in Las
> Vegas, New York, Washington, or anywhere else.

A smart tactician like Bobby should have stuck to his wiretap comments and not ventured into the land of microphones and other bugs.

Kennedy had been pressured into making a statement that was provably untrue. Whether Kennedy knew it, only he could say. The FBI, however, always kept meticulous records on such activities, and Hoover was able to come up with an August 17, 1961, memorandum in which the attorney general gave the FBI permission to use electronic surveillance in New York City. The memorandum—probably routed through Courtney Evans—was signed by Robert F. Kennedy, indicating his approval.

This incident illustrates how the FBI picked up the reputation for unauthorized electronic surveillance. But it also shows how Hoover, determined to win this particular political battle, ultimately lost the larger struggle for the public's good will. The same thing happened when the director scuffled with Martin Luther King Jr. So intent was Hoover on showing that King had been wrong about the diligence of the bureau in the South during the civil rights movement, that he called King a "notorious liar." The bad blood created by their feud hurt the bureau in the long run, because the FBI was wrongly perceived to have hindered the civil rights movement.

Similarly, the perception persists that the FBI was illegal-wiretap-happy. The truth is, neither Hoover nor any of his subordinates would have instituted unauthorized wiretaps. Everyone knew the rules. The director would never have entrusted his career to the discretion of three or four agents, nor would any FBI executive. A number of congressmen, from time to time, have claimed their phones were tapped. If so, it must have been the Russians or their wives or their girl friends—it certainly wasn't the FBI.

The suspicion of illegal electronic surveillance led to a move in liberal circles to do away with bugs altogether. Such a move would have disastrously hampered our ability to catch spies and mobsters. The move to outlaw electronic surveillance came to the Supreme Court in a case dealing with Washington lobbyist Fred Black. Had it not been for the help—admittedly ethically dubious—of Supreme Court Justice Abe Fortas, the liberals might have succeeded.

Black was politically influential, with contacts on both sides of the aisle. And he was suspected of income tax evasion. He was also suspected of having connections with the Las Vegas mob. It was because of these latter suspicions that the FBI bugged a "hospitality suite" that Fred Black kept for his special friends. Convicted of income tax evasion, Black appealed the case, alleging that the evidence against him had been obtained by illegal electronic surveillance devices. As a matter of record, this allegation was untrue; the evidence in the tax evasion case was not obtained by bugs. Eventually the case reached the Supreme Court of the United States, where we ran into unexpected trouble.

Thurgood Marshall was solicitor general of the Department of Justice at the time, and he presented the government's case before the Justices. Marshall apparently made an ill-prepared presentation that raised more questions about the electronic surveillance than it answered, and members of the Court began to question him about the gaps in his brief. Finally losing patience, the Court asked him to come back when he was better prepared. In a second presentation, Marshall said that "...the FBI had general authorization from the department for the usage of such devices..." Here he was either inept, or trying to shield the former attorney general from the charge of having authorized electronic surveillance for other than national security cases.

The former attorney general was Bobby Kennedy.

At that point, Justices Fortas and Clark—old friends of LBJ—

began to cross-examine Marshall, and we received word that they were attempting to bring out Bobby Kennedy's role in authorizing bugs and wiretaps.

We had no problem with that strategy. On the contrary, we were delighted at the thought of exposing Bobby's almost obsessive love of surveillance technology. But our source told us something else that alarmed us: The High Court might be planning to issue a "sweeping statement" condemning the use of electronic surveillance in the investigation of crime. Our source indicated that the Court would make an exception only in the event that surveillance was instigated to save a human life. Such a ruling could undermine prosecution of any and all cases in which such devices had already been used—and would tie our hands in the future.

After sending a memo to Mr. Hoover outlining the report, I made a suggestion: "Let me see if I can talk privately with Justice Fortas on this matter." As the FBI's liaison to the White House, I had worked with Fortas when he was still part of LBJ's staff. "He's a reasonable man. Maybe we can find some way to work this out so the Court won't take such a drastic action."

Hoover called me into his office to consider the proposal. Though he hardly knew him, Hoover did not trust Abe Fortas; Fortas was something of a liberal, and therefore suspect in the director's eyes.

"He'll never see you," Hoover said. "He'll consider it a conflict of interest."

"He's disqualified himself from the case," I said. (Fortas's law firm had previously represented Black, the defendant.)

Hoover thought some more.

"Well, you can try it," he said, still skeptical.

I immediately placed a call to Fortas, and he got back to me that evening.

"I'd like to talk to you about a delicate matter," I said, "but you may consider the conversation a breach of judicial ethics. If so, then just tell me."

He laughed.

"We've discussed delicate matters before," he said.

"Yes, but this involves a case currently before the Supreme

Court—the Black case. I know you've disqualified yourself, but it's possible you wouldn't want to talk about it with me."

He immediately put me at ease.

"Deke, I'll be happy to talk to you about that or any other matter—as long as it's confidential. I have breakfast about 7:45. If you'll join me tomorrow morning, you can tell me what's on your mind."

I accepted his invitation and was ushered into his house at exactly 7:45. We talked about other things until we'd finished breakfast. Then we got down to business.

I told him what was going on—that the FBI had not violated established procedures in the Black case, that Thurgood Marshall's vague presentation was perhaps a stratagem to avoid revealing the full facts in the case, that Attorney General Nicholas Katzenbach apparently was trying to cover up for his old friend Bobby Kennedy, who had authorized specific telephone taps and had reestablished the general practicing of bugging.

"As you know," I told Fortas, "the Supreme Court has requested information on this case, and the director intends to give specific, honest, hard-hitting answers to the Court's questions. But we're afraid that Katzenbach will throw away our answers and present his own version to the Court."

Fortas nodded.

"I agree. Bobby wants to be president, and he's trying to capture the liberal vote from Humphrey. In fact, he's already got some of it. But if these people were to find out he'd approved of wiretapping or bugging—particularly on a widespread basis—he'd lose all the ground he's gained."

Fortas was a strong supporter of Lyndon Johnson. At that point we both assumed that Johnson would be a candidate for reelection in 1968. Humphrey had been put on the ticket in 1964 to secure the liberal wing of the Democratic party, and everyone believed he would run again with Johnson. But many people also believed that Bobby Kennedy might challenge the sitting president.

As for the Black case, Fortas was very forthcoming.

"After Marshall's presentation, the members of the Court held a confidential meeting. Though White and I had disqualified ourselves, we sat in on the discussion. We decided not to remand the case to a lower court, but to investigate the use of devices and then make a decision on the Black case. Everybody except White figured that if we remanded the case, Katzenbach would pick his own lower court judge and ensure victory. There are a couple of Justices who don't like either Kennedy or Katzenbach. They won't be pushed around."

That sounded encouraging.

"I'm here to listen to whatever counsel you have to offer," I said. He immediately understood what we wanted from him.

"The problem at hand," he said, "is to determine how the FBI's evidence showing Kennedy's role in electronic surveillance can be channeled to the Supreme Court." Fortas used few words but his strategy was clear. By getting to the Court the evidence that it was Bobby who authorized the surveillance, the liberals on the Court would be faced with a clear and difficult choice: If they made a big deal of the Black case, using it as the grounds on which to issue a broad prohibition against surveillance, inevitably Bobby's enthusiastic role in ordering bugs and taps could come out. Only by letting the Black case sink beneath the waves—probably by remanding it to the lower court—could Bobby's name be left out of matters. The FBI had a good chance of getting what it wanted—no ban on surveillance—but LBJ would win either way; even if he lost on surveillance at least Bobby would be humiliated.

Fortas asked me "What kind of evidence do you have?"

I showed him several memoranda from our files, including the New York memorandum Kennedy had signed. After he had looked them over, he was convinced.

"In light of these documents," he said, "there's no doubt in my mind that the FBI acted according to the law—and under specific direction from Kennedy and the Justice Department. At the same time, I think you're right to worry that Katzenbach might just ignore this evidence and mislead the Court."

He stared at the documents for a long time, deep in thought.

"I think the best thing for me to do is to slip in the back door of the White House and talk to the president about this matter. I'll tell him the whole story. By the way, is the president aware of these memos?"

"You bet," I told him. "In order to protect the FBI, we've advised both the president and Marvin Watson." Watson was Walter Jenkins' successor as appointments secretary to the president, or, as he would be called nowadays, the president's chief of staff.

"That's good," said Fortas. "But I think he might want to know what I think about this matter—from the perspective of the Supreme Court."

Then he outlined a plan, one that would put Katzenbach and Kennedy in "the back seat" where they belonged.

"I'll recommend to the president that he call in Katzenbach immediately and say he's extremely concerned about this matter and that he wants to appoint an arbitrator to listen to all the evidence and then make a complete report to the Supreme Court." He went on to suggest former Secretary of the Army Ken Royall, or ABA president Ross Malone, or former ABA president (and future Supreme Court Justice) Lewis Powell as arbitrators. Hoover regarded Powell as naive and weak, so Fortas cut Powell from the list.

"Now I'm going to get right on this." Fortas told me. "I'm going down to Jacksonville today, but I'll try to talk to the president before I leave. If I can't get in to see him, I'll discuss it with him on Thursday morning."

I thought we'd concluded our business, but he brought up another subject.

"I've already taken steps to disqualify myself from the Hoffa case," he said, "but it will be going on for years, as will the Black case and the Baker case. Do you know of any electronic surveillance that Kennedy may have authorized during the investigation of Jimmy Hoffa?"

"On one occasion," I said, "Kennedy specifically asked an agent to place a microphone on an attorney named Haggerty. We protested, but he ordered us to do it anyway."

Fortas nodded.

"I suspected as much. When that case comes up before the Court, I'll make certain that Kennedy's role is brought to light."

I was beginning to realize that he knew a great deal more about this whole complicated picture than I had supposed. He was a remarkably shrewd man who knew many people in Washington, was a careful listener, and had the knack of putting together the pieces of very complicated puzzles. Fortas never did tell me what he said, and I didn't want to ask, but he did what needed to be done. The Supreme Court reversed Black's conviction and sent the case back to the trial court for a new trial, with instructions that relevant parts of the transcripts of the FBI's surveillance should be made available to Black. In the end, Black finally did go to jail.

"Let me ask you something else," he said. "Do you know a former FBI man by the name of Courtney Evans?"

"Oh, yes, I remember him well." (Evans was the man who had attempted, unsuccessfuly to substantiate Bobby's claim that he had never authorized electronic surveillance except in national security cases.) I told Fortas that when we had confronted Evans with documentary evidence to the contrary he conceded we must be right. I told Fortas that we specifically asked Evans if Bobby Kennedy had been furnished information that came from the microphone surveillance of Black. He admitted that he'd frequently briefed Kennedy on the matter. Then we asked him whether Kennedy knew that such information came from a bug. Evans said that on one specific occasion Kennedy must have realized that the information could only have come from a planted microphone.

Fortas shook his head.

We talked about other matters for awhile until Fortas took his leave. On the way to the door he told me that he was always willing to help the FBI, that Johnson had great respect for the bureau, and that the current controversy surrounding our use of microphones and telephone taps was the result of Bobby Kennedy's practices, not those of the FBI.

Of course Fortas's involvement in the matter was blatantly unethical. Having disqualified or "recused" himself from the case he should not only have refrained from voting on it, as he did, he should have played no role in the matter and certainly should not have participated in the Court's discussion of the case. And as a member of the Court fully participating in the discussions of the case he should not have been meeting privately with one party in the case—the government—and he certainly should not have been secretly orchestrating the government's strategy! In any event, it worked. The Black case did sink beneath the waves, there was no broad ban on surveillance issued at that time, and Fred Black was denied what might have been quite a significant footnote in American constitutional history.

The funny thing about the Hoover-Kennedy feud was that Hoover had once upon a time been a sort of Bobby Kennedy booster. A writer once asked Hoover about his feud with Bobby—whose appointment as attorney general had been criticized by many in the press, particularly since the president had earlier indicated he would not appoint his brother.

"As a matter of fact," said Hoover, "I advised him to make that appointment."

The writer and his agent were genuinely surprised.

"I told him, 'Mr. President, you've appointed a man to State whom you don't know—Dean Rusk; and another to Defense whom you hardly know—Robert McNamara. You need someone in the cabinet you can confide in, someone in whom you have confidence. I suggest you ignore the newspapers and go ahead and appoint your brother.'"

Then Hoover brought his fist down on the desk and snarled, "Worst damn piece of advice I ever gave!"

4

·····················

The Gay Director?

FROM MY CHILDHOOD through my days at the FBI, J. Edgar Hoover was a national hero—the stern protector of the nation. To be sure, however much Hoover deserved his reputation as head G-man, that image was largely crafted through the director's keen eye for good publicity. But the days of good publicity for Hoover are gone. Currently he is portrayed by the Left as an icon of oppression. And that isn't all. His name has become a punch-line for comedy routines about homosexuals and cross-dressers. When he is thought of years from now, Hoover will probably be remembered as the highest-ranking official in government to have dressed in drag.

What an amazing accomplishment that is for Anthony Summers, the disingenuous biographer who has almost single-handedly propagated the absurd story that J. Edgar Hoover was a cross-dressing homosexual. He accomplished this by quoting a woman with the credibility only Summers would accept—Susan Rosenstiel, a convicted perjurer (about which more later). She claimed to have seen Hoover decked out in a dress at a homosexual party:

According to Mrs. Rosenstiel, Edgar was dressed as a woman in full drag. "He was wearing a fluffy black dress, very fluffy, with flounces, and lace stockings and high heels, and a black curly wig. He had makeup on, and false eyelashes. It was a very short skirt, and he was sitting there in the living room of the suite with his legs crossed. Roy [Cohn] introduced him as 'Mary' and he replied, 'Good evening,' brusque, like the first time I'd met him. It was obvious he wasn't a woman, you could see where he shaved. It was Hoover. You've never seen anything like it. I couldn't believe it, that I should see the head of the FBI dressed as a woman."

When Anthony Summers' *Official and Confidential* was first published, I read it with disbelief. It was not so much a book about Hoover and the FBI as a string of opinions, rumors, and undocumented charges. I read the narrative from cover to cover because it was ostensibly about the FBI, but it was strange to read about people and happenings that seemed only vaguely recognizable, as if total strangers had been assigned the familiar names of friends and colleagues. It was a macabre experience.

Summers charges in his book that Hoover and Tolson were homosexual lovers—and makes the allegation as if it were fact. It so disgusted me that I simply put it out of my mind. Even when it was repeated in newspapers and echoed on TV talk shows, I concluded that the fair-minded people of America would reject so ridiculous an accusation based on such flimsy evidence, that their good sense would see through the fraud. But then, in talking to friends and acquaintances, I discovered that, in the wake of Summer's book, Hoover's homosexuality was widely accepted as undeniable truth.

"Tell us about Hoover and Tolson," people would say.

"Was it obvious?"

"Did everybody know what was going on?"

When I told them that neither man was a homosexual, that Summers had no evidence at all of any such relationship, that he was repeating rumors spread by Hoover's enemies, they didn't disbelieve me, but they were astonished. They had accepted the charges as fact because they assumed no one would make them without conclusive evidence.

I think it's significant to note that no one who knew Hoover and Tolson well in the FBI has ever even hinted at such a charge. You can't work side by side with two men for the better part of twenty years and fail to recognize signs of such affections. Contrary to what Summers would have you believe, neither Hoover nor Tolson was the least bit effeminate. Both were tough and manly. Hoover was a bull dog. Tolson was a strapping, healthy fellow in his youth. He played first base on the FBI's champion baseball team, and there wasn't the slightest sign of weakness or "prettiness" in his face. He was certainly more of a man than Mr. Summers, and I've seen both at close quarters.

Tolson was Hoover's second in command. Tolson—and Tolson alone—had his complete trust. The two were close personal friends as well as co-workers, and they spent many off-duty hours together going to the races, attending boxing matches and other sporting events, and eating at restaurants. A bachelor who devotes his entire life to a job has to have at least one close male friend. For Hoover, that friend was Clyde Tolson.

Tolson entered the bureau in 1926 and quickly rose to the rank of assistant director. In later years he was associate director, second in command to Hoover. He was a quiet man with a keen analytical mind who fine-tuned his own thoughts and sensibilities to those of his superior.

This ability to be of one mind with J. Edgar Hoover was both Tolson's strength and his ultimate weakness. On the one hand, he was the perfect lieutenant who knew without asking what Hoover would think or do in a particular situation. On the other hand, his slavish devotion to the director blinded him to Hoover's shortcomings and prevented him from dissenting when dissent was in order.

Tolson was brilliant—perhaps even brighter than Hoover—but when Hoover was present, Tolson lapsed into silence and did little more than nod in agreement. I always believed he would have served his friend better had he been less subservient.

George Allen, intimate of presidents from Roosevelt to Eisenhower, was also a close friend of Hoover's. After Hoover and Tol-son had died, Allen gave an assessment of the relationship between the two men in a 1974 interview. When writer Ovid Demaris asked Allen directly whether Hoover and Tolson had been homosexual lovers, Allen's response spoke for all who knew Hoover well:

> That's ridiculous. Clyde was sort of an alter ego. He almost ran the FBI. He's not only a brain but the most unselfish man that ever lived. He let Hoover take all the bows, all the credit. He was a great administrator, worked all the budget stuff, and could speak for Hoover on anything. You can't take it much further than that. They were very, very close because he needed Clyde so much.

A shrewd observation from a man who knew Hoover well in a social setting, and could sense the real bond between Hoover and Tolson.

Clyde was extremely useful to the director, a man essential to the management of the bureau. The word "stooge" is a little too strong, because Tolson derived enormous dignity from his position in the FBI, and Hoover treated him with crisp respect, at least at the office. But Allen speaks of some condescension in social settings. He also points out that even when the two were relaxing Tolson called Hoover "Boss."

Bob Wick, one of the four assistant directors who reported to my office, confirmed Allen's evaluation of Tolson's role at the bureau, saying that he was "the best detail man I have ever known. He had a photographic memory. He could look at a memorandum and spot something wrong in one second. He was so good at this sort of detail." Wick correctly noted that Tolson was Hoover's sounding board and participated in virtually all major decisions. As for Tol-son making decisions on his own, Wick said, "Tolson could decide many things on his own. Most of the time they talked it over."

I firmly believe that, for all the time he spent with Hoover over a forty-four-year period, Tolson knew the man little better than I did. Tolson was the perfect subordinate—a tight-lipped confidant, a good companion for a day at the races or a night of boxing at Madison Square Garden, pleasant company on a rainy Sunday afternoon. But I doubt that he was Hoover's close friend in the fullest sense of that word.

In December of 1963, when Tolson was near death in George Washington Hospital following open heart surgery, Hoover called me into the office at 2:00 A.M. His first words were: "I almost lost him." I waited for him to talk about Tolson's condition, the prognosis, but Hoover had more important matters on his mind—the kidnapping of Frank Sinatra, Jr. The young man had been released by his captors and was, at that very moment, being escorted by FBI agents to his father's house. Hoover was extremely anxious to tell the boy's father that his son was safe. After making the call, he said no more to me about Clyde Tolson, nor did he return to the hospital to keep a worried vigil. He was driven home and he went to bed. I'm convinced he slept contentedly, knowing Tolson would continue to serve him as a daily buffer and a sounding board.

That's what Tolson was to Hoover—an almost indispensable figure at bureau headquarters, but not quite a friend. The only person for whom he held a deep and abiding affection had died years earlier, and all that was left of Annie Hoover was her Bible. Hoover's capacity to feel deeply for other human beings, were interred with her in the old Congressional Cemetery near Seward Square.

Summers isn't interested in understanding the real Hoover or Tolson, only the kind of lurid allegations that are sure to sell books. To sustain those allegations, Summers relies heavily on the testimony of corpses. They are convenient witnesses because they can't be cross-examined. If the world were to end tomorrow and the graves were to give up their dead, I suspect that Hoover would be vindicated by more than one resurrected body quoted by Anthony Summers. In many cases, Summers doesn't bother to give any authority at all to his statements; he just floats them into the ether.

It's interesting to see the manner in which Summers and the media have treated the subject, given the current fashion to approve of and promote homosexuality. A good deal of recent literature on the subject has been especially sympathetic toward homosexual lovers who, in another era, had to hide their affections and behave as if they were "straight" to maintain their jobs and respectability in a "homophobic" society. The late Randy Shilts, one of the most skillful propagandists for "gay rights," has said that the relationship between Hoover and Tolson was typical of that earlier time. Summers nevertheless treats what he calls their homosexual relationship with condescension, contempt, and heavy irony. Had he so treated any other homosexual couple of that era, he would have been attacked by every politically correct reviewer in the country for being "homophobic." Yet, since the subject here is J. Edgar Hoover, these same reviewers have been among Summers' most ardent admirers.

To this observation, some of them would counter, "Yes, but Hoover was hard on homosexuals in the FBI, dismissing every one of them he found, persecuting them like the fascist he was. We don't let those people off so easily." Fair enough, but the main thrust of Summers' attack is not on Hoover's hypocrisy but on his supposed effeminacy. Summers smirks at the showcase in Hoover's office containing "delicate china" (it was his mother's). He digs his reader in the ribs when he talks about the charge that Hoover wore perfume. He rolls his eyes at the remark of a magazine writer that Hoover walked with mincing steps. He repeats jokes about Tolson being a woman. In short, his attack on Hoover is precisely the sort that homosexuals most resent. Yet no one has gone after Summers. No one has called his book "homophobic."

This is clearly a tipoff to the true state of affairs. The intellectuals of the Left have allowed Summers to indulge in this kind of smear because they suspect Hoover wasn't really a homosexual and that Summers's ridicule of him is merely a ploy to sell books and in so doing destroy Hoover in the eyes of his natural constituency— the straight conservative community.

It's necessary to examine in detail the quality of Summers' cases. Consider this early passage in his book, in which he dicusses the friendship between Hoover and Melvin Purvis:

> Edgar dropped his usual rigid formality when he corresponded with Purvis, calling him "Dear Melvin" or

"Dear Mel," and signing himself "J.E.H." and even
"Jayee." Understandably nervous, Purvis stuck to
"Mr. Hoover" until Edgar told him to "stop using
MISTER," then moved on to "Dear Chairman" or
"Dear Jayee."

When Edgar's letters to Purvis concerned official
business, he laced them with a puerile brand of humor.
As a cure for a U.S. attorney suffering from "mental
halitosis," his standard epithet for anyone who disagreed with him, he proposed "the Mussolini treatment—a quart of castor oil administered in equal
doses, three in succession."

In unofficial notes, Edgar kept harping on the way
women fell for Purvis, not least his own secretary,
Helen Gandy. At one point he taunted the younger man
with claims that Gandy, a good-looking woman in her
mid-thirties, had been seen locked in the embrace of
another bureau official. In the fall of 1932 he assured
Purvis that, should he come to Washington for the Hal-
loween Ball, Gandy would come dressed in a "cellophane gown..."

Edgar began his fortieth year, 1934, still keeping up
a constant correspondence with his protege Melvin
Purvis. The letters were increasingly intimate, with
Edgar worried whenever the younger man caught a
cold. In one note, written around the time Clark Gable
was shooting to stardom in *It Happened One Night*,
Edgar teased Purvis about the way a newspaper had
described him. "I don't see how the movies could miss
a 'slender, blond-haired, brown-eyed' gentleman," he
wrote. "All power to the Clark Gable of the service."

It is hard to interpret the correspondence as anything
other than a homosexual courtship, even though Purvis
is not known to have had any such tendencies. Edgar's
oddest letter to him, a handwritten one dated April 3,
1934, was a bizarre mix of schoolboy humor and sexual innuendo:

Dear Melvin:

I received the Tru-Vue and films, magic trick, and
your sassy note. What did the True-Vue and films
cost? I asked you to get them for me and I intend
to pay for them. The films were both educational
and uplifting but I thought they would include a
series on "A Night in a Moorish Harem" or was
it a "Turkish Harem"? Nevertheless it was some
night and I am still looking forward to your
producing a set. Of course my interest is solely as
a censor or chairman of the Moral Uplift Squad.
The bombs are the best yet. I have already caused
Miss Gandy to jump two feet and that is something considering the fact that she is now in the
heavyweight class. The damned magic trick has
me almost "nuts" trying to figure out how it is
done... Well, son, keep a stiff upper lip and get
Dillinger for me, and the world is yours.

                    Sincerely and affectionately,
                    Jayee

I've quoted extensively to include all the evidence for the Summers statement that "[i]t is hard to interpret the correspondence as
anything other than a homosexual courtship..."

Indeed, the more you examine these quotations, the more het-
erosexual they seem. The references to Miss Gandy—surprising as
they are to those of us who knew both Hoover and his secretary in
their later years—are clearly part of the bantering between two
bachelors interested in women.

As for the newspaper description that Hoover cites, it contains a
discernible measure of irony, since Purvis is not in the field to look
pretty but to catch criminals. There are several legitimate ways to
interpret this brief passage, removed from its context. But no one
except a sensationalist could properly say it was an example of
"homosexual courtship."

Finally, the letter quoted in its entirety contains only one "sexual" reference—to a "Harem." Again the talk is about women, with Hoover suggesting that he hoped to see a "True-Vue" with such a series on it. Then, tongue-in-cheek, he assures Purvis that his motives are pure, those of the "censor" or of "the Moral Uplift Squad." The clear implication—Hoover might like to look at some girly pictures.

And that is all the evidence Summers offers to support his claim that Hoover's correspondence reveals a homosexual courtship—these quotations, nothing more. And this twisted leap of logic merely hints at the lengths to which Summers will go to transform the highly conventional Hoover into a sexual deviant and cross-dresser.

Next, Summers quotes a succession of writers who, he claims, either hint at Hoover's homosexuality, or speak of it in more open terms. Some of his examples are gossip about two male friends who spent a lot of time together, the same kind of gossip that might well have been spread about Mutt and Jeff. Other examples are so far-fetched as to be contemptible:

- *Colliers* magazine, in the 1930s, published the following description: "Mr Hoover is short, fat, businesslike, and walks with a mincing step... He dresses fastidiously, with Eleanor blue as the favorite color for the matched shades of tie, handkerchief and sox. A little pompous, he rides in a limousine even if only to a nearby self-service cafeteria."

- Robert Ludlum, in his 1978 novel, *The Chancellor Manuscript*, writes that Tolson's "soft pampered face—struggling for masculinity—had for decades been the flower to the bristled cactus."

- And Summers writes: "Yet another reporter observed that Edgar kept dainty china in his office beside the crime trophies. 'He is different,' commented a foreign diplomat, 'from any police officer I ever knew, in that he uses a distinctive and conspicuous perfume.' Edgar ordered a senior aide to say 'very, very diplomatically' that he never used perfume. In fact, he did."

- Summers cites a *Time* article that observed of Hoover that he was "seldom seen without a male companion, most-frequently solemn-faced Clyde Tolson." He suggests that a reporter's reference to Hoover's elusiveness ("as mysterious as a Garbo smile"), and to the fact that Tolson had the hotel room next door to the director's are journalistic "hints" of homosexuality. He reports that when Lou Nichols named his son "John Edgar," unnamed agents joked that if Lou had had a daughter, he would have named her "Clyde." Summers even mentions a Truman Capote proposal to a magazine that he write an article about Hoover and Tolson called "Johnny and Clyde."

In his summary paragraph of this segment of the book—consisting of little more than a catalog of rumors, innuendoes, and passages tortured to yield hints of homosexuality—Summers reveals the illusory nature of his case:

> Scholars have pointed to many photographs, some of them pictures of Clyde taken by Edgar, that survived from Edgar's private collection: Clyde asleep, Clyde in a bathrobe, Clyde by the pool. Yet the two friends never openly set up house together. Clyde continued to maintain his own apartment when Edgar bought a house for himself after his mother's death. At the office, say former colleagues, the two men showed no unusual affection for each other. For the forty-four years they were intimates, the deception must have been a constant strain. But a deception it was.

Summers devotes a chapter to Hoover's relationship with Senator

Joseph McCarthy and quotes a definition of "McCarthyism," which reads in part: "the use of indiscriminate, often unfounded accusations, sensationalism..." When he copied that definition out of the dictionary, he must have blushed.

The verifiable material in this collection of "charges" is insignificant or irrelevant and the partially significant material is unverifiable. Let's take these passages one at a time. No one knows what a *Colliers* writer in the 1930s meant by the phrase "mincing steps." The passage seems to suggest that Hoover was something of a "dandy"—and indeed he was. I am reminded of Scott Fitzgerald's reference, in *The Great Gatsby*, to the "effeminate swank" of Tom Buchanan's clothes. Buchanan was a former athlete who was married to the heroine, Daisy, and kept a mistress on the side. Mr. Summers would probably deduce from the phrase that Buchanan was having a homosexual affair with Nick Carroway.

Ludlum's description of Clyde Tolson is unrecognizable to those of us who knew him. Clearly Ludlum is attempting to give credibility to his fictional work by working some of the current gossip into the texture of the narrative.

As for the photographs of Tolson lounging around, Richard Gid Power, in *Secrecy and Power: The Life of J. Edgar Hoover*, writes this:

> Hoover did not expect these albums to survive his death, but they escaped the notice of Tolson and Hoover's secretary when they destroyed Hoover's personal effects in accordance with his wishes. These albums consist almost exclusively of photographs of Tolson in front of the various backdrops of their vacation resorts. Although the photographs convey a feeling of affection, when the two men appear together in a photo they are never seen touching one another, except in two groups photos in which all present had their arms around each other's shoulders. On the other hand, Hoover took several photos of Tolson while he was sleeping, a situation in which many men might find it embarrassing to be photographed. Other photos show the two men in bathrobes or barechested at the beach.

> The photos convey the sense of a caring, emotionally
> involved eye behind the lens, and whether it was a
> lover's eye or a close friend's, it was still qualitatively
> different from a business associate's.

Note what Powers has written: "Hoover did not expect these albums to survive his death..." Undoubtedly this conjecture is sound, since Hoover ordered the destruction of his personal effects. Under those circumstances, it is important to consider what pictures were not included in Hoover's album. No nude photos of Tolson. No snapshots of the two locked in an embrace. No homoerotic materials. Yet even Powers goes too far, I think, in postulating an "emotionally involved eye behind the lens." The photographs Hoover took of Tolson were the sort you'd find in anyone's album—informal poses of friends in unguarded, casual moments. As for the shots of Tolson sleeping, who hasn't taken such pictures when the opportunity arose, perhaps to say afterward, "Here's how you look when you're asleep"? Again, the evidence offered is open to several interpretations, the least plausible of which is a homosexual liaison.

Summers cites Hoover's unbending opposition to homosexuals and homosexuality as further evidence that he was himself a homosexual. He quotes Hoover as saying, "No member of the Mattachine Society or anyone who is a sexual deviate will ever be appointed to the FBI." And in the very next paragraph he offers even more evidence along those lines:

> Both Edgar and Clyde kept up the macho front all their
> lives. They let it be known they liked smutty jokes, and
> would call senior colleagues to offer off-color gags—
> always about women—for inclusion in speeches. Edgar
> once gave a transparent "striptease" pen, inscribed
> "J.E.H.," to President Truman's attorney general,
> Howard McGrath. One New Year's Eve, at Gatti's
> restaurant in Miami Beach, Clyde was seen presenting
> the sexagenarian Edgar with his birthday present—a
> Jayne Mansfield doll.

Now there's a smoking gun for you! At first it's difficult to understand why Summers would include materials so damaging to his case. But, of course, he had to take up this question since everyone who knew the two men were well aware of their interest in women, their locker-room banter, their enjoyment of a good off-color joke. So Summers says it was all an act, a coverup, a sham.

Summers also reports that William C. Sullivan—who hated Hoover toward the end and slandered him repeatedly—said he had rummaged through Hoover's desk one night and found "lurid literature of the most filthy kind... naked women and lurid magazines with all sorts of abnormal sexual activities." Once again, even if you believe the account, Sullivan found no homosexual materials, only girly magazines.

Summers even resorts to long distance, retrospective analyses by a couple of college professors, who apparently never met Hoover but were still willing to pontificate about his sexuality. His choice of at least one is particularly instructive.

> Where sexuality is concerned, one must be careful in attaching labels to people. Commenting on Edgar's behavioral patterns, however, two leading medical specialists have reached similar conclusions. Dr. John Money, professor of Medical Psychology at Johns Hopkins University School of Medicine, felt Edgar probably had a bisexual, but strongly predominant homosexual orientation.

Dr. Money, Summers' "leading medical specialist," believes that society is moving toward a time when sex with partners of both sexes will be both normal and normative. He has also written an introduction to *Boys and Their Sexual Contacts* (a book by a pedophile that is a blatant apology for pedophilia), calling it "one of the most valuable works of research scholarship on the topic of pedophilia that has ever appeared in print." I suspect I could easily find a couple of retired professors who would be willing to speculate about John Money and his motives for making such a judgment of Hoover.

In an attempt to give even greater credibility to this thesis, Summers claims that Hoover consulted a psychiatrist "[p]robably in late 1946, in the wake of continuing rumors that he was a homosexual...." Predictably, the psychiatrist he names has since died, but Summers quotes the doctor's gossipy widow as saying, "He was definitely troubled by homosexuality and my husband's notes would've proved that.... I might stir a keg of worms by making that statement, but everybody then understood he was a homosexual, not just the doctors." Note the "would've." It seems Dr. Ruffin burned them, along with other patients' files, shortly before he died. A responsible thing to do, which leads one to ask: Would a psychiatrist with any sense of professional ethics have shared case histories with his wife?

Those of us who were close to Hoover knew the identity of his doctors, often associated with them socially, and occasionally invited them to the FBI Academy at Quantico. None of us ever heard of this psychiatrist.

Summers even attempts to suggest that Hoover's love of flowers, which he often sent to friends, was somehow effeminate, a mark of his homosexuality. He quotes a former florist's assistant who delivered flowers for Hoover as saying, "One time I was given a key for an apartment in the Wardman Park Hotel. It had dramatic decor, white furniture with a contrasting carpet. There was a sealed envelope with the flowers. I didn't know if it was for a lady or a gentleman. I didn't ask any questions..."

As another piece of evidence, Summers cites the fact that the FBI instituted a wiretap "on John Monroe, a Washington influence peddler who held Edgar's attention not least because he reportedly claimed the director was a 'fairy.'" Here he can't even say that some discredited FBI agent or underworld character actually accused Hoover of being homosexual. The most he can say is that Monroe "reportedly claimed" Hoover was homosexual.

In reporting about activities during World War II, Summers purports to quote a British officer who visited Hoover's home as follows:

> "There were," Stephenson would recall, "nudes on the stairway, pictures of rather suggestive male nudes, all over the place." He would soon meet Edgar in the

company of Clyde, and recognize them as a homosexual couple. Stephenson thought Edgar remote, complex, very different from himself.

Two things about this passage are striking. One, Hoover had no male nudes in his house whenever I went there. Indeed, it was so out of character that I can only believe Stephenson either remembers someone else's house or else never said what Summers quotes. Besides, as puritanical as he was (and as concerned as he was with his spotless image), Hoover would never have displayed such art work, even if he'd owned it, to be talked about by casual acquaintances and female guests.

Hoover did have the famous nude study of Marilyn Monroe on his stairwell, which is probably all the British officer saw. In a later passage, Summers speaks of the Monroe picture, but also, mistakenly, of other female nudes on Hoover's wall. His strained explanation: "They were there, some assumed, to deflect speculation about the director's homosexuality." If so, why display male nudes?

As for Stephenson immediately recognizing Hoover and Clyde as a homosexual couple, I saw them together for decades and never concluded any such thing; nor did anyone else who knew them. A casual acquaintance would have seen no more than we saw—two men who were quite masculine; who never touched each other physically; who were coolly efficient in their dealings with others; and who were not overly friendly toward each other, even in social situations. In short, none of Summers' testimony squares with my experience or with that of anyone else who knew Hoover and had been in his home.

One of Summers' favorite techniques is to infer from flimsy evidence that someone believed or knew Hoover was homosexual, then later in the narrative to speak about the previous incident as if it were not inference but established fact. Thus, when he first speaks of Hoover's visit to the psychiatrist, he writes that Hoover's physician, "puzzled by a strange malaise in his patient," referred Hoover to a psychiatrist, Dr. Ruffin, and that this happened "probably in late 1946." By the next page, it's a fact: "By 1946, when he first consulted Dr. Ruffin...." And many pages later, he writes: "It was at this time that Edgar's worry about his homosexuality drove him to consult Dr. Ruffin, the Washington psychiatrist." Notice that the doctor's puzzlement over "a strange malaise" has become Hoover's "worry about his homosexuality." Still later we're told that Hoover was sent to Dr. Ruffin because of recurring nightmares.

In like manner, Summers quotes a Truman-era document, with names deleted, that referred to Hoover. It read that "CENSORED gave me some very bad news about J. Edgar Hoover. I only hope it is only gossip. Geo. suggests I see the president alone." Of this passage, Summers writes: "The 'bad news' was very probably about Edgar's homosexuality." By the next page, it is nondebatable fact. "Here was the president of the United States being bothered with FBI gossip about his aides' dalliances with women, when he had just been briefed on Edgar's behavior. In Edgar's case, by comparison, there was at least cause for concern. A homosexual FBI director, in charge of the nation's internal security, was a classic target for any hostile intelligence service—especially that of the Soviet Union." The leaps in logic are mind-boggling, and illustrate the workings of Summers' mind—a contempt for hard facts and credible sources.

In another spot Summers claims that Hoover and Tolson held hands in public, not only at the Stork Club but at the race track as well—an extraordinary charge. One of the accusers, a lower-echelon mob figure named Seymour Pollack, is quoted as saying: "I used to meet him at the race track every once in a while with lover boy Clyde, in the late forties and fifties. I was in the next box once. And when you see two guys holding hands, well come on!... They were surreptitious, but there was no question about it."

Another rumor was repeated by a retired policeman who passed along an alleged report from an unnamed cab driver, who said he'd seen Tolson and Hoover at Washington's National Airport: "He said Hoover was waiting and rented the cab. It was Tolson who came off the plane. And he said he never saw so much kissing and ass-grabbing in his life. It was the kind of thing that made you feel the rumors were true."

The hand-holding incident was supposed to have happened in the late 1940s and early 1950s, and the National Airport story, though undated, was clearly vintage. No homosexual couple during this period would have dared behave this way in public. Even today, with homosexuals riding high, such public displays are rare. And these men were the two top ranking officials in the FBI, one of whom was known by sight to virtually every American.

Summers goes on to say that Hoover's homosexuality was well known in certain gangs, that rumors persisted concerning photographs the Mafia had of Hoover and Tolson, and that they blackmailed the director into leaving Meyer Lansky alone, which was why "[t]here was no serious federal effort to indict Lansky until 1970, just two years before Edgar died." Most of this misinformation comes from the mobster Pollack, and obviously neither he nor Summers is aware of the amount of documented effort the FBI expended trying to put Meyer Lansky behind bars.

The story told by Susan Rosenstiel, however, is the linchpin of Summers' construction. She is the one witness Summers can quote with any direct evidence that the director was a sexual deviant. If true, it goes a lot further to making Summers' case than all his innuendos and assumptions combined. Rosenstiel not only says she saw Hoover in drag with Roy Cohn, she offers up a second sighting, this time wearing a red dress and a boa. "He was dressed like an old flapper," she insisted, "like you see on old tintypes."

Rosenstiel's tales might be more persuasive were she not a convicted perjurer with a grudge against Hoover. It's important to remember that in Rosenstiel's sensational divorce trial there was a controversy over property that she allegedly stole, she lied under oath, and she was convicted for perjury and served time on Rikers Island. Apparently she blamed Hoover for damaging information her husband obtained concerning her activities, which weighed against her in court.

It's difficult to say whether her Hoover story was an act of revenge or whether, in her blind rage, she somehow convinced herself that some drag queen she'd encountered was the director of the FBI. Whatever the reason, she'd been trying to peddle this story to Hoover's critics for years. But even his staunchest enemies recognized her unreliability and dismissed the story as ridiculous or fraudulent. Anthony Summers was the only one who saw fit to publish it.

With the exception of the Rosenstiel anecdote, which is quite specific, virtually all the other sources are second-hand repetitions of rumors, speculations, or tales told by the dead. Summers's sources—when he bothers to identify them—are no more than a handful of gangsters, perjurers, discredited cops, left-wing ideologues, and catty homosexuals.

In short, Summers builds the kind of case that could have been made against any man who remained a bachelor all his life—a case constructed out of rumor, suspicion, and the general attitude among his detractors that of course "everybody knew." A man with as many enemies as Hoover was vulnerable to malicious slander of this sort, but Summers is almost alone among Hoover's biographers to give credence to the petty malice of society's outcasts.

To their credit, several of Hoover's well-known detractors have dismissed these charges as absurd and unworthy, as have fair-minded journalists. This wealth of adverse opinion of the book from quarters unfriendly to Hoover is probably more persuasive than the testimony of Hoover's close associates.

Perhaps the most damaging analysis of the book was written for *Esquire* (May 1993) by Peter Maas, an old Hoover basher. As Maas puts it, "I've been a Hoover foe from the first." And indeed he has. A friend of Bobby Kennedy, he hounded the director in print for years and years, and in his review of *Official and Confidential* he calls Hoover "a fatuous, personally corrupt, evil ass." Yet even he cannot stomach the methodology Summers employs and the conclusions he reaches. Knowing the history of the question better than most, and having interviewed many of the people Summers quotes, he dissects the allegations with great skill.

For example, of the charges that mobster Meyer Lansky was blackmailing Hoover with homosexual photographs, Maas, whose resources are considerably vaster and more responsive than Summers', goes to the most reliable authority he can find, a man who was Lansky's closest friend and associate for over fifty years—Vincent "Jimmy Blue Eyes" Alo:

> Hoover is dead. Lansky is dead. Alo, while still remarkably alert, is pushing ninety years of age. Now long out

of the business, he's spent time in the federal slammer. Throughout a good deal of his life, he was constantly harassed, bugged, and surveilled by Hoover's FBI. I got to Jimmy about the pictures that Lansky allegedly had of Hoover and Tolson. He said, "Are you nuts?"

Maas openly ridicules Summers' claim by pointing to the ample evidence that Hoover and the FBI were almost obsessive in their pursuit of Lansky. "And you don't have to apply for them [the facts] through the Freedom of Information Act. They're right there for anyone to see, including Summers, in a first-rate biography of Lansky by Robert Lacey titled *Little Man: Meyer Lansky and the Gangster Life.*" Then Maas offers a devastating illustration:

> Here's one example. The FBI field office in Miami, where Lansky was residing, complained to headquarters that too many of its agents were expending too much time and energy monitoring Lansky. At the time it said, "There are more important and active top hoodlums in the Miami area."
>
> Did Hoover breathe a sigh of relief? Well, hardly. What he did was to teletype back under his name the following in capital letters:
>
> LANSKY HAS BEEN DESIGNATED FOR QUOTE CRASH UNQUOTE INVESTIGATION. THE IMPORTANCE OF THIS CASE CANNOT BE OVEREMPHASIZED.... THE BUREAU EXPECTS THIS INVESTIGATION TO BE DILIGENT AND DETAILED.

Nor did Hoover let it go at that. He ordered that a "highly confidential source"—i.e., a bug—be used regarding Lansky. The two bugs were deployed in Lansky's home, neither of which produced anything of value.

Finally, Maas addresses the transvestite story. Again he knows the territory, and probably heard the apocryphal tale years before Summers picked it up and thought he'd struck gold. But Maas and other Hoover haters were more discriminating in their choice of sources, more honest about whom they invited into the pages of their attacks. Of the allegations that Hoover cross-dressed and cavorted in drag with Roy Cohn, he writes:

> The trouble is that the sole source for this is Susan Rosenstiel. The trouble also is that she'd been trying to peddle this story for years. Among those she had approached was Robert Morgenthau, a former U.S. attorney in New York and current Manhattan D.A. On paper, she couldn't have made a better choice. Morgenthau had tried, unsuccessfully, to convict Cohn three times for various transgressions. He and Hoover were not on speaking terms. Morgenthau discovered that Rosenstiel—no paragon of civic virtue—had dumped Susan and an ugly divorce ensued. She hated Hoover, convinced he put FBI agents on her to help her husband's cause. "I didn't believe her then," Morgenthau told me, "and I don't now."

In his final evaluation of the book, Maas reminds his reader once again that he is no Hoover lover. But he shows that he values something more than the final destruction of Hoover's tattered reputation, a vocation for which Summers apparently has little concern:

> Come on, you say, so what? Isn't there a little poetic justice here? Hoover on the receiving end for what he'd been dishing out. Hey, right on! But there's a flip side. The material, at best, belongs in a supermarket tabloid. At least you're forewarned. But for a book like this, published by a reputable house—with an ad headline that screams, "At last, the truth about J. Edgar Hoover"—does grievous harm to serious investigative

journalism. Poll after poll shows the media sinking in
public esteem and credibility. Every so often, you have
to wonder if the public doesn't have a point.

These criticisms do more to expose Summers and the falsity of
his charges than anything the rest of us could say. Unfortunately,
the Summers book has received considerable attention from the
press. J. Edgar Hoover was not a homosexual. Those who knew
him well are unanimous in that opinion. And those who carefully
read the Summers book must reject the charge.

5

Hoover the Man

IF NOT THE MYTHIC DRAG QUEEN of recent portrayals, what sort of man was J. Edgar Hoover? That's a hard question, even for those of us who worked with him daily. I once wrote in the preface to an article: "I never knew J. Edgar Hoover. This was true even though the FBI was my career for almost twenty-nine years and I was in contact with him daily, either in person or by telephone, over the last fifteen of those years." Anyone who says he's depicting the "real J. Edgar Hoover" is deceiving himself or others.

Long before the Left had succeeded in trashing Hoover and the FBI, when I was a young man, the director was a glamorous figure and the bureau was synonymous with excitement and adventure. I remember the day I decided to enter the FBI. It was 1941, and with war looming, my fraternity brothers and I were talking about how we would serve our country the following year, after graduation. As we talked, a news bulletin broke on the radio—the FBI had just captured eight Nazi saboteurs who had come ashore, some in Florida, some on Long Island, New York.

"Man, that FBI is one hell of an outfit," said one fraternity brother.

And suddenly it hit me: Why not the FBI? We had all been raised on stories of G-men—the exploits of Melvin Purvis, the killing of John Dillinger and Baby Face Nelson and Pretty Boy Floyd, the stern and incorruptible J. Edgar Hoover.

In June of 1942, I had graduated from Stetson College with a B.A., and completed one and a half year's legal training at Stetson Law School. I was eager to join Hoover's team. But time and lack of money caught up with me and I had to leave Stetson before getting the J.D. degree required for FBI agents. My application to become a special agent was rejected so I accepted an entry-level job as a clerk with the bureau, and soon I was classifying and identifying fingerprints in the cavernous Identification Division in Washington, D.C.

But I still had ambitions to be a full-fledged FBI agent—to pack a gun and wear a snap-brimmed hat. I knew the bureau needed agents because of the wartime caseload and an increasing drain on manpower by the military. So I kept making inquiries and knocking on doors. One day I got an appointment to see Assistant Director Stanley Tracy, and I thought my big moment had come. He listened to my well-rehearsed speech, read my resumé, and gave me a quick, straight answer.

"No. You're too young and inexperienced."

I left his office angry but not discouraged. I waited a while, then asked for an interview with Associate Director Clyde Tolson. He refused to see me. But he did grant me an appointment with one of his assistants, Inspector Robert E. Lee. We hit it off from the start. In his report of our meeting, he described me as "a rugged ex-college football player who, although lacking a few credits for a law degree, does have a B.A. and law school training." He concluded, "I recommend approval to enter training as an agent."

Tolson agreed—and that was it! I was promoted from a $1,440 a year clerk to a $3,200 a year agent trainee. On the day of my appointment I sent a telegram to my mother, Eula DeLoach, who still took in boarders at our house in Claxton, Georgia, as she had done ever since my father died in 1929—when the Great Depression began and I was just nine years old.

After my basic training at the FBI's version of boot camp—the FBI Training Academy in Quantico, Virginia—I was assigned to the Norfolk, Virginia office and then after a while I was sent to Cleveland, Ohio. I didn't find myself engaged in the sort of exciting work I had hoped for. While in Norfolk I had to solve a case of a stolen jar of navy pickles. And most of my time in Ohio was spent monitoring the uneventful comings and goings of the state Communist party chief.

Perhaps the most rewarding assignment I undertook while in Ohio was an interview in Barberton, checking the background of an applicant for an important federal post. The person I was interviewing was a physician, and after I'd asked him routine questions about the applicant, the doctor continued to make small talk, asking me questions about my job, inviting me to talk about my background. I was unaware that he was interviewing me.

Finally he said, "Are you busy this evening?"

"No, not really," I said. "I'll probably try to catch up on a little paperwork at the office."

"You're not married, are you?"

"No sir, I'm still a confirmed bachelor."

He smiled.

"Good," he said. "I have an eighteen-year-old sister-in-law whom my wife and I plan to take to dinner. She might be a little young for you, but why don't you join us and be her date for the evening? We won't be out late."

As it turned out, I hoped the evening would last forever. My date turned out to be a beautiful blue-eyed blonde with a gorgeous figure and a lovely tan. Her name was Barbara Ellen Owens, and that night was just the beginning. Later, after six months of seeing each other regularly, I persuaded her to take her chances in life with me.

In December of 1943—prior to our marriage—all single agents under twenty-five years of age and with no dependents were advised by FBI headquarters that their deferments would be withdrawn. I was neither surprised nor disappointed. As an inexperienced new agent, I had been performing mostly perfunctory tasks. I had not captured any Nazi spies or saboteurs, and, like most young Americans of that day, I dreamed of military service and an heroic war record. I was also interested in politics, and it occurred to me that an ex-FBI agent with World War II combat ribbons might make a formidable candidate for office. So I took military leave from the FBI and joined the United States Navy.

I volunteered—and fully expected—to be sent to the Far East, where the U.S. fleet was now challenging the Imperial Japanese Navy. Instead, I was ordered to report to the U.S. Naval Air Station at Norman, Oklahoma. The combination of my gridiron achievements, legal education, and FBI experience had somehow marked me for the navy's athletic program, and I spent my entire tour of duty in Oklahoma, which was as far as I could get from either ocean. As soon as I could manage a discharge, I returned to the FBI.

Barbara Owens and I were married on April 22, 1945, in Cincinnati, Ohio; and our first child, Barbara Elaine, was born while I was still in the navy. (By the time our family was complete, we would have six more children—Deke, Jr.; Tom; Theresa; Greg; Sharon; and Mark.)

After a two-week refresher course, I was sent back to Akron, Ohio, as the only resident agent in that robust postwar town. There, in the streets and alleys of Summit County, working closely with the local and state police, I came to know the practical side of law enforcement—the things not included in standard textbooks. My days and nights were long and exhausting, not always coordinated with the timetable of a happy family life; yet Barbara learned to live with an FBI agent and to accept the extra burdens that such a life placed on her shoulders.

In June of 1947, Assistant Director Hugh Clegg, head of the FBI Training and Inspection Division at the Washington headquarters, came to Akron to address the graduates of the police academy. Afterward, he accepted my invitation to join Barbara and me for drinks in our small apartment. A week later a letter arrived transferring me to Washington as an agent supervisor. The promotion came as a complete surprise. I can only conclude that Clegg had been impressed by the high degree of respect the people of Akron had for the FBI.

I was excited and pleased, but some of the more experienced agents in Ohio warned me not to accept the new assignment.

"You'll get lost in the shuffle."

"The field is the only place for a real FBI man."

"Washington is no place to raise a family."

This pessimism puzzled and disturbed me, but I didn't feel I could turn down a promotion. And my brother-in-law, the Barberton doctor, encouraged me to take it.

"It's a step forward," he reasoned. "You can't decline a promotion. It would indicate a poor attitude, an unwillingness to try new things, to accept new responsibilities. Serving at FBI headquarters will broaden your experience and improve your qualifications."

He smiled.

"It's only natural that you enjoy being 'Mr. FBI' here in a smaller city, but surely you don't want to serve in a one-man resident agency for the rest of your career. Go to Washington!"

I took his advice and headed for the capital city.

I was assigned to the Atomic Energy-Applicant Section of the Domestic Intelligence Division. My duty was to supervise field investigations of people seeking employment inside atomic energy operations; for example, truck drivers. This was routine work, simplified by guidelines that were detailed, precise, and clear. But I did well, and worked my way up through the FBI bureaucracy until I finally caught Hoover's eye. I was made an inspector, a job that sent me all over the country supervising investigations. This role taught me the most about being a G-man. The experience served me well when I was promoted to help Assistant Director Louis Nichols run the public relations and congressional relations shop at the bureau.

Soon after Nichols retired in 1957, Hoover named me acting assistant director, and in 1959 the "acting" was dropped. I was thirty-eight years old.

I remained assistant director for six years. Then, in 1965, Hoover promoted me to the FBI's number three slot—assistant to the director. In that position I was in command of the bureau's three investigative divisions, as well as the public relations division. I was responsible for general criminal investigations, all special investigative matters (for example, organized crime, fugitives), intelligence and internal security cases, and the public affairs of the bureau.

When I was promoted to this high-level position, many Washington reporters believed that Hoover was placing me in line to take over as director when he and Tolson retired. He had no such idea in mind. As it turned out, I served for five years and then retired, while Hoover remained as director until he died two years later.

The five years as assistant to the director were the most exciting of my life. With Hoover and Tolson slowed by age, and with the director's willingness to delegate substantial authority to subordinates he deemed competent, I was in the thick of some of the greatest—and most terrible—events of our time. And yet even to me Hoover remained an enigma.

Clyde Tolson could have written the most accurate and detailed character sketch of Hoover, but I'm convinced that even Tolson would have failed to capture the essence of this obsessively private man. He was too elusive, too contradictory, too defensive to sit still for a formal portrait, the kind that hangs in the galleries of major museums or appears in two-parts in the *New Yorker* magazine. Even the surviving photographs show a man with a stern face, with an occasional mirthless smile that hardly alters his expression. None of these snapshots betray him.

The young Hoover seems little different from the old man. As best we can tell from scant evidence, the young Edgar was a stiff and serious little boy, raised by old-fashioned parents dressed in dark and formal clothes. It's easy to imagine his hearing the constant refrain to play quietly. But he clearly loved his mother, Annie Hoover, more than anyone in the world—and perhaps she was the only person he ever did love. He lived with her until she died, and then he lived alone. He kept reminders of her in his office—including pieces of her china—but discarded or packed away most of the awards and letters of commendation he got from presidents and other famous people.

The rest of his early biography is largely rumor and speculation, as are his college years and his first days in government service. His private life was as genuinely private as that of any public figure in the nation's history. People knew more about the emotional side of Calvin Coolidge than they did of J. Edgar Hoover.

His nieces, who remembered him from their adolescence, give us some clues, offering a picture of Hoover the devoted son and his doting mother. But in other respects they do little more than deepen the mystery.

"Nanny," as they called Annie Hoover, kept house for "J. E.," and he lavished her with the kind of gifts a man would give a wife, such as expensive jewelry—and a canary that he bought from the Birdman of Alcatraz. But mother and son had their disagreements; she preferred the shades drawn at all times, and he preferred the sunlight pouring in. So the two kept up a silent battle. Every morning after he left for work, she would pull down the shades and live in half-light all day; and every afternoon he would come home to a cool, dark house, and go from window to window opening up the shades again. They would never argue about this, but each would stubbornly persist—day after day, year after year.

According to the nieces, in the early years, the Hoover household was very social. Hoover's mother would entertain relatives and friends on Sunday, serving wine and other alcoholic drinks. Later, when Hoover became master of the household, this stopped, perhaps because Prohibition had arrived.

One night when one of his nieces was going out, he warned her to be careful. "If you're in a place that's raided," he said, "don't give your right name." Standard avuncular advice for that era. One must remember that the FBI was not responsible for violations of the Volstead Act.

Hoover's niece Anna gives a very interesting insight into Hoover's care of his mother and a possible reason for his failure to marry:

> Nanny was around seventy-eight when she died [in 1938]. We always thought it was cancer, but it was in the days when nobody mentioned cancer. She was bedridden nearly three years. I often thought this was one reason why he never married. He didn't have a chance. When he might have married, there was his mother and there was no room in the house for another woman and he simply did not have enough money to run two establishments.

His niece Margaret had a slightly different explanation for Hoover's failure to marry—ambition:

> I think he regarded women as a kind of hinderance.
> You know, they sort of got in your way when you were
> going places. I sometimes have thought that he really—I
> don't know how to put it—had a fear of becoming too
> personally involved with people.

Hoover once told me something that confirms this opinion. While in his office one day, he said, "DeLoach, I've often been asked why I never married. The truth is, that if I had—and gotten the wrong woman—my life and career would have been ruined forever."

Margaret elaborated on Hoover's unwillingness to commit himself emotionally, which, she said, extended to members of his immediate family:

> I think you would have to say that J. E. was not a fami-
> ly person. I don't remember Aunt Lillian too well
> [Hoover's sister]. She married a man called Robinette
> and moved out to the country. She used to come to
> visit, bringing the young children, Fred and Marjorie,
> but I have only a faint recollection of that. Her hus-
> band died and she was crippled for many years. I've
> heard that J. E. never visited her, but I don't have any
> personal knowledge of that. I do know that he got to
> her funeral late and left early.

Most of the hostile biographies of Hoover talk about his racial bigotry as if it were as obvious as his pug nose. The Left hurls this charge around indiscriminately, an ad hominem attack that always seems to draw blood, even when there's little evidence to support it. In the case of J. Edgar Hoover, such an attack is as predictable as it is false. The Left was constantly attacking Hoover—and for several reasons.

In the first place, he was head of an agency that was the epitome of American authoritarianism. The FBI investigated and arrested people who challenged the majesty of the federal government; and during the latter part of Hoover's tenure, the Left was antigovernment and anti–law-and-order. Leftists funded and supported the New Left activists and encouraged the antiwar movement. After building up the power of the federal government and the executive branch during the New Deal, New Frontier, and Fair Deal years, they began to see dangers in a strong centralized government and "an imperial presidency." Lyndon Johnson became the first "dangerous" chief executive, and J. Edgar Hoover was his gestapo chief.

A second reason why the Left hated Hoover was because of his conservative views, which he voiced at every opportunity. Critics were particularly disturbed by his relentless pursuit of the Communist party, which the American Left insisted was no more dangerous than any other political party—perhaps slightly less so than the GOP. Consequently, they regarded Hoover's anticommunist stance as malignant and subversive, contrary to everything for which the nation stood. In other words, they regarded Hoover in precisely the same way Hoover regarded the communists.

A third reason leftists hated Hoover was because of his public confrontations with the Rev. Martin Luther King Jr., who, by the late 1950s, had become a superhero. To challenge King after the success of the Montgomery bus boycott was regarded as an act of lese majesty. Leftists so idolized the civil rights leader that they refused even to consider that he might be flawed or that his movement might have come under malign influences.

For all these reasons, no doubt, they said Hoover was prejudiced against blacks. He was not. To be sure, when Bobby Kennedy and the NAACP demanded that the bureau admissions standards be lowered to achieve a better racial balance, Hoover refused, citing the necessity to maintain the highest possible level of performance in carrying out duties that were often dangerous and even life-threatening. Contrary to bald assertions by journalists—during those years we hired a number of qualified black agents and administrative personnel. Not only did the director show no resistance to minorities in the FBI, he personally sent me to lecture at law schools with the primary objective of inviting black students to consider joining the bureau once they had attained their degrees—then a requirement for all agents.

The record will show that the blacks we recruited during that period were excellent agents. The percentage was not higher because opportunities for qualified blacks in the private sector were much more lucrative than in government service. In fact, we believed we had attracted a higher number of blacks into the FBI than would ordinarily have been hired because we actively and aggressively recruited them. And this happened in some measure because of J. Edgar Hoover's personal intervention.

I might add that in all the years I worked with him, talking with him almost every day, I never heard him utter a single racial epithet or say anything that suggested he regarded any minority with contempt. For a man of his time, he was remarkably free of such prejudices—more so than some of the presidents for whom he worked.

On the other hand, Hoover's attitude toward women in the bureau is open to legitimate criticism. As director, he refused to allow women to become agents. They could work as secretaries and file clerks. They could perform intricate tests in laboratories. But he would not permit them to become full-fledged agents and to perform the same duties the men performed.

Most of us disagreed with this policy. We knew, for one thing, that female agents were badly needed in the field. There were times when they could have gone places men couldn't go, done things that men couldn't do. In fact, we often did assign women to work with our agents, but because of policy, they were described as "auxiliaries" or "affiliates." These assignments usually involved posing as wives of agents who were working undercover, and they were given to women classified as secretaries and file clerks. I worked with women frequently in extortion and espionage cases, but again they were not agents, and I had to make certain they were never exposed to any danger.

I'm sure Hoover would have explained his attitude toward women agents in old-fashioned terms. He saw them as daughters, sisters, and mothers; and his attitude was always mannerly and protective. I suspect that in many ways every woman was his mother, a woman of another century, to be coddled and protected. Such an attitude may well explain why he never established a close relationship with a woman that ended in marriage. It may have been the one area of Hoover's life in which he was deferential; and a man who is too deferential usually never gets to first base.

Hoover was a vain man in many respects, but he loved to tell stories at his own expense—and was good at it, when the mood struck him. He often told about the time when he had flown to rural Minnesota in sub-zero weather to assist in the search for a kidnap victim and the abductor's hideout. During the course of the operation, he stopped by a small general store to buy warm clothing. He saw a group of men sitting around a pot-bellied stove, and, aware that they seldom saw celebrities in such a remote village, he decided to spend a little time with them, chatting about the hard winter and the mission that brought him to their neck of the woods. Then, after shaking hands all around, he left, full of the glow that comes with a gratuitous act of good will. Shortly thereafter, the kidnapper was caught and the victim returned to the community.

Later the store proprietor wrote him to say the boys around the stove agreed that "Hoover wasn't much of a president, but he seems to be making a pretty fair policeman."

Another story he told involved an arrest that he himself had made. During the 1930s, before his duties as director became too cumbersome, Hoover often spent time in the field, working side by side with his agents. Contrary to what some biographers have suggested, those who knew him then said he had little fear of danger, even while capturing armed and dangerous gangsters, with machine guns spitting fire and bullets whistling by. One of the criminals on the "Ten Most Wanted" list was Alvin Karpis, a bank robber noted for being clever and utterly without mercy. So defiant was Karpis that he mailed cards and letters to Hoover from robbery sites all around the country. In these letters Karpis mocked the FBI's attempts to track him down, challenged Hoover to a duel, and even threatened to gun him down. Hoover was so enraged at this arrogance that when he received a wire saying Karpis had been spotted in New Orleans, he gave orders to maintain a stakeout and left immediately for the airport, determined to take charge.

When he got to Louisiana, he told agents he wanted to make the arrest himself. They all waited until Karpis and a companion were leaving their hideout and about to get into a car. Then Hoover ran forward and jammed a gun in Karpis's ribs.

Karpis recognized Hoover immediately, put up his hands, and said, "Well, you've got me, Edgar."

"Get in the car," Hoover growled, and followed the prisoner into the back seat. Three agents also piled in, one of them, a young man who had accompanied Hoover from Washington, took the wheel, and they sped off into the night. After about fifteen minutes, Hoover noticed that they had been cruising round in circles.

"Don't you know where you're going?" he asked.

The driver shook his head.

"Where's the FBI office?" Hoover asked.

"It's in the post office building," said one of the others.

"And where's the post office?" Hoover asked.

None of the agents knew.

At this point, Karpis chimed in.

"Is it in the old post office or the new one?"

"The old post office," the agent said.

Karpis said, "Then you want to turn right at the next light, go three blocks, and take a left. You'll be right there."

"You seem to know this town pretty well, Alvin," Hoover said.

"Not really," Karpis said, "but I know where the old post office is. I planned to rob it."

Years later, Karpis would deny that Hoover made the arrest personally, but eye witnesses corroborated Hoover's version.

Another anecdote was perhaps his best. When former Supreme Court Justice Frank Murphy was attorney general, both he and Hoover attended an American Bar Association meeting in El Paso. El Paso, Texas is just across the border from Juarez, Mexico, a city that is little more than a cluster of night spots and brothels catering to American tourists. One of the FBI's big informants was a madame who ran one of the more notorious establishments, so Hoover and Tolson arrived a day early and drove over to Juarez to find out if the woman had any new information about the mob. The prostitutes all saw Hoover enter the establishment, and some may even have recognized him.

The next night, after Murphy had arrived and given his speech, he mentioned that he would like to see the scandalous red light district. So Hoover hired a driver to take him and the attorney general, a renowned prude, on a brief tour of the joints. When they arrived at the same brothel, one of the girls ran up to the car, peered in, saw Hoover, and said, "Hey, you back here again tonight?"

The blue-nosed Murphy turned to Hoover in righteous indignation, and Hoover swore that for a few moments his job was in real jeopardy.

Reports, memorandums, and requests were routed to the director through Tolson. Tolson handled some of the lesser problems, but passed the important matters along to Hoover. Usually Hoover would make marginal notes on a memo in distinctive blue ink and send them back to their point of origin. At one time I had a file cabinet full of these memos. Sometimes the remarks were merely neutral observations. Sometimes they were heavily ironic. Often he would do no more than underline a sentence or a phrase to indicate he'd noted a particular thought. On occasion he would send back a stern rebuke, neatly penned in the margin or at the bottom of the page.

As time passed, blue ink became an inseparable part of the Hoover legend, and everyone understood when someone asked, "What did the blue ink say?" or "Was there any blue ink on the memo when it was circulated?"

One day a memo on internal security that had been sent up to Hoover came back with a message in the familiar scrawl: "Watch the borders! H." Telephones began to ring all over the building, everyone asking the same question: "Is there anything going on in Mexico or Canada that we should know about?" "Maybe we ought to call the Immigration and Naturalization Service." Somebody said, "Why don't you just ask Hoover what he knows that we don't know?" But no one wanted to show his ignorance. So we called Customs and they didn't know any more than we did.

Several days later a supervisor was again reviewing the memo when the answer to the question jumped out and smacked him in the face. The memo had been typed with the narrowest possible margins. Hoover, always fastidious, had picked up his pen and in annoyance had scrawled, "Watch the borders!"

Helen Gandy and a few other members of Hoover's personal staff were authorized to sign his name to routine correspondence. But in my twenty-eight years with the FBI, only one man could imitate the director's deliberate blue-inked scrawl so well that it was indistinguishable from the real thing: G. Gordon Liddy. Unfortunately, he could not put that peculiar talent to legitimate use, since he wasn't authorized to sign the director's letters. But he was not a man to waste his talents.

One day Liddy bought a broad-point fountain pen of the sort Hoover used. Then he appropriated a bottle of Hoover's blue ink and several of his personal routing slips. Whistling at his desk, he filled the pen with ink and checked one of the routing slips to Milton A. Jones, chief of the Crime Research Section and Liddy's immediate boss. In his best Hoover scrawl he wrote on the slip: "This is atrocious. I want an explanation. H."

While Milt was out to lunch, Liddy placed the slip on his desk, where—bare and unattached to any other document—the note could not have been more conspicuous if it had been on fire. At first glance, anyone would have come to an obvious conclusion—the director was mad as hell about some important memo, and the routing slip had been separated from the document.

Sure enough, when Milt came back from lunch, his eye immediately fell on the memo. A hard-working, conscientious agent, he swallowed a couple of times and turned the memo over and over, looking for a clue. Then he searched his tidy desk for any trace of the missing memo. His eyes modulated from deep worry to wild panic. Finally, with a deep sigh, he picked up the receiver to share his concern with the division front office. At that point, Liddy—who had been watching this pantomime from nearby—let Milton in on the secret. Milt smiled uncertainly while Liddy doubled over with laughter.

In my library today, I have a book autographed by its author, G. Gordon Liddy, and next to his name is an irreverent inscription written in the unmistakable scrawl of J. Edgar Hoover. A quarter of a century later, Liddy could still do it from memory.

Hoover wrote memos the way he spoke—short, clipped, to the point. When I first came to the bureau, he addressed me as "Mr. DeLoach," both in correspondence and in person. Later, when he knew me better and I was in a position of significant authority, he dropped the "Mr." and began "Dear Deloach." He addressed me as "Dear Deke" in correspondence after I'd left the bureau. As a matter of fact, he only called me by my first name once—on a rare occasion when he came to dinner at my house—a dinner, I might add, that was given in honor of 50 or so newspaper editors who were attending a convention in Washington.

As for going to his house, I did so infrequently. Once a year, he would invite Tolson, John Mohr, and me to come to dinner. Significantly, it was not his birthday he was celebrating, but usually the anniversary of the day he was named director of the FBI, as if at that moment his life had really begun.

Hoover, like most of us, had his small vanities—and a few large ones as well. He loved publicity, basked in the warm sun of public adulation, and dressed with a fastidious precision that suggested he spent many minutes before the mirror each morning. One story illustrates this vanity, and what it cost the rest of us.

One night, as he was preparing to attend a formal dinner at the White House, Hoover had a difficult time getting into the trousers of his tuxedo. Realizing that he had put on a good deal of weight, he immediately went on a "sort of" diet. (He eliminated starches and desserts, but continued to drink his Jack Daniels every evening.) But he wasn't about to go on a diet alone.

The day after his tuxedo trousers pinched him, orders were dispatched to all field offices and to headquarters: Henceforth agents would conform to the suggested weight standards of the Metropolitan Life Insurance Company—or else.

"Or else" meant no increase in grade or salary, no transfer to offices of preference, removal from an office of preference if already assigned. Repeated failures to meet the standards—with surprise "weigh-ins" as a strategy to trap the guilty—would mean probation.

Most agents were in excellent physical condition and well within the prescribed limits, and some others made the adjustment easily. But many agents—particularly former college or professional athletes who had not stayed in condition—found it tough going. They had to go on crash diets, and did it with much bitching and moaning.

Those of us at the top echelon of the bureau had usually managed to anticipate and escape some of the more rigid policies. It was easy, for instance, to find an excuse to be out of town when a firearms practice was scheduled. But the weigh-ins posed a special problem, since we couldn't very well hide our excess pounds.

One afternoon Hoover selected three top executives to be weighed-in by him personally. We were called down to the fourth floor dispensary and invited, one by one, to step on the scales. All of us were overweight by Metropolitan Life standards, ranging from about one to twelve pounds. Hoover watched the weigh-in, glowering at us in disgust.

When word spread around headquarters of our failure to make the right weight requirements, we were immediately nicknamed "the Dreadnoughts." But it was Hoover's ire that made us go on diets and lose the extra weight. Hoover, however, never got on a scale for anyone, and we noticed that he didn't seem to get any smaller around the waist either.

After we had tracked down the killers of three civil rights workers in Mississippi, Jeremiah O'Leary of the *Washington Star* wrote a lengthy profile of the director. Learning of the article, I suggested to Jerry that, in the interest of accuracy, he let me see it before publication. He was an old friend, and we both understood that he would not be bound by any suggestions I made.

Two days later a galley proof of his article reached my desk; the story contained a glaring Hooverism, a boast the Old Man had made to O'Leary that we'd heard all too often: "I have just taken my annual physical, am in perfect condition, and weigh only 193 pounds, the weight specified by the Metropolitan Life Insurance Company for a man of my height."

I took the proof to Tolson's office, shut the door, and handed him the manuscript.

"This is a copy of O'Leary's article about his interview with the director," I said. "We've got a problem."

"What kind of problem?"

"The director told O'Leary that he weighs 193 pounds and is within life insurance health guidelines for a man of his height."

"So?" Tolson said.

"He's five feet, nine-and-a-half inches. If you check the Metropolitan chart, you'll see that he's thirty pounds overweight. We've been giving FBI agents a lot of flak for being overweight by just a few pounds. They're going to be mighty upset when they see this statement in print."

Tolson slammed his fist down on the desk.

"The boss is NOT overweight!" he fairly shouted.

"I guarantee you he is," I said.

Tolson glared at me for a moment, his eyes cold and hostile.

"Call John Mohr," he said. Mohr was assistant to the director for administration.

I called Mohr on Tolson's intercom.

"Yes sir!" Mohr barked back.

"John," I explained, "this is not Clyde Tolson. This is DeLoach."

"Oh, yeah, Deke," he said. "What's up?"

"I have a question for you. As you know from your personal records, the director is five feet, nine-and-a-half inches tall and weighs 193 pounds. You administer the FBI fitness program, so is he or is he not overweight?"

There was a long pause.

"I don't have to answer a fool question like that, do I?" Mohr growled.

"O.K., then," I said. "Let me rephrase the question. Let's say that an unnamed individual is five feet, nine-and-a-half inches tall and weighs 193 pounds. How much overweight would that unnamed individual be?"

"Hang on," he said. Almost a half minute elapsed. Then we heard his voice again. "Almost thirty pounds."

Tolson slumped in defeat.

"Well, I'll be damned," he said in a barely audible voice. Then he glanced at me with a hang-dog look. "Call the boss and tell him."

"Maybe you ought to tell him," I suggested.

"No," he said in obvious discomfort. "It would be better coming from you."

"Better for whom?" I asked.

Tolson wasn't about to make that particular call, so I knuckled under and made the call, suggesting to the director that the statement in the O'Leary article might cause trouble. To my surprise, he quickly understood the problem and agreed with me that we should ask O'Leary to delete the reference to his weight and the Metropolitan chart.

He never did get his own weight down, even though the bureau continued to deal ruthlessly with agents who allowed themselves to go over the weight recommended by the Metropolitan Life Insurance Company.

Some critics have suggested that Hoover was an obsequious man, that he fawned over presidents and catered to powerful members of Congress. He certainly knew how to survive in the system, and he tried to get along with both the White House and Capitol Hill. But he was afraid of no one. Indeed, at times his independence was alarming. A case in point:

I was attending a boring meeting of a commission one Saturday on Hoover's behalf—the director had better things to do on a Saturday, like going to the races. Someone slipped me a message, saying the president wanted me to call him immediately.

I left the room, found a phone, and made the call.

When President Johnson came on the line, he got right to the point.

"Deke, Edgar has written several letters to Congress objecting to the establishment of Soviet consulates in the United States. I've got to change his mind. Get in touch with him, say I want you and him to be at the White House at two this afternoon. The attorney general, the secretaries of defense and state, and the director of the CIA will be there. We need to talk."

I was happy to leave the commission meeting, but I did so with substantial misgivings. Would J. Edgar Hoover leave the racetrack, even for a meeting with the president and a third of the cabinet? I went to his office, where Helen Gandy, as usual, was busy with her usual Saturday chores.

"I have to talk to the director right now," I told her.

She looked at me with scorn and amazement.

"You know he's never to be disturbed at the racetrack!"

"But the president wants him to meet this afternoon at the White House—with the secretaries of state and defense, the attorney general, the..."

"I want no part of this," she said. "Bother Mr. Hoover at your own risk."

I went into my office and very, very reluctantly placed a call to the clubhouse at Bowie, my fingers crossed. The voice that finally came on the phone was gruff and irritated.

"Yes!"

I explained the circumstances—apologetic, but not penitent. After all, I'd been told to call by the president himself.

Hoover was in no mood for explanations.

"You tell the president I'm in travel status and can't be reached. Tell him I'm not expected back in Washington until six this evening. Goodbye!"

I heard the crash of the receiver and knew I'd talked to the director for the last time that day.

I called the president and relayed the message exactly as it had been delivered to me. There was momentary silence.

"Bullshit, Deke," the president said. "I know where he is."

There was a longer moment of silence. Johnson was contemplating the situation, trying to determine whether to unload on Hoover. It was a clear act of insubordination. No one else in government would have dared to defy Lyndon Johnson so openly. Finally Johnson spoke.

"All right, goddamnit," he said quietly. "The two of you be in my office at ten o'clock Monday morning, or you'll both be fired."

We were there at 9:45, and Hoover listened attentively as Lyndon Johnson outlined in a firm voice the necessity for establishing the Soviet consulates—better relations with the Russians, additional trade, the strengthening of the American economy. Hoover listened, noting Johnson's cold no-nonsense eyes, which were sending out a strong message—Try to argue with me, you sonofabitch. Just try it."

The director had played enough political poker to know when to fold. Those in government who make a practice of disagreeing with the president may enjoy temporary satisfaction, but their pleasure will be short-lived. So Hoover began to soften his objections—which were well-founded. An increase in Soviet consulates would mean more spies, more work for the FBI, and greater risk to the security of the nation's military and diplomatic secrets. As director of the FBI, he would have been a fool not to oppose an increase in consulates.

Yet, because of his desire to remain at the race track, he had forfeited the moral high ground and was forced to agree to write a letter to several key members of the Senate, moderating his opposition to the new consulates. The next day I drafted the letter and the director signed it—a letter that took the senators off the hook so they could vote their consciences. After the smoke had cleared, Hoover had gotten his day at the races and the Soviets had gotten their consulates. It was not even trade.

Hoover loved favorable publicity but he was annoyed by criticism. Columnist Jack Anderson was one of those who raked him over the coals for his acceptance of favors from Sid Richardson and Clint Murchison, and Hoover never forgot it. From that time forward he would snarl at the mention of Anderson's name. Word of Hoover's displeasure got back to the columnist, who decided to tweak the Great Man's nose.

It was 1971, and the bureau was being criticized for its surveillance practices, including examining the garbage of criminal and espionage suspects, so Anderson sent his team of investigators to inspect Hoover's trash can and report the results to the nation. Then he published the report.

- Hoover dined on crab bisque, sliced onions, and peppermint-stick ice cream

- He followed this meal with Gelusil antacid tablets, from which Anderson concluded that "the living legend" had "gas on his stomach"

- He also drank at home—Jack Daniels, black label.

On reading this information in the *Washington Post,* Hoover became furious. He let it be known at the office that he would like to have a trash compactor, one that Anderson later described as a machine that "could squeeze his garbage into an inseparable, unsearchable block." Since his forty-seventh anniversary at the bureau was approaching, everyone chipped in to buy Hoover his compactor and it was presented to him at a ceremony. Those of us who attended tried to keep a straight face, but it was hard.

Perhaps the nearest thing to a genuine scandal in Hoover's life was the association with Sid Richardson and Clint Murchison that Anderson had written about. Richardson and Murchison were Dallas millionaires who owned a number of race tracks nationwide. This ownership was through an organization called Boys Incorporated, which was a charitable foundation. Actually, the foundation was a tax dodge, and eventually the IRS disallowed the exemption, since the amount the little boys got from the operation fell short of what Richardson and Murchison got by millions and millions of dollars.

Since Hoover loved the horses, he annually vacationed in Southern California, where there were three fine tracks—Del Mar, Santa Anita, and Hollywood Park. At some point he became friendly with Richardson and Murchison. At some slightly later point his friends began picking up the tab for his visits, or rather, he and Tolson stayed free at a resort Murchison owned—the Hotel Del Charro.

In the early 1970s, Hoover and Tolson graced $100-a-day suites, an enormous figure for that time, and one neither could have afforded on his salary. When you added the meals and extras, the bill was something that might have raised the eyebrows of the Aga Khan. For a few days they lived in sheer opulence, after which they returned to the grubby world of the federal bureaucracy.

It goes without saying that accepting such hospitality was, at the very least, indiscreet—particularly since Hoover held such an important post in the eyes of the general public. On the other hand, only the most fanatic of Hoover's detractors could believe that Richardson and Murchison were somehow buying "protection" from Hoover. It was a clear case of hero worship on the part of two old Texas right-wingers and a small touch of hedonism on the part of J. Edgar Hoover. Murchison and Richardson were too sophisticated to believe that the director of the FBI could help them with any problems they might face in the Treasury Department, and I'm certain it never occurred to Hoover that he might be selling his soul to his two friends.

They would sit around the breakfast table, talk about horse racing and the menace of international communism, and then part company. It's even possible that Hoover attempted to pay his check each time, only to be told—as he anticipated—that the matter had "already been taken care of." Whatever the protocols observed, this was no case of bribery—and no federal laws were violated at the time, though today a federal bureaucrat can't even allow a reporter to pick up the lunch tab.

Hoover also collected honoraria at a time when it was legal to do so, but he saw to it that FBI personnel wrote his books, articles, and speeches. The cash returns were divided among the FBI Recreational Association, Tolson, an outside editor, and Hoover himself. The research and writing were mostly done on government time. And of course he also used FBI staff—notably, but not exclusively, Helen Gandy—to take care of his personal and household needs, including the payment of his bills, preparation of income tax returns, and some of his gardening. Even in those days such misuse of government employees was understood to be a breach of ethics, though I doubt Hoover gave it a second thought.

The casual acceptance of gifts and the use of FBI employees to perform personal tasks shows that Hoover, at least in later years, became careless about ethical matters. I suspect he was shocked and angered when such charges were made against him, because he thought of himself as above reproach. But the truth was, having been director of the FBI for so long, he behaved as if he were above such petty rules and considerations. He knew he could not be bought, so he cut himself some slack; and now, twenty years after his death, his reputation suffers as a consequence.

Though Hoover was careless about such ethical matters—and though he was tight-fisted—he was not greedy nor was he for sale. Billionaire Howard Hughes once made Hoover the kind of offer that few people could refuse. As Hoover's close friend George Allen reported the conversation, Hughes said to Hoover, after he had offered him a job lobbying for him: "You name the price and I'll pay you anything you like, give you a lifetime contract—any amount of money."

Hoover replied, "I appreciate your offer, but I'm not interested in any job."

Had he been obsessed with money he could have spent the last years of his life driving up to Capitol Hill in his Rolls-Royce, calling on his old friends in Congress, and talking up the latest Howard Hughes venture. That he turned down the Hughes offer without thinking twice is some measure of his character, and should help those interested to put his other financial indiscretions into perspective.

On the other hand, the older he got the more he worried about the future—and one of his concerns was financial. Frugal though he was, he clearly brooded about his income after retirement. Since he didn't like to give speeches anyway, it came as no surprise to me when Tolson relayed an order from Hoover to turn down awards, honors, and speech invitations that didn't include an honorarium.

"The boss is tired of accepting plaques," Tolson said. "They don't amount to anything anyway. Money is the only real incentive."

Then he went on to talk about his own investments in oil, which had ballooned into a portfolio worth well over $700,000. He grinned at me.

"Pretty good for a small-town boy from Iowa, wouldn't you say?"

I held my tongue.

Shortly after this policy was announced, I got a call from Meade

Chamberlain, vice president of Mutual of Omaha. The company's management had reviewed a list of prominent Americans who might qualify for the corporation's Golden Plate Award and had concluded that J. Edgar Hoover was easily the most deserving candidate. The board of directors wished him to accept the award and make a few remarks at a banquet to be held in Washington. The award brought with it a $10,000 honorarium.

I was certain that Hoover would accept, if only for the money—a substantial amount in those days.

"The director has a heavy schedule," I said solemnly, "and some of us have been urging him to slow down. But I'm sure he'll want to give your offer careful consideration. Could you give me some more details?"

Chamberlain explained that the banquet would be held at the Mayflower, that the director could approve the guest list and add any name he wished, that the master of ceremonies would be Dr. Charles Mayo of the celebrated Mayo Clinic, and that the banquet would be videotaped and shown the following Sunday on national television.

As I listened, I knew that Hoover would snap up this invitation like a hungry alligator, but I played it cool.

"Mr. Chamberlain," I said, "I would like Mr. Hoover to accept this award, and I'm going to urge him to do so. I think he'll probably be receptive because he has a high regard for Mutual of Omaha and the Mayo family. Let me get back to you as soon as I can confer with him."

As soon as I hung up, I hustled down to Clyde Tolson's office and relayed what Chamberlain had told me. Tolson didn't register more than passing interest until I told him about the $10,000 check that came with the award.

"Mutual of Omaha, hmmm," he mused. "I'm sure the boss will accept an award from Mutual of Omaha."

He was right. Hoover agreed, and without any prodding.

Chamberlain and I sent out invitations to a star-studded list of guests, drawn up jointly by Mutual and my front-office staff. Acceptances came back from members of Congress, the Joint Chiefs of Staff, and the cabinet, as well as from White House staffers, CEOs of major corporations, and lesser figures.

I spoke to Hoover about the tape of the banquet and suggested that I fly to New York the morning after the banquet to help news commentators Chet Huntley and Bob Considine edit the tape—just in case.

He glowered at me.

"No need, DeLoach. They're pros. They don't need you."

As the banquet date approached, our plans were right on schedule. Then Murphy's Law kicked in. Without warning, Hoover decided he wanted major changes in his speech. He also wanted a rundown on those who had accepted the invitation, as well as those who had declined. Then he began rearranging the seating at the head table. Finally, at 4:00 P.M. on the day of the event, Meade Chamberlain called, a note of urgency in his voice.

"Deke," he said, "could you possibly assign a couple of FBI agents to spend some time with Dr. Mayo at the Mayflower?"

I expressed my bewilderment.

"Well," said Chamberlain, "the good doctor gets nervous when he has to make a public appearance; and in the past, he's been known to hit the sauce. At all other times he's a sober man. If a couple of FBI agents were to stay with him and keep him away from a Scotch bottle..."

"I suppose we could give him a tour of the bureau and drive him around Washington," I said, "but if he wants to drink, there's no way we can stop him."

Chamberlain agreed; and later, when Hoover, Tolson, and I stopped by Dr. Mayo's hotel suite, he had just come back from his tour and was in fine shape. But after a brief conversation, he excused himself, went back into the suite's kitchen, and we saw him through the door, a bottle of Scotch tipped up, his Adam's apple working furiously. By the time we went down on the elevator, his knees were wobbling, and he was slurring his speech.

After he was seated, I watched him anxiously, hoping he would eat his dinner and drink some coffee, but every time I looked his way, he was ordering another Scotch from the waiter. When he rose to his feet to speak, he was cross-eyed.

He stood for a moment, swaying, fumbling in his pockets.

"Where in hell are my notes?" he said.

Finally, as the audience watched with growing embarrassment, he fished them out of his inside pocket and began to unfold them slowly and deliberately.

Tolson leaned over to me.

"Boy is he loaded! I'll bet the boss is about to have a kitten."

I felt like sliding under the table.

"I've got a framed piece of paper and a check here somewhere."

He began groping under the lectern and came up with the plaque and check.

"Now, let's see who the hell this is for. Hoover. Can't be for Herbert Hoover. Can't be for vacuum cleaner Hoover. Must be for J. Edgar Hoover. Anyhow, the check amounts to $10,000. Bet the poor bastard can use this money—he's been a government employee for so long."

At this point I wished I'd stayed in the navy and never heard of the FBI.

Beside me, Tolson was half-crazed.

"DeLoach, this is terrible," he hissed in my ear. "Do something!"

"What do you suggest?" I asked.

"Tell Chamberlain to ease the doctor away from the mike and get him out of here," he said weakly, knowing it was a useless suggestion.

Nevertheless, I gave it a try. Meade Chamberlain sighed and shook his head.

"It's too late now," he moaned. "We've got to suffer through it."

The doctor staggered on while the audience either gaped in wonder or sought refuge in their own drinks. Finally he came to the actual presentation.

"Now, we've got to let Hoover accept this money by making a few remarks," he said. "I hope he won't be as long-winded as those congressmen are. Hoover, come on up here and get your money—but be sure you pay the taxes on it."

The director shortened his remarks considerably, received an ovation, and was congratulated by scores of old friends and admirers. After the last goodby, as we were returning to the limousine, Hoover turned to me and said pointedly, "What time are you leaving for New York to edit that film?"

Chamberlain overheard the conversation and offered the use of the Mutual of Omaha plane, which was waiting at National Airport.

"There's only one problem," he said. "You've got to help me get Bob Considine on the plane."

Considine, the newsman, writer, and wit, had matched the doctor drink for drink and was asleep on a sofa in the Mayflower lobby, a bottle of Old Rarity cradled in his arms. Chamberlain hoisted his shoulders, I grabbed his legs like the handles of a wheelbarrow, and we struggled out to a waiting cab, which took us to the airport. After more heaving and pulling, we got the world-famous writer, newsman, and wit strapped into the seat of a corporate jet. Then Chamberlain gave the word, and we took off. By the time we landed, Considine was beginning to remember who he was and where he was going. By business hours the next morning, he was again the consummate newsman. We edited the tape, bleeped out the good doctor, and came up with a respectable show. In retrospect, however, I wondered if it was worth the $10,000.

Shortly after the 1964 election, Hoover again began to worry about the future—this time with genuine cause. In January of 1965, he would turn seventy, the mandatory retirement age for civil servants. The very idea of retirement terrified him. His life had clicked away like a finely tuned engine for as long as he could remember. He had breakfast at the same hour, came to work at the same hour, moved all day among people who worshipped him and did his slightest bidding, left at the same hour every night, and had none of the responsibilities that most ordinary men have to bear. After all, Helen Gandy paid his bills, made certain that the cook and cleaning woman and gardener were on the job, called the plumber and electrician when a drain stopped up or the lights went out, and made certain that his laundry was done and his suits were pressed. She didn't tuck him in at night, and he slept alone. Otherwise, he had it all.

When he walked away from the FBI, all of these petty responsibilities would follow him home and clutter up his tidy life. He would no longer have a driver, free travel, instant access to the White House, and literally thousands of people to do his bidding. He would be nothing more than one more retired bureaucrat, easily replaced, soon forgotten—an old man pottering among his roses. Or so he began telling himself as the day for his retirement drew near.

Of course, federal regulations provided for the rehiring of retirees on a year-by-year basis, in his case at the discretion of the president. But Hoover well knew the vicissitudes of presidential politics, and he didn't like the idea of having to come every year to the White House, hat in hand, to beg for his job.

I knew his hopes and fears, so I wasn't surprised when Tolson called me into his office one day in the fall of 1964 and asked me to sit down.

"DeLoach," he said, "just how close are you to President Johnson?"

I wasn't exactly sure what was coming, so I shrugged my shoulders.

"You can answer that question as well as I can."

"I think you're much closer to him than anyone in the bureau, including the boss. That's why you're the man to talk to him about the director's retirement."

"What do you want me to say?"

"We want you to ask the president to waive the mandatory retirement age in his case."

He went on to explain that a lawyer in the FBI's Training and Inspection Division had determined it would not take an act of Congress to do the job—merely an executive order, something Lyndon Johnson could manage with a stroke of the pen. He could do it one time and the question of Hoover's age would be forever moot.

"I'll do what I can," I said.

I made an appointment to talk to the president. When we were sitting in the Oval Office, I told him what Hoover wanted. After I'd finished, Johnson shook his head.

"Do you realize what you're asking me to do?" he said.

I told him I thought I did.

"I don't think you do. If I waive mandatory retirement, Edgar will stay in there until he dies. And if that happens, I won't be able to name you director of the FBI."

I wasn't expecting to hear that, and I was speechless.

"I'm going to ask you one more time," he said. "Do you really want me to do this?"

He looked at me with a steady, questioning gaze. I realized that he was putting Hoover's fate into my hands—and offering me the Old Man's job at the same time. Of course he was right. Crotchety, dictatorial, set in his ways, at times petulant, somewhat past his prime—Hoover was nonetheless in fairly good health. He could last another ten years, maybe longer. And each succeeding president would have to live with Johnson's decision or else risk the ire of the American people by destroying one of their living gods.

On the other hand, if Johnson failed to take positive action, then Hoover's departure would be automatic. Of course, there would be some congressional pressure to rehire him on a year-by-year basis, but Lyndon Johnson could handle his old friends in Congress. Besides, many of them resented Hoover's power and feared that the rumors about his "secret files" might be true. If Johnson wanted to, he could end Hoover's career. And he was asking me to decide for him.

What made my position doubly tough was the fact that I wanted the job. Tolson was too old and in ill health. I was still under fifty—mature and experienced enough to assume command, but young enough to provide long-term leadership. There were a lot of changes to be made, and I thought I knew what they should be. Ironically, every time a reporter or columnist had speculated that I might succeed Hoover, the Old Man would signal his disapproval by cutting off all communication until I crawled on my belly, begging his forgiveness for imaginary sins.

I'd endured this kind of treatment ever since I rose to a position of high visibility in the bureau. Now I had Hoover's future in the palm of my hand.

Yet I couldn't say the one thing that Johnson wanted me to say, that I wanted him to deny my request. I'd been sent to do a job. I had accepted the assignment. If, at this point, I used the occasion for my own advancement, I would be betraying the trust of a man who had always believed in me. Lyndon Johnson, a man thoroughly familiar with ambition, knew precisely what he'd asked me to do and was quietly waiting for my response.

"I want you to give the Old Man what he wants," I said finally.

Johnson shook his head and sighed. I know he thought I lacked what it took to succeed in the political world, and perhaps he was right. But he accepted my decision.

"All right," he said. "I suppose I'd rather have the old bastard inside the tent pissing out, than outside the tent pissing in. Go into the next office and dictate to Mildred what you want me to say in an executive order."

Hoover stayed in office till the day he died.

6

....

The Assassination of JFK

BEFORE LEAVING THE TEXAS HOTEL in Ft. Worth on November 22, 1963, John F. Kennedy made a prophetic remark to his old friend Kenneth O'Donnell, assistant to the president. He said that if anybody really wanted to shoot the president of the United States, it would be an easy task. All he'd have to do was station himself somewhere in a high building with a telescopic rifle. From such a vantage point, nobody could stop him. After making this casual remark, the president prepared to leave for the airport.

John F. Kennedy was not the only person concerned with presidential safety that morning. Shortly after 8:00 A.M., Gordon Shanklin, special agent in charge (SAC) of the FBI's Dallas office, held a meeting with his agents, reminding them one more time that the president of the United States was scheduled to tour downtown Dallas later in the day.

"If there is any indication of any possibility of acts of violence against the president or the vice president," Shanklin said, "if you have anything, anything at all, I want it confirmed in writing."

The agents took such requests for information very seriously. They had already passed along information to the Secret Service concerning someone from nearby Denton who'd made threats against Kennedy. The FBI had also reported a tip that the president's speech at the Trade Mart would be picketed. And Agent James Hosty had picked up some street pamphlets highly critical of the president and had taken them to the Secret Service office—just in case.

Hosty was one of the agents who sat in silence on that November morning as Gordon Shanklin asked if they had any additional information that might be useful to the Secret Service. One of Hosty's case files contained the record of a disgruntled defector to the Soviet Union who had returned to the United States and was now living in the Dallas–Ft. Worth area. Hosty had filed a brief report on the man only four days earlier. His name was Lee Harvey Oswald, and he'd recently sent Hosty an alleged threatening note.

Calvin Coolidge once said, "Nobody ever got into trouble for something he didn't say." It's not true. Ask Jim Hosty. His silence that morning and his subsequent actions in the wake of the assassination would become a matter of great controversy for decades.

Dallas and Ft. Worth were only a few miles apart, and most people made the trip from one to the other by automobile. But to save time, the presidential party flew from Ft. Worth to Dallas's Love Field, a flight of about ten minutes.

Once at Love Field, President Kennedy, the First Lady, Governor and Mrs. John Connally, and Vice President and Mrs. Lyndon Johnson climbed into open automobiles, surrounded by Secret Service agents, and rode in a motorcade along Harry Hines Boulevard and through the streets of downtown Dallas. The parade route had been published in the newspaper the day before. The crowds jammed the sidewalks, 250,000 people waving and cheering as the president and his entourage passed.

When the motorcade reached Dealey Plaza, it turned right, then turned left again. During those crucial moments, the open automobile in which the president was riding slowed to a crawl. Just before the car picked up speed to move onto Stemmons Freeway, Lee Harvey Oswald squeezed off three rounds from a sixth-story window right above the president's limousine. For a practiced marksman, it was like shooting pigeons on the ground.

Both the president and Governor Connally were bleeding from bullet wounds. Mrs. Kennedy, who had seen her husband's head blown to pieces not two feet away, panicked and tried to climb across the trunk of the car, but was pushed back by a Secret Service agent. Several people in the crowd started to scream, and the driver hit the gas pedal. The limousine zoomed under a triple underpass and out onto Stemmons Freeway, followed by the other vehicles in the motorcade. With sirens screaming, they headed toward Parkland Hospital, which was back on Harry Hines Boulevard.

Special Agent in Charge Shanklin was in his office when a secretary knocked and entered. She told Shanklin a young clerk had been monitoring the Dallas police frequencies and had something to tell him. Shanklin agreed to see him and the young man came in and blurted out his message: "Some shots were fired at the president's car." Then he gave a few more details. Shanklin first called Agent Vincent Drain into his office, then dialed Hoover's number in Washington.

"SAC Gordon Shanklin, Dallas office," he said. "Let me speak to the director."

Hoover knew that Shanklin would not make a direct call unless it was important so he got on the line immediately.

"Gordon Shanklin. The president has been reported as shot in Dallas."

Several historians have remarked that Hoover received the news dispassionately, devoid of human feelings, quickly considering the proposition with a cold and analytical eye. It was always his way in times of stress. It was his greatest asset in a job that frequently placed him in the middle of situations where life and death hung in the balance. On such occasions he became a machine, spitting out orders almost automatically, measuring his words with the precision of a jeweler.

He asked a few questions, then told Shanklin, "Offer the full services of our laboratory and fingerprint division." It was an offer he would shortly regret. He also told Shanklin, "Find out how badly he's hurt and call me back."

Shanklin hung up and said to Vince Drain, "Get to Parkland at once." He also told Drain to "offer our laboratory facilities if we can help." At that point, the bureau had done all it was legally entitled to do. The FBI had jurisdiction only over federal crimes, and—astonishingly—it was not against federal law to kill the president of the United States, not in 1963. President Kennedy had been shot in Dallas, Texas, and the case belonged to Dallas Police Chief Jesse Curry—at least for the moment.

Back in Washington, Hoover hung up and asked Miss Gandy to place a call to Bobby Kennedy. While she was dialing, Hoover summoned Tolson to his room. Next he called in Al Belmont, assistant director in charge of Investigative Activities. Then he tried to call me. My secretary told him I was at lunch.

"Get him back immediately. Tell him the president's been shot, that he may be dying."

Meanwhile, Agent Doyle Williams had rushed to Parkland Hospital, plunged through the doorway into the emergency room, and was roughed up by two Secret Service men, one of whom clipped him in the jaw. They held him up against a wall, a machine gun trained on him, while he fished out his government ID. Only then was he allowed to take his station and act as Shanklin's eyes and ears.

Agent Hosty was eating lunch in a restaurant a block away from FBI headquarters when the president was shot. He'd seen the motorcade roll by minutes before the assassination. A waitress told him she'd just heard over the radio that the president and vice president had both been shot. Hosty paid his bill and dashed out the door. When he got back to the office, he was told to go to his car, turn on the radio, and listen for instructions. First he was ordered to Parkland Hospital. When he got there, he was ordered back to headquarters to go over his case files to see if anyone he'd investigated looked like a presidential assassin. One of the files he examined was that of Lee Harvey Oswald, but Hosty still couldn't believe Oswald was a killer.

I was seated in a restaurant in the bowels of the World Bank in Washington with Erle Cocke, the Bank's deputy director. We were both active in the American Legion and were there to talk about the organization. I didn't know anything had happened until shortly after 1:30, Washington time. We'd eaten and were winding up our discussion when a waiter came up to me with a questioning look on his face.

"Mr. DeLoach?"

I nodded.

"There's a telephone call for you," he said. "It's your office. An urgent call, sir."

I frowned. I knew my secretary, Marie Robusky, would never interrupt me unless some crisis had arisen. Nothing overly important was pending at the bureau. I thought of my family as I excused myself and followed the waiter to the phone. I grabbed the receiver and said, "Hello."

Marie was sobbing.

"Mr. Hoover wants you back in the office immediately. The president's been shot in Dallas. They think he's dying."

I felt suddenly numb.

"I'll be there as quickly as I can," I said.

As I hurried back to the table, Erle could see the shock and disbelief in my face.

I started to tell him what had happened, then hesitated. I didn't know anything for certain, so I decided to err on the side of discretion. I'd learned long ago that casual words over lunch could end up on the front page of the *Washington Post*.

"Erle," I said, "this is a major emergency. I've got to leave right now. I apologize, but this won't wait."

He nodded his understanding and I moved quickly between tables and out the front door. I was on the wrong side of the street for a taxi; I crossed against the light and almost got hit by a car. I hailed a cab and on the way back to the Justice Department tried to come to terms with what I'd just been told.

Less than a week earlier, my wife, Barbara, and I had attended a reception for the federal judiciary at the White House. As we were standing around talking, Bobby Kennedy, who was then attorney general, came up, grabbed me by the sleeve, and said, "Deke, I want you to meet the president." The introduction had been brief and formal. Bobby had told his brother, "Mr. President, this man has been of great service to us."

I'd been astonished. Bobby had seldom said a kind word about the FBI—and particularly its administration. Shaking the president's hand, I'd mumbled a few polite words, and wandered back into the social crush, weaving my way between Supreme Court justices, appellate judges, and executives of various government agencies. I'd tried to appear nonchalant, but Barbara could tell by the look on my face where I'd been. Even though I'd met a lot of important people in Washington, it was an introduction I wouldn't forget.

As I rode across Washington, I remembered the energetic young man whose hand I'd shaken just a few days earlier. Then I thought of his brother, the man I knew and had worked with over the past two years, and the whole tragedy seemed more human, more personal—infinitely sadder. At that point, we turned onto Pennsylvania Avenue, and I began to steel myself for what lay ahead.

Once on the fifth floor, I started to go straight to Mr. Hoover's office, but I decided to stop by and check with Marie first. At this stage of my career, I was assistant director of the Crime Records Division, and one of my responsibilities was to maintain liaison with the White House, Congress, and the press. When I entered the office I saw at once that the place was in a state of uncharacteristic turmoil. Everyone was on the phone or rushing from one room to the next.

Marie looked up at me with a grief-stricken face.

"What do we know?" I asked as she followed me into the office.

"We now know that he's been shot, that he's seriously wounded, that he may be dead."

"Do they have anybody in custody?"

"We don't know," she said. "All we know is what I've told you."

"And is that much for certain?"

"Yes, sir," she said. "The director got a call from SAC Shanklin. But it's on the television networks now."

I turned on the television that sat across from my desk and watched as the flickering black-and-white images became the face of Walter Cronkite. For the next twenty-four hours, I would be watching the screen as I talked to callers from every corner of the nation, picking up information from all three networks, changing direction in midsentence to reflect the latest news bulletin.

My phone had been ringing since I entered the office. All lines were tied up, and Inspector Bob Wick, Don Hanning, and the other agents working under me were already on the phone, handling as many inquiries as they could.

"O.K.," I said. "If that's all we know, then I guess I'm ready to take calls."

And the calls came—from newspaper reporters, from the networks, from Capitol Hill, from heads of other government agencies. At the start I realized I couldn't take them according to strict priority, since virtually everybody who was calling was important. So I began to field them in order.

"Deke, what happened?"

"Do you know anything more than we're getting on the tube?"

"Is he still alive?"

"Does the FBI have any idea who shot him?"

"Where's the vice president?"

"Is this a plot against the government?"

Some of the calls involved rumors.

A black informant of the Washington field office called to tell me he'd overheard someone say, "Now that we've got the president, we're going to get Senator Byrd." I didn't take this tip too seriously, but we notified Senator Byrd and the Capitol police, then sent an agent to check out the story. The Associated Press in St. Louis wanted to confirm a rumor that Bobby Baker, the former Capitol Hill wheeler-dealer, was involved. I told them that no one at the FBI had heard such allegations.

In Parkland Hospital, FBI Agent Vincent Drain stood by as doctors worked quickly, quietly, desperately trying to bring their patient out of the lengthening shadow of death. Drain watched in morbid fascination as one surgeon took a scalpel and quickly slit the throat of the president of the United States—a tracheotomy to try to facilitate breathing. (Many sensationalists later claimed this surgical cut was the result of a frontal or forth shot. This is absolutely false.) Drain focused on the chest of the patient, but there was no sudden heaving. It was obvious to everyone in the room that John F. Kennedy was dead.

Another call to Hoover came from SAC Shanklin. The president had died in Dallas's Parkland Hospital. Marie came into the office to tell me. I stopped for a moment to offer a silent prayer. Then I took the next call.

In Dallas, after the shots had been fired, a man entered the Texas Book Depository and walked up to a slim, youthful employee, standing just inside the door. "Secret Service," said the man, flashing his ID. "Where is the phone?" The employee gestured in the direction of the telephone, and the man hurried over to make his call. He had lied to the employee, as any good reporter would have done under such circumstances. He was Robert MacNeil of NBC, and he was about to file the story of his life—the assassination of a U.S. president. But he had missed the opportunity for an even greater story. The employee he had fooled with his quick flash of ID had just shot the president.

Having jettisoned the murder weapon, Lee Harvey Oswald quickly left the building, walked a few blocks, caught a cab, then a bus. But a man named Howard Brennan had reported seeing a man fire the shots from the Texas Book Depository window, and he gave a description to Dallas Police Sergeant D. V. Harkness. Soon Dallas police radios were broadcasting the description all over town: "White male, approximately five feet, ten inches tall, weighing 165, in his early thirties."

One of the police officers who heard this broadcast was John Tippit. He was cruising in a squad car through Oak Cliff, technically within the city limits, but several miles from downtown Dallas, with a business center and residential neighborhoods of its own. Tippit spotted a man walking down Tenth Street who matched the description of the assassin, a little shorter perhaps, but close enough. He pulled up beside the pedestrian, asked him a few questions, then got out of the patrol car. As he stood facing the suspect across the hood of the car, the young man whipped out a pistol and fired five shots. Four of them struck Tippit, who crumpled slowly to the pavement, attempting to draw his weapon even as he slipped into unconsciousness. The man who fired the shots started running. Tippit lay dead on the pavement behind him.

Meanwhile, police at the Texas Book Depository had found the rifle, a 6.5 Mannlicher-Carcano bolt-action, and gave a name to the description of the killer—Lee Harvey Oswald, an employee at the Depository. And Oswald was missing. The police were no longer trying to solve a murder mystery; they had launched a manhunt.

After shooting Officer Tippit, Lee Harvey Oswald panicked. If he'd had any detailed plan for shooting the president, it had long since fallen to pieces. Now he'd killed a policeman, and soon the area would be swarming with patrol cars. He abandoned the sidewalk and began to cut across lawns and backyards, hoping to elude the net he knew would soon be closing around the area.

He emerged on Jefferson Boulevard and heard a siren wail. A police car was tearing down the street in his direction. He stopped, turned, and pretended to look at the merchandise in the window of Hardy's Shoe Shop. The police car went careening by, and for the moment it appeared as if Oswald had escaped once again. But he had made a mistake. Johnny Brewer, manager of the shoe store, had noticed this peculiar behavior. Why would a man turn away to look in a store window—just at the moment when most people would be watching the speeding police car? Brewer had also been listening on the radio to the ongoing story of the Kennedy assassination and had just heard that an officer had been shot in the neighborhood.

At that moment, Oswald saw the Texas Theater, which had opened only a few minutes earlier. The cashier, Julia Postal, was not in the ticket booth. She had walked out to the curb to talk to the theater manager. On an impulse, Oswald ducked inside the theater without buying a ticket.

Brewer, still suspicious, talked to the cashier, who, after hearing the description of the man, agreed that he was indeed a suspicious character. She called the Dallas Police Department and told them, "We have your man." Skeptical at first, the officer on the other end of the line heard the description and became increasingly attentive.

In a matter of minutes, the lights in the Texas Theater went on and police swarmed down the aisles. One spotted Oswald out of the corner of his eye, wheeled, and barked "On your feet!" Oswald stood up, raised his hands, and said, "It's all over."

James Bookhout, one of Shanklin's Dallas agents, called FBI headquarters there to report that Officer Tippit's likely killer had been picked up by the police in Oak Cliff. His name? Lee Harvey Oswald. The word went from office to office, and when James Hosty heard it, he must have felt sick inside. He went immediately to Shanklin and told him about the file on Oswald.

Shanklin asked what was in the file, and Hosty summarized the contents, adding that nothing there would indicate that Oswald was capable of shooting anyone. Shanklin immediately called Will Fritz, head of the Homicide Division of the Dallas Police Department.

"I want to assure you," he said, "that the FBI will cooperate with you in any way possible. Remember that our laboratory and fingerprint division are at your disposal."

Then he made a request.

"We know a little something about Lee Harvey Oswald. One of our agents has a file on him. I wonder if he could come and sit in on your interrogation of Oswald?"

"Sure," said Fritz. "Send him over."

When Hosty arrived at Fritz's Office, Fritz invited him to join the ongoing interrogation of Oswald. Agent Bookhout was already there. Hosty showed Oswald his ID, then sat down. Fritz allowed Hosty to question Oswald, assuming the FBI agent knew the subject better than anyone present.

"Have you been in Russia?" Hosty asked.

"Yes," Oswald replied, "I was in Russia three years."

"Did you ever write to the Russian Embassy?" Hosty continued. He was trying to establish whether Oswald would lie concerning verifiable facts. Initially Oswald refused the bait.

"Yes, I wrote."

Then Hosty asked a question that surprised and disturbed Oswald.

"Have you ever been to Mexico City?"

Oswald began to lose his composure. The FBI knew more about his movements than he'd imagined.

"No!"

Hosty, remaining calm, didn't question Oswald's answer. Instead, he said, "When were you in Mexico City?"

At this point Oswald leaped up. Pounding his handcuffed fists on the table he shouted: "I know you! I know you! You're the one who accosted my wife twice!"

Fritz restrained him.

"Take it easy. Sit down," he said.

"Oh, I know you."

"What do you mean he accosted your wife?" Fritz said to Oswald.

"Well, he threatened her," Oswald said. "He practically told her she would have to go back to Russia [Oswald's wife was Russian]. He accosted her on two different occasions."

That was Oswald's only moment of panic, the one time during a long afternoon of interrogation when he came close to breaking. The rest of the session he was evasive, arrogant, and condescending—a man more and more confident of himself even as more and more evidence mounted against him.

Sometime during or shortly after the Oswald interrogation, Jack Revill, a lieutenant in the Criminal Intelligence Section of the Dallas Police Department, who had talked to Agent Hosty briefly when he came over to interview Oswald, offered the following summary of their conversation:

> Captain W. F. Gannaway
> Special Service Bureau
> Subject: Lee Harvey Oswald
> 605 Eisbeth Street

Sir:

On November 22, at approximately 2:50 P.M., the undersigned officer met Special Agent James Hosty of the Federal Bureau of Investigation in the basement of the City Hall.

At that time Special Agent Hosty related to this officer that the subject was a member of the Communist party, and that he was residing in Dallas.

The subject was arrested for the murder of Officer J. D. Tippit and is a prime suspect in the assassination of President Kennedy.

The information regarding the subject's affiliation with the Communist party is the first information this officer has received from the Federal Bureau of Investigation regarding same.

Agent Hosty further stated that the Federal Bureau of Investigation was aware of the subject and that they had information that this subject was capable of committing the assassination of President Kennedy.

This memo was written during the frantic time immediately following the death of the president, since by 1:30 A.M. Saturday morning, Oswald was no longer merely "a prime suspect" but had been officially charged with the assassination. And the motive of the memo was clear from the statement in paragraph four emphasizing that this was the "first information" received from the FBI concerning these alarming "facts" about Oswald.

But of course they weren't facts, nor was it likely that Hosty had said what Officer Revill claimed he'd said. As Hosty's own file clearly showed, Oswald was not a member of the Communist party, despite his addiction to Marxism. The FBI had informants who regularly attended local Communist party meetings, and Oswald was never there, nor did his name show up in any of the party's correspondence. Indeed, one of the reasons Hosty had not taken Oswald too seriously was because of his very lack of involvement in Communist party activities.

Second, neither Hosty nor the FBI had any information that

Oswald constituted a serious threat to the president. On the very day the memo was written—and with such a threat uppermost in his mind—Gordon Shanklin had called twice for a review of all files, once before Kennedy was shot and once afterward. Neither time had Agent Hosty thought Oswald worth mentioning as potentially dangerous. He knew the Secret Service only investigated people who had made direct or indirect threats against the president. Oswald had done nothing of the sort.

So did Officer Revill lie in his statement? Probably not. After reviewing the matter, we concluded that in all likelihood he had reported what he thought he'd heard. Hosty had undoubtedly told him about Oswald's defection to Russia and his Marxism. To Revill, "Marxism" had probably translated into Communist party membership—and a dangerous figure.

Regardless of how the misunderstanding occurred, Police Chief Curry—anxious to shift the blame for the assassination to the federal level—put the report in his drawer and waited for the most opportune moment to use it.

Surprisingly, Oswald, the prime suspect in Officer Tippit's killing, sat in Dallas police headquarters for a long time before anyone in the media realized he was the Book Depository employee wanted in connection with the assassination of the president. When someone made the connection, the press swarmed all over the place like red ants. They also began to call me. Everyone wanted to know what prior information the FBI had collected concerning Lee Harvey Oswald.

In Dallas, Marguerite Oswald, mother of Lee Harvey Oswald, arrived at City Hall. She was there to provide her son with the warm wet blanket of protective love that had all but smothered him since he was a small child. She refused to talk to the Dallas police. Instead, she said, "I want to speak to the FBI."

Two agents, both named Brown, met with her in a small room. She began with an extraordinary statement, one that others would echo in the future. She said, "I want to talk with you gentlemen because I feel like my son is an agent of the government, and, for the security of my country, I don't want this to get out."

Perhaps sensing their doubt, Mrs. Oswald said, "I want to talk to FBI agents from Washington."

"Mrs. Oswald, we are from Washington," one of them told her. She was skeptical.

"I understand you work with Washington," she said, "but I want officials from Washington."

The agents, knowing at this point that whatever information she gave them would probably be useless, nevertheless tried to encourage her to talk to them.

"Well," one said, "we work through Washington."

"I know you do," she said. "I would like Washington men."

At length they convinced her that they were worth talking to, and she told them her bizarre tale, first cautioning them to keep their lips sealed.

"For the security of the country," she told them, "I want this kept perfectly quiet until you investigate."

They nodded.

"I happen to know that the State Department furnished the money for my son to return to the United States, and I don't know, if that would be made public, what that would involve, and so please will you investigate this and keep this quiet."

She went on to assure them that "Congressman Jim Wright knows about this," and gave the agents the names of State Department officials who could corroborate the story.

The FBI already knew everything Marguerite Oswald was reporting—and then some. The State Department had indeed lent Lee Harvey Oswald money for such a purpose, as they did routinely for many Americans stranded in foreign countries without the price of a ticket home. In this instance, Oswald had repaid the loan. But Mrs. Oswald, for reasons any parent could understand, was anxious to find some way to exonerate her child from the terrible charges he faced, some explanation that would buy him sympathy and grace.

The two agents thanked her for her information and escorted her out the door. They had treated her courteously, and for the moment she seemed satisfied. But she would be heard from again and again and again. In the years to come, hers would be one of the most persistent voices accusing the U.S. government of duplicity in her son's arrest and death. Every few months a new book or magazine article would feature quotes from this distressed woman, most of them vague accusations. Like many of the liberal journalists who exploited her, she simply would not believe that Lee Harvey Oswald had alone planned and executed the assassination of the president. That day, when she left the two agents shaking their heads, she was on her way to becoming a permanent footnote in the pages of American history.

During the day, FBI strategy for handling the Kennedy assassination was developing according to a familiar pattern. Hoover was making some decisions himself, but he was also asking the rest of us for recommendations. He was delegating responsibility, not only to get the best expert advice, but also to hedge against possible disaster. If anything went wrong—and it sometimes did—he could always point an accusing finger at the man who'd recommended a particular course of action. Over the years, FBI failures were never the fault of the director. The press always blamed some poor bastard who'd given Hoover bad advice. I'll say this: When he asked us for recommendations, we never offered them without considering every possible outcome that might bring official censure.

Now the director talked to each of us in turn, either face to face or over the intercom. Among those he consulted were Tolson, Al Belmont, Gordon Shanklin, assistant directors, special agents in charge nationwide, and key agents in our laboratory. In addition, all off-duty agents were called and ordered to report for duty immediately.

With Hoover spitting orders, and with the rest of us offering reasoned suggestions, a comprehensive plan took shape. At FBI headquarters in Washington, Belmont would supervise the entire operation. He would be aided by Assistant Director Alex Rosen and Inspector James Malley of the General Investigative Division. William C. Sullivan would be in charge of investigating the degree to which the assassination posed a threat to internal security. As assistant director of the Crime Records Division, I would work closely with Belmont in the investigation and also continue as liaison with Congress, the White House, and the press.

As for the field operation, Inspector Malley would lead a team of forty-nine special agents and forty support personnel. They would leave for Dallas almost immediately to join the massive investigation and lend assistance to the force already on the scene. All information collected around the nation that pertained to the assassination would be channeled to Dallas. This order covered calls, letters, teletypes, airtels, interview reports, and memoranda. All leads were to be prepared on duplicate lead sheets, one copy of which would be retained to follow the coverage of the lead, the other given to the agent who was assigned the lead. Results of investigations were to be typed on multiliths, which were to be read for accuracy.

Already we were getting tips and leads from well-meaning citizens, crackpots, and publicity seekers. We established a "Communications Index" identifying each communication by date, type of communication (call, wire), with a brief comment on the subject matter. (This index later proved invaluable and was maintained for approximately four years after the assassination, when the volume of correspondence finally began to subside.)

Shanklin would continue to run his own operation, which provided the bureau with the bulk of its manpower. The Dallas office consisted of some one hundred agents, about half of them assigned as resident agents in cities surrounding Dallas. Over the years they had been doing a quietly competent job. Now they would be the focus of the world's attention. Already news reporters and television crews were flying to Texas from all parts of the world.

At one point during the development of this strategy I looked out the office window and was surprised to see that it was getting dark outside. I thought fleetingly of home, Barbara, and the children. But I knew I'd be there all night and that if I were lucky, I'd catch an hour of sleep on the sofa in my office. It was always that way on big cases, and this was the biggest case of all.

Late that afternoon, an FBI agent boarded a plane at Love Field in Dallas. He had with him a box that contained three fragments of the president's skull. Two had been found inside the car and one in the gutter on Elm Street, right in front of the Texas Book Depository. These fragments would be the first of many pieces of physical evidence from the crime to be analyzed in our Washington crime laboratory—the most advanced facility of its kind in the world.

At Andrews Air Force Base, where Air Force One had landed with the newly sworn-in president and the late president's body, a Secret Service agent gave FBI Agent Elmer Todd a small object, a bullet. Todd took the bullet immediately to the FBI's Fire Arms Identification Section, where Agent Robert Frazier received it with great interest.

"Where did it come from?" he asked Todd.

"It fell off a stretcher in Parkland Hospital."

As Frazier looked at the object, his interest grew. A ballistics expert who worked with such specimens daily, he was pleased to see that the bullet was not flattened, shattered, or fragmented. After examining the size, he raised his eyebrows.

"The first reports claimed that the gun was a 7.35 Mauser. This is very interesting."

After measuring the round, he nodded.

"Just as I thought. This is not a 7.35. It is a 6.5 millimeter. Did the Secret Service man know which stretcher it was on?"

"No," said Todd. "The man who found it thought it came off of Governor Connally's stretcher."

After examining the bullet at some length, Frazier was able to come to an additional conclusion.

"It's not foreign made," he said. "It's American."

The fact that the bullet was in good shape and made in the United States greatly simplified Frazier's task and that of the Fire Arms Identification Section. In murder mysteries, ballistics tests are always perfectly executed and conclusive. You look through the microscope and see a perfect match—by no means the case in many instances in the real world. When bullets strike bone they tend to flatten or shatter. Often identification is difficult—and sometimes impossible.

Also, foreign-manufactured ammunition was frequently hard to identify, whereas virtually all ammunition made and sold in the United States was known to Frazier and his colleagues. With this bullet, his task could be done quicker and more precisely.

By 7:00 P.M. Eastern Standard Time, President Kennedy's body had arrived at Bethesda Naval Hospital, located in the Maryland suburbs of Washington. Accompanying the casket were two FBI agents, Francis O'Neill and James Sibert. They were not there to protect the remains of a president. That was the job of Roy Kellerman and his Secret Service agents. The FBI representatives were there to ensure the integrity of the examination that was to follow and to report back to headquarters. They remained as observers during the autopsy.

Outside the hospital the sky was dark and the streets were alive with the lights of automobiles on their way into Maryland—federal bureaucrats winding their way home, their eyes on the crawling cars ahead, their attention focused on the radio. As the traffic was beginning to thin, J. Edgar Hoover got a call from Lyndon B. Johnson, sworn in as president and already back in Washington.

The new president informed Hoover that he wanted the FBI to conduct an exhaustive investigation of the assassination and to have a report on his desk by Monday morning. He told the director to assume whatever powers the executive branch had to offer to accomplish this task. Actually, the president had no real powers to give. He certainly had the authority to order the FBI into the case, but this order did not supersede the Tenth Amendment, which gave the state of Texas jurisdiction over murder committed within its boundaries, and the state had in turn delegated its authority to local police departments. Johnson's order might help with the Secret Service; it would do nothing legally to shake the evidence loose from Chief Jesse Curry and Captain Will Fritz.

In the past Hoover had sometimes found it necessary to work with less than full authority. The FBI adhered rigidly to most of the restrictions imposed on it; but occasions arose when Hoover believed the end justified the means, that regulations should give way to expediency, particularly in national security cases. These occasions occurred far less frequently than his critics want you to believe—but this was clearly one of them.

Soon FBI officers all over the country were working on the case. In the New York office, agents were soon identifying and contacting all companies that sold firearms through the U.S. mail. By 10:00 P.M. that night, they had located the manufacturer of the weapon, Crescent Firearms of New York, and also the mail order house to whom that particular rifle had been sold—Klein's Sporting Goods, Inc. of Chicago, Illinois. The Chicago office located William J. Waldman, vice president of the company, and he accompanied our agents to the company's headquarters, where the group began to rummage through company files. A little after midnight they discovered the invoice for the rifle Oswald had used. It had been in a shipment of ten cases purchased from Crescent on March 4, 1963.

Fortunately, Klein's Sporting Goods kept microfilmed photostats of all sales, so the purchaser could be identified. Unfortunately, the orders were filed according to the date received—and Klein's had sold a lot of rifles.

The post office box to which the gun had been sent had been rented by Lee Harvey Oswald. The company had received the order in March of 1963 with payment in the form of a money order. The money order was signed by A. Hidell.

At Bethesda Naval Hospital, doctors finishing up their autopsy ran into a problem. They had no bullet for the entry wound they found in the right strap muscle. At that point, William Greer, the Secret Service agent who had driven the automobile and who was in attendance at the autopsy, told the doctors about the bullet that had fallen out. FBI agents Francis X. O'Neill and James W. Sibert were on hand, taking notes on the findings to make certain the Fire Arms Identification Section had every bit of information available.

In Dallas, Shanklin was running into some difficulties with Curry and his subordinates. Despite the fact that President Lyndon Johnson had ordered the FBI to take full charge of the investigation, the Dallas Police Department continued to maintain that the jurisdiction was theirs—as, in a strictly legal sense, it was. We requested that all evidence be sent to our laboratory in Washington, but Captain Will Fritz of Homicide was saying he needed the evidence right there in Dallas for his own investigation.

Then Jesse Curry made his move. We began to get calls from the networks and wire services telling us that the chief of the Dallas Police Department had just been on television, claiming that the FBI had had Lee Harvey Oswald under surveillance. The callers wanted to know if Curry's statement was true. When the first call hit, I could only say that I'd check the story and get back as soon as possible with an answer.

I immediately dialed Gordon Shanklin in Dallas.

"It's not true," he said, and explained to me about Hosty and the status of the Oswald case.

A file, he told me, had been opened on January 12, 1961, as the result of a letter from the District Intelligence Office of the Eighth Naval District, New Orleans, Louisiana. Among other facts, the file contained the information that Oswald had attempted to defect to the Soviet Union in October of 1959; had married a Russian woman; had returned to the United States; had formed a chapter of the Fair Play for Cuba Committee in New Orleans, which listed a fictitious "A. J. Hidell" as its president; had moved back to his native Texas; had taken up residence locally; had not joined the Communist party; had made a trip to Mexico only two months earlier. Hosty had interviewed Marina Oswald because she was a resident alien, but had never found Lee at home.

I put a hold on further calls and dialed Clyde Tolson. He told me to call or see the director. I buzzed Helen Gandy and told her I had to see the Old Man. When I reached the inner office, the director was on the phone, and this one time he didn't bother to rise or to come around the desk to greet me. I learned from listening to his conversation that he knew about the capture of Lee Harvey Oswald. No surprise. He'd probably talked to Shanklin earlier. He saw me, and barked into the receiver, "Hold on a minute."

"Mr. Hoover," I said, "the Dallas chief of police is on national television, saying the FBI has had this Oswald under surveillance."

"Is it true?" he asked, a worried look on his face. If so—and if Oswald were indeed the Kennedy assassin—it would mean we had either lost touch with him during surveillance or, worse, stood by while he shot the president of the United States. As always, the director was concerned with his own reputation and that of his bureau.

"No," I said. "It's not true. I just talked to Shanklin. We have a file on Oswald because he defected to the Soviet Union, but he hasn't been under surveillance. The agent in charge of the case has never even seen the man."

Hoover nodded with grim satisfaction. He understood just what kind of file we had on Oswald and how many files of this sort we maintained nationwide—literally thousands.

"Call Curry and tell him that's a lie, that he's to make a public retraction as soon as possible."

I started to leave, but he held up his hand.

"And tell him if he doesn't offer the retraction, we'll cut off all privileges."

The phrase had a very specific meaning. Ordinarily the FBI responds to all official requests for fingerprint and laboratory assistance from law enforcement officers all over the free world. But this cooperation is not mandated by law. It is a courtesy extended by the bureau, and one that can be withdrawn at the pleasure of the director. Hoover withdrew the privilege only rarely. That he was threatening to do so now—in the middle of this extraordinary investigation—was some measure of his anger and frustration.

I went back to my office, immediately called Gordon Shanklin, and he in turn spoke to Dallas Police Chief Jesse Curry. Within minutes Curry was back on television with a correction—of sorts. But it was insufficient to stem the Old Man's fury; and in succeeding days, after more evidence of hostility and incompetence on Curry's part, the FBI did in fact cut off his department's privileges.

Early Friday evening, November 22, we sent out instructions to all FBI offices nationwide "to immediately contact all informants, security, racial and criminal, as well as other sources, for information bearing on the assassination." The dispatch requested that all offices "establish the whereabouts of bombing suspects, all known Klan and hate group members, known racial extremists and other individuals" who, on the basis of available evidence, might have been involved in a plot to kill the president of the United States.

In 1976, the Senate Select Committee, commonly referred to as the "Church Committee," published its final report, which stated that the FBI sent a teletype dispatch to all field offices "rescinding" this order, implying that the bureau was somehow remiss in not pursuing such leads. That is untrue. In fact, on Saturday, November 23, with the case against Oswald firmly established, FBI headquarters instructed all field offices "to resume normal contacts with informants and other resources." This merely meant that agents throughout the country could contact their informants in the normal course of business rather than waking them up in the middle of the night, as the previous day's communique had ordered.

Eventually I took a break and called Barbara. We spoke only briefly. She already knew I'd be working round the clock, so we exchanged a few comments on the grisly events of the day, discussed the children's reaction, and speculated on my chances of coming home the next night. All the while the phones were ringing in the background, and I had to get back to work.

In Dallas, the police department was gathering evidence, much of which it jealously guarded. By this time the tension between local and federal authorities was obvious. Chief Curry had attempted to saddle the bureau with primary blame for the assassination, and Hoover had responded with a demand for a retraction and a stern threat.

Unaware of this tension, Agent Drain dropped by the Dallas police laboratory to see if any new evidence had been uncovered. Lt. J. C. Day had just lifted a handprint from the rifle.

"The metal is rough," he'd told his assistant. "If it was smooth, this print would be sharper."

Day showed Drain what he'd found, and Drain again offered the resources of the FBI Identification Division, which had the most comprehensive file of fingerprints in the world. Day, apparently more aware of the rivalry than Drain, refused, saying it was up to Chief Curry to make such a decision. Drain left, empty-handed and frustrated.

Soon Chief Curry began to receive phone calls from local bigwigs, urging him to turn the evidence over to the Federal Bureau of Investigation for a day or two. Annoyed by these intrusions, Curry dug in his heels, set his jaw, and refused to cooperate with the FBI. Given the importance of the callers, he wondered who had generated these invasions into what he clearly viewed as his exclusive business.

The telephone campaign bore the unmistakable fingerprints of Hoover, who was annoyed to distraction by Curry's accusations against the bureau and who had powerful contacts in the Dallas-Ft. Worth area. Texas big-wigs Clint Murchison and Sid Richardson were among his few close friends, and they in turn knew everybody in local and state politics. There were also members of Congress who were sympathetic with the FBI or owed Hoover favors—and more than one who feared him. He undoubtedly made four or five calls in rapid succession, then sat back and waited until his contacts got back to him, reporting on their conversations with Chief Curry.

Again, Curry had the law on his side. The matter was indubitably within his jurisdiction. But cooperation among all available law enforcement agencies would clearly help everyone. The idea that the Dallas Police Department could, without any support from the FBI, carry on a complete and thorough investigation of the assassination was absurd.

Our fingerprint files, our Fire Arms Identification Section, and our New York office were all crucial in developing the tissue of evidence that ultimately made the case for Oswald's guilt. The Dallas Police Department could not have done it alone in the length of time necessary to satiate the demands of the general public. They too contributed key evidence, but the FBI pinned Oswald to the wall.

Earlier in the afternoon the day of the assassination the Washington office had asked the Dallas office for a biography and description of Lee Harvey Oswald. It was to be an essential element of the report we were preparing for President Johnson. But in the course of the day's frantic activities, our people in Dallas forgot about this request. Late in the evening, we again asked for the information.

Agent Manning Clements asked James Bookhout if he'd gathered the information, and Bookhout said he was unaware anyone had asked him to do so. Some of this information was in the file, but Clements concluded that the easiest way to fill in the gaps was to go down to the Dallas city jail and interview Oswald. He asked Captain Will Fritz for permission and received it. When Clements spoke to Oswald, he, too, made no objection. Indeed, he was cooperative, supplying a list of family members, dates of birth, height, weight, addresses, schools, cities of residence, and employment record. While Oswald was out of the room, Clements also went through his wallet, which was lying on the captain's desk. In short order he had all the information he needed for a preliminary biography and physical description.

It was almost midnight, the night of the assassination, when District Attorney Henry Wade finally persuaded Chief Curry that it was foolish not to ask for assistance from the FBI, and its famous laboratory, its capacity to track down leads all over the country, and its offices in New Orleans and New York—cities where Oswald had once lived. Wade was a man with tremendous clout in Dallas County. He enjoyed the same kind of reputation locally that Hoover had earned nationally—as a crime fighter. Curry could go to war with Washington without alienating his local constituency. If he fought with Henry Wade, he would lose on his own home field.

So very, very reluctantly, Curry agreed to hand over all physical evidence to the bureau as soon as possible. But there was a catch. He would give us less than twenty-four hours to work with it. We could fly the exhibits to Washington immediately. The FBI would sign for each piece. We could work on the evidence all day. But we would have to have everything back in Dallas by the stroke of midnight, otherwise we would all turn into pumpkins.

Drain heard the conditions, heaved a sigh, and agreed. Then he called Gordon Shanklin to pass along the news. Shanklin in turn called Washington. Al Belmont took the call.

"We'll be waiting," he said.

Shanklin then phoned the commanding general at Carswell Air Force Base in Texas.

"One of our agents is taking evidence in the assassination to Washington. We have a directive that you will help us fly it up and wait for it to come back."

It was after 1:00 A.M. when Agents Sibert and O'Neill left the site of the autopsy at Bethesda Naval Hospital and returned to the Justice Department building, most of the lights still blazing on its upper floors. In the Fire Arms Identification Section, Robert Frazier was waiting for them impatiently. He knew this would probably be the most important case he would ever work on, and he was still wide awake. When Sibert and O'Neill came through the door, he asked them immediately, "Did you find anything?"

They knew exactly what he meant. He wanted pieces of the grisly puzzle, and they had something for him in a salve jar—two tiny slivers of lead, precisely what Frazier wanted to see.

"Here are some metal fragments from the president's head," Sibert said.

Frazier looked at them dubiously. One weighed 1.65 grams, the other only 0.15 of a gram.

"Is this all you found?"

They told him the frustrating truth. X-rays showed that there were thirty or forty fragments still lodged along the skull and embedded in the brain. The doctors decided not to attempt to retrieve them, since they were too small.

Frazier knew that fragments of the bullet (or bullets) were still missing. So where were they? One possibility was in the SS-100-X—the president's automobile. It had been flown to Washington and was now over at an M Street garage, guarded by Secret Service agents. Frazier got a group together, and they all drove over to M Street.

With the help of the Secret Service, they rolled out the car, removed the plastic cover and the leatherette convertible top. One of the FBI agents, a photographer, took pictures from all angles, including the interior of the trunk. Then Frazier and his crew began to examine the automobile, patiently, carefully, with precise attention to every detail. They measured the crack on the windshield, gleaming in the artificial light like a spider web. Then they ran their fingers across it, outside and inside. Outside the spider web was smooth to the touch. Inside it was sharp and grooved. They carefully scraped the cracks with a knife and captured tiny bits of metal along with the ground glass. Later they would discover that the metal was identical with the slivers found during the autopsy.

After carefully harvesting the windshield, they examined every other likely inch of the automobile—tires, fenders, upholstery, dashboard, floor. On the back seat and on the rug they discovered dried blood and brain tissue, which they examined for metal fragments. They also found fragments of metal—more pieces of the puzzle—on the floor. Two of them were fairly large. Maybe large enough! Frazier was encouraged. It was tedious and exacting work, but every little piece in place clarified the picture.

By 1:30 Saturday morning, November 23, the evidence was there to charge Lee Harvey Oswald with the assassination of the president of the United States. It had been gathered by both the FBI and the Dallas Police Department, despite the attempt on the part of Chief Curry and his subordinates to exclude both the bureau and the Secret Service from its investigation.

Meanwhile, at Carswell Air Force Base, Agent Drain was waiting in a car with the crucial pieces of evidence Chief Curry had finally been willing to surrender. He was soon joined by Winston Lawson, a Secret Service agent, who had been ordered to accompany him.

"I remember you," said Drain. "You were at headquarters this morning." Drain told Lawson he would be happy to have him aboard.

When they were airborne, Lawson asked Drain if he could take inventory of the evidence. Lawson recorded the evidence as consisting of the following:

1. A live 6.5-millimeter rifle shell found in a 6.5 Mannlicher-Carcano rifle on the sixth floor of the Texas Book Depository building.
2. Three spent 6.5-millimeter shells, found on sixth floor of the Depository inside the northeast window.

3. One blanket found in garage of Mrs. Ruth Paine, 2515 Fifth Street, Irving, Texas.
4. Shirt taken from Lee H. Oswald at police headquarters.
5. Brown wrapping paper found on sixth floor, near rifle, believed to have been used to wrap the weapon.
6. Sample of brown paper used by School Book Depository and sample of paper tape used for mailing books.
7. Fragment of bullet found in the wrist of Governor John Connally.
8. Smith and Wesson .38 revolver, V510210, taken from Lee H. Oswald at Texas Theater.
9. .38 bullet recovered from the body of Officer J. D. Tippit.
10. One 6.5-millimeter bolt action rifle, inscribed "1940, Made in Italy," serial number C2766. Also inscribed on the rifle was a crown similar to an English crown. Under it was inscribed "R-E." Also inscribed was "Rocca," which was enclosed in rectangular lines and was on the plunger on the bolt action on the rear of the gun. On the four-power scope of the gun was inscribed "Ordnance Optics Inc., Hollywood, California, 010 or 010 Japan." Also inscribed was a cloverleaf and inside the cloverleaf was "OSC."

Back in Washington headquarters, most members of the bureau had surrendered to physical and emotional exhaustion. I was still on duty. By 3:00 A.M. the calls had almost ceased, and I'd seen enough of the grim images on the black-and-white television screen: the solemn and often tearful statements of famous people and anonymous passersby; the speculations of reporters and commentators; the arrival in Washington of the current president and the casket of the former president; the already famous Zapruder film, run again and again, with its jerky image of John Kennedy pitching suddenly forward and his terrified wife trying to scramble out of the car.

Weary and numb, I turned down the sound, left the screen to flicker in the gloom of the office, and stretched out on the sofa. As soon as I closed my eyes, the phone rang, and I had to leap up and grab it. This happened virtually all night. Sometimes it was the press. Sometimes it was Al Belmont or Gordon Shanklin.

I didn't get a full hour of sleep the entire night, and by dawn the phones were ringing as persistently and frequently as the previous day. Saturday morning, November 23, between calls, I was able to drink some coffee and eat something, though I had little appetite. Hoover called Belmont and me to receive reports and give additional orders. He spoke to us numerous times during the day.

A little after 5:00 A.M., Drain arrived at the Justice Department, evidence in hand, accompanied by Lawson. At that point, the evidence was apportioned according to expertise, with most of it going to Frazier and the Fire Arms Inspection Section. Virtually everyone had been awake for most or all of the night, but they were bright-eyed and alert. They had been told the terms of the agreement Drain had reached with the Dallas Police Department and Chief Jesse Curry. They had slightly more than one full working day to complete their respective investigations. Outside it was still cold and starry. It was late in the fall, and no trace of dawn colored the sharp edges of buildings or the remaining dark leaves of trees. By the time the sun had risen they would be hard at work, and when it set in the late afternoon, they would have to be finished. No one had time to be sleepy.

Agent Robert A. Frazier had been with the bureau for over twenty years, examining weapons and identifying bullets and cartridge cases to determine whether they had been used in specific crimes or fired from particular weapons. The Kennedy shooting, though certainly a challenging case, did not pose extraordinary problems for either Frazier or his team of experts. He had seen bullets more fragmented, had successfully reconstructed more difficult puzzles. According to his own testimony before the Warren Commission, he had made "in the neighborhood of 50,000 to 60,000" firearms comparisons and had "testified in court about 400 times."

He was a connoisseur of rifles and bullets, and no one living knew more about them. When you were as experienced as Frazier in any field, you came to a point where you instantly and instinctively knew things that other people could not discover by hours and hours of diligent concentration. But by the end of the day— when the evidence had to be gathered up and dispatched back to Dallas, hand-carried by the weary Vincent Drain—even Frazier could draw only a limited number of conclusions. Some questions could never be answered, given the impact of the bullet and the scattering of metal fragments. But this much Frazier could say for certain by the time he had to give up the evidence: The bullet found on the stretcher and the two larger bullet fragments found in the president's limousine had been fired from the C2766 Mannlicher-Carcano rifle found in the Texas Book Depository "to the exclusion of all other weapons."

By 6:45 A.M. on Saturday, we were able to say with some degree of certainty that the information on the documents used to order the murder weapon was in the handwriting of Lee Harvey Oswald, that he was, in effect, A. Hidell. This new evidence complemented the information gleaned the previous night. And by then we had also identified the handprint the Dallas police had found on the rifle. It belonged to Oswald.

The accumulation of such evidence and the formal charging made my job much easier on Saturday than the day before. I was able to offer details of the case to members of Congress and other government officials, though I still had to be selective in what I said. Many of the people who contacted me were still shaken and close to tears. Members of the press, though less emotional, were more irritable and impatient than they'd been the previous day. Like me, most of them had been up all night, and they were under tremendous pressure to turn up something—anything—that would beat the competition.

By Saturday evening the calls had diminished to the point where we could actually handle them efficiently and courteously. The nation, over its initial shock, was now sad and silent. Utterly exhausted, my throat raw, I finally gave up and went home, assuring myself, in my ignorance, that the crisis had passed. But in a city the size of Dallas, more than one crazy fool walks the streets.

7

....

Jack Ruby

JACK RUBY WAS AN INTENSE MAN who had admired John F. Kennedy and was emotionally devastated when the young president was assassinated in Dallas. Heavy-set and often overdressed, Ruby looked like a Mafia boss in a Hollywood movie. He owned two nightclubs—the Carousel Club, a downtown strip joint, and the Vegas Club, a rock 'n' roll hangout in the Oak Lawn area. Both were cheap and sleazy, but they didn't cater to the criminal element.

In the ongoing drama of the assassination, Ruby appeared at first as a character actor, showing his face in scene after scene, never taking part in the central action. A little after noon on Friday, at the very time Kennedy was shot, Ruby was in the *Dallas Morning News* office, just five blocks away from Dealey Plaza. He was placing a weekly ad for his nightclubs; and while there, he also protested a black-bordered advertisement in the *News* that morning which read, "Welcome, Mr. Kennedy." It was signed with the name "Bernard Weissman." Ruby thought the ad was inhospitable.

Ruby was still in the *Morning News* building when he learned that the president had been fired at. It's conceivable that if a window had been open he could have heard the shots. Later in the day, he would call back and cancel his ads, substituting an announcement that both his clubs would close for the weekend out of respect for the deceased president.

Later, one reporter would claim to have spoken briefly with the nightclub owner at Parkland Hospital less than an hour after the shooting. But Ruby denied being there, and none of the photographs and video tapes of Parkland on that day corroborate the reporter's story.

That Friday night, Ruby was on the third floor of the Dallas Police Department. He'd come because he was increasingly obsessed with the assassination, unable to stand at a distance and watch the developments as a bystander. The police should never have let him enter—but they were unaware that he'd done so. Newsman John Rutledge described how Ruby gained access to the building:

> I saw Jack and two out-of-state reporters, whom I did not know, leave the elevator door and proceed toward those television cameras, to go around the corner where Captain Fritz's office was. Jack walked between them. These two out-of-state reporters had big press cards pinned on their coats, great big red ones. I think they said "President Kennedy's Visit to Dallas—Press," or something like that. And Jack didn't have one, but the man on either side of him did. And they walked pretty rapidly from the elevator area past the policeman, and Jack was bent over like this—writing on a piece of paper, and talking to one of the reporters, and pointing to something on the piece of paper, he was kind of hunched over.

While at the police station that night, Ruby, standing on a tabletop with several other newsmen, got his first glimpse of Lee Harvey Oswald. A little later he watched District Attorney Henry Wade field questions at a press conference. After the questioning, Ruby went up to Wade and introduced himself: "Hi, Henry. Don't you know me? I am Jack Ruby. I run the Vegas Club." He was beginning to feel the pull of history.

After Ruby left the police department, he drove to KLIF radio, where he habitually hung out with the staff and announcers. He talked about the assassination, telling one employee that he had closed down both his nightclubs because he didn't want to remain open at such a time in the nation's history. As he left KLIF, Ruby told one of the station's announcers that right-wing "radicals" were partially responsible for the president's death.

About 4:00 A.M., Ruby showed up at the composing room of the *Dallas Times-Herald,* where he spoke excitedly about the assassination with some of the employees.

Later that morning, after a few hours of sleep, he drove down to Dealey Plaza and engaged a police officer in a conversation about the assassination. The policeman pointed out the sixth-story window from which Oswald had fired the shots, and Ruby looked at the wreaths that had been laid there in memory of the president.

On Saturday afternoon, Ruby made up his mind to be at the city jail the next morning to witness Oswald's transfer to county facilities, which would be open to the press. He was heard telling a friend that he would be "acting like a reporter," saying, "you know I'll be there."

During the rest of that day and night, Ruby became increasingly depressed and angry over the failure of competitors to close down their clubs in honor of Kennedy. He paced up and down, talking to himself. Friends and family noticed that he was morose and distant, and later remembered: "There was something wrong with him," "He was jabbering."

On Sunday morning, Ruby got up, drove downtown, wired an employee some money, then walked one block to the Dallas city jail, where he entered the building, using the auto ramp. Once in the basement, he mingled with reporters and officers, awaiting the transfer of Lee Harvey Oswald. When Oswald appeared, Ruby was no longer content to stand by and merely watch history take place. He had decided to become a major player. As two officers hustled Oswald toward him, Jack Ruby stepped forward, drawing his pistol.

Back in the office on Sunday, I remember feeling some satisfaction at the progress we'd made. The efficiency of the FBI was reassuring in a period of national crisis, and that knowledge took away some of our pain. For the first time in two days my television was turned off, and I was going over reports that had been piling up on my desk—most of them from Dallas, some of them from agents in other parts of the country, all of them relating to the Kennedy assassination.

"Oh, my God," someone shouted from a nearby office. I heard another cry somewhere farther down the hall. Then the intercom came on. "Deke, somebody just shot Oswald!"

Shot Oswald? I couldn't believe it! How could anyone have shot a man in a secure jail? Then I remembered. They were transferring him from the Dallas city jail to the Dallas county jail this morning. I turned on the television just in time to see the replay.

It all happened again right before my eyes in slow motion: the basement crowded with police officers and reporters, the sudden surge of excitement, the burst of flashbulbs, the appearance of Oswald flanked by two detectives, from the right the appearance of a hulk in a wide-brimmed hat, Oswald's apprehensive glance, the lunge, the muffled explosion, the look of instant agony on Oswald's face, the convergence of a mob of officers. It was the first murder ever to occur live on television, and that blast would echo in the memory of millions of Americans.

I heard profane exclamations from all over the office, and I knew exactly how they felt. We'd had a perfect case in the making. We'd hoped we might even get a confession. The investigation would be wrapped up and tied neatly in ribbon by Christmas—a gift to the nation and punishment for a man who had not only murdered another human being, but had committed a crime against the people of the United States. Now our case was moot.

Someone stuck his head into my office.

"What do you think Oswald's chances are from what you could see?"

I shook my head.

The phone, which had been silent most of the morning, suddenly started jangling. It had begun all over again.

Immediately after Oswald was shot, Gordon Shanklin dispatched two FBI agents to Parkland Hospital, the same place Kennedy had been taken to only two days earlier.

"We're here to take any confession Oswald might make," they said.

The physician in charge nodded.

"O.K.," he said, "but you'll have to put on surgical masks and gowns and wait in the hallway. If he's conscious and talking, I'll let you come in. Right now he's unconscious."

They did as they were instructed, but they were never called inside. Lee Harvey Oswald died on the operating table without ever regaining consciousness.

Within the hour, we received word that Oswald was dead. Suddenly, the case we'd been pursuing—Oswald's assassination of the president—had become just a little less urgent than it had been at the start of the day, and in addition to the assassination, we were investigating a new crime—the murder of our chief suspect. Immediately we wondered if the Dallas Police Department would attempt to exclude us from the investigation, on the same grounds—jurisdiction. This time, however, we had a foothold. We were told that we could investigate the possibility that Lee Harvey Oswald's civil rights had been violated. That was an area within our jurisdiction, and we proceeded to respond as quickly as possible.

In the Dallas office, Shanklin immediately assigned Special Agents Manning Clements and Bob Gemberling to take charge of investigating Oswald's shooting as well as Kennedy's. They divided the responsibilities between them. Clements headed the "Ruby Squad" and Gemberling the "Oswald Squad." Each man had about twenty-five agents under him.

Agents Gemberling and Clements had been given a gargantuan task, one Gemberling hadn't completed by the time he retired in 1976. The two teams, utilizing all the resources and personnel of the FBI, collected an enormous amount of information on both Ruby and Oswald. No investigation in the nation's past had been conducted with such painstaking care, with such attention to minute detail.

Our agents followed leads that were so farfetched they were laughable. They also pursued tips that seemed grounded in fact and pointed to conspiracy. Yet in the end, the FBI concluded that both shootings were precisely what they'd appeared to be from the start—lone acts, each perpetrated by an unbalanced man caught up in the raw excitement of contemporary history.

On November 29, just one week after the death of John F. Kennedy, President Lyndon Johnson announced that Chief Justice Earl Warren would head a commission to evaluate all the evidence pertinent to the Kennedy assassination. According to published reports, when the president asked him to undertake this enormous task, Warren broke down and cried.

The Warren Commission took as its purview the study and evaluation of all data gathered by investigative agencies, whether municipal, state, or federal; and the two FBI committees were ordered to report directly to the commission. Accordingly, Gemberling submitted his first report on November 30, one day after the commission was established, eight days after the death of the president. The document, submitted through FBI headquarters in Washington, was 515 pages in length and contained virtually all of the basic facts that were to provide the substance of the final report by the Warren Commission. Though portions of this report have been challenged by everyone from Mark Lane to Oliver Stone, none of the information has ever been proven erroneous.

Because the press was already speculating about a possible conspiracy, still hoping to implicate the radical right, the commission was particularly interested in all information about the life of Lee Harvey Oswald. So after Gemberling had submitted his lengthy report, the bureau also provided the seven members and their staff with a complete history of Lee Harvey Oswald's life, the kind of detailed personal narrative you would find in the definitive biography of a famous figure. The narrative covered his time in nursery school, elementary school, and high school, his decision to drop out of the tenth grade, his enlistment in the Marine Corps at the age of seventeen, his military career, his defection to the Soviet Union, his life there, and his return to the United States.

We provided the commission with a well-documented account of his employment record, finances, and places of residence since birth. We scrutinized his travels outside the United States: Russia (October 1959 to June 1962) and Mexico City (September 26 to October 3, 1963). We examined his affiliations with foreign organizations, notably his connection with the Fair Play for Cuba Committee. And we investigated all allegations against him and either proved or disproved them with persuasive evidence or credible witnesses.

In the end, the Warren Commission—after sifting through a mountain of evidence that might have topped the Washington Monument—came to the same conclusion as the FBI: Oswald shot President Kennedy without the aid of any conspirator; Jack Ruby shot Oswald by himself.

For a while it appeared as if the Warren Commission report would treat the FBI respectfully, or so we heard from Congressman Gerald Ford, our chief contact on the seven-man commission. At that point, with the bureau's position apparently secure, Hoover was in a benevolent mood. He even had a long, fatherly conversation with Jim Hosty, in which he told the Dallas agent not to worry about the future, that the whole matter would soon be forgotten. What Hosty did not know was that Hoover was ready to throw him or anyone else overboard if the situation changed and the bureau—or the director—were put at any risk.

Then the wind changed. According to Ford, Chief Justice Warren was pressing the rest of the commissioners to issue a report critical of the bureau. In the beginning, it appeared as if five members were opposed to such criticism and only two in favor. But by the time Warren had finished lobbying them the vote was four to three in favor—with John Sherman Cooper, Allen Dulles, and John J. McCloy joining Warren in voting for a mild and qualified reprimand.

When he heard this news, Hoover's benevolence vanished. Rain clouds formed in his office. He wasn't about to shoulder the blame. He decided to spread it around. When I heard about his intentions, I wrote a memorandum suggesting he delay any administrative censure against the agents involved.

"In a few months this will all blow over," I said. "Then we can review the actions of everybody working on this case. Censuring them now will result in bad public relations. In the meantime, the FBI can surely weather the storm." Other assistant directors joined with me in this advice.

I knew it was futile even then. He'd made up his mind. He thought it would be best to show the American public that in such cases the bureau could move swiftly despite the mildness of the alleged derelictions. Consequently he took disciplinary action against seventeen agents. Twelve of these received what agents called "slap on the wrist" letters, mild rebukes—but signed by the director himself. Most agents and administrators picked up a few such letters along the way; but these were usually more than outweighed by the "atta boy" letters Hoover wrote in abundance.

He took more severe action against five agents. Hosty's supervisor in Dallas was busted back to agent and reassigned to Seattle. The case agent in New Orleans was transferred to Springfield, Illinois. One supervisor in Washington headquarters was sent back to the field, though Hoover couldn't reduce his pay, since he was a war veteran and was protected from such arbitrary action under the Civil Service Law. A second Washington supervisor was reassigned to the Washington field office.

Jim Hosty took the biggest hit. First Hoover attempted to fire him because of his failure to anticipate Oswald's behavior; but Hosty, also a war veteran, challenged the action before a Civil Service review board and won. Then Hoover suspended him for thirty days without pay and reassigned him to Kansas City, where a good friend of Hosty's was the special agent in charge. Hosty's fellow agents in Washington and Dallas, convinced that he was being persecuted, took up a collection to cover his salary loss, giving Hosty an all-expenses-paid vacation. Resettled in Kansas City, he thought the whole matter was behind him. Unfortunately, he was wrong. The whole matter would be resurrected more than ten years later.

Following the investigation of the Kennedy assassination, the FBI's relations with at least two law enforcement agencies were strained. Most obvious was the bad blood between the bureau and the Dallas Police Department. Hoover had made it official—all privileges had been withdrawn, and this punishment did not apply exclusively to the Kennedy case, but to every single case from that time forward until Hoover chose to rescind his decision. Today the director of the FBI could not engage in such selective retribution. In those days Hoover could do as he pleased. With a single stroke of the pen, Hoover had put the Dallas police in a time machine and zapped them back to the days of Bonnie and Clyde, when nobody cooperated with anybody.

Obviously this rift had to be mended, but neither Hoover nor Dallas Chief Curry had any intention of giving an inch. Maybe Curry didn't know that his only chance for absolution lay in a full admission of culpability and an abject plea for forgiveness. Maybe he knew what was required and wasn't willing to humble himself. Whatever his reasons, the chief made no move to appease Hoover, and the impasse continued well into 1964. At that point, two non-combatants got together to effect a reconciliation.

I was scheduled to make a speech before a veterans' organization in Dallas. The day before I left, Marie buzzed me on the intercom to tell me that Eric Jonsson was on the line.

"Who's Eric Jonsson?" I asked.

"He's the mayor of Dallas."

Then I remembered. He'd been elected quite recently, the candidate of a nonpartisan group called the City Charter Association, which represented Dallas business interests. Jonsson himself had been the CEO and co-founder of Texas Instruments, one of the major manufacturers in the Dallas-Ft. Worth area, and a giant in the aerospace industry.

I got on the phone immediately.

"Mr. DeLoach," he said, "I understand you're going to be in Dallas tomorrow. I wonder if you could have breakfast with me. There's something I'd like to discuss with you. Perhaps you can guess what it is."

I told him I thought I knew the subject, that I'd be happy to meet with him.

The next morning, as we were finishing coffee, Mayor Jonsson, an extraordinarily friendly and courteous man, put the question to me directly: "What would it take to mend fences between your agency and the Dallas Police Department?"

I explained Chief Curry's inaccurate statements and Hoover's attitude in response. We both understood who had made the decision, who was in charge. I could offer advice, but there was no guarantee Hoover would listen.

"If Jesse Curry apologizes in the right way," I told Jonsson, "I believe the director will accept his apology." Jonsson leaned forward and spoke more quietly.

"Suppose Jesse Curry is no longer chief of police?"

"In that case," I said, "we would have a whole new ball game."

He nodded and was silent for a moment. I had the feeling he was searching for the right words.

"We can't allow this situation to continue," he said. "It's important to the future of this city for our police to be on friendly terms with federal law enforcement agencies, and particularly the FBI. We've always had a good working relationship. That has to be reestablished. I can promise you that soon—very soon—Chief Curry will be gone."

"In which case," I said, "I will certainly tell Mr. Hoover about our conversation and strongly recommend that we reinstate privileges as soon as that happens."

He smiled thinly.

"And not before?"

I returned his smile.

"And not before."

When I got back to Washington, I told Hoover what had happened, and he nodded. It sounded good, but we would wait and see. Shortly thereafter, Chief Curry left the Dallas Police Department, and J. Edgar Hoover immediately reinstated the department's privileges. He wasn't one to hold a grudge—at least not when his enemy's head was delivered to him on a platter.

The lingering ill feeling between the FBI and the Secret Service following the Kennedy assassination posed a slightly more complicated problem. Each was sensitive about its role in the shooting and its aftermath. Rightly or wrongly, both were accused of failing to monitor Oswald's movements more closely prior to the shooting, and both brooded over these charges. The FBI fretted that it might have advised Secret Service agents that Lee Harvey Oswald lived in the area and had exhibited erratic behavior. The Secret Service took to heart the allegation that it should have broadened its own survey of potential assassins to include troubled misfits like Oswald. At the same time, each agency circled the wagons to defend its own personnel and reputation. The result: serious name calling, which led to a growing bitterness that threatened the ability of the agencies to work together.

It was a bad time to quarrel. The nation needed to believe that the president of the United States was safe while driving down the streets of America. As the quarrel worsened, Father Daniel J. Power, S.J., head of development at Georgetown University, called me and said, "Deke, why don't you and Jim Rowley have a quiet lunch with me at my office at the university?" Rowley, chief of the Secret Service, was a former FBI agent whom I knew and liked; we both accepted.

It was the first of a number of such luncheons. Following each, I wrote a memorandum to J. Edgar Hoover with the increasing conviction that Rowley wished to cooperate rather than, as Hoover suspected, make the FBI a scapegoat for his own agency's shortcomings.

Eventually we worked out a number of administrative procedures that strengthened the relationship between the Secret Service and the FBI and ensured greater protection for the president and his family. Today, it is far less likely that a Lee Harvey Oswald could slip through our net.

This reconciliation was all the more essential because the new president, Lyndon Johnson, issued an executive order allowing the president to use the FBI for protection as well as the Secret Service. Had Rowley and I not worked out our differences, such efforts would have been difficult, at best.

As everyone knows, rumors surrounding the Kennedy assassination persevered, even after the Senate Select Committee on Intelligence and the House Committee on Assassinations had issued reports. The old conspiracy theories continued to circulate, and a new generation of theorists arose. Every few years the television networks aired skeptical retrospectives; and in 1991, Hollywood activist Oliver Stone took his bizarre version to the screen. At the time the film was released, a national poll indicated that a majority of Americans did not believe Lee Harvey Oswald had acted alone, even though few if any of those surveyed had examined the evidence of the Warren Commission.

The remarkable vitality of these conspiracy theories is a testimony to the power of the press in general and the electronic media in particular. They have kept the doubts and suspicions alive, despite an overwhelming body of evidence to the contrary. But why? Why have they chosen to perpetuate a dark and irrational view of American government and society?

The answer surely lies in the expectations of reporters and commentators during the first hours after the assassination and the failure to see them realized as the story unfolded. From the moment shots were fired at Dealey Plaza, the predominantly liberal press assumed that the assassin was a man of the Right—a Klansman, a neo-Nazi, a John Bircher. After all, the incident had occurred in Dallas, a stronghold of political conservatism, home of billionaire H. L. Hunt, Congressman Joe Pool, General Edwin Walker.

In the hysteria that followed the assassination, reporters and broadcasters forgot that the Dallas city government was securely in the hands of a bipartisan coalition of moderate businessmen like Democratic Mayor Earle Cabell and Republican Eric Jonsson of Texas Instruments, who shared a vision for the city that included a strong role for minorities and a "progressive" political agenda.

From the beginning, commentators on all three networks were hinting—if not stating outright—that the right wing was responsible for the assassination. Walter Cronkite said over and over that the president was shot while en route to deliver a speech attacking the radical right. And when Kennedy's casket was being lowered into the grave, Cronkite called him the first president to be martyred in the cause of civil rights.

When it turned out that the assassin was a Marxist who had connections with the liberal far left Fair Play for Cuba Committee, the liberal media first went into shock, then into denial. Things simply couldn't have happened that way. Somehow, some way, the right wing had to have been responsible. So the Left withdrew into one of two great fantasies.

The first fantasy held that in some mysterious, indefinable way the atmosphere of "extremism" and "hatred" in Dallas had subtly affected Oswald's mind and provoked him to violence. The most ambitious attempt to sustain this hallucination was William Manchester's *The Death of a President*, a huge volume written with the cooperation of the Kennedy family and published in 1966 with great fanfare. In his narrative—hurriedly written and littered with innumerable factual errors—Manchester cites crime statistics, newspaper editorials, political flyers, and election results to build his case against "the City of Hate." It wasn't Lee Harvey Oswald who killed John F. Kennedy, he seems to argue, but Dallas itself, using the hapless (and apparently helpless) Oswald as a lethal weapon. A mere twenty-five years later, the proposition seems totally absurd, but for several years after the assassination, it absolved the Left of guilt and transferred responsibility to its wicked step-sister, the Right.

The second fantasy is more satisfying to the Left and therefore more enduring—the conviction that somehow there was a well-planned conspiracy behind Oswald's act, that he was merely the creature of larger and more sinister forces—right-wing industrialists, the CIA, the FBI, that is, the demonology of the 1960s. The children of this era came to view the American system as one giant plot against humanity, and they continue in their paranoid delusion. Hence the success of Oliver Stone's movie and the continuing belief by a majority of the American people that in the early 1960s, their government deceived them, plotted against them, and perhaps even murdered their president.

In fact, the FBI did consider most, if not all, of the conspiracy theories, as well as those speculating on such specific questions as the number of shots fired, the direction from which they came, and the nature of the wounds sustained by both President Kennedy and Governor Connally. Contrary to popular opinion, no one has disproved the bureau's original conclusion that Lee Harvey Oswald, acting alone, fired three shots from the sixth floor of the Texas Book Depository, killing the president of the United States.

Most of the conspiracy theories were based on one of several false assumptions: that more than three shots were fired, that more than one gunman was involved, that at least one of the bullets that struck the president was fired from "the grassy knoll" in front of him.

Many of these theories depended in part on the idea that the autopsy at Bethesda Naval Hospital was somehow flawed. In response to the heated public dialogue following the release of Oliver Stone's *JFK*, the American Medical Association decided to review the autopsy findings and determine whether navy doctors had indeed participated in a grand cover-up.

In the May 1992, the *Journal of the American Medical Association* (*JAMA*) published the first of two articles exploring allegations that the autopsy findings were untrustworthy. The conclusions dealt a severe blow to conspiracy theories. *JAMA* stated unequivocally that the physicians who performed the autopsy on the night of November 22 had established beyond reasonable doubt that the president was struck by only two bullets, which hit him from above and behind his head.

In addition, *JAMA* revealed a fact hitherto unknown—that far from working with no information concerning events in Dallas, one of the Bethesda doctors had contacted the emergency-room doctors who had worked on the president at Parkland Hospital. This helped the team in Bethesda to perform the autopsy with greater understanding of the wounds they were examining and to make more educated judgments in their final evaluation.

In the October 7, 1992, issue of *JAMA,* editor George D. Lundberg, M.D., stated: "A series of unbiased experts, forensic scientists, pathologists, and radiologists over the years have re-examined the Kennedy autopsy findings, using written materials, testimony of Humes [James Joseph Humes, M.D.], Boswell [J. Thornton Boswell, M.D.], and Finck [Pierre Finck, M.D.], the Zapruder film, photographs, X-rays, and microscopic slides." Lundberg concluded that these experts have almost unanimously supported the published findings and interpretations of the autopsy team and the Warren Commission, the single dissenting voice being that of Cyril H. Wecht, M.D. Yet even he agreed in 1966 and wrote in 1973 that "all shots were fired from the rear."

The calm expert testimony in the most distinguished medical publication in the United States countered the emotional outcries of the amateurs. It was, of course, no surprise to those of us who had continued to follow the case. The autopsy findings were confirmed by the Warren Commission in 1964; and in 1968, an impartial panel of four pathologists and radiologists examined all available evidence and made a sixteen-page report to Attorney General Ramsey Clark. Another vote of confidence came in 1969, when Dr. Pierre Finck testified at the trial of Clay Shaw, during District Attorney Jim Garrison's sensational and unwarranted prosecution. It was in part because of Dr. Finck's convincing testimony that Garrison's case collapsed in court.

Many critics of the FBI and the Warren Commission have based their objections on reports that witnesses heard firing from the grassy knoll in front of Kennedy's car. At least one witness reported seeing a puff of smoke from that direction. Indeed, the grassy knoll figures prominently in most conspiracy theories.

On the question of whether a sniper was firing from the grassy knoll we again had concrete evidence to the contrary. A woman named Mary Moorman had photographed the motorcade and the surrounding landscape at the very moment Oswald fired down at John F. Kennedy, and hers was only the best of several such snapshots we examined. In this photograph, the grassy knoll is clearly visible, as are all the people waiting there. You can blow it up to the size of a billboard, and you'll see no gunman there—not a single suspicious figure.

There is yet another source for conspiracy theories—the so-called "acoustical evidence" introduced late in the debate by a second wave of dissenters. When talk of the grassy knoll had died down to a whisper in the dusty libraries that stocked the more than eight hundred assassination books, a new gaggle of doubters produced sounds allegedly recorded from an open microphone on the motorcycle of an officer escorting the presidential party. Some "experts" insisted that this recording picked up one or more shots from the vicinity of the grassy knoll, indicating the presence of a second gunman.

In response to this theory, a later Dallas County sheriff, Jim

Bowles, prepared a 130-page journal entitled *The Kennedy Assassination Tapes—A Rebuttal to the Acoustical Evidence.* Bowles was supervisor of communications at the time of the assassination. As a former motorcycle officer, he was well qualified to study and evaluate the evidence.

Bowles's conclusion: The radio transmission came from a motorcycle traveling at thirty to thirty-five miles per hour in the vicinity of the Dallas Trade Mart two-and-a-half miles from the scene of the shooting. By carefully analyzing all sounds heard on the transmission, Sheriff Bowles was able to expose what he finally termed a "preposterous deception."

Experts at both the FBI Technical Services Division and the National Academy of Sciences, in the light of Sheriff Bowles's study, reviewed the "acoustical evidence" and concluded that the tapes did not necessarily reveal: (1) that a gun had been fired from the grassy knoll; (2) that the sounds recorded were gunshots; and (3) that the sounds originated in the assassination area. Yet the "acoustical evidence" lives on in legend.

In 1975—more than ten years after the Warren Commission hearings—Jim Hosty suddenly found himself the center of renewed controversy. Apparently it all began at a Dallas party attended by several FBI agents, their wives, and at least one reporter. The conversation moved from Watergate to the impending congressional hearings on the Kennedy assassination, and one of the wives speculated that Congress might reopen the question of the note Oswald left Hosty a few days before he shot the president. Someone asked for clarification, and the reporter took out pencil and paper. The next day, Tom Johnson of the *Dallas Times Herald* called then-Director Clarence Kelley, and the whole story broke into the open: Shortly before the assassination, Lee Harvey Oswald had dropped by FBI headquarters in Dallas and had left an allegedly threatening note for Agent Hosty, proving he was a violent man. Furthermore, the note had been destroyed.

The congressional committee picked up on the story and sent investigators around the country to talk to everyone who had worked in Dallas headquarters at the time. One of the people questioned was the woman who was at the reception desk at the time Oswald delivered the note. According to Hosty—who has good reason to remember the details—the receptionist told three different stories. The first time she was questioned, in 1963, she said Oswald threatened to kill Hosty. The second time, in 1975, she said it was a letter bomb. The third time, before the congressional committee in 1976, she said Oswald threatened to blow up the Dallas police station. But she also admitted that she gave the note to Agent Kyle Clark, who looked at it, said there was nothing to the threat, and told her to pass the note along to Agent Hosty.

It was at this point that the conspiracy theorists began to cry that the FBI had engaged in a coverup. They were able to make much out of the note's destruction. But the most sinister interpretation is that the note was later destroyed merely because it was embarrassing. At worst, it showed that Hosty had fallen down on the job—not that there was some grand conspiracy. In any case, Hoover never knew the note existed, and was dead by the time the controversy erupted. Had he known of the note in 1964, he would have used it during his disciplinary action against Hosty.

Clearly, it was a breach of FBI regulations to destroy the note. Hosty claimed that Gordon Shanklin ordered him to do so, though he admitted he should never have obeyed. Shanklin testified that he could not remember telling Hosty to do it, but did not deny the charge. No one knows for certain what did happen. But it may be relevant that when the question of the note was revived in 1975, Shanklin told the bureau he was retiring because of a "serious personal problem," effective the next day.

There is no reason to pursue this matter. Shanklin, a good agent, has since died. Hosty, also a good agent, retired after years of successful service in Kansas City. But it's important to note that everything we know about the note suggests that it did not contain a serious threat, that its contents did not intimate Oswald was a danger to the president, and that under then-existing policy it was not the kind of information that would have been passed along to the Secret Service.

Chances are the note was as innocuous as Hosty said it was. Besides, FBI agents soon learn to ignore the threats and ravings of people who are clearly unbalanced. All sorts of wild people are attracted to FBI offices. During the Kennedy investigation, a Cleveland man called to assure us that Jacqueline Kennedy was a communist, that she knew the president was going to be killed, and that it was done with her permission. And in Dallas, a man came to headquarters, asked for an agent, and when he was ushered into an office began to shout: "George has no business out there! Abba is no kin to me. Peggy is no kin to me. All them people are no kin to me. I'll get the military after you all." No one in the Dallas office, of course, prepared for a possible military invasion. They showed the man to the door. The first time you hear a wild-eyed man say he'll blow you up with fifty pounds of dynamite or disintegrate you with his ray gun, or blow up your headquarters, you're a little unnerved. After a while, you get used to it. If you checked every threat, jailed every loudmouth, you would paralyze the bureau and destroy the federal prison system. So you weigh each case individually—and sometimes you make mistakes.

Since then, both the FBI and the Secret Service have reassessed their criteria for persons who might prove a danger to the chief executive. In 1963, we reported only those known to have threatened the president or expressed unusual hostility—people who had written letters, talked openly about assassination, or mumbled their homicidal intentions within earshot of friends and relatives. Examining the case of Lee Harvey Oswald—and comparing the Kennedy assassination with the murders of Lincoln, Garfield, and McKinley—both the FBI and the Secret Service have widened their nets to include a number of people who would have been overlooked in 1963. Current practice requires many more agents and hours of investigation, and there are those who say the efforts are largely wasted. But we have every reason to believe that today, under new regulations and procedures, a Lee Harvey Oswald would be caught before he could harm the president.

One thing is certain, speculation concerning the assassination of President Kennedy will continue. Even the FBI has not given up on the case. As recently as June 17, 1993—following the death, two days earlier, of former Texas Governor John Connally—the bureau endorsed the idea of retrieving bullet fragments from Connally's body, since he had been wounded in the wrist and thigh by the same bullet that pierced the president's throat.

The *New York Times* reported the story on June 18, 1993, with a Washington dateline: "FBI officials here and in Dallas said they favored trying to recover the fragments if the Connally family consented. 'If the family will allow this to be done, we could put this to rest,' said Oliver B. Revell, Special Agent in Charge of the FBI office in Dallas. 'Conspiracy theorists are not going to let this get away.'"

As the *Times* explained, an examination of the fragments could support the findings by the Warren Commission and the FBI that this was one of the three bullets fired by Oswald and by no other person or persons. But the Connally family objected strenuously to having the body exhumed for this purpose. Said a spokesman for the family, "Mr. Connally was available for thirty years for that purpose, and in all that time no such request was made by any responsible authority. The family will resist any efforts to disturb the body."

I would certainly agree with that decision. Even if an examination proved that the metal fragments in Connally came from the bullet that wounded Kennedy, critics would still claim that other shots were fired, other assassins involved, other evidence suppressed. Nothing will ever satisfy the conspiracy theorists. They have staked too much on their wild hypotheses—many have built whole careers spinning conspiracies. The simple fact remains: Lee Harvey Oswald, acting alone, killed John F. Kennedy.

8

....

Mississippi Burning

IN MANY WAYS THE YEAR 1964 saw the high tide of the civil rights movement. In 1963, the Rev. Martin Luther King had instituted a successful drive to desegregate retail stores and other business establishments in Birmingham, Alabama—perhaps the most militantly segregated city in the South. For years, blacks had called it "Bombingham," because of the frequent and sometimes deadly use of explosives by the Ku Klux Klan and other white terrorists. Yet, during Easter week, King had led a small army of blacks into the downtown section and, enduring the attacks of Bull Connor's men, who used fire hoses and dogs against the demonstrators, gained the sympathy of the entire nation. The brutal actions of Connor and his local force had so stirred the American people that by the following year it appeared as if a federal civil rights bill—one guaranteeing all citizens access to public accommodations—might actually pass Congress. That summer, King and the Southern Christian Leadership Conference (SCLC) had been engaged in a fruitless struggle at St. Augustine, Florida, but by the fall they would see the greatest triumph of their movement: the passage of the Civil Rights Act of 1964.

Some Southern politicians tried to stem the coming social revolution by invoking the Tenth Amendment and whipping up white racist sentiment, primarily among the lower classes. In Mississippi, the chief obstructionist was Gov. Ross Barnett, who made segregationist speeches for the home folks, all the while negotiating behind the scenes with Attorney General Robert Kennedy to facilitate the entrance of James Meredith into the University of Mississippi. In part because of Barnett's histrionic posturing, in part because the state was the most rural in the South and hence the least open to change, and in part because of the brutal slaying of Medgar Evers in 1963, Mississippi became the chief target for many of the civil rights groups in the year 1964. Poor and ignorant Mississippi whites—by then abandoned by the demagogues who had stirred up their anger and traded on their bigotry—were increasingly frustrated by what they saw as the collapse of civilization itself, unaware that many of the Jim Crow laws they thought immemorial had actually been passed between 1895 and 1905. Consumed by racial hatred and frustrated by what they regarded as the treachery of their own politicians, they cast around for some means to fight back. For some, it was the Ku Klux Klan.

The Klan in the 1960s was not a large organization. It was certainly nothing like the Klan of the 1920s, which numbered over 4 million members, but quickly dwindled and was disbanded in 1944. For a while, the revived Klan numbered no more than a few hundred men in Mississippi. But these desperate fanatics were consumed by ideological rage and were willing to do anything—even to kill. And as their exploits were publicized they attracted new members until eventually there were over two thousand of them in the Magnolia State alone—an insignificant fraction of the population as a whole, but enough to poison an entire society.

The Klan was led by Imperial Wizard Sam Bowers—grandson of a Mississippi congressman, World War II veteran, and part owner of a vending machine company. Bowers believed the civil rights movement was a "Jewish-communist conspiracy" that threatened the very survival of the United States, and he attracted members from among the uneducated by warning of coming disaster.

Opposing the Klan in Mississippi was a civil rights coalition called the Council of Federated Organizations (COFO)—an umbrella group that coordinated antisegregation initiatives throughout the state. In 1964, COFO's goal was to register 400,000 black voters to overthrow the white power structure by electing candidates open to social and political change.

To mount a successful drive, COFO was enlisting youthful workers from all over the United States. A number of young people from Northern states, moved by idealism and a desire for adventure, came to Mississippi to join in the struggle and help register voters. A leader of COFO publicly estimated the number of new recruits at thirty thousand—a wildly exaggerated figure. But Sam Bowers and his group of cold-eyed followers took the COFO estimate seriously and felt that they and their "way of life" were victims of an enemy invasion. They began to brood on plots to thwart the enemy.

It was to this hostile world that COFO's Northern recruits came— full of hope, eager to help, seemingly unaware of just how much animosity they had stirred up, how much danger they really faced. One of these was Michael Schwerner, known as "Mickey" to his family and friends.

Schwerner—a New Yorker whose Jewish grandparents had emigrated from Europe—had joined in civil rights demonstrations in New York City and Baltimore, as had his wife, Rita. Both had been sentenced to jail. Both had enlisted in the Congress of Racial Equality to fight segregation in Mississippi. Schwerner had written on his application to join CORE: "The Negro in the South has an even more bitter fight ahead of him than in the North, and I wish to be a part of that fight... I would feel guilty and almost hypocritical if I do not give [it] full time."

Mickey and Rita Schwerner were undoubtedly warned about the potential danger they faced in Mississippi. James Forman, then executive secretary of the Student Non-Violent Coordinating Committee (SNCC), told new recruits: "I may be killed and you may be killed. If you recognize that, the question of whether you're put in jail will become very, very minute." But those were just words. They didn't fully define the broiling rage in the hearts of embittered klansmen, nor did they tell how dark and cold and permanent a grave could be in the stagnant waters of Bogue Chitto Swamp.

Shortly after they arrived in Mississippi, the Schwerners met a young black man named James Chaney. Chaney, twenty years old and slight of build, was intrigued with the COFO campaign to register voters and soon joined in the effort. He acted as handy man, driver, and chief liaison for the Schwerners on their trips into the black community. Like them, he had been warned that what he was doing was dangerous. His mother had raised the matter and he had replied: "That's the trouble now, Mama. Too many people afraid." White men who had once treated Chaney with casual contempt were now in the mood to kill, but at the age of twenty you don't really believe you can die.

Andrew Goodman was approximately the same age as Chaney. Like Schwerner, he was Jewish and a New Yorker—an anthropology student at Queens College who had come South to enlist in the struggle. Goodman was a member of the SNCC and had only been in Mississippi for about a day when he tied in with Mickey Schwerner and James Chaney on a last desperate adventure. He had come to attend an orientation program funded by the National Council of Churches, and he, too, had heard the dire warnings.

The Rev. James Lawson, later a major figure in the civil rights movement, had told the two hundred young people present: "Just your walking into Canton, Mississippi, or Ruleville or Shaw, just your being there could be a catalytic agent that evokes violence." Another speaker told them: "Most of the people that you meet there are going to be just about as afraid of you as you are of them... I would suggest a little track practice between now and then because I really believe it's going to be bad." And like the other volunteers, Andrew Goodman received a Security Handbook that told him he should maintain telephone contact at all times. The handbook also advised that if anyone should fail to return on schedule, those remaining behind should immediately contact the local police or the FBI. These were standard precautions, yet Goodman, like the others, was willing and even eager to begin his work with COFO and the Schwerners.

Mickey Schwerner had already traveled three times to the Longdale Community near Philadelphia, Mississippi, to persuade the members of the Mt. Zion Methodist Church to allow COFO to use the church building as a center during the summer. Each time he had encountered opposition from fearful church members, and the matter was still unresolved by the middle of June. But these meetings had not gone unnoticed. The local Ku Klux Klan was keeping a watchful eye on the bearded Schwerner, whom they contemptuously called "Goatee."

On the night of June 16, klansmen invaded the church, where its all-black membership had been meeting to discuss church finances. Though most members had left, klansmen confronted the several who had remained in the parking lot to talk. The invaders shouted: "Where are the white people who were here?" When the blacks denied that any whites had attended the meeting, the klansmen beat them, almost killing one of the men. Later that night, someone returned to the church and burned it down.

On the 18th of June, FBI agents in Jackson learned about the brutal attacks and the torching of the church. They reported the incidents to their principal office in New Orleans and were told to investigate immediately. At the time, the bureau had no headquarters in sparsely populated Mississippi, where comparatively few federal crimes were committed—though recently the case load had increased rapidly.

On Friday, July 19, two FBI agents arrived in Longdale, Mississippi, to begin the investigation. Their arrival probably escaped the notice of Mississippi klansmen, because something else happened that day to occupy their attention. The U.S. Senate passed the Civil Rights Act of 1964, one of the most revolutionary pieces of legislation ever enacted. Ten years after Brown v. Board of Education had struck a crippling blow to Jim Crow, the U.S. Congress had delivered the coup de grace. All over northern Mississippi Klan members and their sympathizers were gathering in small groups in county squares, at country stores, and in back rooms to mumble and mutter about the news from Washington and to threaten dire revenge. It's impossible to estimate the degree to which anger over the vote in Congress led to the tragic events that followed, but passage of the Civil Rights Act must have played a part.

On Saturday, Schwerner heard about the beatings and the burning of the church. At COFO headquarters he learned more details and got first-hand reports from some of the blacks who had been at Longdale. "I'll go up there tomorrow and see what I can find out," he told one staff member.

Early Sunday morning, Schwerner, Chaney, and Goodman left Meridian and headed toward Philadelphia in their Ford station wagon. At Longdale, they stopped to talk to Ernest Kirkland, one of their contacts; and he suggested that they go see Cornelius Steele and his wife.

"They were there that night," Kirkland told them.

On their way, the men stopped and examined the charred remains of the Mt. Zion Methodist Church. Then they drove on to the Steele house.

Schwerner took the initiative in questioning Cornelius Steele, but Steele could supply little information. He said several cars and a truck had pulled up suddenly, and a bunch of white men had poured out. The only one he could describe was a man with a roll-brimmed straw hat who sat in the car and watched the other whites beat up the church members.

"Can you tell us how the church was burned and who did it?" Schwerner asked.

"I don't know anything about what happened after we left the church," Steele said.

"Will you come to COFO headquarters in Meridian next Tuesday and give us an affidavit on what you do know? We're going to bring suit against Neshoba County for this."

Steele agreed to come.

Then Schwerner, Chaney, Goodman, and Kirkland went to see Junior Roosevelt Cole, one of the men who had been beaten at the church the previous Tuesday. He told the group precisely what had happened.

"They almost killed me," he said. "One man flashed a light in my face and somebody said, 'That's the son of a bitch!' They dragged me out of the car and began hitting and kicking me. I thought my jaw was broken but the doctor said it wasn't."

After talking with Cole, the four men dropped Kirkland at his house and then headed back to Meridian. As always, Schwerner had set a specific deadline for his return—4:00 P.M. When the deadline passed, his friends at COFO headquarters in Meridian began to worry. At 4:45, they notified the COFO office in Jackson that the three had neither returned nor called in, as they had promised to do. By 5:30, COFO officials began to call law enforcement officers in the area—the Neshoba County sheriff's office, the police department in Philadelphia, the Philadelphia jail. They didn't contact the FBI until 10:30 that night.

Back at FBI headquarters in Washington, we were aware of the disappearance of the three men by the next day, Monday morning. Though we had no concrete evidence, we began to consider the possibility that they had met with foul play and that the Ku Klux Klan might have been involved. The Civil Rights Division of the Justice Department asked us to notify the Mississippi Highway Safety Patrol and the Neshoba County Sheriff's Department that the men were missing and give them a description of the missing vehicle. We did so immediately, then waited until noon. The three young men still had not turned up.

At that point, Hoover ordered our Meridian office to investigate the disappearance. After conferring with COFO officials, Resident Agent John Proctor and another agent traced the itinerary of the three to Ernest Kirkland, who told them he'd last seen the young men at around three in the afternoon. When the agents checked in with Neshoba County Sheriff Lawrence A. Rainey in Philadelphia, he gave them fresh information, which he said he'd gotten from his deputy, Cecil Price.

"They were here all right. Price arrested the nigger for driving seventy miles an hour in a thirty-mile zone, and he held the other two for investigation. When they paid a twenty-dollar bond for speeding, Price told them not to hang around Philadelphia, but to be on their way. And they drove out of town."

The agents interviewed Price, who confirmed the sheriff's story.

"Why were Goodman and Schwerner held for investigation?" one of the agents asked.

"Well," the deputy said, "they told me they had spent the day in the neighborhood of that burnt-out nigger church over there at

Longdale. I figured they might have had something to do with the church-burning."

"When did you last see them?" the FBI agent asked.

Price said that he and a deputy, Richard Willis, followed the three COFO workers to Highway 19 and watched their station wagon disappear down the road and into the night.

"That's the last I saw of them," Price said.

Sheriff Rainey, Deputy Price, and the other local law enforcement officers seemed only mildly interested in the fate of the three men. When questioned by reporters, Sheriff Rainey said, "If you want to know what I think, it's all a publicity stunt to raise money for COFO. They're around somewhere laughing at the commotion they've stirred up."

Back at FBI headquarters in Washington, we were becoming increasingly alarmed at this studied nonchalance. And so, Monday at 6:20 P.M., only twenty hours after the last person had admitted seeing them, John Doar of the Civil Rights Division of the Justice Department proposed that henceforth the disappearance of the three should be treated as a kidnaping, a presumptive federal offense. This meant the FBI was taking charge of the investigation.

In response to this order, the director sent five New Orleans-based FBI agents and an inspector to Meridian. By coincidence, one of the FBI's top men, Inspector Joseph Sullivan, was on a routine inspection tour of our Memphis office. A tough veteran of twenty-three years, Sullivan was six feet, two inches and had seen action in some of our toughest cases. Physically intimidating and irreproachable in conduct, he was ordered to Philadelphia, Mississippi, to participate in the investigation. Later, agents would be brought in from all parts of the country. The first of these reinforcements were in Mississippi by Tuesday morning, intent on finding the three missing civil rights workers as quickly as possible. We knew that with the passing of every hour their chances of being found alive would diminish significantly.

As our agents attempted to work with local authorities, they were increasingly struck by a new spirit abroad in Mississippi— contempt for federal authority. Local law enforcement officers were minimally cooperative. They responded either curtly or else with patronizing smiles, as if to say, "We know where they are, but we'll be damned if we'll tell you."

The same was true of many ordinary citizens, particularly the men. Usually people treated FBI agents with respect, awed by the presence of a member of the federal government and the reputation of the bureau. But in the Mississippi of 1964, that awe had been replaced by open hostility. Potential witnesses would reply in words of one syllable, staring at the floor or else out the window. Their words were uncivil and their eyes flashed rebelliously. Agents walking down the sidewalk would be shouldered into the street. In some instances passersby spat in their direction.

Meanwhile, back in Meridian, Resident Agent John Proctor was on the verge of a breakthrough. Like many resident agents, Proctor had made friends in the community and in the surrounding area. In those days, FBI agents generally followed one of two career courses. Those who were ambitious and hoped to advance in the bureau angled for an assignment at Washington headquarters. Those who enjoyed field work were usually happy to stay in one location for their entire career, rearing families in familiar surroundings, putting down roots in a town or city, widening associations, and wielding greater and greater influence in the community as the years rolled by. In so doing, they inevitably increased their usefulness to the bureau, since their knowledge of their territory continued to grow as did their list of contacts. Resident Agent John Proctor was one of these.

On noon of Tuesday, less than twenty-four hours after the FBI had been ordered into the case, Proctor got a call from an old friend, Lonnie Hardin, superintendent of the Choctaw Indian reservation in Neshoba County. Hardin got right to the point.

"I understand the FBI is looking for some people up this way."

"You better believe it," Proctor said, struck by Hardin's serious tone of voice. "This thing could be rough."

"You better come up here, John," Hardin said. "I may have something for you. I don't want to talk about it on the phone."

"I'll be there as fast as I can," Proctor said, and hurried to his car.

When he arrived at Hardin's office thirty-eight minutes later, he was not disappointed. Hardin told him that a Choctaw Indian had come by his office late Monday afternoon to say that he and a companion had been walking along the edge of the swamp near a bridge that crossed Bogue Chitto Creek. They had spotted the charred husk of an automobile—a station wagon—in the bushes along Highway 21. The wreck was still smoking.

Proctor thanked Hardin, drove to the bridge, and quickly located the remains of the station wagon. On the outside, the paint was blistered and peeling. The inside had been completely gutted by flames, and when Proctor peered through the window he could see only ashes and blackened springs. He half expected to find three bodies, charred beyond recognition, but as best he could tell there were no human remains. Of one thing he was certain: This was the car in which the three young men had been riding, a 1963 Ford station wagon with the still-legible Mississippi license tag—H25503.

He knew he was the first law enforcement officer on the scene, and he had long since ceased to trust the local cops, particularly on an issue involving civil rights. Since his radio was tuned to the frequency used by the Mississippi Highway Patrol, he decided to communicate his news to FBI headquarters by telephone.

Remembering that he'd passed a farmhouse a mile down the road, he drove back and, posing as a salesman, made a collect call to his office in New Orleans. An agent was soon on the line to take his report.

"We've found the car of the missing men," he said. "It has been burned, but the license number checks and it's the same model they were driving."

When the agent asked Proctor if there were any bodies, he hesitated. He had taken a quick look, and he was reasonably certain of the answer; but at this point what he said would become part of the official record. Suddenly he grew cautious.

"I'm sure there were none in the car," he said, "but I'll make another check to be a one hundred percent sure."

At this point the FBI was assuming that its agents were just as likely to be targets of white supremacists as civil rights demonstrators and local blacks. Proctor and the agent accompanying him were roaming about in uncharted territory. Killers were on the loose. Three young men had already disappeared, and the grim discovery of the burned car greatly increased the odds that they had been murdered. The New Orleans agent was taking no chances.

"I want you to call me back in fifteen minutes," he told Proctor.

"It's three-quarters of a mile there and three-quarters of a mile back," said Proctor.

"I don't care how far it is," the agent said. "I want a call every fifteen minutes."

In Washington, we received word that the car had been found, and we immediately dispatched a team from our laboratory to fly to Mississippi to search the area and sift through the ashes for evidence. Searchers found beer bottles near the car site, but none that yielded fingerprints. In the car, they found the charred remains of a man's wrist watch and a set of car keys. All of this evidence was sent back to our laboratory in Washington for examination and evaluation. The watch and car keys, it developed, belonged to Mickey Schwerner.

At this point we were probably dealing with a triple murder. By morning the case would be discussed on every television news program and on the front page of every newspaper in the country. I immediately informed Hoover of the latest development, and he in turn called President Lyndon Johnson, who had asked to be informed of any new developments.

When the president hung up the phone, he faced a grim duty. Mr. Nathan Schwerner and Mr. and Mrs. Robert W. Goodman were just then arriving for an appointment. He had to tell them about the discovery of the charred station wagon. They were intelligent people and understood fully the meaning of such evidence. They wept in the Oval Office while the president of the United States tried to console them.

Nathan Schwerner was understandably bitter, and he condemned law enforcement agencies at every level.

"It's perilous just to cross the state line in Mississippi. They're animals down there. The police don't protect people, they beat them and persecute them. Nobody seems to care what's happened. What really gripes me is that the FBI and the Justice Department took so long to get into this."

Actually, we'd entered the case hours earlier than we ordinarily would have, and we'd already turned up a crucial piece of evidence, one that local authorities had overlooked or else deliberately ignored for several days. In fact, by the time Mr. Schwerner made his statement it was too late for the FBI or anyone else to help his son. The only thing to do was to find his killers, and we began to do just that almost immediately.

These facts notwithstanding, critics of J. Edgar Hoover continue to suggest that somehow the director was reluctant to pursue the investigation, that the FBI was not diligent in its investigation of civil rights cases during the early 1960s, and that LBJ had to twist Hoover's arm to get him to open an FBI office in Mississippi. That was not the case.

By early July, more than four hundred FBI agents were operating in Mississippi, and pressure was building from a number of quarters to establish a full-time bureau office in the state. Walter Jenkins called to tell me how the White House staff felt.

"Deke," he said, "the president wants you and Mr. Hoover to consider opening an office in Jackson. He also thinks the director should go down there personally and hold a press conference, see the governor, and try to quiet criticism by the newspapers and television commentators. Would you see what you can do?"

I promised to push the project, knowing full well that Lyndon Johnson had his eye on the upcoming Democratic Convention and the election in the fall. He wanted law and order in Mississippi, but he also wanted to be reelected president.

The president's obvious political motivation aside, no one in the bureau was philosophically opposed to a Jackson headquarters. We had always assumed the time would come when economic and physical necessity would dictate such a move; in fact, we had once maintained an office in Jackson, but closed it down in 1946 because the case load didn't justify it. But now, with the advent of the civil rights movement, we could anticipate a good deal more business in Mississippi.

Consequently, at FBI headquarters in Washington we reviewed the files of the defunct office, reexamined current logistics, studied current caseloads, and tried to project their growth. The final report to the director indicated that the crush of criminal investigations in the state—more than 1,300 current cases—demanded a permanent headquarters. Mr. Hoover, convinced by the bare facts, agreed with the recommendation and instructed John Mohr to look for the most appropriate office space.

In addition to Sullivan and the five agents from New Orleans, we also dispatched Roy K. Moore to Jackson, Mississippi, on special assignment. Moore, a tough ex-Marine, initially operated under the wing of the New Orleans office and was the agent who identified two informants within the Klan who were willing to supply information for money. Consequently, he picked up and passed along information unavailable to other law enforcement officers. Moore told us from the beginning that the three men were dead and that they had been murdered by the Ku Klux Klan.

As Moore's evidence began to mount, we also sent Al Rosen, assistant director of our Investigative Division, to the scene of the crime. Rosen, with thirty-five years experience, was intelligent and cagey, a patient man who could sniff out pertinent evidence where others might see only incidental trivia. He was to be in charge of overall operations and report back to Washington. The measure of the FBI's commitment to solving this case could be taken by the assignment of these two men to Mississippi.

Yet even as we were moving into high gear, civil rights groups were calling for yet more radical measures. The National Association for the Advancement of Colored People (NAACP) was holding its national convention, and delegates paraded in front of the Justice Department, waving signs that said: "STOP MISSISSIPPI TERROR"... "NAACP DEMANDS ACTION NOW"... "EQUALITY, JUSTICE FOR ALL IN MISSISSIPPI." The leaders of the organization had drafted a resolution that was long on indignation and short on good sense; it called for the federal government to protect lives by "taking over the administration of the state of Mississippi." They met with Bobby Kennedy and told him they wanted "preventive action rather than ambulatory action such as picking up the bodies afterward."

In Mississippi tensions mounted and the danger of violence loomed large. Authorities in Philadelphia heard that a caravan of twenty black civil rights leaders was on its way to conduct its own investigation, and state and local law enforcement agencies braced for a possible riot. They surrounded the Neshoba County courthouse, imposed a curfew on local citizens of both races, and sent officers to turn back the caravan.

It was into this broiling scene that Al Rosen stepped the next morning. He confirmed what we had already concluded—evidence suggested the three civil rights workers were dead and that the main task was to search for clues and for the bodies of the victims. Rosen also determined that while the Neshoba County sheriff's office and the Philadelphia police force were untrustworthy the Mississippi State Police were cooperative and reliable.

Secretary of Defense Robert McNamara had offered the use of the Marines in the investigation, and Rosen recommended we accept. The search would be widespread and cover difficult terrain, including the Bogue Chitto Swamp. A large detachment of men already trained to fight in the bushes and bogs of Vietnam could make a substantial contribution to the search, Rosen told Hoover, and he agreed. But when this news hit the press, Southern Democratic leaders protested. Recognizing that the resemblance to Reconstruction would cost him votes, Johnson rescinded the order to send in the Marines and announced that instead sailors would join the FBI and state police in the search.

Hoover gave orders to transfer still more agents to Mississippi. Not only did he want to increase the number of trained law enforcement officers searching for the missing men, but also hoped to intimidate the Klan further by flooding the streets of small Mississippi towns with FBI agents. He wanted them to feel the heat wherever they went, to conclude that there was no place to hide. Among the throng of agents sent to the state was a highly select group of Counter Intelligence Program (COINTELPRO) agents. Many were big bruising men, highly trained in the tactics of interrogation; their job was to interview every member of the Mississippi Klan.

The COINTELPRO operation moved forward—but only by inches. Mississippi Ku Klux Klan members didn't spill their guts at the first frown, nor did they slip up in casual conversation. Their Klaverns (local groups) were small, tightly knit, and staffed with local people of intense pride and unshakable determination. Most members had known one another all their lives, and were little inclined to betray lifelong friends.

Contrary to popular myth, the Klan had little success recruiting members among state and local lawmen. Police officers had their own social ties with one another from years of close fraternization—training school, joint investigations, shared dangers, and efforts to uphold and upgrade standards of law enforcement. Their own professional organizations gave them a sense of belonging: Most did not need to be in the Klan. Still, many people suggested that the local police and the Klan were synonymous. Because FBI agents were seen working with the police, many critics said they were also cozy with the Klan. The Rev. Martin Luther King criticized us over the years for our cooperation with local law enforcement personnel. Yet it was this cooperation and camaraderie that eventually helped to expose the KKK, identify the perpetrators, and issue warrants for their arrest.

On the other hand, if the Klan was unsuccessful in recruiting policemen in large numbers, they did recruit some, both at the local and state levels. Our COINTELPRO operation gradually began to discover who these officers were. But it was a slow and difficult operation, since klansmen maintained their own discipline and nurtured a strong team spirit that made them among the toughest adversaries we'd ever faced.

By engaging the Ku Klux Klan in northern Mississippi, we discovered that we had forfeited much of the authority we usually brought to conflicts with law breakers. In dealing with auto thieves, organized crime, and the Communist party we could always count on our opponents avoiding confrontation at all costs and being intimidated by the enormous power and authority of the federal government. To put it simply, most people were scared of the FBI.

We soon began to realize, however, that many members of the Mississippi Klan weren't intimidated at all. It was as if we were foreign invaders fighting on somebody else's sacred soil. On other cases, when we walked into buildings or knocked on doors and flashed our badges, people cringed and broke into a cold sweat, or else stumbled all over themselves to provide us with information. In Mississippi, people snarled at us and called us names. As we walked by groups of men on the streets, we could hear them mutter "Nigger lover!"... "He's with the Federal Bureau of Integration"... "They're for the niggers and Jews—not the white people."

They also watched us, knew where we were staying, and would often make late night phone calls, most of them threatening, some obscene. As one agent put it:

> We had never run into anything like this before. This was nothing less than intimidation. Those people actually were beginning to believe the law didn't apply to them. We got word to fight back—and to have a face-to-face showdown with anyone who made a threat against an agent. This could be bare-knuckle stuff, but we had to do it in self-defense.

Some of the hostility was just bluff and bluster by people who had neither the intention nor capacity to carry out their threats. One merchant in the area swaggered around his store, telling his customers just how he intended to deal with the FBI: "If one of those FBI agents comes into my store, I'm going to beat hell out of him."

Someone must have spread the word, because it got back to our people in Mississippi. The next day, a lone agent entered the front door and asked for the owner. The tone of his voice caught the attention of every customer in the place.

When the merchant came from the back of the store, the agent told him, "You stated last night that if an FBI agent came in here, you were going to beat hell out of him. Well, sir, I'm an FBI agent. I'm not armed. And I'm waiting for you to try to beat hell out of me."

With all eyes on him, the merchant hesitated for an instant. Then tried to maintain that he had said no such thing, that somehow, some way, this was all a misunderstanding. The agent let him stammer and backtrack for a while. Then he said, "I think in the future it would be better if you didn't make threats." The agent left the merchant standing in silence.

Not all citizens of Neshoba County were so hostile. Many were appalled at the poisonous atmosphere, and a few actually gave us information that furthered our investigation. One person, when questioned by agents, made a cryptic statement that proved to be enormously useful.

"Why don't you find Wilmer Faye Jones and ask him what happened when he was arrested early in June and why he left town?"

It turned out that Jones, a nineteen-year-old black youth, had left Mississippi and was now living in Chicago. When FBI agents heard his story, they understood why their source had suggested the interview. Like the civil rights workers, Jones had crossed the Ku Klux Klan. According to his story, he had taken a ring to a local jewelry store to be sized. The clerk who waited on him was a young white woman of about twenty-one. The next day he had called back and talked to her about the ring. Apparently she said he had asked her for a date.

A few minutes later, he was arrested by a constable and driven to a service station on Highway 21, where he was questioned by Sheriff Rainey, who implied that he had stolen the ring, though the sheriff never made the charge. The law officers then drove him to the jewelry store, where he was identified by the girl. Afterward, he was taken outside and placed in the back of the sheriff's car, where Deputy Sheriff Price asked him if he had tried to date the white woman. Jones denied the allegation.

At that point he was hauled to jail and kept there without charges until shortly after midnight. Then he was released. As he stepped onto the dark sidewalk, he saw two white men under a lamppost. One had a shotgun, and the other an automatic pistol.

As Sheriff Rainey, Deputy Sheriff Price, and the jailer watched, the two men forced Jones to walk toward their car. As they walked, a shotgun pressing against Jones's spine, the three policemen watched. Three more men were standing by the car. Jones was forced into the front seat of the car and handcuffed. One white man, whom the others called "the Preacher," seemed to be the leader. He got into the front seat on the right side of Jones, and one of the other men drove. The other three white men got into the back seat; and as they drove away, Sheriff Rainey waved.

They drove Jones to an abandoned farmhouse where they jabbed guns into his back and told him they intended to kill him. One even said he was going to throw him into a forty-foot well.

They questioned him about his conversations with the white woman and also about his relationship with civil rights groups and about his religious views. Finally, they released him, told him to get out of town and gave him money for a bus ticket. They also told him to send them any information he picked up on civil rights groups in Philadelphia. Then they drove him back to town, where he bought a bus ticket and left town.

This was the story Wilmer Faye Jones told to FBI agents. It was a detailed narrative with specific descriptions of the men involved and remembered snatches of dialogue. Jones told it without great emotion. No one in the FBI who heard or read the statement disbelieved it.

As they listened to Jones's narrative, moreover, the agents began to realize why their informant had sent them: the experience of Wilmer Faye Jones bore an eerie resemblance to what they had ascertained about the last known hours of Schwerner, Chaney, and Goodman. Like Jones, the civil rights workers were engaged in activities that offended the Ku Klux Klan. Like Jones, they had come to Philadelphia. Like Jones, they had been arrested and taken to jail. Like Jones, they had been involved with Deputy Sheriff Price. Like Jones, they had been detained, then inexplicably released late at night. Had Schwerner, Chaney, and Goodman also met up with the Preacher and his gang after being released? And were they driven to the same spot?

The FBI asked Jones to return to Philadelphia, hoping he could lead them to the place where the five white men had taken him. After driving around the countryside for two days, Jones recognized the farm and even showed them the well.

"This is where they brought me," he said. "This is the place."

The FBI spread out and combed the farm and the surrounding countryside. They found a number of old wells and other likely places to hide corpses, but they never found what they were looking for; and until they actually recovered the bodies of the three civil rights workers, they had no case.

Meanwhile, the time had come to open the FBI office in Jackson. But the building wasn't ready. Roy Moore, the special agent in charge, gave me the good news and the bad news.

"It looks like an office," he said, "but it's more like a Hollywood set."

"What do you mean?" I asked.

"Well, let's put it this way," he said. "Don't you or Hoover lean against any of the walls when you come down here, or they'll fall over. We haven't had time to secure them."

But we couldn't wait any longer. Hoover wanted this investigation centered in Mississippi; and Lyndon Johnson, knowing that most political storms begin with a cloud no larger than a man's hand, wanted everything in place prior to the Democratic Convention. So we scheduled a press conference for the Hollywood set.

On the morning of July 9 at 6:45, Special Agent Bill Gunn and *Washington Star* reporter Jerry O'Leary met me at Andrews Air Force Base. There we boarded an eight-passenger White House Jetstar for the flight to Jackson. Two other journalists met us there: Jim Lucas of the *Washington Daily News*, and Frank Holman of the *New York Daily News*. All three newsmen were old friends. I was godfather to one of O'Leary's children and had worked with the others over the years in presenting the FBI story to the general public. Each had been following the Mississippi civil rights struggle closely, knew the commitment of the bureau to solving this case, and could be counted on to give an objective and even-handed account of our operations. That's all we could hope for.

When we arrived at Jackson, we were met at the airport by SAC Roy Moore, who briefed us on the progress of MIBURN (our shorthand for the operation we had named Mississippi Burning). The only good news he could offer: there was no more bad news.

When I saw the new office, my heart sank. Only three rooms were ready—the reception room, the office of the assistant in charge, and what would be SAC Moore's office—and even these were unfinished. The press conference was to take place in Moore's new office, and I cautioned the three reporters about the walls; but Agent Gunn forgot and leaned against one of them, which almost toppled over.

Except for the walls, our blueprint for the director's appearance the next day was perfect in every way—like the game plan of every football team, losers as well as winners. But I couldn't have anticipated the reaction of the press to his arrival. When he and Tolson stepped off a second Jetstar at precisely 10:00 A.M., reporters and photographers broke through the flimsy barrier erected to restrain them and ran wildly toward the two men. Moore and I quickly laid hands on Hoover and Tolson and propelled them through the mob and into their car, telling the reporters that they would have the opportunity to question the director at a press conference that afternoon. In Washington headquarters we often forgot that to the rest of the country Hoover was larger than life, a folk hero as awesome as a movie star or a president—and that also applied to the local press.

Jackson's mayor, Allen C. Thompson, and Colonel Birdsong of the State Police joined us in a small motorcade to the old and gracious Governor's Mansion, where Governor Paul Johnson greeted us in his office on the second floor.

Happily, the director was at his best.

"Governor," he said, in a strong and friendly voice, "the president asked me to tell you that there will be no interference in your state by federal troops or authorities as long as you can prevent any wholesale disruption or breakdown of law and order."

Governor Johnson replied in kind, expressing grief over the violence that had occurred thus far, pledging to hold the line on law and order. When the two men discussed the Ku Klux Klan, Hoover was able to cite our successful attempts to infiltrate the Klaverns. And he took the opportunity to mention the many indignities suffered by FBI agents at the hands of malcontents and diehards. He specifically mentioned incidents in which agents had been spat upon, received harassing calls at home in the dead of night, endured threats to their wives and other family members, and opened a car door to find a rattlesnake inside.

"We'll stay within the law," he told Johnson in a matter-of-fact tone, "but the next time a klansman challenges an agent to fight, the challenge will be accepted."

Johnson was taking all of this in, nodding his head in understanding and agreement. But Hoover hadn't finished with him yet. He turned to me and said, "Give me the names of the two klansmen who are presently members of the Mississippi Highway Patrol."

I gave him a slip of paper with the names, and Hoover handed it to the surprised governor, who took it from him as if it were a water moccasin. For a second he was speechless. Then he said he would take care of the matter immediately. Next Hoover gave him the names of several police officers in scattered localities who were also Klan members.

After visiting with Attorney General Joe Patterson, we returned to what we presumptuously called "the new FBI office" to conduct the press conference. When the press gathered, in a far larger crowd than expected, I realized that if everyone present inhaled and exhaled at the same time, the walls might collapse on us like the straw hut of the first little pig.

Hoover, unaware of impending doom, read the opening remarks we'd prepared for him. He immediately challenged the state's law enforcement bodies.

"There will be attempted resistance, some possibly very violent," he said, "but this must be met by the united will, the united strength of the Congress, the courts, the president, and the law of the land. The key to law and order in Mississippi remains the extent to which state and local authorities recognize their responsibilities and discharge them."

When it was his turn to speak, Governor Johnson picked up the challenge.

"When I first took office, I told the people of Mississippi that ignorance, hate, and prejudice would not sit in the governor's chair as long as I was there, and that law and order would be maintained at all costs. This is as true today as it was then."

This united front was precisely what we'd hoped for. It played well in the nation as a whole; and more importantly, it played well in Mississippi, where we needed the aid and support of ordinary citizens to solve this particular case and ultimately check the power of the revitalized Ku Klux Klan.

After the formal remarks, we opened the question-and-answer period, and predictably the press zeroed in on the MIBURN case. The director responded sharply and decisively.

"This investigation will be continued until the three missing civil rights workers are found and those responsible for their disappearance are brought to justice."

In my own prior briefing of the press, I had taken pains to explain precisely why the FBI could not undertake the task of protecting civil rights workers as they moved into dangerous communities. I tried to make them understand that we had neither the statutory right nor the personnel to become bodyguards—even of federal officials, including the president of the United States. I had gone over this question many times with Jerry O'Leary.

Thus I was somewhat taken aback when O'Leary—of all the reporters present—raised his hand at the press conference and asked bluntly, "Mr. Hoover, is the FBI going to give protection to civil rights workers, and if not, sir, why?"

Hoover replied instantly.

"We most certainly do not and will not give protection to civil rights workers. The FBI is not a protection organization. It is purely an investigative agency, and the protection of individual citizens, whether natives of this state or those coming into the state, is a matter for local authorities. The FBI will not participate in such protection."

It was an issue he had addressed many times before in refusing protection for members of Congress, other federal officials, and diverse political groups—some on the Left, some on the Right. And no one ever quite accepted those limitations on our mission.

Even the press, which was supposed to be more circumspect and analytical about such matters, seemed puzzled and hostile. This attitude would remain undiminished in the years to come. Paradoxically, there was not one reporter present that day who didn't abhor the idea of a national police force. Yet that's precisely what they were calling for in their news stories, editorials, and columns.

Well, at least none of the walls fell down.

After the press conference, we drove back to the Sun 'n' Sand Motel on the outskirts of Jackson, and as the sky reddened over the tops of the pine trees, we prepared for the last scheduled event of the day—a meeting with all agents assigned to the MIBURN investigation. Hoover was exhausted, yet he ended his trip with a rousing pep talk, vowing to spare no expense of money or manpower.

Afterward, the director, Tolson, Al Rosen, and I went back to Hoover's suite, where Al dropped a bombshell.

"Two of our informants in the Klan—a minister and a member of the State Highway Patrol—have some information they're convinced will lead to Schwerner, Chaney, and Goodman."

We leaned forward to listen.

"Unfortunately, these two solid citizens aren't willing to spill their guts for moral or patriotic or religious reasons. But there is something that will make them talk."

"Money?"

"You got it! Money."

"How much will it take?" Hoover asked.

"They haven't named a figure," Rosen said. "But I think we can probably swing the deal for $25,000."

"Make the offer," Hoover said curtly, and then turned to me. "DeLoach, have the money ready at FBI headquarters."

Rosen got up and left to set up the deal. Hoover, Tolson, and I remained to rehash the events of the day, have dinner, and update plans to resolve the MIBURN case. Finally we all admitted we were exhausted and went to bed. Tolson told me Hoover was to receive no phone calls until the next morning. Gunn and I were sharing a room next door to Hoover's suite, and we turned off the lights at around 11:15. I was asleep before the second hand had made one complete sweep. Less than an hour later, Gunn awakened me.

"There's a guy on the line who says he has to talk to the director."

"Who is it?" I said, still in a daze.

"He won't say."

I took the receiver and identified myself.

"What do you want?" I said groggily.

A gravel voice spoke.

"If Hoover and the rest of you bastards walk out of your room at eight o'clock tomorrow morning, you'll get the hell shot out of you!"

"We'll be there," I said, "and we'll be looking for you..."

I heard a click on the other end of the line.

"...you son of a bitch."

I wanted to go back to bed, but I knew I couldn't. Angry, I threw on some clothes and went out to find the agents cruising the area. I spotted a nearby radio car parked under a huge oak tree and recognized Roy Moore in the front seat.

"Double the number of agents on surveillance," I told him, "and make sure they stick close to the motel area."

I left him calling for reinforcements and went back to the motel room. Bill Gunn was still awake and a little curious.

I told him what I'd done and then lunged for my bed.

"That should be the end of the shit calls for tonight," I told him, and fell asleep within seconds.

At 2:00 A.M. I awoke again, this time to the sound of Bill's voice. Whomever he was talking to, he seemed subdued and excessively polite.

"Yes, ma'am," I heard him say. "Yes, ma'am. You're absolutely right, ma'am. Yes, ma'am."

After several more "yes ma'ams" he finally hung up.

"What in hell was that all about?" I asked.

"Some klansman's wife," he said, yawning.

"What in God's name did she have to say at this time of the morning?"

"She said you and Hoover and all the rest of the FBI were nothing but a bunch of LBJ-nigger-lovin' sons of bitches. She also said for us to get out of town or we'd be shot."

"Oh," I said, and turned over to go back to sleep. But a thought struck, and I sat up in bed.

"Bill," I asked, "why were you agreeing with everything she said?"

The next day as we walked out of the motel into the Mississippi sunshine the only people who ambushed us were reporters. We knew we might be close to breaking the case, but all we could offer was a replay of what we'd already said. But as we took off and headed toward Washington, the deal we'd authorized Rosen to make was going down. Soon—very soon—we might have all the evidence we needed to find the three missing men and close the case.

The minister and the highway patrolman held out for $30,000.

Rosen had miscalculated only slightly; needless to say, Hoover authorized the extra $5,000. It was a small price to pay for the solution to a major crime that might take weeks of additional investigation and millions of tax dollars. After they received the money, our informants told Inspector Joseph Sullivan and SAC Moore that the bodies were buried in a dam on a large farm a few miles outside Philadelphia.

Sullivan asked how the three civil rights workers had been murdered.

The informants told him they'd been killed after a high speed chase. They were captured, then shot. Afterward the bodies were taken and buried in the dam, which was then under construction.

"They were buried under at least twelve feet of earth," one of the informants said, "But I'm not going to say who did it."

"Who owns the farm?" asked Sullivan.

"Olen Burrage."

In retrospect, two things were significant about this revelation. First, it was obvious that this knowledge was common to a good many people—passed around among klansmen in absolute trust. It was like the secret a fraternity keeps among the membership—the handshake, the motto, the details of the investiture. Two men were willing to sell the secret, but a good many more had kept it and cherished it like some shared treasure.

Second, the informants were willing to give us the information we needed to recover the bodies and to begin building our case—they knew the details of the murder and who had pulled the trigger—yet they wouldn't give us the names, as if to retain the illusion that in the final analysis they hadn't squealed.

As soon as Sullivan and Moore had the information, they went to Rosen, who called Washington. We decided not to rush out to Olen Burrage's farm with earthmovers and tear into the dam. Although Sullivan was convinced the information was accurate, we were by no means positive. It was possible that the informants believed they knew the location of the bodies and were mistaken. It was also possible, though less likely, that we were being conned. In all likelihood, Sullivan and Moore were right, but we decided to explore all possibilities before risking public embarrassment.

After a day of questioning, during which agents once more interviewed Sheriff Rainey, Deputy Sheriff Price, and other local officials, Sullivan gathered his agents back in Meridian and told them that the next day they would be digging for bodies. He asked Resident Agent Proctor to bring picks and shovels, and he set the departure time at 5:00 A.M.

The next morning they met, drove up to the farm, and began hiking through fields and woods looking for the dam. They found a dam all right, but it was covered with growth. No one had broken ground there in recent months. With the sun mounting in the sky and a lot of countryside to cover, Sullivan decided to call for help.

"Drive to the Naval Air Station," he told two of his agents. "Get them to fly you over this area and see if you can spot the dam from the air. Take a walkie-talkie with you and tell us where the dam is in relation to our car. We'll wait here."

They had to wait for almost two hours, but eventually navy helicopters began to sweep the area, and shortly thereafter one of the agents shouted over the walkie-talkie.

"We've spotted the dam. It's a big one. It's about four or five hundred yards south of where you are parked."

When Sullivan and his crew arrived there, they were immediately discouraged. The dam was enormous—547 feet wide, 11 feet thick, and 20 feet high. Clearly picks and shovels wouldn't get the job done. They knew they would have to call in bulldozers, and that posed a whole new set of problems.

Sullivan called Washington for permission to rent heavy equipment, and we immediately approved. Roy Moore made the arrangements, and the Hyde Construction Company agreed to furnish one bulldozer and one dragline. Then they got a search warrant to rip into the dam.

Early on the morning of August 4, the equipment arrived in Philadelphia, and agents served a warrant on Olen Burrage, owner of the farm. Within thirty minutes the property was swarming with Hyde employees and busy FBI agents. They had brought tarpaulins and military rations. They were prepared to camp out on the site for several days, in case someone found out what they were doing and tried to remove the evidence.

But it didn't take several days. Around 3:00 in the afternoon the air became suddenly rank. Flies swarmed around the spot where agents were digging. Then the bulldozer scooped one more time and exposed a black boot. It was the kind Michael Schwerner had been wearing when he disappeared, and he was still wearing it. Agents unearthed the body and found Schwerner's wallet still in his hip pocket. A little after five o'clock they uncovered Andrew Goodman's body, and less than ten minutes later the remains of James Chaney.

We had learned from our informants that the Klan sometimes tapped telephones, so I had worked out a voice code with SAC Moore: he was not to refer to "bodies" but rather "oil wells." After the first discovery, Moore called me in Washington and delivered a coded message.

"We've uncapped one oil well," he said.

"Good work," I told him. "Give me an immediate report if there are others."

Before 5:30 I received the last call from Sullivan.

"We've uncapped the third oil well."

"Sit on the story until I call you," I said.

I called Hoover and gave him the news. He was his predictably unemotional self.

"Call the White House and let them know. Then prepare a statement for immediate release."

I called Walter Jenkins at the White House, but he wasn't in, so I talked to Mildred Stegall.

"Deke, Walter and the president are in a National Security Council meeting," she said.

"Will you please get a note to Walter," I said. "Tell him I must talk to him right away about the Mississippi case."

Everyone likes to be the bearer of interesting and important news, but that wasn't why I was so anxious to talk to Walter. A number of people had been present at the discovery of the bodies, and some of them were not FBI personnel. In addition, Olen Burrage knew we were digging in his dam. He must have passed the word along to still others, because a gaggle of reporters was waiting at the farm gate, fully aware that we were in the middle of an excavation. From past experience, I knew a story this big would leak in a matter of minutes. So I was relieved when Jenkins called me back almost immediately.

"Walter," I said, "we've found the bodies of the three civil rights workers. They were buried in a dam on a farm near Philadelphia. Will you pass the word to the president and call me back immediately? We can't sit on the news long. The reporters are pushing us hard."

Walter said he would move as quickly as possible and get back to me. I sat and waited—five minutes, ten minutes, fifteen minutes. No call. Any second I expected the television networks to break in for a news bulletin. If they did, their correspondents would report only a part of the story, with every chance of getting some of the details wrong. If we issued our own release and answered their questions, the story would be accurate the first time around and save us hundreds of hours of clarification and correction.

Finally, I decided to call back and chew Walter's butt. Obviously he hadn't understood what I'd told him. I dialed the White House, asked for Jenkins, and when a voice answered, I unloaded.

"This is Deke again, Walter. Damn it, I can't hold this news much longer. Why in hell haven't you called?"

"Deke," said an oddly familiar voice, "this isn't Walter."

Then who the hell was it? I thought. I was just about to ask that question when the voice continued.

"This is the president. Walter gave me your message. We're notifying the families of these men before the news is released."

I told the president I thought that was an excellent idea.

"I want you and Edgar to come over to the White House and appear with me on network television when we make the announcement of these developments."

I told him we would be there.

The autopsy report revealed that all three men had died from gunshot wounds—five in all. Each of the white victims had been killed by a single .38-caliber bullet. There were three .38-caliber bullets in the body of Chaney. One of the bullets found in Chaney was fired from a different weapon. The other four came from the same gun. Two people had fired the shots—and from close range.

So we could now prove that Schwerner, Chaney, and Goodman had been murdered—something we'd known in our hearts from the very beginning. Finding their killers, however, posed enormous problems. We searched the terrain surrounding the dam but found no additional evidence. No guns, no spent shells, no tire prints. That meant we would have to requestion the local residents—a task that had been fruitless and painful.

But the climate in Philadelphia had changed. At the outset, the responsible citizens of this rural town had told themselves that no one they knew could possibly have committed such a crime, that the disappearance of the three young men was a hoax, that the FBI was a national police force determined to enforce a Washington political agenda. Or perhaps they were merely hoping against hope that their community was somehow innocent of what appeared to be a particularly grisly crime. They had seen Mississippians stereotyped in Hollywood films and television dramas as ignorant and vicious rednecks. They knew they didn't conform to those stereotypes, and they resented anyone who came to Philadelphia to prove otherwise.

With the discovery of the bodies they could no longer maintain an illusion of local purity. The stench of the newly unearthed corpses had reached their nostrils, and they were sick and ashamed. The following day, agents walking the streets were greeted with shy smiles and friendly waves. No more muttered profanities, no more threats and boasts.

In addition, people were willing, even eager to give information. Blacks came forward to tell tales of false arrest, police harassment, and even brutal beatings by law officers waving guns. And always the names of the officers involved were the same—Sheriff Rainey, Deputy Sheriff Price, Officer Richard Willis, and a few others. We had long suspected that these men knew about the killings. We were becoming more and more convinced they were accomplices.

Then we got a big break. A police officer, Sgt. Wallace Miller of the Meridian Police Department, came to us—guilt-ridden and eager to unburden himself. He was a member of the Ku Klux Klan in Lauderdale County and knew precisely what had happened to the three civil rights workers, though he had taken no part in the killing. Meeting night after night with one of our agents, he gave a surprisingly detailed account of the Klan's activities in Neshoba County over the past months. He named names, dates, and specific movements. It was as if he'd been trained as a double agent.

The killings had originated with the desire to teach "Goatee" a lesson he would never forget. At first they were simply going to give him a good beating.

"At a meeting in May," Miller told us, "one of the [klansmen] got up and said, 'We've got to get Goatee. I make a motion we go and get him.' Somebody said, 'What do you mean "go and get him?"' And the man said, 'I mean beat the hell out of him and the niggers.'"

"Somebody else said Goatee needed a beating, all right, but first we ought to investigate where he lives because he might have a machine that takes pictures of anybody coming around or have a radio to send out a warning. One fellow said, 'For all we know, he might be an FBI agent.'"

"There was talk about how to get into the apartment where Goatee lived. A salesman volunteered to go over and see if he could sell the Schwerners a vacuum cleaner and get a look at the apartment.

"Two weeks later the salesman said the Schwerners wouldn't let him past the door. There was some more talk about going after Goatee. But then a klansman from Philadelphia said, 'Don't you bother Goatee.' He reached in his pocket and pulled out a paper. He said, 'This is an elimination order. If you go over there now, you may mess things up.'"

So the killing of Schwerner had been carried out by members of the Philadelphia Klavern. And it appeared as if they might have been "ordered" to commit the murder by some higher authority in the Klan. But how to bring Schwerner to Neshoba County, where law enforcement officials were involved with the Klan? A Philadelphia klansman gave Miller the answer to that question: They burned down the Mt. Zion Methodist Church, and "Goatee" came into enemy territory, right on schedule.

Miller said that after the young men were released from jail, three cars, one driven by Deputy Cecil Price, had chased them down the highway at speeds of 100 mph. They had finally stopped them near House, Mississippi; and it was there that the three activists were executed.

"After they were killed," Miller told us, "the group split up. Part of them took the bodies to Olen Burrage's farm and buried them with a bulldozer. Two of the men were supposed to take the station wagon over to Alabama and burn it—but for some reason they didn't."

So there it was. We now knew precisely how the killings had taken place, and we also knew some of the participants. But this was hearsay evidence—nothing that would hold up in a court of law. We needed more evidence—hopefully an eye witness or a confession. Our best bet to gather such evidence was—Sgt. Wallace Miller.

"Wallace," the agent said, "if you keep on as if nothing has happened, you can perform a service for your country and for Mississippi. Don't you see? If we work together, we can smash this thing."

Miller agreed and became an FBI informant. We paid him travel expenses for out-of-town trips, and we promised him protection if he got into serious trouble. Always more a policeman than a klansman, he embarked on an effort to ingratiate himself further with the leadership of the Ku Klux Klan. And he was not the only informant we'd placed in the organization.

Meanwhile, instead of lying low after the discovery of the three bodies, the Klan was planning more ambitious crimes. In an ill-timed move, COFO had come to Neshoba County to register voters and had set up operations in the Evers Hotel, a two-story building that catered to blacks. County officials tried to evict the civil rights workers, but the owner wouldn't cooperate. The business community formed a committee to address the "problem" but came up with no plan.

At that point, the Klan developed its own melodramatic solution: Murder the entire COFO contingent. As one of our informants told us, "There is a plan to dynamite the Evers Hotel. The dynamite is going to be moved from Meridian into Neshoba County." Forewarned, we took immediate steps to locate the dynamite.

Again, our informants came through. We learned that the cache of explosives was located in the home of one James C. Rutledge, a jobless truck driver. We procured a search warrant, and on October 8 we searched Rutledge's house and found two-thirds of a box of dynamite, as well as blasting caps and a fuse. We also found Klan literature, and Rutledge admitted that he was a member.

With Rutledge's arrest, even the average klansman could figure out that someone in their midst was talking to the FBI. Leaders met in secret, worried that Rutledge might talk. As one of our informants reported, the discussion dealt with desperate remedies: "One of the men from Meridian thought Rutledge should be eliminated. He suggested renting a room on the third floor of the Lamar Hotel across the street from the Lauderdale county jail. A sharpshooter could shoot Rutledge when he appeared in a jail window."

We determined that such a shot was impossible, but we warned Meridian police of the possible attempt on Rutledge's life. We did not take such plots lightly. We knew the Klan was composed of desperate men, and the remainder of summer and early fall confirmed our view. Twenty-seven black churches were burned in three months. Bombs went off in the houses not only of blacks, but also whites—such as the blast that tore through the house of Natchez Mayor John Nosser, who had been trying to act as a peacemaker.

In early September, the FBI submitted a report on civil rights violations in Neshoba County. The document was 2,673 pages long and focused on the Schwerner-Chaney-Goodman case and the harassment of blacks by local law enforcement officers. By the end of the month, we were bringing cases of rights violations to the federal grand jury in Biloxi. These indictments, however, did not include the killing of the three civil rights workers, since in most cases murder is not a federal crime.

Because the cases we presented to the federal grand jury involved some of the same people we suspected of killing Schwerner, Chaney, and Goodman, we were disturbed when State Circuit Judge O. H. Barnett ordered a Philadelphia grand jury to investigate the murder of the three civil rights workers and then sent the following telegram to J. Edgar Hoover:

YOU ARE RESPECTFULLY REQUESTED TO
INSTRUCT ALL YOUR AGENTS THAT HAVE
INFORMATION REGARDING THE DEATH OF

THREE CIVIL RIGHTS WORKERS WHOSE BODIES
WERE FOUND IN NESHOBA COUNTY, MISSISSIP-
PI, IN AUGUST TO APPEAR IN PERSON AT THE
COUNTY COURTHOUSE IN PHILADELPHIA, MIS-
SISSIPPI AT NINE O'CLOCK A.M., MONDAY, SEP-
TEMBER 28, 1964, PREPARED TO TESTIFY
BEFORE A GRAND JURY ABOUT THIS MATTER.

This would have forced the FBI to lay its whole case on the table, including the names of our informants and the evidence we had uncovered. Had we revealed the identity of our sources, it would have ended their effectiveness and jeopardized their lives.

I therefore drafted the following telegram, which we sent to Judge Barnett over Hoover's signature, putting an end to the matter.

FBI AGENTS REFERRED TO IN YOUR TELEGRAM
WILL BE UNABLE TO TESTIFY BEFORE STATE
GRAND JURY AT THIS TIME REGARDING DEATH
OF THREE CIVIL RIGHTS WORKERS, AS THEY
HAVE BEEN INSTRUCTED BY THE ACTING
ATTORNEY GENERAL NOT TO DISCLOSE
BEFORE THAT GRAND JURY ANY INFORMA-
TION RELATING TO MATERIAL OR INFORMA-
TION CONTAINED IN THE FILES OF THE
DEPARTMENT OF JUSTICE, OR ANY INFORMA-
TION OBTAINED IN CONNECTION WITH ANY
OFFICIAL DEPARTMENT OF JUSTICE INVESTIGA-
TION. IN THE CIRCUMSTANCES, I ASSUME THE
AGENTS WILL BE EXCUSED FROM APPEARING
BEFORE GRAND JURY ON MONDAY.

Neither Judge Barnett nor the Philadelphia grand jury was pleased with our decision, but the federal grand jury in Biloxi saw things our way. They indicted Sheriff Rainey, Deputy Sheriff Price, Officer Richard Willis, Officer Otha Neal Burkes, and former Sheriff Barnett on charges that they had violated the civil rights of six black prisoners in their custody. These indictments were based on evidence gathered while looking for the killers of the three civil rights workers. Acting on the indictments, FBI agents arrested the five men in Neshoba County and brought them before U.S. Commissioner Esther Carter, who fixed ridiculously low bonds of $1,000–$2,000, which they were able to meet. For the moment they were free.

Meantime we were beginning to gather invaluable information from our contacts inside the Klan. In addition to stories of murder plots, we gradually learned the names of several klansmen who had been involved in the killing of Schwerner, Chaney, and Goodman. One was James Jordan. Another was Wayne Roberts. Still another was Doyle Barnette. Intimidated by the presence of the FBI and a continuing investigation that threatened to implicate them, Jordan and Barnette left Neshoba County. However, we located both and began to question them. Eventually they admitted their involvement, and we were able to develop a full and detailed account of the murder—who was involved, how each phase of the plot developed, what individual participants said and did, how the victims reacted and what they said, how Roberts killed Schwerner and Goodman and Jordan killed Chaney, how they took the bodies to the dam and bulldozed them under, and how they went their separate ways after promising each other to keep their mouths shut.

Jordan denied that he had participated in the shootings. However, Barnette's testimony, the more reliable account, identified both Roberts and Jordan as the killers:

> Before I could get out of the car Wayne Roberts ran past my car to Price's car, opened the left rear door, pulled Schwerner out of the car, spun him around so that Schwerner was standing on the left side of the road with his back to the ditch, and said, "Are you that nigger lover?" and Schwerner said, "Sir, I know just how you feel." Wayne had a pistol in his right hand, then shot Schwerner.
>
> Wayne then went back to Price's car and got Goodman, took him to the left side of the road with Goodman facing the road, and shot Goodman.

When Wayne shot Schwerner, Wayne had his hand on Schwerner's shoulder. When Wayne shot Goodman, Wayne was standing within reach of him. Schwerner fell to the left so that he was lying alongside the road. Goodman spun around and fell back toward the bank in the back.

At this time Jim Jordan said, "Save one for me!" He then got out of Price's car and got Chaney out. I remember Chaney backing up, facing the road, and standing on the bank on the other side of the ditch, and Jordan stood in the middle of the road and shot him. I do not remember how many times Jordan shot. Jordan then said, "You didn't leave me anything but a nigger, but at least I killed me a nigger."

Our ballistics experts examined the physical evidence and determined that Jordan had fired into Chaney's body, as Barnette had reported; but a shot to the head had killed the black youth, and that bullet was fired from the same weapon as the bullets that had killed Schwerner and Goodman. Jordan claimed he had not been present at the killing but had been dropped off down the road. We could prove that he had shot James Chaney. With Barnette's testimony and solid ballistics evidence, we were ready to move on those involved.

Of course, the Justice Department couldn't charge them with murder—a state crime rather than a federal crime. So SAC Roy Moore and Inspector Joseph Sullivan met with Governor Johnson and Mississippi Attorney General Patterson to discuss the question of jurisdiction and to map out the best possible strategy to net all the fish. Since the grand jury was not currently meeting in Neshoba County, any action at that level would have to be delayed. In addition, there was the possibility that a local justice of the peace would demand complete and immediate disclosure of all evidence and witnesses, just as Judge O. H. Barnett had done.

As a consequence of these and other considerations, we decided to charge the killers with civil rights violations in federal court. On the night of December 3, we filed a complaint charging nineteen men with conspiring "to injure, oppress, threaten, and intimidate

Michael Henry Schwerner, James Earl Chaney, and Andrew Goodman... in the free exercise and enjoyment of rights secured to them
by the Constitution and laws of the United States."

We started rounding up the suspects on the morning of December
4, including Sheriff Rainey—in fact, we arrested Rainey and Price
together as they came into the office shortly before 9:00 A.M.—and
before the end of the day, all were in custody. We had completed
our investigation in slightly less than six months. The federal case
seemed strong, and we had supplied the state with signed confessions that could be used to prosecute a number of participants in
the murder.

Over the months, civil rights leaders like the Rev. Martin Luther
King had been highly critical of our performance. Now they were
singing our praises.

I only wish the final resolution of the case had been as satisfying.
It was three years, two months, and five days after the FBI had
uncovered the bodies in the red clay dam before the trial began. The
evidence was overwhelming, and no one was surprised that eight of
those charged were convicted. These included Imperial Wizard Sam
Bowers, Sheriff Lawrence Rainey, and Deputy Cecil Price.

What surprised and shocked us was the nature of the sentences
the judge handed down. Two klansmen received ten years. Two
received six years. Three got off with only three years. All were eligible for parole long before their sentences expired.

9

....

King vs. Hoover

IN DECEMBER OF 1964, at a dinner party, the wife of an FBI agent seated next to me turned and said, "I think Mr. Hoover's criticism of Martin Luther King is one of the most courageous things the director's ever done."

I couldn't let the remark pass with polite agreement. I'd lain awake nights thinking about what Hoover had said.

"It was a public relations disaster of the first order," I told her, "and it'll haunt the FBI for years to come."

Most of the people at the table agreed with her, but I was the only one present who had taken the full measure of King's reputation and his standing among members of the press. And I would be the one who would have to deal with the consequences of Hoover's remarks.

At that moment, King was nearing the zenith of his popularity. He had led the Montgomery bus boycott—the first great civil rights demonstration of the 1950s—and had done so using the techniques of nonviolent protest, a strategy designed to win public sympathy and support. Few people now remember that the Montgomery boycott did not begin as a movement to desegregate the buses, but only to gain fair treatment under existing laws. But because of the boycott, the courts eventually ruled that Jim Crow public transportation was unconstitutional. King and his followers won a greater victory than they had intended and became the heroes of the new television industry, which found in the fierce confrontations between demonstrators and Southern police the first great story for TV news.

After Montgomery, King and his lieutenant, Ralph David Abernathy, moved on to even greater triumphs. And in Birmingham they finally found a perfect adversary to further their agenda—Public Safety Commissioner Theophilus Eugene "Bull" Connor, who ordered his men to use fire hoses and dogs to turn back demonstrators. TV cameras filmed the confrontation, and the nation recoiled in horror. The result was the 1964 Civil Rights Act—legislation that, among other things, ended segregation in privately owned accommodations that served the general public.

Near the close of the Birmingham campaign, in order to influence passage of the Civil Rights Act then before Congress, King and other civil rights leaders, with the help of the National Council of Churches and several unions, organized the famous March on Washington, during which he made his famous "I Have a Dream" speech. The mall was jammed with tens of thousands of people and millions more watched the spectacle on television. At that point, King ceased to be merely a regional black leader and became a figure of mythic proportions, someone who had captured the imagination of a significant number of Americans, white as well as black.

Shortly after King's star had ascended to these breathtaking heights Hoover developed an intense animosity toward the civil rights leader, one that grew, like the biblical mustard seed, from a small kernel into a huge living thing that cast an enormous shadow across the landscape. That kernel was little more than a brief comment by King in a November 19, 1962, article about the civil rights movement in the South. A *New York Times* reporter quoted King as saying:

> One of the great problems we face with the Federal
> Bureau of Investigation in the South is that its agents

are white Southerners who have been influenced by the mores of the community. To maintain their status, they have to be friendly with the local police and the people who are protecting segregation. Every time I saw FBI men in Albany [Georgia], they were with the local police force.

When Hoover read it, he got angry. For almost forty years as head of the FBI, he had worked hard to maintain the bureau's reputation for fairness. In addition, he knew that all FBI agents were aware that he would not permit attitudes and behavior remotely similar to those described in King's allegations. Finally, without lifting a phone or cracking a file, he knew full well that white Southerners were not disproportionately represented in the bureau's Southern offices. Like members of the armed forces, agents went where they were assigned—and they were assigned where they were needed. King was either badly misinformed or else had deliberately misrepresented the facts to gain sympathy from the predominantly non-Southern readership of the *Times*.

Even so, Hoover—with his usual prudence and thoroughness—ordered an immediate investigation of FBI operations in Southern offices. This investigation included detailed personnel surveys and the examination of hundreds of civil rights cases. Investigators could not find a single case in which derelictions occurred that might reflect on the equity or objectivity of our agents. They also found that non-Southerners abounded in all offices. Four of the five agents assigned to the Albany, Georgia office were Northern-born, Northern-reared, Northern-educated.

Indeed, King and his small band of activists were treated well in Albany, Georgia, so well that his campaign there was the least successful of his career. As one commentator put it, "The Albany police could have been mistaken for the local Welcome Wagon." Chief of Police Laurie Pritchett, one of the shrewdest lawmen in the region, had trained his men to deal with protestors without using force.

Because of this diplomatic approach, King's invasion of Albany was a frustrating defeat. The Southern Christian Leadership Conference (SCLC) not only lost face, but lost money. The checks came in only when people were moved to anger witnessing gross mistreatment on their television screens. In the Albany campaign, all they saw was the warm and friendly face of Laurie Pritchett. At this point, stalemated by Pritchett, King lashed out in anger at the FBI, and soon Hoover responded in kind.

In a move to set the record straight and force King to admit his error, we instructed our Atlanta office to make an appointment with him to discuss his public allegations. He would be asked to substantiate his charges or else to make a public statement repudiating them.

The special agent in charge (SAC) in Atlanta called King at the SCLC office to set up the appointment. Told that Dr. King was not in, he left a number and asked that King return his call. The days became weeks. The weeks became months. The SAC tried several more times and received the same treatment. Dr. King was out. Yes, the message would be placed on his desk. And again no return call.

Hoover brooded about it and concluded that King was merely trying to grab headlines with his statement—at the expense of the FBI. It was an outrage—an affront Hoover neither forgot nor forgave. It was the single wellspring of the director's ongoing animosity. From that day forward, he never believed anything King said.

Meanwhile the FBI watched King's activities with growing alarm. As the civil rights leader rose in public favor, his potential for good or ill increased proportionally. Yet we had gathered information about King and his associates that was troubling. We learned that King was being advised by past and current members of the Communist party, and that the party seemed pleased with the situation.

This information came to us at a time when the Soviet Union was doing its best to destabilize American society. We weren't sure how King fit into those plans. We wondered whether he was, to use Lenin's phrase, "a useful idiot" or someone acting on his own and deliberately attempting to foment riot and insurrection.

In attempting to find the answer to that question, we discovered something else to worry about—King's sexual adventures, pursued openly and unashamedly on a number of occasions. Such behavior seemed incongruous in a leader who claimed his authority as a man of God. So extravagant was his promiscuity that some who knew about it questioned his sincerity in professing basic Christian beliefs and in using the black church as the home base of his movement. When Hoover learned of King's prodigious sexual exploits, he narrowed his eyes and pursed his lips. He was straight-laced about such matters and saw extramarital sex as evidence of moral degeneracy—an opinion that many Americans still shared in the early 1960s, before Hollywood taught that promiscuity was ennobling.

Hoover's anger bubbled on the backburner for more than a year, finally boiling over, unwisely, at a press reception he held in 1964.

Members of the Washington press corps were forever seeking interviews with the director, who was shy on such occasions and tried to avoid them. In vain did reporters try to overcome this shyness with politeness, intimidation, bribes, and subterfuge. Then there was a breakthrough. A group of female journalists—including top-flight reporters Sarah McClendon and Miriam Ottenberg—organized the Women's National Press Club, which became a force to reckon with in the capital. The WNPC routinely demanded—and got—interviews with senators, representatives, cabinet members, and White House officials. So when they asked Hoover for an audience early in November of 1964, he couldn't think of a reason to turn them down. He stalled for a few days, then agreed to meet with them on November 18—for a "briefing session."

We knew "briefing session" meant a monologue by the director in which he would give them a history of the agency and some highlights of current policy. Then Inspector Bob Wick had an idea to improve our standing with the women.

"Why don't we serve coffee?" he said. "That way it'll be a more informal, more sociable occasion."

"You're out of your mind," I said. "The Old Man won't allow it. He won't let anybody in the bureau drink coffee on duty. What makes you think he'll have it served right there in his office?"

"Just let me ask him," Wick said.

"O.K.," I said, "but you're wasting your time."

I forwarded the request to the director's office; and, lo and behold, he agreed. He probably remembered coffees and teas his mother had attended and thought it might appeal to these women as well, since to Hoover all adult females were "ladies" in gloves and hats. Whatever the reason, when the women filed in on the 18th, coffee was waiting for them in a handsome silver pitcher.

It was an intimidating group—eighteen women in all—and only Hoover, Wick, and I to face them. Since the session was billed as a "briefing," we'd compiled several sheets of facts and statistics covering a range of pertinent topics—fugitives arrested, robberies solved, major cases handled, stolen autos returned, investigations in progress. We also presented each woman with a financial report on the substantial amounts the FBI had saved the U.S. government as the result of fines, savings, and recoveries over the past eleven months.

The women took the handouts, thanked us, and stuck them away in their briefcases. Then, while they sipped their coffee, Hoover launched into his standard lecture, outlining the glories of past and present in a staccato delivery that did little to enliven the subject matter—which consisted of canned data anyone could have extracted from FBI reports or one of the director's public speeches. Their eyes begin to glaze. He sensed he was losing his audience and decided to give them something a little juicier.

"I want to dispel a number of current misconceptions about the assignment of bureau personnel in civil rights cases," he said. "Seventy percent of the FBI agents assigned to the South in November 1962 were born in the North, contrary to the assertions made by Dr. Martin Luther King that these agents were overwhelmingly Southern."

The women snapped to attention like West Point plebes. King was the hottest name in the news at that time. As they leaned forward, Hoover went for broke: "In my opinion, Dr. Martin Luther King is the most notorious liar in the country."

I rose halfway out of my chair and looked at Wick. He had turned ashen. At the word "liar," I had seen more than a dozen hands hurriedly jotting down the quote. Wick rolled his eyes. We both knew the remark would keep our phone lines burning for weeks to come. I grabbed pencil and paper, scrawled a note, and passed it over to Hoover. It read, "Don't you think you should insist that the remark about King was off the record?"

Hoover, warming to his audience, shoved the note aside, so I passed him a second note: "Why not state that the remark about King should remain in this room?" He read it, while rattling on about other things, and ignored my advice. Ten minutes later, sensing that the meeting was coming to an end, I passed a third note: "Could we keep the King remark off the record?"

This last attempt produced an outburst.

"DeLoach advises me to tell you ladies that my calling Dr. King a notorious liar should be off the record. I won't do this. Feel free to print my remarks as given."

I understood how he felt. King had insulted the entire bureau. Then King had arrogantly refused to discuss the matter or answer our phone calls. On top of that, Hoover knew the company King was keeping, the manner in which he was behaving. What he didn't know was that he had engineered a public relations disaster for the FBI and for himself.

Most people had forgotten King's complaint, which by then was two years old. Suddenly Hoover had revived the charges himself. The FBI was now engaged in name-calling with the darling of the national press, a contest we could never hope to win. After all, few people knew about King's communist associates or his sexual orgies.

After the director had given the assembled women carte blanche, Sarah McClendon expressed their gratitude.

"Oh, Mr. Hoover, I'm so glad you're going to let us print your remarks."

Hoover gave me a look of triumph, a tilt of the chin that said, "Mind your own business, DeLoach." And the women ran from the room as if the ceiling were falling, anxious to get to their typewriters.

The headlines are history. Nobody needed to prompt Dr. King. He saw the high, weak lob coming down on his side of the net, and on November 19, 1964, he sent the director the following telegram:

I was appalled and surprised at your reported statement
maligning my integrity. What motivated such an irresponsible accusation is a mystery to me. I have sincerely

questioned the effectiveness of the Federal Bureau of
Investigation in racial incidents, particularly where
bombings and brutalities against Negroes are at issue,
but I have never attributed this merely to Southerners
in the FBI. This is part of the broader involvement in
the protection of Negroes in the South and the seeming
inability to gain convictions in even the most heinous
crimes perpetrated against civil rights workers. It
remains a fact that not a single arrest was made in
Albany, Georgia, during the many brutalities against
Negroes. Neither has a single arrest been made in connection with the tragic murder of four children in Birmingham, nor in the case of the three murdered civil
rights leaders in Mississippi. Moreover, all FBI agents
inevitably work with local law enforcement officers in
car thefts, bank robberies, and other interstate violations. This makes it difficult for them to function effec-
tively in cases where the rights and safety of Negro citizens are being threatened by these same law enforcement officers. I will be happy to discuss this question
with you at length in the near future. Although your
statement said that you have attempted to meet with
me, I have searched in vain for any such request. I have
always made myself available to all FBI agents of the
Atlanta office and encouraged our staff and affiliates to
cooperate with them in spite of the fact that many of
our people have suspicions and distrust of the FBI as a
result of the slow pace of justice in the South.

As soon as we read the message, we knew it had been written for
the press rather than for the director; and sure enough, King immediately released the wire to the media. The FBI switchboard was
flooded with calls from reporters. One of the women who had
attended the November 18 briefing phoned and said she understood that Dr. King was to meet with the director. She expressed a
desire to sit in on the meeting. Hoover's grumpy reply: "I have no
appointment with King and do not intend to make one."

But after taking a beating in the press day after day, Hoover finally gave in. In his wire, King had implied that he wanted to discuss this disagreement with J. Edgar Hoover, so I suggested to Clyde Tolson that I phone King and see if he did indeed want a meeting. Tolson agreed, but said I should ask Hoover, not him. When I phoned the director he turned sour at the suggestion, growled for a minute or two, then said to go ahead with my plan.

"But make sure the meeting is in my office," he warned, "and no press. Do you hear me, no press!"

I called King's headquarters three times, but each time I was told, "Dr. King isn't available. We'll give him your message." The same old dance routine. After the third call, I decided to let the matter ride, assuming that if we didn't call them, they would begin to worry and call us.

Sure enough, in a few days Andrew Young, King's executive assistant, called me.

"We could meet with you on December 1 [1964], at 3:00 P.M." There was a certain imperiousness in his insistence on such a precise time and place; but when I passed the demand along to Hoover, he nodded his head and said, "All right. Give them what they want—but no press present and no press conference afterward."

As I expected, King's office notified the media of the impending dialogue, and representatives of all branches of the media flooded our office with phone calls and inquiries. By noon of the first day of December, the switchboards were blinking constantly.

As the result, the hallway outside Hoover's office was packed with reporters and photographers. King didn't arrive until almost 3:30, and as he approached from the direction of the attorney general's office, he wasn't spotted by the press. I plunged through the crowd of irritable reporters, intercepted King and his entourage, and steered them directly into Hoover's office. As we eluded the mob, he introduced me to his companions—Andrew Young, Ralph Abernathy, Walter Fauntroy.

The director charged around his desk as usual and shook each hand. I was pleased to see him on his best behavior. It was a good sign that things might go well. As we all sat down, I got out my notepad and looked at my watch. It was 3:35.

King began by saying, "I'm grateful for the opportunity to meet with you about these issues. If you don't mind, Rev. Abernathy will speak first for us."

Abernathy was courteous and even cordial. He told the director it was a great honor to meet a man who had done so much for his country and had accomplished so much in the field of civil rights. The tone and content of his opening remarks suggested that he had done his homework and was well aware of Hoover's personality and ego. Rather than go into specific areas of disagreement, Abernathy concluded by saying that blacks had many problems, particularly in the South, and that the Southern Christian Leadership Conference hoped this meeting would help their people "rise up from their bondage."

Abernathy's speech was biblical in tone but confined to the vocabulary of daily conversation. King spoke in slightly more erudite language. He began by saying it was "vitally necessary" for him and his followers to maintain a working relationship with the bureau. Then he said something that brought Hoover forward in his seat.

"Many Negroes have complained that the FBI has been ineffective, but I, myself, discount such criticism. And I want to assure you that I have been seriously misquoted in the matter of slurs against the FBI."

Hoover raised his eyebrows, pleasantly surprised.

"My only complaint," King continued, "is the fact that I have seen FBI agents who have received civil rights complaints consorting the next day with local police officers who have been charged with brutalities."

Hoover nodded without responding.

At that point, King hastened to say, "I personally appreciate the great work of the FBI in so many instances related to civil rights, particularly in Mississippi, where constructive developments have been significant. The FBI is a great restraining influence against injustice, and, by the way, I have never urged Negroes to refrain from reporting information to the FBI. To the contrary, I have encouraged them to report many incidents. Indeed, I sincerely believe there are good relationships between Negroes and the FBI in the South—and especially in Atlanta."

Hoover again nodded. I couldn't tell whether King's conciliatory speech had made an impact on him, but I thought perhaps it had.

Then King stated emphatically that he had never made any personal attacks against the director, that he had simply tried to articulate the feelings of blacks in the interest of furthering the overall strategy of nonviolence.

At this point, Hoover interrupted and began his monologue. He said the FBI had "put the fear of God" into the Ku Klux Klan, that he knew the identity of the Klan members who had murdered the three civil rights workers, and that these killers would soon be brought to trial. He acknowledged that some of the sheriffs and deputies in rural Mississippi had participated in racial crimes, but explained that the FBI was laboring under some of the same frustrations and restraints as the black leadership. And he pointed out that the small army of bureau agents now in Mississippi was so successful against the Klan that members were sullenly referring to us as "The Federal Bureau of Integration."

As for the charge that the FBI was consorting with racist law enforcement officers, Hoover said, "I'll be damned if the FBI has associated with any of these people, nor will we be associating with them in the future. We're in full sympathy with the civil rights movement, but we need cooperation and assistance in order to solve cases."

King nodded without comment.

Hoover then explained to King and the others that several years earlier he had made a special point to transfer Northern-born agents to the South in order to avoid just the kind of charges that King had been quoted as making.

"However," he said, "I'm certain that all of our agents—regardless of their origins or color—investigate their cases impartially and diligently. They're not stupid. They know they're rated and promoted on the basis of how well they handle complaints and crimes—especially those that involve highly sensitive issues."

He then launched into a standard speech that many of us gave over the years: the FBI is only an investigative agency; it operates under severe legal restrictions.

"I'm sorry we can't protect civil rights workers, black or white.

But you must understand that we have no authority to protect any-one—members of Congress, cabinet officers, even the president. It's just not in our job descriptions.

"Also," he continued, "we cannot recommend prosecution or declination of prosecution. We cannot make on-the-spot arrests. We can merely investigate. Then it's up to the Department of Justice to determine whether to prosecute."

Here he was referring to charges that the FBI was responsible for failure to bring to trial and convict the murderers of the three civil rights workers. The FBI, he continued, had also complained about the almost imperceptible grind of the wheels of justice. Hoover told King and his group that he was as frustrated as they were, and they all nodded gravely. I thought we were making real progress in explaining our mission and its limitations.

The director concluded his review of the issues by telling the four civil rights leaders that he welcomed legitimate complaints about the shortcomings of bureau personnel.

"I want to know immediately if any of our agents has been unavailable or has mishandled a report of a civil rights violation. If one of our agents is in the wrong, he'll be called on the carpet—fast!" I instinctively nodded in agreement. Those of us in the FBI knew the statement was true.

Then, after he'd covered all the reported complaints, he added a footnote.

"I would like to give you some advice, Dr. King," he said. "One of the greatest things you could accomplish for your people would be to encourage them to register and vote. Voting registrars in the South now have to be much more careful than in the past, and there are fewer attempts to prevent Negroes from registering. For one thing, we're monitoring registrations and voting procedures very carefully. And by the way, we're also monitoring restaurants that have been accused of discrimination."

He said he was in favor of equality in public accommodations and in schools, though he added that he didn't think children, black or white, should be bused ten or twelve miles. He went on to suggest that the SCLC turn its attention to preparing black people to cultivate knowledge and skills so they would be eligible for better jobs.

At this point, someone asked him why there weren't more black agents in the FBI.

"I'd like to have more black agents," he said. "The ones we have already are as good as any in the bureau. The problem is, we require not only a college diploma, but in most cases an advanced degree of some sort. Negroes who have such degrees generally choose to go into jobs that pay higher than we do. We won't water down our qualifications simply because of the color of a person's skin."

Dr. King began to talk more freely at that stage of the discussion, and in response to Hoover's advice, he said he intended to go to Selma, Alabama, in the next month or so to register voters.

"Do you suppose," he asked, "that FBI agents could be present to prevent violence?"

"Certainly agents will be sent to Selma," Hoover said, "but I can't assign them to protect anybody. They'll be there to observe violations of civil rights laws and to report those violations to the Justice Department."

As the afternoon wore on, I was increasingly surprised. The exchange was going well. Both men obviously loved to talk; but Hoover dominated the conversation, which might have continued into the evening, had the director not been scheduled for additional appointments. What I found particularly interesting was the diplomacy both men displayed in failing to confront Hoover's published charge that King was "the most notorious liar in the country." King never asked for an apology. Hoover never offered one.

When King and his group left Hoover's office, after shaking hands all around, it was the end of their public feud, except for one brief flareup. But there was still distrust on both sides, and Hoover by no means became an admirer of Martin Luther King.

In fact, what little trust Hoover had been able to build in King was soon scuttled—but by no fault of the director's. Shortly after our meeting, Coretta King received a package meant for her husband. It was a tape-recording of King's sexual activities in the Willard Hotel in Washington. When King heard the voices, he correctly concluded that it was an FBI tape. Along with the tape was an abusive and anonymous message. In his autobiography, Ralph Abernathy reports their almost automatic reaction:

> He ran the tape forward while the squeaky voices chattered in high speed. Then there were other sounds and he slowed the tape down. Clearly what we were hearing were whispers and sighs from a bedroom. After a minute of this, Martin suddenly reached over and punched the stop button.
>
> "That's enough. It just goes on like that," he said quietly. We sat in silence for a moment, staring at each other.
>
> "J. Edgar Hoover," I said.
>
> "It can't be anyone else," he said.

In fact, as Abernathy later acknowledged in his book, it was someone else. As we ourselves later determined, it was Assistant Director William C. Sullivan, at that point riding dangerously high on his ego. Yet both Abernathy and King quickly, almost instinctively, blamed Hoover, who would have been horrified at what Sullivan had done. Clearly neither King nor Abernathy had learned anything from their interview with the director. Such a move was not his style. He was no coward. Had he taken a notion to confront King with his immoral conduct, he would have done so at the meeting in his office. The person who had sent King the tape and the note clearly had the sensibilities of a bushwhacker.

On the other hand, Hoover was just as disgusted as Sullivan with King's private life. In January 1964, I recall seeing one of Hoover's typical "blue-ink" comments on a memo concerning King's adulterous behavior. He called King a "tom cat" who was possessed by "degenerate sexual urges."

(Sullivan once brought one of the tapes to my office and started to play it for me. I listened for a minute or so, then told him to turn it off. The dialogue was sickening. No decent human being could have enjoyed eavesdropping on such conversations. I was happy to see the tapes sealed by a federal court. As published leaks have already indicated, they contain nothing of political or social significance—no smoking gun, no significant self-revelations. Just raw and vulgar sex talk.)

Our surveillance of King began in 1962, when Hoover sent a letter to Attorney General Robert Kennedy to inform him that one of King's closest advisors was Stanley D. Levison, an alleged member of the Communist party, USA. Reliable sources had confirmed that Levison had written a speech King had delivered to the AFL-CIO convention in Miami a month earlier. We also had evidence that Levison had advised King on such matters as organization, administrative procedures, political strategy, tax matters, and speeches. Levison had prepared press statements for King to give to the news media concerning such controversial issues as race riots and the Vietnam War. He even helped King raise money by arranging musical concerts for the benefit of the SCLC.

We learned about Levison's influence on King from very reliable informants—two brothers who were key figures in the National Committee of the Communist party. These brothers, Morris and Jack Childs, were ostensibly communists who had joined the American Communist party and moved up the ladder of its hierarchy, rung by rung, over a twenty-eight-year period. In fact, the Childs brothers, both trained in Russia by the Soviets, were double agents working for the United States government. In the eyes of the Soviets they were so trustworthy that they became the conduit for secret funds (more than a million dollars annually) funneled to the American branch of the party from its big brother in Moscow. Every year a Childs brother would travel abroad, pick up the cash, and smuggle it back into the United States. Needless to say, neither one was ever caught by U.S. customs, so their credibility with the Soviets increased as the years rolled by.

We nevertheless used the information they passed along with great discretion. We knew about virtually every high-level initiative the communists launched, but we made certain that our words and actions never revealed the true measure of that knowledge, since, as a rule, it was more important to have reliable informants in the top echelons of the party than to take action on the specific intelligence we received.

The case of Stanley Levison was an exception to that rule. Jack

Childs knew Levison as a member of the Communist party just prior to the time that King launched his civil rights campaign with the Montgomery bus boycott. We knew that Levison had become friendly with King and that he probably did so on direct orders from the party. We were convinced that he wanted to exploit King and his organization in order to create civil disorder and political chaos. We were even concerned that the Communist party might ultimately capture the movement.

This concern was grounded in more than a paranoid delusion that there were communists behind every social upheaval. We knew better than that. But we also knew from the Childs brothers that Levison had hired one Jack O'Dell, a man with a long record of Communist party ties, to work in the high-profile New York office of the Southern Christian Leadership Conference, where he remained for two crucial years, playing a key role in the policy decisions and public statements of the organization.

Anyone who wonders why the FBI tapped Martin Luther King's telephone need look no further than the presence of Stanley Levison and Jack O'Dell among King's inner circle. We wanted to know if two men with communist ties were running the operation or if King himself was still in charge. Why, we asked ourselves, would King allow Levison to dictate strategy and write virtually all major policy statements? And why would he assign a man of O'Dell's shady character to a key position on his staff when he was in contact with black people of greater skill and stature who were eager to help?

The Justice Department repeatedly warned King that he was dealing with known communists, and on June 22, 1963, President Kennedy personally took King into the Rose Garden and advised him to break off the relationships, but King stubbornly refused to do so. At that point, having learned from the Justice Department that King had been warned by President Kennedy, we tapped King's phone and bugged his hotel rooms.

For the room bugs our authority was a standing order from an earlier attorney general (and later from a second) that allowed us to use such devices in national security cases.

As for the phone taps, Bobby Kennedy authorized them without hesitation. Assistant Attorney General Burke Marshall of the Civil Rights Division, who had established close relationships with King and Abernathy during the early 1960s, would later say that Bobby approved of the taps because "there didn't seem to be any course of action left."

The wisdom and ethical propriety of that decision are still being debated today. I would argue that both Bobby and the FBI acted properly, given the circumstances at the time. King's followers numbered in the millions; and, from our perspective, his behavior was increasingly disturbing. We had no choice but to investigate the close association of such a potentially powerful organization with people who embraced an ideology dedicated to the overthrow of the American government. The bureau would have been derelict in its investigative responsibilities had it failed to determine who, if anyone, was behind King's phenomenal rise as a black leader. Black supporters as well as white deserved to know whether King was in control of his own movement, part of a larger and more sinister movement, or a "useful idiot."

Actually, if the press had been doing its job, our surveillance might have been unnecessary. But few publications questioned what was going on in the back room of the civil rights movement. Nor were the watchdogs of Congress growling, much less barking. Everyone seemed awed by Dr. King's reputation. Most publications accepted without question King's commitment to peaceful solutions for social problems. If they had studied his writings and his training techniques, they might have been more inclined to doubt his professed motives. Peace is what he got in Albany from Laurie Pritchett, and peace meant boredom and inertia. What Dr. King wanted was what he got in Birmingham and Selma—confrontations, injuries, and deaths.

To further his cause, he had to provoke whites to violence, to taunt and defy local law enforcement officials until they lost their heads. Commissioner "Bull" Connor of Birmingham and Sheriff Jim Clark of Dallas County, Alabama, were the people who gave King what he really sought. Without them (and the Ku Klux Klan in both Alabama and Mississippi) his strategy might well have faltered, and at that point the forces of law and reason would have

216 • HOOVER'S FBI

been called in to effect the will of the Supreme Court and the American people, which was soundly against segregation.

As the civil rights movement developed, the question we kept asking was "Is his main goal the achievement of equality under the law or the continued disruption of American society?" So we were particularly interested to see what King would do after the stated goals of the original civil rights movement had been achieved—when all legal barriers hindering blacks from participating in society had been struck down. We found out after the 1965 Voting Rights Act, when King and his organization moved into Chicago with the announced purpose of correcting economic inequities. No longer was he confronting legal discrimination on the basis of race. He was demanding that Chicago housing patterns, based largely on historical custom and the relative income of homeowners, be changed by law.

His tactics included marches into white ethnic neighborhoods, where violence was a certainty. Mayor Richard Daley was fearful that there would be injuries or even lives lost and that the bloody spectacle would end up on CBS Evening News. When King learned that the greatest bloodshed would be provoked in Cicero, he announced he intended to march into Cicero.

In 1967, King moved even farther away from his original agenda by injecting himself into the controversy over the Vietnam War. On April 4 of that year, in a speech at New York's Riverside Church, he praised the Vietcong leadership; called the United States "the greatest purveyor of violence in the world today—my own government"; charged that America had betrayed the Vietnamese people "both north and south"; and maintained that our troops had "caused a million civilian casualties in Vietnam." He urged young Americans to avoid the war and become conscientious objectors.

At this point, the White House boiled over. The war had become President Johnson's *bête noire*; and although the administration's civil rights legislation and "Great Society" programs had been the answer to every liberal's Christmas list, the war continued to cause troubles for the president within his own party. Now Martin Luther King had turned up the heat, using his considerable moral authority to urge increased civil disobedience. As one White House aide

To Cartha D. De Loach
With warm personal regards
J. Edgar Hoover
4.29.66

In my view this is the most authentic portrait of
Hoover ever done, far more true to the man than
most photographs. But Hoover, preferring a more
formal, aloof image, disliked the sketch, so he
gave it to me!

The day I was made an Inspector in the FBI.

One of the most satisfying experiences an FBI agent can have—arresting a Top Ten Fugitive, in this case Perlie Miller in New Hampshire. I am on the right.

Working on an extortion case in Charlotte, NC. I am on the left.

Hoover was gruff and distant in most of our professional dealings, but always warm to my family.

Two old war-heroes page through the memories.

As far as Hoover was concerned one of the most important assignments of my career was to persuade LBJ to waive the 70 year mandatory retirement age Civil Service requirement so Hoover could stay on the job. Here LBJ officially presents Hoover (and several Congressmen) with the waiver, which meant I would never be Director. I am on the upper right.

One of many lunches with LBJ. Clockwise from bottom center: LBJ, Ramsey Clark, Thurgood Marshall, Fred Vinson, Jr., Clyde Tolson, me, Walter Yeagley, and J. Edgar Hoover.

One of my regular early morning briefings of LBJ in the oval
office of White House.

(below) With Vice President
Hubert H. Humphrey at a
banquet at the former
Shoreham Hotel.

(above) American Legion Convention in Las
Vegas with J. Edgar Hoover. His well-timed
entry caused spontaneous applause and interrupted the speech of then Secretary of State,
William P. Rogers.

With Attorney General Ramsey Clark, the "Bull Butterfly."

Here I am using the widely acclaimed "FBI" television series to ask the nation's help in pursuing a Top Ten Fugitive.

"I'm sorry, Dede - no matter what blandishments you use, I simply will not run for a third term!" Affectionately

With Efrem Zimbalist, Jr., star of "The FBI."

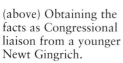

(above) Obtaining the facts as Congressional liaison from a younger Newt Gingrich.

(right) With commentator Paul Harvey and former Supreme Court Justice and Secretary of State Jimmy Byrnes.

Hoover hated reknowned investigative columnist Jack Anderson, but we were always friends.

AUSTIN, TEXAS

Feelings of friendship and gratitude, of admiration and pride are all a part of bidding farewell to Deke DeLoach.

His competence and dedication have made him one of the finest public servants I have ever known... and the strength of his character and principles one of the finest men.

Deke's friends are wishing him the best this evening. I know how well he deserves it. May the years ahead bring him every happiness.

Sincerely,

Mr. Milton Kronheim
2900 V Street, N.W.
Washington, D. C. 20018

July 8, 1970

I'll always be proud of this letter sent by LBJ to Milton Kronheim ("Mr. Washington") on the occasion of a testimonial dinner Kronheim threw for my retirement from the FBI.

told me bluntly: "The president was tear-ass when he read King's remarks."

The White House staff was not alone in resenting the speech. The liberal *Washington Post* was also angry. In a featured editorial, the *Post* said King's speech "was filled with bitter and damaging allegations and inferences that he did not, and could not, document.... He has no doubts that we have no honorable intentions in Vietnam and thinks it will become clear that our 'minimal expectation is to occupy it as an American colony.' He has conjured up an American napalm war in Peru so that he could denounce it.... Many who have listened to him with respect will never again accord him the same confidence. He has diminished his usefulness to his cause, his country, and to his people. And that is a great tragedy."

Carl Rowan, the black columnist and former director of the U.S. Information Agency, was also critical: "King delivered a one-sided broadside about a matter on which he obviously has an abundance of indignation and a shortage of information." And he added pointedly, "Key members of the House and Senate have been told by the FBI that King is listening most to one man [Levison] who is clearly more interested in embarrassing the United States than in the plight of either the Negro or the war-weary people of Vietnam."

Meanwhile, King was plunging ahead with his antiwar activities. He joined with the Spring Mobilization Committee (SMC) to end the war. The SMC had organized a "Call to Vietnam Week," to be highlighted by a big parade in New York on April 15, 1967, with protests staged simultaneously in other major cities. The "Week" had been planned in December 1966 at a conference of SMC delegates. The FBI learned from its sources that a number of communist groups participated in that planning session, among them the Communist party, USA and the Socialist Workers party.

Martin Luther King had granted one of his SCLC aides, the Rev. James Bevel, a leave of absence to serve as national director of SMC. For this reason, it did not surprise us to learn that King was to be one of the parade's Grand Marshals and to lead the huge broil of people, many of them dedicated revolutionaries.

As mid-April approached, antiwar demonstrators surged into New

York City from all parts of the country, and on the day of the demonstrations around 100,000 people amassed at the rallying point in Central Park. Draft-dodgers tore up their draft cards. One group set fire to an American flag, while onlookers cheered. Nearby, flying high and free against the backdrop of New York's skyscrapers, flew the flags of the Vietcong. No one made a move to burn or deface them. At the beginning of the parade, Dr. King stepped out to cheers and took his place at the head of the line and led the group of demonstrators into downtown Manhattan. The event received massive media coverage as a consequence of his participation.

In retrospect, this event seems to blend easily into the receding landscape of the Vietnam era, a time when America went slightly crazy. But at the time, the event was profoundly shocking, even to many people of the Left. For one thing, it was probably the first time in history that a large group of people had publicly declared their support for the enemies of their own government during a shooting war. Had such a parade taken place in 1942—and even then a minority of Americans opposed U.S. entrance into World War II—its leaders would probably have been imprisoned, had they not been first torn to pieces by angry bystanders.

Nine months after the New York parade, Dr. King gave a speech commemorating the centennial of W. E. B. DuBois. While praising DuBois, he again attacked the United States as the chief instigator of the world's ills. It was perhaps an appropriate occasion for such an attack, given the beliefs of DuBois, who wrote: "I have studied socialism and communism long and carefully in lands where they are practiced and in conversation with adherents, and with wide reading. I now state my conclusion frankly and clearly: I believe in communism."

The FBI had no evidence that Dr. King was himself a member of the Communist party. Judging from his speeches and actions, we tended to believe that he was not a member, since he operated with far less discipline and far less cunning than seasoned communists. But he obviously leaned heavily on both Levison and O'Dell, who, in turn, aimed him and pulled his trigger with apparent ease.

Thus, in late March of 1968, he led a march in Memphis, Tennessee in support of a strike by Local 1733 of the American Federation of State, County, and Municipal Employees, the union of sanitation workers, both black and white, who were demanding the right to negotiate with the city. This time the issue was clearly economic—a typical labor-management dispute. King led a march composed primarily of his black supporters, and some of the marchers went wild. Young blacks smashed windows, fired shots, looted stores, and engaged in pitched battles that left one dead and scores hurt. King was convinced that they were members of a more radical group and called for the march to cease. (It was the whites who were supposed to turn violent.) Even as protestors were being arrested and unchecked mobs were surging through the street, Dr. King fled the scene by climbing into a stranger's car.

When King announced that he would organize a second "nonviolent" march, a U.S. district judge issued a temporary restraining order forbidding King and his followers from marching. King denounced the order, saying it was illegal and unconstitutional, and declared that he would not obey it. He returned to Memphis to lead the protestors in defiance of the very federal judiciary system that had given him such strong legal support in the past.

In an article he wrote for the April issue of *Look* magazine, King warned Americans that if they did not follow the pathway he was recommending, the consequences would be grave: "I think we have come to the point," he wrote, "where there is no longer a choice now between nonviolence and riots. It must be militant massive nonviolence, or riots."

Shortly after he—or Stanley Levison—wrote this veiled threat, King was gunned down in Memphis by a white racist named James Earl Ray. The assassination caused wild and destructive anarchy over a three-day period. Many buildings—residences as well as commercial property—were burned to the ground, most of them black homes and stores serving black patrons. Thousands and thousands of people were arrested—the overwhelming majority of them black. Twenty-eight people were killed, all but two black. Hundreds were injured. Tens of thousands of blacks found themselves homeless. In some localities, the National Guard was called out to protect property and lives. Such was the racial climate at the time Martin Luther King died, his legacy of nonviolence. By then if we didn't question what his motives had been—that is, whether he had deliberately provoked violence—we certainly questioned his wisdom.

10

······················

The Hunt for
James Earl Ray

ON APRIL 23, 1967, two men at the Missouri State Penitentiary picked up a large box, used for hauling dozens of loaves of bread, and loaded it onto a delivery truck bound for the prison farm. Apparently neither man noticed that the box was unusually heavy. The driver of the truck cruised to the gate, eased to a halt, and was approached by a uniformed guard. It was a routine stop. The guard, who knew the truck and the driver, glanced in the back, and waved them on.

Inside the box, balled up, red-faced, holding his breath until the truck began to move again, was a thirty-nine-year-old convict who had already attempted two escapes over a seven-year period and had failed. As the truck gained speed and rounded a bend, he began to breathe again. He was outside the walls of the prison, but he knew he still had a long way to go.

He scrambled out of the box, hoping that no car or truck was trailing him. Again he was lucky. One more bit of luck and he'd be free. Calculating the right moment, the right place, he leaped off the back of the truck. The driver didn't see him through the rear-view mirror. He'd made it. This time he was on his way. And it would cost Martin Luther King Jr. his life.

At FBI headquarters in Washington, April 4, 1968, it had been one hell of a day. Hoover had come to work in a sour mood and immediately begun scrawling blue-ink notes in the margin of every memo I sent him. When I went into his office, he started growling.

"Do you know what the Bull Butterfly's done now?" The "Bull Butterfly" was his name for Ramsey Clark, attorney general of the United States under Lyndon Johnson. It was Hoover's contemptuous equivalent of the phrase "paper tiger."

I said I didn't, and he proceeded to tell me. Hoover believed the Bull Butterfly had encouraged the Civil Rights Division of the Justice Department to use the FBI for an investigation that was nothing more than political grandstanding. And in part he blamed me. The Bull Butterfly was my responsibility.

Clark was awed by Hoover, who treated him like a small child—someone who should be neither seen nor heard. I was easier to get along with. Consequently, when Clark wanted to communicate with the bureau, he usually came to me.

That would have been fine with Hoover had it been his idea. He really didn't want to mess with either the attorney general or the president. On the other hand, neither did he want a subordinate—no matter how loyal or capable—to be singled out as the official conduit for the FBI.

So that day, in dealing with communications from the Bull Butterfly, he was scrawling such messages as: "DeLoach should handle, the AG wants to talk to him anyway." Or, "DeLoach should take up with the White House." (By that time I was liaison for the White House as well.) Hoover was at war with Clark, and I was in the line of fire. By day's end, the pressure gauge was registering in the red.

I was relieved when, sometime after five, I got the usual call from the director's telephone office.

"The director's just left the building."

The "all-clear" had sounded. I planned to go home early for a change; so I waited fifteen minutes, grabbed my coat, and hit the door.

Driving home in slow, heavy traffic, I was thinking of a relaxing drink and dinner. But when I got there, the household was in chaos. Barbara was about to leave for a church meeting. Daughter Theresa had a cold and fever. The other children were hungry, with no dinner in sight.

"Why don't you fix hamburgers?" said Barbara, as she gave me a quick kiss and disappeared into the bedroom to get ready.

I took off my jacket, rolled up my sleeves, found a package of hamburger meat in the refrigerator, and carried it over to the sink. I'd just ripped off the cellophane and plunged my hand wrist-deep in ground round when the telephone rang.

"It's your office, Daddy," nine-year-old Sharon announced.

"My God," I said, "I just got home."

I washed my hands and took the receiver.

It was Bob Jensen, special agent in charge (SAC) of the Memphis office. His call had been routed through our Washington switchboard. From the moment he began to talk—in a quiet, overly controlled voice—I knew something terrible had occurred.

"Deke," he said, "at approximately 7:00 P.M., our time, Dr. Martin Luther King walked out of his room at the Lorraine Motel, 406 Mulberry Street. Several aides and friends were with him. A single shot, believed to have been fired from some distance away, ripped into Dr. King's face. An ambulance took him to St. Joseph's Hospital. The bullet entered his right cheek, near the corner of his mouth, and apparently passed through his spinal column."

For a moment I was stunned. I knew King had excited a lot of adulation and a lot of animosity, but it had never occurred to me that someone would shoot him. Particularly since he was no longer in the limelight.

"Tell the Memphis police we'll do everything we can to help— run down leads, give them data on fingerprints, criminal records, ballistics—whatever they need."

"Anything else?"

"Yes, keep me constantly updated on developments. I'm going to switch you back to headquarters so you can talk to Al Rosen."

He said goodby, and I hung up the phone with a sinking heart. The repercussions would be enormous.

Barbara came through the kitchen, on her way out to the garage. "What was that all about?" she asked.

Suddenly very tired, I said, "Some idiot shot Martin Luther King."

"Oh, no!" she gasped, then shook her head. "Promise me you'll eat something before you go back to the office."

At that point, food was the last thing on my mind. I was worried about protests, riots—in Chicago, Detroit, Los Angeles, Washington, in all the major cities. I picked up the phone and dialed Hoover's private line. When he answered, I gave him the bare facts. He listened carefully.

"Offer them whatever help they need."

I told him Jensen was doing that right now.

"One more thing," he said. "Do not accept responsibility for the investigation, this is a local matter. Under the jurisdiction of the local and state police—not the FBI."

Then he sighed.

"I guess you'd better advise the Bull Butterfly."

In addition to my regular phone, up in my bedroom, I had a hotline to the White House, installed by order of President Johnson. I thought this was an occasion to use it. The White House operator located the attorney general almost immediately.

"Yes, I know," Clark said. "I heard it on the radio. And I think the FBI should investigate. Get as many facts as you can. I'll call the president."

I knew better than to protest. But now I was in the line of fire again. I called the director back.

"Clark says he wants us to take over the case."

"He would," Hoover grumbled. There was a long silence on his end of the line.

"O.K. Go ahead. You assume charge." He hung up!

My other phone rang. It was Jensen.

"King's dead," he said. "About a block away, a white male abandoned a rifle and a bag containing some personal effects and fled the area. This happened immediately after the shooting. It looks like the shot came from a rooming house that overlooks the Lorraine Motel, where King was staying. The address is 422$^{1}/_{2}$ South Main Street."

I was taking notes.

"Who has the physical evidence?" I asked.

"We're making arrangements to fly it to Washington right now," said Jensen.

"Good, because the AG wants us to take over the case."

Jensen was silent for a moment. I knew he was considering everything that such a responsibility involved. He would immediately be in the national spotlight, with reporters and photographers snapping at his heels and telephone calls coming in from all over the country. Of more concern to him, perhaps, was the fact that until the case was resolved, he would be the point man for the bureau, the guy with a thousand opportunities to screw up. It couldn't have been a comforting thought.

"O.K." he said.

"As you well know," I told him, "this has to be solved as soon as possible, so we need a full-court press—all your people on the job till they drop."

I called both the director and the AG to report the conversation.

"The president wants both of us to fly to Memphis tomorrow," Clark said. "We'll be using a White House jet."

I thought of the Old Man and wondered what he'd think of this arrangement. I was still in the crossfire.

"Why don't you call the director and brief him?" I said.

Clark agreed, though I had the impression he didn't relish making the call. In three or four minutes, my phone jangled angrily.

"Don't let the Bull Butterfly make a sideshow out of you and turn this investigation into a political circus," Hoover barked. "You make it clear this is the FBI's case."

At that point I was talking on my regular line, but as I hung up, the phone in my bedroom rang again. This time it wasn't Clark but President Johnson, ready to stage the event himself.

"Deke, it will be better if you and Ramsey fly together. You should say that you're down there primarily to kick off the federal investigation. Try to be with Ramsey at any press conference to give him support."

I assured him I would do just that, trying not to think about what Hoover had just told me.

"Do your best," the president said, and hung up.

I took a few more calls, then decided to drive back to the office on the premise that on-the-scene management was preferable to staying at home and attempting to supervise operations by telephone. The office was already bustling, with agents manning telephones and staff members shuttling files from one office to another. I was glad to see Al Rosen, assistant director of our Investigative Division, who moved hurriedly down the hallway, gave me a quick nod, and shook his head. I knew how he felt.

I got an update from Jensen. The rifle and bag would be on a midnight plane out of Memphis. Thus far no suspect was in custody. Agents had interviewed several people at the rooming house where the sniper probably fired the shot. I passed this word along to Hoover.

Later a man came into my office with a sheet of paper in hand and identified himself as an aide to the assistant attorney general in charge of the Civil Rights Division of the Justice Department. He handed me the sheet, a department memorandum.

"Here's the official request to conduct a full investigation of the King assassination. We're treating it as a possible violation of Title 18, Section 241 of the U.S. Code."

It was what I expected. This statute "prohibits conspiracies to injure, oppress, threaten or intimidate any citizen in the free exercise or enjoyment of any right or privilege secured to him or her by the Constitution or laws of the United States." Clark had cast a wide net to bring King's murder under Justice Department control. Our legal ground might be challenged, but the decision was sound.

I initialed the memorandum and sent it along to Rosen, with a scribbled note: "We've got to solve this one fast, Al. As you can see, our jurisdiction, as set forth in this memo, will barely pass muster. But it's the only cover the department can use to get the full resources and manpower of the FBI into the case. Push it!"

When I called Hoover, he agreed. He was as anxious as anyone to find King's killer, even though he disapproved of the man and had quarreled publicly with him.

I kept in constant communication with Jensen throughout the evening, but also spoke to others. First I called Ivan Conrad, the ever-patient scientist in charge of the FBI laboratory, and told him, "Bring in all your people and keep them on standby. When this evidence arrives, we'll need lab analyses immediately."

"Do you know exactly when it's coming?"

"Jensen says he's gotten everything from the local police. An agent will be boarding a plane around midnight. That's after 1:00 A.M. our time. He should arrive here around 5:00 A.M."

"We'll be standing by," said Conrad.

I called Les Trotter in the Identification Section.

"We'll have everything shortly after 5:00 A.M. Be sure technicians are available to do fingerprint examinations."

"They're ready right now," he said.

At 1:05 A.M. Jensen called again.

"We can now confirm that the shot was fired from a second-story window of the Main Street rooming house."

"How far away from King was the sniper?" I asked.

"Slightly more than two hundred feet. And a guy named 'John Willard' rented a room only yesterday afternoon. He's now missing."

I immediately told the agent supervisors to run a search on John Willard in our files and central index. "There'll probably be more than one. It's a common name. It may also be an alias, but do what you can."

With the evidence Jensen was sending, it appeared as if we had a strong case in the making. What we didn't have was "John Willard," and I knew that a manhunt could last for months, even years. I put the thought out of my mind.

The next time I talked to Jensen, I asked him to keep me posted on any information regarding the suspect—up until the time the AG and I boarded the plane, which was now scheduled to leave from Andrews Air Force Base at 7:00 A.M.

Clark called for the latest information, and then Hoover.

"Be careful what you tell the Bull Butterfly," the Old Man said. "He'll blab everything to the press and disrupt the investigation."

"Yes sir," I said, wobbling on the tightrope.

Shortly before 5:00 A.M., a bureau supervisor called to report that a "John Willard" had been arrested on a fugitive warrant in April 1958 by the Memphis Police Department. Following that arrest, he was released to Mississippi authorities, since he'd received a sentence of three-years probation in the town of Pono-toc. His crime—arson.

It sounded promising. "Pass it along to the SACs in Memphis and Jackson," I told him.

At 6:45 A.M., I drove through the gate at Andrews Air Force Base and up to the large hangar that houses presidential jets. The plane was already out and on the runway. Ramsey Clark and two of his staff were there. One, a young black named Mark Wilkins, winked at me. We had met before. Clark would later whisper to me that Wilkins was coming "to help diffuse the situation in Memphis," as if some explanation were needed. I told him I knew Wilkins, that he was a bright young man and a good choice.

We landed in Memphis at 7:45 local time and were met by Bob Jensen. He'd been told not to bring the press along, so he was there alone, except for an agent who would drive us. As we sped across town, he gave us an update. Nothing had really changed since our last conversation. Still no John Willard.

At Jensen's suggestion, we stopped in at the local FBI office for a brief visit, moved on to the U.S. attorney's office, and then to the office of Frank Holloman, Memphis commissioner of safety and formerly a top-flight FBI agent. These visits were more symbolic than functional, a gesture to show everyone involved in the investigation that the full power of the federal government was at their disposal, including the attorney general of the United States.

After we'd made the rounds, we returned to a large room in a federal suite of a downtown building, and only then did Jensen call in the press. I was surprised at the number of journalists there—reporters, photographers, camera crews from all over the world, crammed into a room much too small to contain them comfortably.

Clark led off, telling the assembled group that the president was shocked and saddened by Dr. King's assassination, that all the resources of the Justice Department and FBI were now focused on the search for the killer. He introduced me and his staff members, then began to field questions.

We soon realized that some of the people waving their arms for recognition were not press members but black militants, the very people who had been attacking King's nonviolent strategy in Memphis only a couple of days earlier. They began to interrupt both the legitimate press and those of us responding—making accusatory speeches, demanding swift and decisive action by the administration and the FBI, implying that we might deliberately drag our heels. That the attorney general and a high-ranking official of the FBI were already in Memphis did little to assuage their anger.

We kept our tempers until the press conference ended, then, walking away from the meeting down a long corridor, Clark exploded.

"A lot of phonies out there! They had no right to be in on a press conference. They'll just make things worse."

That was the understatement of the decade. This band of Black Power advocates had been growing in numbers and influence—and at the expense of Martin Luther King and the Southern Christian Leadership Conference. They had denounced King as a coward and an Uncle Tom. Now that he'd been murdered, they intended to exploit his death to further their own cause—the violent disruption of American society. Before midnight, sections of several of the nation's major cities would be in flames.

It was late afternoon when we arrived at the Memphis airport. There we saw a grim scene. Several of King's supporters were carrying his casket onto an airplane for the return flight to Atlanta. Clark sent one of his staff members to find out who was aboard. He came back to say that Mrs. King was in the plane, along with family friends. Clark turned to me.

"Deke, I think I'll go aboard and pay my respects to Mrs. King. Do you want to come?"

I thought about it a moment, then shook my head.

"In view of Mr. Hoover's longtime feud with her husband, I think she might resent my coming."

He nodded, then walked over and boarded the plane. Andrew Young was standing on the cement runway nearby, and since we had met, I walked over and expressed my sympathies. He was courteous and thanked me.

"We'll do everything we can," I said. "I'm sure we'll get him."

Young nodded without conviction. He seemed to have been numbed by the shock of King's death. He was articulate and friendly, but I felt he was somewhere else.

After only a minute or two, Clark emerged from the King plane, and we reboarded our own aircraft. Just before we climbed aboard, Jensen gave us some disturbing news, relayed from his office. Blacks were starting fires and looting stores in Washington.

Once airborne, the twinkling lights of Memphis disappeared quickly in the gathering darkness behind us. On the flight back we were silent and thoughtful. Most of us had been awake for thirty-six hours, but no one could sleep. Twice we got reports from the cockpit. The public affairs office called to say that our national press coverage had been excellent. News reporters saw the attorney general on the scene promptly and interpreted his response as an indication that the White House was deeply concerned. In addition, commentators viewed my presence as evidence that the FBI was conducting an aggressive investigation.

We were encouraged until we approached Washington. What we saw stunned us. A smoky haze hung low over the city, despite unlimited visibility in every other direction. From several miles out we could see leaping flames. The sight reminded me of an old print I'd seen, a view of the capital during the War of 1812, when the British had sacked and burned the city.

Clark went up front and asked the pilot to fly as low as was permissible so we could assess the extent of the damage. What Jensen had reported hardly prepared us for the destruction below. It looked as if whole neighborhoods were aflame.

Driving home from Andrews Air Force Base, my head began to throb—in part because I'd gone so long without sleep, in part because I was beginning to feel the full pressure of the King investigation. It was difficult to sort out all the problems, but three things were clear: (1) this crime was probably committed by a crazy bigot, (2) the black community was in a state of frenzy, and (3) we would never be able to find the killer fast enough to dam the flood of criticism and abuse that was coming our way, much of which would be a direct consequence of the Hoover-King feud.

The next morning as I drove into work—listening to radio

reports of rioting, burning, and looting in cities like Chicago and Los Angeles—I considered assigning a special inspector to the case. Bob Jensen was a capable and experienced SAC, but few FBI officials had ever been called on to supervise an investigation so potentially explosive. I finally decided to stick with Jensen. An agent familiar with the area who had worked closely with Memphis agents could do a more effective job of coordinating the investigation and save us priceless time. If any serious problems arose, we could always dispatch a special force later.

Al Rosen and I got together as soon as I came into the office. We looked over the information we'd gathered thus far to see what we could make of it. We knew that in a major case it is always imperative to interview potential witnesses as soon as possible, before details fade from memory. In this case, the eye witness accounts of the suspect were better than we sometimes got, though there were inconsistencies.

The agents who interviewed the manager of the rooming house had reported that he had rented Room B-5 to a white male who had arrived between 3:00 and 3:30 on the afternoon of April 4 and had paid one week's rent in advance—$8.50.

The man hadn't been required to sign a register. (This was not the Ritz Carleton or even the Ramada Inn.) He gave his name as "John Willard." A female resident whom agents questioned saw the man only once, but she gave us a description—thirty-five years old, five feet eleven inches, medium build, neat in appearance. Two roomers reported that they saw a man fitting that description dash from the rooming house moments after the fatal shot had been fired.

One of the witnesses heard a sound "similar to a gunshot" and, when he opened his door to look out, saw a man "about six feet tall, in his thirties," running down the hall toward the stairs leading to South Main Street. Under his arm, the man carried a long object, wrapped in a blanket.

The second tenant said he caught a glimpse of "Willard" as the resident manager was showing him to Room B-5. This tenant described the suspect as "about five feet ten or eleven inches tall, about 165 pounds, and in his early thirties." The witness had been repairing a radio in the kitchen when he heard "a sound like a gunshot" come from the common bathroom shared by all the tenants on that floor. The witness opened the door, looked out, and saw a man running down the hallway toward the stairway leading to South Main Street. "He was carrying a long bundle," said the witness, who identified the fleeing man as the same person he had seen entering Room B-5 with the manager about three hours earlier.

As the suspect fled from the rooming house, he passed a nearby junk shop. A juke box was blaring, and two customers were looking through old 78 phonograph records near the front of the store. It was a couple of minutes after six. The two customers and the shop owner heard a "plop" on the sidewalk next to the front door, just as a man ran by. One of the customers was facing the street and saw a bundle near the shop's entrance. He also saw a man dashing down South Main Street. A moment later, this same customer heard the sound of tires screeching and immediately spotted a white Mustang tearing north on South Main. The customer caught only a glimpse of the runner, but described him as a white male, maybe thirty, about five feet, eight inches, and weighing around 165 pounds. According to this witness, the suspect had dark hair, an average build, and a neat, clean appearance.

The second customer who looked up after hearing the "plop" also saw a white man running rapidly down South Main past the shop. Within moments, this customer saw a white Mustang speeding north past the store. His description of the suspect: five feet eight inches tall, and weighing about 160 pounds.

The proprietor saw essentially the same thing—a white man running south past the store window. When the proprietor stepped outside to find out what was going on, he saw a white car, "possibly a compact," pulling rapidly away from the curb just south of his store. He described the man he'd seen on foot as twenty-five to thirty years of age, "or possibly older," with dark hair, neat and clean. He was between five feet, ten inches tall, and weighed 175 pounds or more.

Rosen and I talked over these narratives, given shortly after the event by people who had been on the scene. Despite the usual inconsistencies, we had a pretty complete account of what the suspect had done from the moment he pulled the trigger until the moment he'd made his getaway. We also had a fairly good description of the man. As a consequence, we could begin to form a tentative picture of "John Willard."

"It's not the John Willard we have on file."

"No. Too young."

"A racist. Maybe a member of a hate group."

"Well groomed, yet somebody who would feel at home in a flop house."

"Not too bright. Obviously hadn't planned the crime very well."

"No conspiracy here. He did it alone. No evidence he had help, either in planning or execution." If he'd had help, his escape plan would have been better and left fewer witnesses.

We considered whether to prepare a portrait parle (a facial likeness based on a description by an eyewitness) but decided to hold off for one day and see what the investigation turned up. Additional evidence might produce something better than an artist's portrait.

Of course, we turned all information over to the attorney general, so he would know where the investigation stood at every stage. By midafternoon we found he'd been leaking everything we gave him to the press—just as Hoover had predicted. The switchboards were swamped with calls from well-meaning citizens who had just spotted the Mustang, which no one should have known about, on the road leading out of Canton, Ohio, or Rosebud, Texas, or Two Egg, Florida. Back in his office, the director was spouting flame like a volcano—every third sentence condemning the Bull Butterfly. I didn't blame him. I was prepared to shove the next report down Clark's throat, since we had to check out every "sighting" of the Mustang.

In record time, our laboratory analyzed the contents of the bundle the suspect had abandoned. The Memphis police had found the following objects:

1. A brown and green herringbone-patterned bed-spread wrapped around a cardboard box that had originally contained a Browning Mauser rifle, a 30.06 Remington Gamemaster rifle, model 760, on which was mounted a Redfield telescopic sight, and a box containing nine cartridges. In the Gamemaster

rifle were an empty ammunition clip and an empty shell casing.

2. A blue, zippered suitcase, 20" by 30", containing, among other items, a road map of Georgia and Alabama, a road map of the United States, a pocket transistor radio, and a pair of binoculars, together with a sales slip dated April 4, 1968, and a paper bag that traced the purchase to a Memphis store. Among miscellaneous toilet and personal items was a safety razor that bore a price sticker from a store in Whitehaven, Tennessee, a Memphis suburb near the Mississippi border.

The Memphis police had turned over all this evidence to the FBI on the night of April 4. I'd told Bob Jensen to hand-deliver everything to the FBI laboratory that same night. And to bring the bullet that doctors had removed from Dr. King's spine the night he'd been shot. Two days later the Memphis office forwarded a pair of men's undershorts and a T-shirt, both taken from the zippered suitcase. There were laundry marks on the items of clothing, but our efforts to trace them to any Memphis laundry had failed. We were frustrated for the moment.

On April 5, agents went to a store on South Main Street to check on the sales slip for the purchase of the binoculars, which had cost $41.55. We also had the paper bag in which the binoculars had been placed. The salesman looked at the slip.

"Yes, I remember him," he said.

"Can you give us a description of him?"

"White guy. Maybe five feet, eleven inches. Weighed—160–175 pounds."

"Tell us about the binoculars."

"They were in the window on display."

"How did he pay for them? What size bills did he use?"

"Let's see. I think he gave me two twenties and a one. And then the change. Two quarters and a nickel."

Not much there. Next, the agents visited the drugstore in nearby Whitehaven. Again they found a clerk who remembered the purchaser—a woman who sold him a safety razor contained in a plastic container, as well as some aftershave lotion. She described "Willard" as shorter and slightly older than previous witnesses, but the discrepancy was not significant enough to suggest we weren't on the right track. (When we finally caught our man we discovered that her estimate of his age came closer than the others.)

While other agents were checking on purchases, Bob Jensen was also directing a team assigned to track down the white Mustang. This was a particularly important clue, because the witnesses at the junk shop had such a positive impression of the make and color of the automobile. We began to canvass motels in the Memphis area to see if the owner of such a car had registered anywhere in town prior to his appearance at the rooming house. Unless he'd appeared in Memphis on the day he shot King, he had to have stayed somewhere.

It took a while, but we finally hit pay dirt. On April 8, agents stopped in at a motel on Lamar Street and found a registration card for one Eric S. Galt, who had checked in shortly after 7:00 P.M. on April 3 and checked out before 1:00 P.M. on April 4. A motel employee remembered the car.

"It was a white Mustang—with Alabama plates. I saw it in front of the room occupied by Galt."

"Did you see Galt at any time?"

"Not once. It was the previous night. He was probably in bed by then."

No one else had seen "Galt" either. But we did have his registration card, which Jensen's people took and sent to our lab in Washington for analysis.

The fact that "Galt" had been driving a car with Alabama license tags encouraged us to check the Alabama motor vehicle records. On April 8, we discovered that the state of Alabama had issued a license tag to Eric S. Galt for a 1966 Mustang. The records indicated that he'd bought the car from a private seller rather than from a dealer. He'd made the purchase on August 30, 1967.

Alabama agents immediately located the seller and questioned him.

"I placed an ad in the local newspaper," he said. "I offered to let the guy try it himself, but he said his driver's license was out-of-state—in Louisiana. So I drove him around. He said he liked the car, though he wasn't too pleased with the white color. Finally he said he'd take the car, and we agreed to meet at my bank the next day to get a notary and witnesses and to close the deal.

"He showed up with a fistful of money. He had at least $2,000 in bills. Most of them looked like twenties. We signed all the papers, and I gave him the keys. He got in the car and drove off. At the time, I wondered about that business of his Louisiana driver's license and his unwillingness to drive the previous day. It sure didn't stop him after he'd bought the car."

"Did you ever see him again?" an agent asked.

"Not him. But I did see the car parked in front of the rooming house where he said he was living."

Back in Washington I was receiving regular reports from Memphis, our lab people, the Alabama office, and others in the South and elsewhere. Needless to say, I had to absorb all this material and try to make new assignments based on the development of the evidence. But my major problem was having to keep Hoover and Clark advised without angering one or both of them.

Perhaps sensing Hoover's distrust, Clark kept up his pressure on me with constant calls: "Are you sure you're keeping me posted? I have a feeling that Hoover knows more about this investigation than I do. You be sure to keep me as current as he is."

"I'll do it," I said.

And he had a point. He had every right to know. So I found myself sneaking over to Clark's fifth-floor office and providing him with all the up-to-date briefings. I felt disloyal and guilty. I was Hoover's man, and I was grateful for the Old Man's confidence in me. Still, I couldn't hide information from the attorney general of the United States, the man the president had asked me to help. Besides, in the final analysis, I was serving the director as well, since a satisfied Clark meant a more independent Hoover. But the situation troubled me daily.

While we were tracing down all leads in Memphis and Alabama, in

Washington we were concentrating on the 30.06 Remington Gamemaster 760—which we had every reason to believe was the weapon that had ended Dr. King's life. Agents in Memphis quickly determined that the rifle abandoned in the bundle dropped in front of the junk shop had been part of a shipment from a Birmingham wholesaler in the spring of 1966. The wholesaler had in turn sold the rifle to a Memphis gun shop on August 31, 1966—almost two years before the killing of Dr. King.

Armed with this information, agents entered the gun shop the day after the assassination and asked to see the sales records. A clerk looked up the transaction.

"Sold to a man who said his name was Harvey Lowmyer. He paid cash for it on March 30—$248.59. But that's not all he bought."

The agents perked up.

"This same guy had come in here the night before he bought the Remington. That night, he bought a Browning Mauser rifle, let's see, with a Redfield telescopic sight. He also bought a box of ammunition."

"Did he talk? Give any reasons for buying the weapon?"

"He said he was going hunting in Wisconsin. By the way, I have his address. Here—it's on South 11th Street."

The agents wrote down the address, and immediately drove to the spot, hoping to surprise Lowmyer. But when they got there, the tenants in the building said they'd never heard of anyone by that name. It was a false address.

By this time we realized that our chief problem would be to discover the true identity of the killer. He'd already used three names—John Willard, Eric Galt, and Harvey Lowmyer—and chances were we still didn't have his right name.

Memphis agents meanwhile continued to follow up on leads. In examining the registry of the Lamar Avenue motel where Galt had stayed, they noted that he listed as his permanent address 2608 Highland Avenue in Birmingham, Alabama. Two Birmingham agents visited the address and found a huge, sprawling white-clapboard rooming house. Its paint was peeling and it listed to one side. Inside, the accommodations were small and spare and cheap. We began to detect a pattern.

When the agents identified themselves to the manager, he was friendly and cooperative. He immediately located a receipt showing that Eric S. Galt had stayed at the establishment from August 26 through the first week in October 1967.

"Do you know whether he had a job?" one of the agents asked.

"No," said the manager. "As best I could tell he was unemployed."

"Did he give you any indication that he was looking for work or had been employed?"

"He didn't talk to me very much," the manager said, "but I think he said once that he'd recently quit his job in a boatyard in Pascagoula, Mississippi. When he left, he told me he'd accepted a job on a boat down in Mobile."

"Was he broke all the time?" an agent asked.

"Not all the time," the manager said. "He once got a C.O.D. package from a camera company in Chicago. The stuff was expensive—but he had the money to pay for it."

We located the company and found out that the cost of the camera equipment was $337.24—a lot of cash for someone who mostly lived in flop houses. The more we found out about him, the odder he sounded.

For example, our agents discovered by asking his neighbors that Galt had signed an agreement to take lessons at a local dance studio—from 7:30 to 8:30 in the evenings. They questioned some of the dance studio employees and got several responses that gave us additional insights into his personality.

"He loved to dance as much as any guy I've ever seen, but he was a lousy dancer."

"Shy and quiet. A loner."

"That's right. He didn't have much to say, and he wouldn't look you in the eye. I noticed that."

The physical descriptions people gave us were similar to those we'd already received, but we did get some additional details that helped us to round out our picture. He had blue eyes and brown hair. His complexion was medium to pale. We also learned that he didn't smoke.

While agents in the Southeast were tracing Eric Galt's movements from state to state, the FBI's National Crime Information Center (NCIC) was doing the same thing with his automobile. We fed data about his white Mustang into the computer and asked the machine if any criminals or criminal violations had been associated with such a make and model. At first, the computer said no. Then on April 11, I got a call from Inspector Jerry Daunt of the NCIC.

"Deke, guess what the Atlanta police want to know."

"Tell me," I said.

"If we have any information on a white 1966 Mustang with Alabama license tags."

"They have the car?"

"Yes. It was abandoned at an apartment complex on the morning of April 5. Two apartment residents saw a man park the car around 9:00 A.M. He was alone."

"Did they give us a good description?"

"You can guess what they said. White. About five feet ten inches. Weighs about 160 pounds. Neatly dressed."

As soon as we got this report, we launched an intensive search for Galt in the Atlanta area. He might be without transportation now. We knew what kind of accommodations he was used to. We began combing the rooming houses and cheap hotels.

Within hours, Atlanta agents had knocked on the right door—a rooming house for transient long-haired males in the northeastern section of the city. It looked like a flop house for hippies. The manager seemed a little defensive, but he admitted that Galt had been registered there.

"He checked in on April 5. Out on the 9th or 10th."

"Do you remember anything about him?" an agent asked.

"Well, he wanted a single room, but we didn't have any. He settled for a double. He paid for a week in advance, plus a deposit on the key. Two days after he checked in, a single became available, so he paid a little more and moved in there."

"Did he have any luggage?"

"No," said the manager, "he had a box and a paper bag. His clothes were stuffed in the box and bag."

"Do you have any idea where he was going?"

"When he came to turn in his key the morning he left, he told me he'd gotten a phone call from a friend and was going to Michigan to work as a welder."

The manager told the agents he couldn't remember Galt's first name and couldn't find any entry in the desk book. When asked what Galt looked like, he gave a description that fit the composite we'd already developed.

When the agents left the rooming house, they were convinced that the manager knew more than he was telling. The Atlanta SAC called and gave me the report that Sunday evening.

"Put an undercover agent in the rooming house," I told him. "Make sure you pick somebody who can look the part. He's got to be sleazy enough to mingle with the clientele. Tell him to get a room as near to Galt's as possible—just in case Galt comes back. If he does, we'll be the first to greet him."

Hours passed. Then days. Galt didn't return. And a trail that seemed hot turned decidedly cold. Meanwhile, black activists were demanding results, blaming the FBI for dragging its feet, calling for demonstrations.

In this atmosphere, Al Rosen and I held lengthy conversations with Sterling Donahue, the inspector assigned to my office, and with agent supervisors on the case, often working till midnight sifting through the evidence and leads, looking for something we'd missed earlier. By this time we had more than five hundred agents nationwide tied up on this case, and we were sparing no expense.

On a case like this, we didn't worry about money. We knew we had to solve this one, otherwise the public, the press, and—most important of all—J. Edgar Hoover, would be eternally riding our tails. But the commitment of so much manpower was another thing. Other cases were put on hold. Our priorities were turned upside down. And yet, to use a navy saying, our prow was dead in the water. Throughout, Hoover was demanding a progress report by 9:00 A.M. every morning; and he called several times during the day, just to remind us we weren't getting anywhere. Clark was equally persistent.

Meanwhile, our undercover agent at the Atlanta rooming house had discovered that, as suspected, the manager hadn't told us everything. When confronted and reminded of the penalty for withholding criminal information, he began to talk. He remembered the full name of his tenant as "Eric S. Galt" and also that Galt had arrived not on April 5, but on March 24.

He'd next seen Galt on March 31, when the rent came due. He confessed he'd entered Galt's room on the morning of April 5th to change the linen and had found a note saying that Galt had gone to Birmingham and would return in about a week. He insisted that this was the last time he'd heard from the suspect and that he'd confiscated the belongings left behind when the rent expired. These items included a portable TV set, a booklet entitled Your Opportunities in Locksmithing, a collection of maps of Birmingham, Atlanta, Los Angeles, several Southwestern states, and Mexico. (King was known to have visited all these places, except Mexico.)

With the suspect's white Mustang impounded, agents were able to trace service stickers inside the door to a Ford dealer in California. The dealer dug out records indicating that Eric S. Galt—with an apartment address in Los Angeles—had brought the car in for servicing on February 22, 1968. Agents immediately went to the apartment management and determined that Galt had indeed lived there—in a bachelor unit that cost slightly more than $100 a month. He'd been a resident from November 1967 to January 1968. But he'd kept to himself, made no apparent attempts to cultivate friendships, and no one saw him receive any visitors. As far as anyone knew, he was unemployed.

From that apartment house, Galt moved to a cheap hotel on Hollywood Boulevard in Los Angeles, where his rent was $85 a month. When he left the hotel on March 17, he gave his forwarding address as General Delivery, Atlanta, Georgia.

Examining all the reports back in Washington, we began to see a clear picture emerging. All the signs were there: the aliases, the movement from one place of residence to another, the reluctance to

242 • HOOVER'S FBI

make friends, the caution, the restraint. Galt was behaving like an escaped convict trying to avoid detection.

But we knew he had one weakness—he liked to dance. So we checked around the Los Angeles area to see if he'd indulged that weakness. Our efforts were rewarded. He'd also taken dancing lessons at a studio in Long Beach. In fact, on December 14, 1967, he'd signed a contract for twenty-five one-hour private lessons and twenty-five one-hour group sessions. The two courses cost him $499—a lot of money for a man who lived in flea traps.

The studio's records showed that Galt took his first lesson on December 5, and he showed up at the studio two or three times a week until February 12. We asked studio employees what they knew about Galt, and their answers were predictable—never mentioned employment, was a loner, was very evasive in the limited conversation he permitted.

But they did remember a few specific snatches of conversation. He said he'd been to Mexico. He said he liked to travel and talked vaguely of going back to sea as a merchant marine. He also said he'd enrolled in a bartending school on Sunset Boulevard with the thought of opening a restaurant.

On April 15, two Los Angeles agents checked the school Galt had mentioned and found he'd indeed been a student there—from mid-January to mid-March. According to a school official, he'd attended classes six hours a day, from Monday through Friday. In fact, he'd "graduated." After graduation, the school had told him about a job opening for a bartender, but Galt had refused, saying he was leaving town to visit a brother.

The agents wanted to know if the school had by any chance taken a picture of the graduate.

"As a matter of fact," said the official, "we have a color photo on file. Would you like to see it?"

"If you don't mind," said the agents, barely able to conceal their excitement. It was the most useful piece of evidence we'd turned up yet. When I heard about the photograph back in Washington, I was certain for the first time that we would eventually get our man.

We immediately took the photograph to the gun dealer in Memphis. He looked at it for a moment.

"That's Harvey Lowmyer," he said, "the man who bought the rifles.

So Galt and Lowmyer were one and the same man. Our suspicion had been proved. Our net was beginning to close.

On April 17, agents went to the rooming house in Atlanta, sat down at a table with the manager, and showed him photographs of several different people, including "Galt."

"Is one of these Eric Galt's picture?"

The manager reached over and picked up the photograph from the bartender's school.

"If this isn't Galt, it sure looks like him."

That same day the photograph appeared on television screens and the front pages of papers coast to coast. A caption identified "this man as the FBI's prime suspect in the slaying of Martin Luther King Jr."

Our agents learned that Galt had carefully cased the hotel on Hollywood Boulevard before moving in on January 21. In fact, he'd spent enough time in an adjoining bar to become acquainted with one of the waitresses. When questioned by FBI agents, she said that he was a "solemn, quiet-mannered person who usually drank straight vodka and sometimes beer."

The waitress had two cousins in Los Angeles named Charles and Rita. Rita had two children living with relatives in New Orleans; and on December 14, 1967, Eric Galt agreed to drive Charles to New Orleans to pick up Rita's children. They left the following day and arrived in New Orleans on the 17th. Two days later, they began the return trip and arrived in Los Angeles with the children on the 21st. In New Orleans, agents had no difficulty locating the motel where Galt had stayed. The motel's records verified what we'd been told in Los Angeles: he was there from December 17 to December 19. Apparently Galt paid all of the travel expenses.

That he'd spent this sum on the New Orleans trip reinforced another theory we were developing. For a man with no job, he always seemed to have money. He'd been able to buy expensive weapons. He'd ordered expensive camera equipment. And now we knew he'd financed a cross-country trip. From this we concluded that from time to time he'd been committing small robberies to make living expenses.

Our investigation was now moving forward, though a little slower that we would have liked. We had a prime suspect, and we were accumulating a wealth of information about him. Unfortunately, much of this information simply reinforced what we had already learned. But there were two big questions we couldn't as yet answer: (1) Where was Galt? and (2) Was he a professional hit man, a man driven by racial bigotry, or some sort of misguided freak?

On the morning of April 17, the SAC of the Birmingham FBI office went before a U.S. commissioner and signed a federal complaint against Eric Starvo Galt. Later that day, Tennessee authorities issued a warrant in Memphis charging Galt with murder. Both public and private donors raised a total of $100,000 to post as a reward for information leading to the arrest and conviction of the person or persons responsible for the killing of Dr. King.

Meanwhile, the FBI continued to gather further evidence. For example, a tourist sticker on the rear window of the white Mustang indicated that the car had been driven to Mexico in the fall of 1967. With the full cooperation of the Mexican police, we found out that Galt had stayed at a hotel in Puerto Vallarta, Jalisco, from October 19 to November 6, and during the following week had registered at another hotel in the same city. We also discovered that Galt had bought a thirty-day automobile policy in October at Nuevo Laredo, Mexico, a town just across the border from Laredo, Texas.

Several agents were assigned to pursue all possibilities suggested by the booklet Your Opportunities in Locksmithing, which Galt had left behind in the Atlanta rooming house. Since the publication contained the name and address of a locksmith school in New Jersey, we contacted the director and discovered that—sure enough—our suspect had enrolled in a correspondence course the school offered. The address he gave was a new one in our books—an apartment in Montreal, Canada. Al Rosen and I speculated on the meaning of this, wondering if Galt intended to make a living in Canada by picking locks and robbing houses.

With the help of Canadian authorities, we learned that Galt had signed a lease for this apartment, beginning on July 19, 1967. He was paying $75 a month. But for some reason he skipped out on his rent less than two months later and headed south.

Among the evidence we had gathered, three pieces delivered to the FBI lab bore identical fingerprints. Both Rosen and I strongly believed that these prints belonged to Galt. Today, with electronic scanning, the task of checking these prints against our files would be simple and quick. But at that time, researchers had to probe fingerprint cards by hand; and the Identification Division of the FBI had some three million fingerprint cards on file.

But we had to make a move. Public outcry was mounting, and the press was beginning to say we would never catch Dr. King's murderer. I couldn't allow the investigation to founder. So I called in Les Trotter, director of the Identification Division (fingerprints), and told him we needed his help on the Galt case. He groaned—and I sympathized with him, but we needed to follow up on the leads we had.

"Les," I said, " we have pretty good evidence that Eric Galt is an escapee—and if so, he should be on our list. How many federal "Wanted" notices do you currently have in Identification Division files?"

He didn't even have to check.

"About 53,000," he said.

"That's better than three million," I said. "You've got to put your people to work comparing Galt's print with those 53,000 wanted criminals."

"When do you want us to begin?" Les said.

"How about today?" I said.

Our fingerprint experts began the monumental task on April 18 at 4:00 P.M.—two weeks after Dr. King had been killed. Special agents who had previous fingerprint training were ordered in from the Richmond, New York, Baltimore, and Philadelphia offices. The technicians pitched in with a purpose, knowing the FBI was under tremendous pressure and that our major cities were powder kegs.

Trotter called me at 9:15 the next morning. I wasn't sure I wanted to hear what he had to say. But the news was fairly encouraging.

"We're getting there. Give us just a little more time."

I was amazed that they'd moved so quickly, but I still wasn't optimistic. I was about to step into our weekly Executive's Conference, and I didn't really want to tell Clyde Tolson one more time that "We're getting there. Give us just a little more time." He would immediately relay this to Hoover as evidence that we were stymied. As I put the last papers into my folder and moved toward the door, the phone rang again. It was Les Trotter, and I immediately caught the note of triumph in his voice.

"Deke, we've got your man! James Earl Ray! Habitual offender who escaped from the state penitentiary at Jefferson City, Mississippi."

"Are you sure?" I said. "I can't believe you probed that many fingerprints in so little time."

"We did it," Les said, "with a lot of hard work and a little luck."

He went on to tell me that the fingerprint examiner had been attracted immediately to the inked impression made by Ray's left thumb. It matched the three identical prints we'd supplied, the ones found on the murder weapon, Galt's new binoculars, and one of his road maps.

So Galt was James Earl Ray.

After advising the director and the Executive Committee of our discovery, I hurried over to tell Ramsey Clark the good news. Since he was holding a conference in the huge formal office of the attorney general, I went through the back door of the anteroom that led into his smaller office. Before I came, I'd told his secretary that I had crucial information he needed to know immediately, so he slipped out of the conference room and met me.

"Any new developments?" he asked anxiously.

I told him what we'd learned.

"Great!" he said. "That's just great! Congratulations. You've done a first-rate job."

Later that day, Rosen and I pored over incoming data and made calls to ask questions and give follow-up instructions. As we gathered additional information, a clearer picture began to emerge, and we began to take the measure of our man.

He was a typical habitual criminal: poorly educated, without scruples, and dull-witted, but with just a touch of animal cunning. In a few hours, we'd compiled a life's history of little more than failure and bumbling stupidity. From his inability to soldier in the 1940s to a one-day job in the late 1950s, he'd been unemployable—a chronic incompetent who couldn't perform the most basic tasks.

His criminal record reflected the same level of incompetence. He couldn't stay out of jail. He was forever being surprised in the middle of burglaries, fingered by casual acquaintances, and tracked down by small-town law officers. When hauled into court, he never had a defense. Fortunate enough to receive light sentences in the beginning of his career, he kept trying and trying until he managed to draw twenty years for his last offense. In one attempt at escape, the pipe he was climbing broke. In another, he stuffed his bed to appear as if he were asleep and then hid—inside the prison—and was quickly caught.

But he had done two things that distinguished him from all the other losers in all the jails and prisons he'd inhabited—he'd escaped from the Missouri State Penitentiary and he'd shot and killed Martin Luther King Jr. These were actions we couldn't have predicted from the banality of his life and the mediocrity of his career. School dropout, military outcast, hobo, jailbird—he was the most sought-after and talked-about criminal in America, an instant celebrity, a name for the history books. So we looked very carefully at the information we'd compiled, searching for clues that might lead us to this very ordinary criminal who had suddenly become extraordinary.

Low-grade criminal though he was, he had thus far eluded capture and with luck could embarrass the entire federal government. And if he stayed at large for any length of time, he might make a substantial contribution to the greatest civil unrest in American history. Students were already rioting on campuses and destroying buildings. Blacks had been in the streets for two weeks. The nation was teetering on the brink of anarchy. And all because some petty criminal had decided to go big-time.

On April 19, we published and distributed nationwide a "Wanted" flyer containing a photograph and description of James Earl Ray. The following day he was added to the list of the FBI's "Ten Most Wanted Fugitives." From the moment Ray was finally identified, he became the object of a highly intensive investigation involving all FBI field offices. His photograph and description were published by newspapers and magazines and telecast throughout North America.

Because Ray had been missing for more than two weeks, we had to assume that he might have left the country. So in addition to widespread probes throughout the United States, Canada, and Mexico, we extended the search to nations outside North America. These included: England, Germany, Rhodesia, the Netherlands, Guatemala, Venezuela, Jamaica, Japan, New Zealand, Australia, Honduras, Italy, and Bermuda. It was probably the most comprehensive manhunt in the annals of American crime.

On May 14 the Washington field office of the FBI had instituted at the Department of State a review of approximately 2,153,000 passports issued to American citizens during the previous year. At our request, the Royal Canadian Mounted Police were also reviewing Canadian passports during the same period. Again we needed a big break—and again we got one.

RCMP troopers, working around the clock, located a passport for "Ramon George Sneyd," issued in Ottawa on April 24. The photograph on the passport was that of James Earl Ray.

Since the passport had been issued in order to fly to London during a two-week period in May, we immediately contacted our counterparts in Scotland Yard. They quickly determined that "Sneyd" had arrived in London on May 7, 1968, using a Canadian passport. But he'd departed for Lisbon, Portugal, on the same date.

We dispatched two agents to Portugal. But—as we later found out—just as they landed in Lisbon, James Earl Ray was winging his way back to London. He slipped in before anyone spotted him, but at that point we knew that he was hiding somewhere in England, Scotland, or Wales—a smaller area than the United States, but still a haystack in which a needle could disappear for weeks or months or years.

Ray—unaware that the airports were under such close scrutiny and confident that his alias would protect him—decided to travel to South Africa. He took a taxi to Heathrow Airport, checked in at the airline desk, and was in the process of answering the usual questions, when suddenly a nearby customs officer heard a fellow officer repeat the name "Ramon George Sneyd." The officer quickly slid in beside Ray and asked him to step into a small private room to answer a few questions.

When confronted with his true identity, Ray lied, saying he was precisely who his passport said he was. But the British authorities were skeptical and they detained him at the airport. His odyssey was over.

The legal attaché of the American Embassy—an FBI agent in England—raced to Heathrow. There he conferred with British officials, checked Ramon George Sneyd's passport, and looked at the man in custody.

Then he placed a call to me.

Back in Virginia it was Saturday morning. Barbara was at church. The children were getting ready to scatter in all directions. I was cooking pancakes—my Saturday morning specialty. I was about to pour the batter onto a hot griddle when the phone rang.

My son Tom groaned.

"It's got to be your office. And just when you're about to put on the pancakes. I'm hungry."

"Phone, Dad," Greg called from the next room. "Your office."

Annoyed, I put down the spatula, turned down the stove, and went into the other room to take the call.

I heard the legat say, "Deke, we've got your man."

Then he added a note of caution.

"We think this is the guy. We're pretty sure, actually. But we don't yet have a positive ID."

No longer annoyed, I felt an enormous sense of relief. Every muscle in my body suddenly relaxed. I hadn't realized how tense I'd been over the past two months. Light and warmth flooded into every dark corner of the room.

"What about fingerprints?" I asked, anxious to put an end to any doubts.

"Not allowed here, unless the subject voluntarily agrees."

Suddenly all the weeks of tension, painstaking work, and loss of sleep boiled up inside me. I wanted to throw the telephone at the wall. Instead I shouted the first thing that came into my head.

"Damn it, man, hand him a glass of water. Then take the glass and lift the latents."

"But..."

"Do it!" I said, and hung up.

I waited for what must have been no more than an hour, but seemed half the day. No one ate pancakes. No one came near me. No one dared to make an outgoing call. Then the phone finally rang.

"Positive!" cried our legat.

"Good man," I said. Then I went in and cooked pancakes.

Later I called Jerry O'Leary at the *Washington Evening Star*, as well as several other key journalists who had been patiently following the story.

"In a couple of hours we're probably going to be announcing a big break in the King case. You might want to stand by."

Then I called the Old Man, who was in one of his favorite weekend haunts—the Waldorf Astoria. As usual, he was low-key and in control.

"Fine," he said. "Have the usual press release prepared."

As soon as I hung up, I remembered the Bull Butterfly. He would have to be informed immediately. I knew that at that very moment he was in New York City, attending the funeral of Bobby Kennedy, who had been assassinated on June 5. I called bureau headquarters in New York and asked that an agent be stationed on the steps of St. Patrick's Cathedral to grab Ramsey Clark as soon as he left the funeral Mass.

"Tell the agent to take the AG to the nearest telephone and have him call me at this number."

A few minutes later Clark called. He was very enthusiastic, commended the bureau in general and me in particular, then expressed his thanks for keeping him informed.

"Pass any further details along to Warren Christopher [then Clark's deputy]."

"We need to have a joint press release as soon as possible," I said, "because the news will break in London and will be on the wires here in a matter of seconds."

"I agree," he said, and told me to coordinate the press release with Christopher. I immediately got in touch with him. We agreed on the text of the lengthy release, and I sent it out.

I settled in my office chair, closed my eyes, and congratulated myself. Not only was James Earl Ray safely behind bars, but J. Edgar Hoover and Ramsey Clark were happy, and we were all living in the Peaceable Kingdom. The lion had lain down by the lamb.

Then my phone rang.

"I'd like to see you immediately in my office."

It was Clark, and he was obviously upset. I went to his office, wondering what in the hell was bothering him. When I arrived, his wife, Georgia, was also there. Apparently they'd come straight from the airport following the funeral. He didn't even bother to take me into a room where we could speak in private.

"This press release!" he shouted, waving the offending document in the air as if it were on fire. "Why weren't the attorney general and the Justice Department mentioned more often?"

"We followed standard procedure," I explained. "We mentioned your name and the department in the lead paragraph. I cleared it with Christopher. We..."

He interrupted me.

"We should have gotten more credit. This is the most important civil rights case ever handled."

I stared at him for a moment. He had shrunk from the proportions of a man to a small boy denied a treat. It had never occurred to me that he was such a glory hog. I wondered what his wife thought of such a childish tantrum.

I carefully—and, it turned out, inadequately—explained to him that the FBI had done all the work, that the release simply chronicled the facts of the case, that we had made no attempt either to exaggerate or to diminish anyone's role in apprehending James Earl Ray.

The more I talked, the wilder he became. Finally I tactfully withdrew and went back down the corridor to my own office.

Fifteen minutes later he was on the line again.

"Who the hell do you think you work for?" he bellowed.

"The FBI and the Department of Justice," I replied in a calm and steady voice. He'd forfeited any small chance he had of intimidating me by his outburst of temper.

"You work for me," he snapped back.

For the first time in my life, I hung up on a superior, cutting the attorney general off in mid-whine. I immediately called Hoover and told him the entire story. He listened carefully, without interruption, though I knew he was deriving some satisfaction from what I was saying.

"You've done a good job," he said. "Stand your ground."

In the end, I realized that Hoover had been right about the Bull Butterfly, his swollen ambition, his obsession with the press, his view of public service as a means of self-aggrandizement. As a consequence, I felt even guiltier about having passed along intelligence to Clark after Hoover had explicitly forbidden it.

Ramsey Clark and I never spoke to each other again. Two days later, still pouting, he asked Hoover to assign one of my assistants to serve as liaison with him in the future. Hoover arranged this reassignment without ever telling me.

The day of Ray's capture, after clearing it with Hoover, I called in two top-flight agents—George Zeiss and Kenneth Bounds—and assigned them the job of bringing Ray back to the United States. Both men had been instructors at the FBI Academy. Zeiss was a rugged six feet four inches, and Bounds was six feet three. Together they weighed almost 450 pounds. When they left, I expected to see them back in a couple of days.

But days dragged into weeks, and the English wheels of justice ground more slowly than the mills of the gods. Bounds' father died while he was waiting, so we brought both men back. In the meantime, Clark sent Fred Vinson, Jr., to London to serve as his representative in the case. Vinson was the son of the late Chief Justice and at the time assistant attorney general of the Department of Justice. Vinson was well liked by our agents, and the legat gave him every assistance in arranging for the return of Ray to the United States.

Finally, after the nation had all but forgotten about James Earl Ray, Vinson's office called to say that the way had been cleared—FBI agents could now assume custody of Ray and fly him to the United States for trial. I again gave the assignment to George Zeiss, and for his partner I chose Harold Light, of the FBI Academy. The two men flew to London in a chartered 707 Air Force jet—at a cost to the taxpayers of $7,000. (I had to answer some harsh questions about that decision even though the flight had been planned by the Justice Department and the White House.) I sent Bounds to Memphis to assist SAC Jensen in receiving the prisoner and turning him over to Tennessee authorities.

The night Ray was scheduled to return, my staff and I stayed up until the wee hours of the morning, checking and rechecking all security precautions on both sides of the Atlantic. Security at the U.S. Naval Base in Memphis, the jet's destination, was reported as "a ring of steel." Still, we took no chances. We gave no advance notice to the press of Ray's intended arrival. We made sure that his assigned cell at the Shelby County Jail had been converted into a minifortress, devoid of any object or instrument he might use to commit suicide. We wanted this assassin to stand trial for his crime and to be convicted in a court of law. We took all these precautions, I might add, even though the Civil Rights Division of the Justice Department had decided to turn over the prosecution of Ray to the state of Tennessee.

That night I sat in my office, manning an open line, seeing in my imagination Jack Ruby stepping out from the crowd of reporters, rushing forward, and jamming the gun into Oswald's belly. I heard the muffled explosion, saw the anguished look on Oswald's face, and I remembered the contempt with which the news media had treated Jesse Curry and the Dallas Police Department, even though Oswald's transfer had been staged for the benefit of the press. This could not, would not, happen to James Earl Ray.

The agent on the line began to speak.

"The 707 is approaching the airport. It's already in a landing pattern. I can hear the engines and see its blinking lights."

"So far, so good."

We waited.

"The plane's touched down. I can see it on the runway."

Now was the crucial moment. Ray was still our prisoner. Soon he would be in the hands of Tennessee authorities. At that point, my responsibility would cease.

"They're getting out of the plane. I can see Zeiss, Light, Bounds, Jensen, and Ray. Our guys look like giants beside Ray. Here come the state police in a car. Zeiss is handing the state trooper something—credentials, I guess. Now they're taking the prisoner. Now they're getting into a car. Now they're cranking. Now they've started off towards downtown Memphis. Zeiss and the others are coming this way."

I breathed a sigh of relief and signaled to Al Rosen, who was sitting in the office, watching. Then I called the director. As for Clark, he could read about it in the morning newspaper, for all I cared.

In retrospect, I can only feel a deep sense of satisfaction at the performance of our agents, who were under great stress. Never once during the entire investigation did any agent say, "To hell with this case! King hated the FBI, so why should we stay up nights trying to find his killer?" To the contrary, scores of agents worked their butts off night after night, as dedicated as if the victim had been J. Edgar Hoover himself.

When we were handed the case, we knew nothing except the bare facts of the shooting. We didn't know the name of the sniper, nor did we have a list of suspects. This was clearly a political act, or else one motivated by blind, irrational bigotry. So from the beginning we knew we would probably be looking for a man who had never met King but who had harbored deep-rooted racial animosities, the kind that welled up from the miasmal slime of a misspent life.

Our big break was Ray's ineptitude in dropping the rifle and bag in front of the junk shop. Had he been bright and bold enough to pack his car first and keep the rifle with him until he had driven across the first wide river, he might have had a chance to escape. But he gave us a little bit to work with—and that was just enough.

Of course, Ray had accomplished what he'd intended. He'd altered the course of American history and gotten the recognition that had eluded him since he was a small child. For a few months, he was a big man—someone whose name and face were plastered on the front pages of newspapers worldwide. Then the name and face faded way—though not completely. Few people in America would fail to recognize the name of James Earl Ray, though fewer and fewer would recognize the gray-faced, gray-haired man who occasionally surfaces in the news. Recently he filed another lawsuit, trying to win parole, still claiming that others had committed the crime for which he was convicted and imprisoned for life.

Predictably, a few people believe him. As in the case of the Kennedy assassination, publicity seekers and ideologues still raise questions about his guilt. Where did Ray get the money to plan and execute the assassination and escape? Why did he take such a risk in killing Dr. King unless he expected some substantial reward? And how did he manage to elude the FBI for so long without help from at least one co-conspirator?

The FBI considered those questions and provided satisfactory answers. We believe that one robbery and two major heists provided him with more than enough funds to carry out his scheme. We had sufficient evidence to suggest that Ray had planned and executed these robberies, but we didn't have quite enough proof to bring him to trial and convict him. Had it been necessary to prove the robbery charges to get a murder conviction, I'm convinced we could have produced sufficient evidence.

As for the motive, bigotry and a failed life were sufficient to prompt such a man to carry out this desperate act. We checked into Ray's background, interviewed people who knew him both in and out of prison, and concluded that his hatred for blacks was almost pathological. He had made remarks that indicated not only his willingness but his intention to inflict punishment on those who strove for racial justice. His animosity was particularly strong against

King. No one who knew him well was surprised that he had committed such a crime.

Ray's escape to Canada and then to Europe was neither as clever nor as well planned as the general public believes. Criminals who spend years in prison know where to buy forged documents; and once Ray could prove that he was Eric Starvo Galt, he could go anywhere in the world with relative ease. (Incidentally, during the investigation, we discovered that the name was borrowed from Ayn Rand's novel *Atlas Shrugged*, a fictional illustration of Nietzsche's doctrine of the "superman." We were surprised that a man as ill educated as Ray might have read such a book.)

The truth is, we moved very quickly to identify Ray and then apprehend him. He was able to remain at large as long as he did only because it took time to chase down leads, spear those fingerprint files, and go through the millions of passport photos in the United States and Canada. Nothing he did threw us off the path or required additional assistance. From the time we found that photograph at the bartender's school, his fate was sealed.

But conspiracy theories still roam the streets of New York and Hollywood, and every so often one of them is let into the house. The House Select Committee on Assassinations—chaired by Louis Stokes, and manned by such congressmen as Walter Fauntroy and Christopher Dodd—took up the King case as well as the Kennedy case, and managed to spend more than $7 million to come once again to an inevitable conclusion: James Earl Ray acted alone when he shot Dr. King. The committee came to this conclusion reluctantly, since several of its staff were anxious to discredit the FBI.

I myself wasted four or five frustrating days working with staff and attorneys, then testifying before the committee. The members asked me very little about the investigation and the evidence gathered in the case. Not a word about Ray's latent fingerprints on the murder weapon. Nothing about the binoculars or the razor kit. Never mind that the fragments of the bullets that struck King could be traced to Ray's rifle. Or that we had a record of the rifle's purchase and a positive ID by the proprietor of the gun shop. These congressmen were oblivious to facts.

Instead, they spent most of their time questioning me in detail about the feud between King and Hoover, about Hoover's animosity toward King, implying that somehow this had an impact on the way James Earl Ray was brought to justice. It was worse than a fishing expedition. It was an obvious attempt to smear the director with innuendo. No one asked me what King might have said about Hoover, whether in public or private.

Truth be told, the old feud did have an impact—it drove us to prove, at every moment, that we were doing all we humanly could do to catch King's killer. That may have made our job harder—or at least more pressure-packed—but as I look back on the case, I still feel that same sense of satisfaction that I felt on the night Ray was handed over to the Tennessee authorities and hauled off to certain conviction. The FBI had never built a better case nor pursued a fugitive with greater patience and imagination.

11

Counter-Intelligence

ESPIONAGE CASES ARE LIKE FINGERPRINTS: no two are alike. Some spies are bright and well educated. Others are stupid and ignorant. Some are glamorous international travelers. Others lead drab, routine lives and earn marginal salaries. Some are young, others are in their seventies. They have only one thing in common. They all exhibit severe character flaws, the kind of weaknesses that make them unreliable friends and all-too-reliable betrayers of their own people. Such was the case of the man I call "the greedy sailor."

At 4:20 in the afternoon on Friday, September 8, 1962, a navy Yeoman First Class called it a day and walked out of his office at Coasters Island, home of the Newport Naval Base in Rhode Island. This yeoman—later described as "a happy-go-lucky twenty-two-year-old sailor"—was Nelson Cornelius Drummond, a native of Baltimore, Maryland. Known by his friends as Neil, Drummond was "regular navy," the administrative assistant to the lieutenant in charge of METU-8, the Mobile Electronic Technical Unit that was an integral part of an antisubmarine detection system. The sailor headed for the parking lot, presumably on his way home.

Twenty minutes later, Marine guards on their security rounds entered Drummond's office. They emptied the confidential waste baskets, checked the windows and file cabinets, turned out the lights, and locked the door. After the Marines had gone to another part of the building, two men—FBI Special Agent Thomas P. Selleck and a naval intelligence officer—moved cautiously along the dark corridor, paused briefly in front of Drummond's office, slipped a master key into the lock, and opened the door. After leaning through the doorway to make certain the room was empty, the officer motioned Selleck inside.

"Good luck," he whispered, as he quietly closed the door, relocked it, and hurried away.

Selleck moved across the room quickly and slid behind a bookcase, a position from which he could see the row of file cabinets lined against the opposite wall. The agent knew he wouldn't be detected. He'd hidden in this same spot three weeks earlier.

He flicked the switch of his miniature two-way radio and said softly, "In position. Over and out."

"Roger," came the reply from one of Selleck's partners, Special Agent Arthur K. Dowd, Jr., who was stationed in a nearby building. Using closed-circuit television, he was monitoring the room. Meanwhile, Special Agent Joseph J. Palguta, a veteran "spy buster," waited in a parked car close to the office.

Selleck turned off his transistor, ending all radio contact. He was on his own. He waited. Thirty minutes. Fifty minutes. Still nothing, except the sound of his own quiet breathing.

Then, at 5:30, he heard the sound of footsteps along the corridor. They grew louder, then they stopped. A key slipped into the lock of the office door. The lock clicked and the door swung open. Selleck squinted slightly, preparing for the sudden glare of the lights. He saw Drummond enter the office, carrying a small travel case. The sailor walked directly to the file cabinet nearest the door, opened a drawer, removed some papers, and slipped them into his case. He shut the drawer and went into the inner office of the lieutenant-in-charge. Through the open door Selleck could see Drummond unlock and open a cabinet, search for a document, find it, and place it in the case with the other papers. Then he closed the cabinet, locked it, turned out the lights, shut the door to the inner office, and left, locking the outer office door behind him.

Selleck looked at his watch. Yeoman Drummond had been in the office suite slightly less than six minutes, but in that time he'd stolen several top secret documents vital to the national security of the United States. And it wasn't the first time. The sailor had been a spy for four years, and Selleck knew that he was on his way to deliver the classified documents to a Soviet agent. Selleck listened until the footsteps in the corridor had died away. Then he flicked on his transmitter.

"Tell me when," he said.

"Stand by," Palguta replied, waiting for Drummond's 1959 blue Oldsmobile to clear the area. Selleck, still behind the bookcase, was poised to move.

"O.K.," said Palguta, "let's hit it!"

Selleck slipped from behind the bookcase, unlocked the door from the inside, and moved quickly, silently down the corridor. When he reached Palguta's car, Dowd was already piling into the driver's seat.

"No need to hurry," said Palguta as the two men slammed the car doors. "We know where he's going, and in order to leave Newport, he'll have to wait for the 7:30 ferry."

Dowd cranked up the dark blue Ford and moved slowly out. When they reached the pier where the Newport-Jamestown ferry docked, Drummond wasn't there.

"Where do you suppose he is?"

"Obviously he'd made a stop somewhere else."

"Don't worry. He'll be here."

Sure enough, shortly before 7:30 Drummond drove up in his Oldsmobile, as if on cue. He eased onto the platform of the ferry, shut off his engine, and stayed there during the brief crossing to Jamestown. When the ferry docked, he drove onto dry land and headed for the Connecticut Turnpike. Dowd followed the Oldsmobile at a discreet distance. Up ahead, the sailor turned onto the New York Thruway and later switched to the Merritt Parkway.

All along the parkway, at strategic intervals on both sides of the divider, FBI agents waited in other cars, ready to join the pursuit. Just as Drummond passed Exit 14 on the north side, near Greenwich, Connecticut, the sailor suddenly braked, swung the wheel sharply to the left, slipped across the median, and took the southbound lane toward Larchmont, New York.

No car followed Drummond across the center strip. All he could see in his rear-view mirror were the headlights of two cars in the distance, cars that had been in the southbound lane when he crossed over. Up ahead, he could see two other cars that gave no sign they were interested in his abrupt change of direction. If he thought about it at all, he must have been certain he was safe. Certainly it would never have occurred to him that he was now in the middle of a tight little escort of FBI cars—two in front and two behind. The hands on his dashboard clock had just passed 11:00 P.M.

Neil Drummond was something of an enigma, even to those who thought they knew him. He had been stationed in London in 1958. A year or so later, a defector told the FBI that a serviceman somewhere in England was giving top-secret information to the KGB. The informant didn't know who the serviceman was, what kind of intelligence he was passing, or how it was being delivered. But he believed the spy was in some kind of clerical position.

With this scant information, we went to work. Through a tedious process of checking the records of literally thousands of soldiers, sailors, Marines, and airmen stationed in England, we narrowed our list of suspects to six noncommissioned males—one from the air force, one from the navy, four from the army. The navy noncommissioned officer (NCO) had been transferred back to the States by the time we identified him as a suspect, and we noted that he was stationed in a highly sensitive position at the Newport Naval Base in Rhode Island.

We zeroed in on the six suspects and soon discovered an important fact about the sailor, Neil Drummond—he was living way beyond his means. For years he had lived a hand-to-mouth existence in a state described by one associate as "abject poverty." In his native Maryland he had been trying to cope with "an avalanche of debts." Recently, however, he had not only paid off those obligations but was able to buy expensive furs for his pretty, twenty-three-year-old wife, acquire two expensive cars, and two homes. He even had enough money left over—$12,000—to buy into a sailor's bar in Newport, where, after returning from late-night trips to New York, he would buy drinks for the house. This remarkable financial achievement moved us to eliminate the other five suspects and to concentrate on Drummond.

His fellow servicemen described him as "gregarious and ebullient, yet tending to be secretive about his personal affairs [and] people with whom he associated when off duty." That, too, tended to confirm our suspicions. We accelerated our investigation, arranging with Naval Intelligence to control, and account for, all classified material that might be available to Drummond. We also pulled out all stops to determine just who Drummond was contacting and what information he was stealing.

First, we put a tail on him—a team of agents who watched every off-duty move he made. Under ordinary circumstances, this might have been risky; but we had our best men on him. Besides, Drummond was so confident after four years of successful espionage that he never thought to look behind him. He was a man utterly confident of his own invulnerability.

Second, we tapped his telephones, both at work and at home. Through this tactic we picked up most of our information. Again, he had no suspicion that he was being monitored and spoke freely with Soviet agents on a number of occasions.

Third to determine precisely which documents he was passing along to his KGB contacts, we trained two closed-circuit television cameras on him while he worked at the Newport Naval Base, one at his desk and the other at the file cabinet holding the secret documents. As the weeks went by, we amassed a complete inventory of the classified information he was giving to the Soviets.

At the same time we were monitoring known Soviet spies, so we sometimes had "double coverage" on Drummond, since he would call on telephones and show up at sites already being monitored by the FBI. The only thing we didn't do was to station an agent under his bed every night, but had that tactic been necessary, I'm convinced we could have gotten away with it, so secure did he feel.

We soon discovered that the burly yeoman, despite his happy-go-lucky reputation, was shrewd and hardboiled—a self-promoter who knew how to strike a bargain and apply pressure. He was a difficult agent for the Russians to control, so demanding and unpredictable that the Soviets had to assign four of the KGB's toughest officers to keep him in line.

The first was Mikhail Stepanovich Savelov, who had recruited him in England and then followed him to the United States. In 1961, Drummond was "taken over" by Aleksandr Sorokin, who was apparently unable to control the yeoman's demands for more money and fewer risks. By 1962, it was apparent that Sorokin could not handle him, so the Soviets replaced their agent with not one, but two agents—Yevgeni M. Prokhorov and Ivan Y. Vyrodov—who tried to direct his operations and placate him during the hectic September of 1962, when our three agents were closing in on him.

We also learned from our surveillance that Drummond had a tough time remembering the multisyllabic Russian names. Instead of attempting to learn first name, father's name, and last name—as good Russians must do—he called all of them "Mike." Savelov was "Mike One," and Sorokin "Mike Two." In due course, Prokhorov became "Mike Three, and Vyrodov "Mike Four."

As if that effrontery wasn't enough, Drummond defied all rules of espionage by showing up at the Soviet Mission to the United Nations on Park Avenue and demanding to see Mike Three—Prokhorov. Our stakeout spotted Drummond the moment he rounded the corner and watched in awe and disbelief as he walked right into the mission. One agent, watching the scene, breathed into the microphone: "That Drummond is something else again. He's shifting gears without bothering to put in the clutch."

We later learned what had happened. As one agent put it, "When Prokhorov saw that big sailor materialize in his office, the Russian almost shit in his pants." But Drummond was too cocky to care. Besides, he needed money; and he wanted to frighten the Soviets into giving it to him. Prokhorov told Drummond he was crazy, but surprisingly he did not drop the sailor from his payroll, as he would have done under ordinary circumstances. As cautious as the Russians usually were, they were not ready to discard a contact who had given them as much information as Drummond had. (By then we knew that he'd been stealing specifications for the entire anti-submarine warning system of the United States naval defenses on the Eastern seaboard.) Instead of throwing him out of the Soviet Mission and removing his name from their Christmas list, Prokhorov merely reprimanded Drummond and told him never to come near the mission again. He also provided Drummond with an unlisted telephone number to use in making contact, day or night.

On September 26, Drummond phoned "Mike Three" at the unlisted number, which we were already tapping. The sailor told Prokhorov he had some "hot material" to deliver, but it was "perishable."

"What do you mean 'perishable,'" Prokhorov had asked.

"I mean, you bring $7,500 in small bills," said Drummond, "preferably tens and twenties, or there's no deal."

"I can't believe you're asking this," said Prokhorov, obviously shaken. "I just gave you $4,000."

"You have no choice," Drummond replied. "You either come up with the money or you don't get this information—or any more—from me."

Then he explained.

"I'm in a bind. I owe a high liquor bill at the joint. And taxes—lots of taxes. And over six grand to the vending machine operators. You know who they are and what they're going to do to me if I don't cough up. Yeah, and the Internal Revenue said they're going to padlock my place [his bar]."

Prokhorov didn't like it, but he finally capitulated yet one more time to Drummond's growing demands. He agreed to meet the sailor on the night of September 28, in Larchmont, New York, an affluent suburb in Westchester County. Mike Three also agreed to bring the $7,500.

When SAC Foster heard the recording of this conversation, he decided it was time for the FBI to make its move. So he boarded a plane on the morning of the 28th, flew to Washington, and gave us a last-minute briefing on the New York espionage squad's plans to follow and arrest Drummond.

"We intend to turn this meeting between Drummond and Prokhorov into a surprise party, hosted by the FBI."

Hoover was skeptical.

"Are you positive about this?" he said.

Better than anyone he knew the dire consequences of failure in such an operation. It was bad enough to arrest a native-born American on insufficient evidence. The newspapers always put our mistakes on the front page and our successes on page A-29. But when two out of three suspects were foreigners—and citizens of the Soviet Union at that—the fallout was even greater. A hasty move could end up provoking a debate in the United Nations and embarrass the president of the United States. In such instances, someone would be publicly hanged. Hoover wanted to make certain he wasn't the corpse at the end of the rope.

That's why he asked Foster, "Are you sure you have all the evidence you need?"

Foster was an old hand at the spy game. In New York City, Soviet espionage agents were as abundant as cockroaches; and he'd worked on a number of such cases. He knew as well as Hoover the pitfalls of insufficient evidence.

"I'm absolutely positive," Foster said. "There isn't a single loose strand in this case. We've given Drummond plenty of rope, and he's used every inch of it."

Hoover nodded, then gave permission for the operation.

We at headquarters were all eager to make the bust and end Drummond's spying. We had been monitoring the investigation for months, and we were outraged by the boldness of Drummond's treachery and his seemingly insatiable greed. So the day went by slowly as we waited for dark and the final chase to begin. Meanwhile, in New York, agents were quietly racing from here to there and back again, picking up arrest warrants, smoothing out last-minute wrinkles in their plans.

As usual, Hoover could have played a role in the final act of this drama; but as usual he declined. He had come to believe in recent years that he had honed the bureau to such a fine edge that his presence was no longer necessary in a field operation of this sort. He had already done his part. The success that followed was the product of his training and example. He never hesitated to take credit and no longer felt that credit would be any the less if he were not there personally. That evening the director watched television, then went to bed at about the moment his agents—Selleck, Dowd, and Palguta among them—were forming the multicar posse to escort Yeoman First Class Drummond along the Merritt Parkway.

Shortly after Neil Drummond had crossed the grassy divider strip on the parkway, Agent Dowd made a similar turn, out of Drummond's line of vision, and worked his Ford back into the pattern of vehicles accompanying the spy southward. The entire convoy followed the Oldsmobile into the quiet suburban town of Larchmont where FBI agents watched as Drummond pulled into the parking lot of a diner on the Boston Post Road. At that point, FBI cars blanketed the surrounding streets, sealing off all escape routes from the parking lot.

After the sailor had sat there for a few minutes, a man left the diner. All FBI eyes were on him as he walked briskly to the Oldsmobile, opened the door, and slid into the passenger's seat. It was Prokhorov.

That was the signal. Selleck, Dowd, and Palguta leaped from their cars and dashed toward the Oldsmobile. They yanked open both front doors and flashed a light into the front seat.

"FBI," barked Selleck. "Get your hands up and slowly get out of the car."

Drummond and his companion stumbled out, their faces incredulous. They couldn't believe this was happening to them.

Meanwhile, a second team of agents entered the diner, collared a man at the counter, who was about to bite into a cheeseburger, and rushed him outside before he could fathom what was happening. He was Ivan Yakovlevich Vyrodov, Prokhorov's cover man and Drummond's alternate contact. He had driven his boss to the rendezvous point and was supposed to serve as lookout. Apparently he had been more interested in his cheeseburger.

As soon as Vyrodov realized what had happened, he refused to answer questions or even to identify himself. Prokhorov adopted the same tactic. Both knew that with their diplomatic cover, they were immune from prosecution in the United States. Then, when we were about to handcuff them, they both began to struggle.

At that moment Drummond surprised everyone by jumping into the fray and helping the FBI agents subdue his Russian contacts. Selleck reacted immediately.

"Get some cuffs on that crazy bastard!" he shouted, sensing the sailor was trying to play the role of the innocent bystander.

The fight was over in seconds, and the suspects were thrown into three separate cars. Then the caravan took off for New York City, about forty miles south of Larchmont. They arrived a few minutes after midnight.

In Washington, we waited for the Manhattan office to call and verify that Drummond had been picked up, along with the two Russians. Inspector Donald E. Moore and Special Agent William A. Brannigan were particularly interested because they were both Soviet specialists and had been deeply involved in the case. At 1:20 A.M. we finally got the call. All three had been picked up. After identifying themselves as "diplomats," Prokhorov and Vyrodov—with State Department approval—had been released.

Even knowing this would happen, we were disappointed.

"Don't worry," our Espionage Section told us. "Those two will really have their tails between their legs when they get back to Moscow. They got caught. Their pictures will be on the front pages of Western newspapers. They will have made their government an object of contempt in the international community. Those guys may be spending the next few winters in Siberia."

"Yeah," said someone else, "but I'll bet the Soviets are happy to be rid of Drummond. He was a real pain."

The sailor had been too volatile, too unpredictable, too greedy. The Soviets had been able to approach him because of his greed, and that same greed had helped to betray them all.

Unfortunately, when he came to trial, Drummond was charged with only two negligible counts—conspiracy to commit espionage (a hazy, theoretical allegation) and attempting to pass six defense documents to the Soviets. These relatively minor charges were all the Kennedy administration was willing to press. Nonchalantly, even indifferent to security threats, Bobby Kennedy seemed to shrug off the fact that Drummond had compromised sectors of our underseas defense system, revealed crucial technology, and cost the navy millions of dollars to redesign and rebuild their electronic installations.

Perhaps because of a careless and lackluster prosecution, the first trial was stalled when one juror refused to vote for conviction. At the second trial, the defendant was convicted only on the nebulous "conspiracy" charge, which carried a maximum of thirty-five years of imprisonment, with plenty of time off for good behavior. As for the charge that he'd been selling documents in the parking lot of the diner, once again the jury was deadlocked—with a lone female juror as a holdout. With FBI agents assigned to the case testifying against him, the woman still couldn't be sure that government witnesses were telling the truth.

After making extraordinary efforts to bring the Soviet Union into the United Nations after World War II, the American government watched as Stalin began to build an empire that soon absorbed most of Eastern Europe and reached out to the far corners of the globe. Dismayed by these imperialist incursions, Americans began to regard international communism as a genuine threat to the United States and to take seriously the warnings of many conservatives that Soviet agents were a danger to national security.

At this point, Senator Joseph McCarthy moved effortlessly into the spotlight as the leader of anticommunist forces in the U.S. government. A man of limited intelligence and little principle, McCarthy was eventually censured. His fall damaged serious attempts to monitor communist activities in this country and to ferret out Soviet agents spying against the United States. It became fashionable among liberals to doubt that such agents even existed, much less that they were systematically engaged in stealing military and diplomatic secrets to bring about our downfall.

It is useless to argue with those who busily rewrite history, and it would take another book to document the acts of espionage, the assaults on the American political order, and the moves and countermoves of the Cold War that constituted the formidable internal threat to our nation that virtually every president from Truman to Reagan recognized.

The American Communist party was a vital part of that threat, constituting a sizable "Fifth Column" apparatus within the U.S. Hoover and the FBI were not, that is, acting out of blind hatred and irrational fear in keeping tabs on the U.S. party. We knew exactly what the party was doing in this country and precisely how dangerous it was. We certainly knew a great deal more than the anti-anticommunists, who were forever telling us that the Communist party, USA, was merely a more doctrinaire version of the Socialist party. And we knew it, in no small part, thanks to a controversial, even infamous, counterespionage program built by the FBI, codenamed COINTELPRO.

COINTELPRO was instituted in 1956. The premise of COINTELPRO—which stood for Counter Intelligence Program—was "Do unto others as they are doing unto you." The Communists in this country were using a variety of techniques to destabilize large segments of American society. They were telling lies, setting one faction against another, planting incriminating evidence on innocent people, and infiltrating legitimate organizations to subvert them. Why not use the same techniques against the Communists? It seemed like a good idea at the time.

The main architect of the COINTELPRO approach was William C. Sullivan, who became famous, even notorious as a consequence. Brash, brilliant, brimming over with self-esteem, something of a bantam rooster, Sullivan had more ambition than was good for a man, combined with a slight deficiency in principle. For years COINTELPRO was his special domain. He ruled it with skill and daring most of the time, but occasionally with reckless abandon.

During the late 1950s, COINTELPRO was exclusively devoted to combatting the Communists, and I must confess that in retrospect I find little to criticize in the way the program operated. Agents joined the Communist party, worked their way up through the ranks, and then began to make as much trouble as possible. They gathered intelligence, harangued leaders at party meetings, recommended disastrous courses of action, and encouraged factionalism. By 1957, there were those who said the Communist party had been so splintered and demoralized by COINTELPRO that it was no longer worth worrying about.

But increasingly, the architect of COINTELPRO—Sullivan—was worth worrying about. In the end, he seriously abused the power of the bureau—and then blamed the director for his excesses.

Early on, Sullivan became a favorite of Hoover, primarily because he flattered the vulnerable director more than any man who ever worked in the bureau. He was forever writing the Old Man letters so obsequious and transparent that I was certain Hoover would be embarrassed and even angered by them. Sullivan compared him to the great men of the ages and to such contemporary giants as Conrad Adenauer and Charles de Gaulle. But I've long since learned that it's difficult to overpraise a vain man. So pleased was Hoover with Sullivan's extravagant compliments that he called me into his office so he could read them to me, commending Sullivan for his loyalty and, by implication, his own shrewd judgement of character.

Bill Sullivan's career as chief court flatterer didn't last forever. Later—when Hoover refused to approve certain illegal acts to obtain intelligence—Sullivan, thinking he had the support of the Nixon White House, became the director's most stinging critic. Embittered and sullen, a spoiled child, he was forced out of the bureau by Hoover and later wrote a highly biased and factually flawed account of his career in the FBI. Later critics of Hoover use Sullivan as a frequent source, repeating his distortions and half-truths, rarely noting that he was the one-time sycophant who abused the powers of the bureau by urging the use of COINTEL-PRO techniques against law abiding political dissidents on the left, as well as other drastic and illegal activities.

Sullivan's ego, in my view, also steered the FBI in the wrong direction on one of the most controversial questions in the history of American intelligence: the "Fedora" case. "Fedora" was the code name of a strategically placed KGB officer serving at the United Nations as a Soviet diplomat; for years the FBI relied on him as a trusted "double agent." But after a series of puzzling incidents and an agonizing reevaluation, the bureau concluded that "Fedora" may never have been working for the FBI—despite long-term assumptions to the contrary. I have always believed we were wrong and that, in reporting Fedora, we betrayed a valuable ally.

When the Nixon administration went to court in an effort to prevent the publication of the "Pentagon Papers," the FBI informed the White House that a complete set of these top-secret documents had already been delivered to the Soviet Embassy. How did we know? The information had come from Fedora.

Some people claim that this report—revealing a leak in the White House security system—was partially responsible for the formation of the so-called "plumbers unit," the group primarily responsible for the Watergate scandal. At the time, one source claimed that President Nixon's efforts to suppress the Watergate investigation was prompted in part by a desire to protect Fedora.

Subsequently, a few FBI agents began to suspect that Fedora was a Soviet triple agent, acting under Moscow's control rather than ours. This assumption was based on some unsettling questions raised by Fedora's confirmation of stories told by other defectors. Among these defectors was Yuri Ivanovich Nosenko, a one-time KGB officer whose credibility had been suspect since his defection from the Soviet Union in 1964.

Nosenko claimed to have been in charge of the KGB file on President Kennedy's assassin, Lee Harvey Oswald, and insisted he was defecting because he was about to be recalled to Russia, where the KGB had learned of his previous contacts with the CIA. Fedora confirmed this. He also backed Nosenko's claim that he was a lieutenant colonel in the KGB. This tidbit of information caught the FBI's attention, since several of our experts believed that Nosenko was lying. And if he was lying, so was Fedora.

When the House Assassinations Committee concluded its long and futile deliberations on the Kennedy assassination, it had to come to some new conclusions to justify its creation and the unconscionable expenditure of tax dollars. Among these new conclusions—that Nosenko had lied about Lee Harvey Oswald.

At this point, Bill Sullivan—one of the four assistant directors who reported to my office—began to indicate his lack of confidence in Fedora. He didn't come right out and say that Fedora was a double agent, but every time the Russian's name came up, Sullivan's lip would curl and he would raise his eyebrows or roll his eyes. Sometimes he would even venture the opinion that "everything we get from Fedora has to be examined very, very carefully"—an attitude I encouraged in dealing with all intelligence sources.

Eventually Sullivan planted doubts in the minds of others, including the head of the Espionage Section, Lish Whitson. All the information Fedora had passed along was suddenly suspect, requiring a complete reevaluation of a significant portion of American intelligence on the Soviet Union. The FBI unofficially turned Fedora's picture to the wall.

The CIA, on the other hand, elected to stand by Nosenko, claiming that he was a legitimate defector and that he had become "a well-adjusted American citizen utilized as a consultant by the CIA." They even went public with this opinion.

Since I was Sullivan's superior—and since I couldn't get him to make a final judgment on Fedora or to offer sufficient proof to justify his suspicions, I decided to try to resolve the matter in my own mind. I called for all the information we'd collected on Fedora, and while it was being gathered, I remembered that a retired agent and good friend of mine had worked constantly with Fedora over the years. He lived in New York, so I called him on the phone.

"Jack," I said, "I've got a problem, and I need your help. I'll buy you lunch in New York if I can pick your brain."

"It's a deal," he said.

Two days later, we met in a small, out-of-the-way restaurant where we could talk without worrying about the rumble of the subway or the clatter of dishes. He had changed little, and he still had the Irish gift of gab. He told a few jokes, reminisced about the old days, and then we got down to business.

I told him about Sullivan's suspicions and gave him a little bit of the latest intelligence on Nosenko. Then I asked him if he thought Fedora could be a triple agent.

He shook his head.

"No," he replied. "I really don't think so."

I could see him turning the idea over in his mind, even as he was rejecting it. No one knew Fedora better than Jack, but I wanted him to give me reasons.

"Why don't you think so?"

"Look at it this way," he said. "We know that informants are historically motivated by at least one of four basic personal incentives. The first of these is revenge—they want to get even with the system or some particular person in the system. The second is reward—money, a soft life, good sex. The third is remorse—a guilty feeling about something they've done. And the fourth is fear—that the KGB will get them if they don't get the KGB first. Fedora's primary motivation was clearly revenge, and his secondary motive was reward."

"How do you conclude this?" I asked.

"Because I knew the man—talked with him, listened very carefully to everything he said. Here was a guy who hated the regime. The party had arrested his brother, prosecuted him on trumped-up charges of 'crimes against the state,' and thrown him in prison. Fedora's brother died there."

"Was he disillusioned with communism?"

"No indeed," Jack said. "All the time I worked with him, he still believed in the communist system, still loved Russia, and was—in his own way—loyal to his people. He was just bitter toward the guys who were running the system."

A good agent could fake a certain amount of bitterness; it would be a predictable ploy to use. But Jack said he knew Fedora too well to be fooled. "I saw too much of him. It was all there, seething inside him. He couldn't have faked it that well."

Besides, Jack said, Fedora wanted the money badly, that was how he had been recruited in the first place.

Fedora had arrived in this country carrying several thousand dollars with which to rent and furnish an apartment. His wife, scheduled to join him, had been delayed. At some point he wanted a little female companionship, so he picked up a hooker and they went out drinking. The next thing he knew, he was lying in a hotel room buck naked with no wallet. The hooker had stolen the KGB money.

Not only was Fedora in a serious financial bind, but if his superiors learned how he'd lost the money, he'd be out of the KGB and maybe on his way to Siberia. Throw in his desire for revenge and he was ripe to become a double agent.

"At first," Jack said, "all he wanted was the money he'd lost. But the more we talked to him, the more he concluded that he'd like to be financially independent in his old age, with a dacha in Odessa."

If the KGB had wanted to plant a triple agent, they would have come up with a better story—disgust with Marxism, a desire for American-style freedom. Besides, Fedora was more careful than a plant would have been.

"He refused any contact on Russian soil by American intelligence agents," Jack went on. "Said it was too risky. If he'd been a triple agent, he would have agreed to such meetings, because it would have given the KGB the opportunity to smoke out our agents stationed in the Soviet Union."

But Jack's final argument was the clincher.

"Fedora wanted only money and unclassified information from us," Jack said. "He never asked for classified data, which is an odd posture for an alleged plant. His main objective seemed to have been to enhance his position in the KGB."

That made sense to me. The KGB would never allow its agents to be arrested, embarrassed, compromised all over the world without demanding more from Fedora than a little money and some unclassified information. At that moment I was certain that Sullivan was wrong, that Jack was right. Fedora was a legitimate informant.

I thanked Jack, said goodbye, and caught the plane back to Washington, where I brooded about the matter for several days. Since I'd already sent for the relevant files, I reviewed Fedora's performance while he was cooperating with the FBI. In those specific instances where the facts were verifiable, Fedora's information held up. I looked over the file again and again, and each time I was more convinced that we were making a mistake in doubting his credibility.

During the years he was working with the FBI, Fedora identified scores of KGB agents operating out of diplomatic offices or commercial establishments such as TASS, AMTORG, Radio Moscow, and the United Nations. In some instances, these agents were apprehended violating federal law, prosecuted, and convicted in American courts. Others were declared persona non grata and expelled from the country. One thing is certain—their identities were compromised and they were subject to much tighter scrutiny and control because of Fedora's disclosures.

Fedora also identified KGB officials operating in other Western countries and unmasked the identity of ranking officials in the hierarchy of the KGB. On one occasion, when the chief of the KGB visited the United States, Fedora supplied us with his identity, travel agenda, and business schedule. We in turn passed this information along to the *New York Daily News,* and as a result, photographers dogged his every footstep. Finally, in a blind rage, the man cut short his trip and fled back to the Soviet Union.

I called Sullivan to my office and went over the Fedora matter, but he'd already taken his stand and didn't want to accept opinions to the contrary. By then it was a matter of pride with him—a question of his personal judgment and integrity. He desperately wanted my job, and later Hoover's job; and I'm sure he believed that any admission that he'd made a mistake would compromise his chances—particularly in a disagreement with me, since he undoubtedly saw me as his chief rival.

Finally, when he realized that I was making sense, he pounded his fist on the table.

"O.K.," he said. "Authorize me to go and interview Fedora myself. I'll ask him so many questions he'll forget who and where he is. I'll trip him up, and the matter will be settled once and for all. I'll report back to you."

I shrugged my shoulders and agreed.

The agent on the case duly arranged a meeting between Sullivan and Fedora in a New York apartment. On the appointed day, Sullivan arrived at the rendezvous and met Fedora. The two men sat down, and Sullivan started to question the man he swore was a triple agent. But he stopped in midsentence and called the agent who had provided the contact.

"No point in going on," Sullivan said. "I've got all the evidence I need."

"What do you mean?" the agent asked.

"That bulge in his crotch," Sullivan said.

"Bulge in his crotch?"

"You didn't notice? Obviously he has a microphone in there."

The agent suppressed a smile.

"No, Bill, you're wrong. We searched him before the interview. Fedora just has big balls."

12

....

Spying on Americans

IN 1968, I WAS SUMMONED to the Oval Office, where Lyndon Johnson motioned me to sit down and immediately began to complain about the mob violence in major cities and on our campuses. Every night the television news featured the latest sit-ins, burn-ins, or loot-ins, and the president was losing patience. Finally he got around to his point.

"Deke," he said, "you and the FBI have got to stop these riots. One of my political analysts tells me that every time one occurs, it costs me ninety thousand votes."

"We're doing what we can to investigate their origins," I told the president, "but we don't have either the manpower or the authority to quell demonstrations, even when they turn violent. But believe me, we are at work."

He was impatient with my answer, and I had to repeat one more time my speech on the statutory limits of the bureau and the need to avoid establishing a national police force. It was an old lecture. He'd heard it before.

But what I told him was true: We had been at work—since earlier in the decade when we realized that not only were mass demonstrations and riots on the increase, but also that they were becoming the major strategy in an organized effort to destabilize American society. There were essentially two types of disruptions fomented by two separate groups. Demonstrations and riots on college campuses were generally started and managed by white student radicals. Urban demonstrations and riots were usually sparked by black revolutionaries.

The two had separate histories and grievances. Violence on the campus began with protests over the Vietnam War and broadened to include a number of social and academic issues, some of them specific, some of them abstract and hazy. Urban riots were both an extension of the nonviolent civil rights movement led by Dr. Martin Luther King and a reaction against that movement. We had to deal with each category separately, though in many instances the two groups merged. Combined they were known popularly as the "New Left."

The chief tactic of the campus radicals was to occupy administration buildings through sit-in strikes. Originally peaceful, these demonstrations gradually became more combative, aggressive, and physical. Soon, in many famous institutions of learning, teachers were no longer permitted to teach their subjects, but were driven from the classroom by students screaming epithets and obscenities. Eventually, the noisy bullying of the mob gave way to unrestricted violence complete with guerrilla tactics and dangerous weaponry. While California colleges and universities probably were hit hardest during this period, virtually every state in the Union was experiencing the same kind of mob violence, which sometimes resulted in property damage and serious injury. The New Left leaders of these nationwide demonstrations and riots were quite explicit in telling their followers and the general public their alarming intentions. Devereaux Kennedy, student body president of Washington University, made his desires crystal clear:

> I want student power to demand "revolutionary
> reforms" that can't be met within the logic of the existing American system. I'm going to say loudly and

explicitly what I mean by revolution. What I mean by revolution is overthrowing the American government, and American imperialism.... This is going to come about by black rebellions in our cities being joined by some white people. People in universities can do a number of things to help it. They have access to money, and they can give these people guns, which I think they should do. They can engage in acts of terrorism and sabotage outside the ghetto... and they can blow things up, and I think they should.

Eventually one group emerged as the "control" of the ongoing campus revolution, an organization that was national in scope, well-funded, and full of people who were preaching the total dismantlement of the government of the United States and the reworking of its social and moral codes. This organization was called Students for a Democratic Society (SDS); and their leaders, like those quoted above, made no bones about their intentions to tear the country apart. Surprisingly to some, this had been SDS doctrine since its founding long before the Vietnam War became a major issue. Carl Davidson, in a 1962 SDS publication called "Our Fight is Here: Essays on Draft Resistance," wrote: "We need to move from protest to resistance; to dig in for the long haul; to become full-time, radical, sustained, relevant. In short, we need to make a revolution."

Before the violence had become more than a small blip on our radar screen, Special Agent Supervisor Ben Fulton and I urged J. Edgar Hoover to issue a warning that trouble was just over the horizon. He agreed, and in his feature, "Message from the Director to All Law Enforcement Officers," he said of the New Left and its leadership:

We have in our midst hatemongers, bigots, and riotous agitators, many of whom are at opposite poles philosophically but who spew similar doctrines of prejudice and intolerance. They exploit hate and fear, spread rumors, and pit one element of our people against another. Theirs is a dogma of intimidation and terror.

Shortly thereafter, the nation watched in bewilderment as afflu-ent middle-class youngsters tore down their own universities. At the University of California at Berkeley, the dean of students mailed a letter to the leaders of all student organizations, specifying regula-tions for solicitation of funds, distribution of literature, and requirements for membership of off-campus societies. This letter, or one very like it, had been sent out every year since Methuselah was a freshman. But this year student leaders, primed for a revolution, immediately proclaimed that the dean's letter was an infringement of their rights as free men and women. Thus was born the Free Speech movement, which sprang up under the leadership of Bettina Aptheker, Mario Savo, and Jack Weinberg.

After shrill speeches and much arm-waving, the students occu-pied Sproul Hall and refused to leave. Eventually the governor ordered the police to storm the building and remove more than 800 people, of whom 732 were arrested. It was the largest sit-in and mass arrest in American history. But leaders of the New Left hailed the demonstration as an unqualified success, proclaiming "univer-sity reform" as one of the major planks in their ever-growing plat-form. With this victory as a model for emulation, the demonstra-tions spread to other campuses.

When the National Council of the SDS announced that it was going to sponsor a March on Washington in April 1965 to protest the war in Vietnam, the FBI was put on alert to discover what we could about the intent and strategy of the march, and to report our findings to the White House.

What we noted first in our report was the shift in emphasis from campus issues to national issues. After having protested everything from campus regulations to the politics of their professors, the stu-dents began to focus on the war. Of course, they had a vested inter-est in stopping the shooting, since many of the young men would be eligible for the draft once they graduated. Just as naturally, they dreamed up high-minded motives for their reluctance to fight—questioning the moral right of the United States to defend the South Vietnamese, despite the treaty that obliged us to do so and the imperialist designs of the Soviet Union.

Those who opposed the student movement accused the young men of cowardice and said they were too young and ignorant to decide international policy. But no youngster likes to hear adults say such things; and besides, demonstrations were now the ultimate adventure, the "in" thing. The idea of returning to the humdrum classroom had no appeal whatsoever. And so they came to Washington.

The surprising thing was how few actually did come. The estimate was only fifteen thousand—a far cry from the hundreds of thousands who took part in Dr. King's March on Washington in 1963. We knew we were not dealing with a huge upwelling of dissatisfaction—at least not at this stage of the game. But we did understand that the movement now had a national agenda, one that coincided with the nation's most dangerous foreign enemies, and that it intended to pursue this agenda on a national stage.

While white, upper-middle-class students were radicalizing American colleges and universities, less affluent blacks were stirring up racial discord in the nation's major cities. The cry there was "Black Power!" and the stated intent of the Black Power leadership was to foment racial warfare, abandoning what they called the failed strategy of peaceful protest by Martin Luther King. The three most important Black Power leaders were Floyd McKissick, in 1966 the national director of the Congress of Racial Equality (CORE); Stokeley Carmichael, former chairman of the Student Nonviolent Coordinating Committee (SNCC); and H. Rap Brown, chairman of SNCC. Each made it clear that he supported violent revolution.

Of these three, Stokeley Carmichael was probably the most outspoken and the most eloquent. A handsome young man with flashing eyes, he moved audiences wherever he went. In August 1966, Carmichael gave this definition of Black Power when speaking before a CORE rally: "When you talk of Black Power, you talk of bringing this country to its knees... of building a movement that will smash everything Western civilization has created... of the black man doing whatever is necessary to get what he needs—we are fighting for our lives." At a rally sponsored by the Free D.C. Movement the following month he proclaimed: "You ought to get together and tell the man that if you don't get the vote, you're going to burn down this city."

H. Rap Brown was equally strident. Prior to a riot in Cambridge, Maryland, on July 24, 1967, he told his audience: "If America don't come 'round, we're going to burn it down, brother—we're going to get our share of it or burn it down." He finished by shouting: "Don't love the white man to death, shoot him to death—if this town don't come 'round, burn it down!"

The white revolutionaries who were leading demonstrations and riots on literally hundreds of campuses nationwide together with these black organizers constituted a growing mass of discontented Americans, mostly in their teens and early twenties, that for a time appeared to threaten the political and social order of the United States. And from the beginning, the FBI was determined to discover the degree to which international forces were manipulating the New Left to serve their own ends. Both the Soviets and the Chinese Communists had a strong interest in the withdrawal of American forces from Southeast Asia. Obviously antiwar riots at home served those ends. In addition, the Communists had always used social unrest—the kind that existed in the black community—to recruit membership and to disrupt noncommunist regimes. They had been courting blacks since the 1920s, though with little success. And we wondered if the New Left might not really be their operation after all.

Because of these concerns, under the aegis of COINTELPRO we placed undercover informants in all of these organizations; we were particularly alert to the presence of communist influence. We had seen the role Stanley Levison had played in advising Martin Luther King, and we strongly suspected that the New Left leaders might be taking their cues from similar advisors.

What we found out was surprising. Despite marginal infiltration, the Communists were largely unsuccessful in taking over black groups during this era. Though Communist Stanley Levison wrote a number of King's speeches and may well have persuaded the black leader to become an antiwar activist, he did not "capture" the Southern Christian Leadership Conference. Likewise, Carmichael, McKissick, and others had their own agenda, one that had little to do with Marxist theory or the internationalist agenda of the party. They were black nationalists, not workers of the world. They thought of themselves as settling scores with a "repressive white regime," and they had little appetite for submitting their plans and dreams for the approval of another white regime in another country. The Communist party, USA, didn't know how to handle these black revolutionaries any more than did the Democratic and Republican parties.

The Communists did make some progress among the student groups. They funneled some money into their activities. They sat in on strategy sessions. They supplied students with ideas and rhetoric, as they had previously done with student groups in Europe and South America. They even placed some of their own among the hierarchy of various organizations. In the final analysis, however, the Communists never gained control of the SDS or any of the other influential national groups.

The problem for the Communists was the lack of discipline and hierarchy among many of these students. They were intoxicated by freedom and resentful of all authority—they were not interested in joining anybody's army, not Lyndon Johnson's army, not U.S. Communist party leader Gus Hall's army. Somehow they had the idea that they could create a society in which no one was responsible to anyone, where discipline gave way to license and hierarchy was melted away by love—the sappy, sentimental world envisioned in John Lennon's song "Imagine." Tom Hayden, the group's most famous spokesman, said, when asked about the purpose of the SDS, "We haven't any. First we will make the revolution. Then we will find out what it is for."

This kind of free thinking was directly contrary to everything the Communists believed in, everything they'd fought for. For them, the revolution had a particular end in mind, one prescribed by Marx and Lenin, an order that was both inevitable and for which one was expected to fight and even die. The struggle demanded not only discipline, but the submission of the individual to the will of the party and the flow of history. But neither Hayden nor his followers were about to submit to anybody.

As Columbia student John Meyer wrote in 1969: "SDS is the nation's leading radical student organization. It is not a Communist front. Its members have outgrown not only the fear of communism, but the thrill of having Communists among them; they have even outgrown procommunism. Individual Communists are accepted in the group as a matter of course, though somewhat condescendingly; they are too establishment, too 'organization-oriented.'"

Nevertheless, that Communists failed to capture the New Left in general, and the student movement in particular, made them no less dangerous to the safety and well-being of university campuses and ultimately to the stability of society itself. The student revolution, whether Communist-led or not, was calling for the violation of federal laws, as well as for violence and mindless destruction. Lest anyone forget the level to which this violence escalated, consider the following events that occurred during a twelve-month period in the state of California, as catalogued by then-Governor Reagan and confirmed in FBI files.

- February 9, 1968: Four fire bombs damaged the Naval ROTC building at the University of California at Berkeley.
- February 19, 1968: A flammable liquid was used to set fire to the porch of the Naval ROTC building at Stanford. The damage was estimated at $35,000.
- May 7, 1968: The Naval ROTC building at Stanford was destroyed. Authorities estimated it would cost $70,000 to replace.
- July 15, 1968: A $100,000 fire destroyed the office and irreplaceable effects of former Stanford President Wallace Sterling.
- August 6, 1968: Two fires were set in the Stanford student activities office.
- September 14, 1968: A bomb blasted the Naval ROTC building at the University of California.
- December 11, 1968: A firebomb was hurled at the administration building at San Francisco State College.
- December 13, 1968: College of San Mateo students, in an act of protest, smashed windows and broke crockery in the college cafeteria.

- January 5, 1969: Someone fired shots into a San Mateo home in the mistaken belief it was the residence of a college trustee.
- January 7, 1969: The home of Philip C. Carlington, Sr., former dean of instruction at the College of San Mateo, was severely damaged by firebombs. He and his family were lucky to escape with their lives.
- January 10, 1969: Someone threw fire bombs into the home of Edwin Duerr, coordinator of internal affairs at San Francisco State.
- January 16, 1969: A firebomb was defused in the state administration building. It had the potential to kill anyone within twenty-five feet.
- January 17, 1969: A mob of strikers smashed windows in a rampage at San Jose State.
- January 20, 1969: Two firebombs exploded on the University of California campus.

In May of 1970, the FBI put out a comprehensive report on the subject, entitled "Nationwide Civil Disturbances: 1969–1970." This report summarized student disruptions for the 1968–69 academic year as follows:

Demonstrations 850
Arrests 4,000
Injuries. 125
Deaths 1
Arsons/Bombings 61
Sit-ins 200

The report went on to note that according to the American Insurance Association, riots and civil disorder caused property damage of more than $31,000,000 in 1969. Incidents involving damage occurred in 350 cities in forty-one states and the District of Columbia.

The 1970 FBI report also described several disturbing developments in the continuing saga of the SDS. The organization was becoming more militant and violent, progressing from a program of protest to one of militant rebellion—with the ultimate goal of overthrowing the establishment. For example, in June 1968, at a conference in East Lansing, Michigan, the SDS held a workshop on "sabotage and explosives," during which participants discussed such activities as firing Molotov cocktails from shotguns, jamming police radio equipment, and dropping thermite bombs down manholes to destroy communications systems.

By 1969, a debate broke out in the organization over the degree of commitment to violent resistance; the SDS split into factions, one of which proclaimed itself more single-mindedly revolutionary in mission and tactics. This faction called itself "The Weathermen," an allusion to the line, "You don't need a weatherman to know which way the wind blows."

The Weathermen position paper of June 1969 called for a clandestine organization of revolutionaries with a unified "general staff." It urged that schools and colleges be closed down because "...kids are ready for the full scope of militant struggle...."

On September 4, 1969, twenty-six women, members of the Weathermen, were arrested for using violent tactics at a local high school. Also in September, Bernardine Dohrn, a Weathermen leader who had recently spent six weeks in Cuba, called for militant demonstrations in Chicago from October 8 through October 11, 1969, to protest the trial of eight defendants accused of violating federal antiriot statutes at the 1968 Democratic National Convention. The real purpose of these October demonstrations, according to an FBI report, was to engage in street action to gain experience in revolutionary tactics. During these demonstrations, the Weathermen and their followers battled police, broke windows, smashed cars, and attacked bystanders. Police arrested over 250 men and women.

The strategy of the Weathermen was further defined at a self-styled "war council" held in Flint, Michigan, in December of 1969, the building of a small, tough paramilitary organization designed to carry out urban guerrilla warfare to bring about a revolution. At the Flint "war council," one Weathermen leader urged the establishment of an underground movement using tactics developed by Arab terrorists. He stressed the need to kill police and to learn the use of guns and bombs.

Three months after this meeting, dynamite explosions in a townhouse in Greenwich Village in New York City killed Weathermen activists Ted Gold and Diana Oughton. The townhouse was owned by the father of Cathlyn Wilkerson, a Weathermen leader. Fifty-nine sticks of dynamite and other explosives were later discovered in a Chicago apartment rented to a Weathermen activist who used an assumed name. This cache matched the dynamite found unexploded in Detroit police installations on March 6, 1970.

In addition to the SDS and the Weathermen, the 1970 FBI report also discussed other student dissident groups, including the New Mobilization Committee to End the War in Vietnam, the Young Socialist Alliance, and the Student Mobilization Committee to End the War in Vietnam, documenting their sympathies with communist ideology and their international ties. The report did not say that these organizations were under the control of the Soviet Union or Cuba, but it did trace the travels of their principal leaders to Eastern Europe and Castro's Cuba.

The report also analyzed the Black Power movement, focusing on the Black Panthers, easily "the most notorious and dangerous" of then-current black militant groups. The Black Panthers was organized in 1966 at Oakland, California, and by 1970 its membership was estimated at some nine hundred members in forty cities—not a large group, but one that had attracted thousands of sympathizers in the white as well as the black communities. Many of these sympathizers followed the progress of the group through its newspaper, *The Black Panther*, which was published every week with more than 100,000 copies distributed nationally.

Though its nominal leader was "Chief of Staff" David Hilliard, its three top leaders were: Huey P. Newton—co-founder and "Minister of Defense" (convicted and jailed for killing a police officer); Bobby Seale—co-founder and "Chairman" (at the time of the report, Seale was in jail and awaiting trial for murder); and Eldridge Cleaver, "Minister of Information" (Cleaver was hiding out in

Algeria). The Black Panthers openly called for the overthrow of the U.S. government, the assassination of the president, and a war of liberation. A 1969 Black Panther pamphlet, "Revolution and Education," written by Cleaver sums up the Panther platform: "In order to destroy the American social order, we have to destroy the present structure of power in the United States, we have to overthrow the government." In 1969 alone, 348 Panthers were arrested for serious crimes, including murder, armed robbery, rape, bank robbery, and burglary. Between 1967 and 1970, Black Panther members were convicted of crimes on more than 450 occasions, and 310 others were awaiting trial for criminal violations.

At least twenty Panther members were killed during the four-year period leading up to the report. The Panthers claimed that they were the victims of "police brutality," but of the twenty, ten died in shoot-outs with police that were initiated by Panthers; four were killed by rival gangs; two were killed by persons unknown; one was killed by a store owner during a hold-up attempt; one died of barbiturate overdose; one was killed by his wife over an extramarital affair; and one was murdered, apparently by Panthers themselves (fourteen were indicted for the crime).

This last case is instructive. In May 1969, the mutilated body of Panther Alex Rackley was found in Connecticut. Rackley had been beaten, stuck repeatedly with an ice pick, scalded with boiling water, and finally shot twice with a .45 caliber pistol. Of the fourteen Panther members indicted, two entered guilty pleas. Rackley was murdered because he was suspected of being a police informant.

As the result of arrests at Panther offices during 1968 and 1969, law enforcement officers uncovered 125 machine guns, sawed-off shotguns and rifles, thousands of rounds of ammunition, assorted knives, machetes, bayonets, homemade bombs, gunpowder, and forty-seven Molotov cocktails. In addition to this cache of weapons, the Black Panther newspaper printed articles on the use, care, and manufacture of firearms and explosives. The newspaper also cautioned members not to buy small caliber weapons. The editors recommended high-powered rifles able "...to knock the pig out of his shoes at a distance of three or more blocks."

In dealing with this increasing violence, the FBI was caught in a cross-fire. On the one hand, President Johnson, conservative Democrats, and most Republicans were calling on us to end these shocking acts, which were filling the front pages of their newspapers every morning and their television screens every night. On the other hand, the Left was crying "fascism" and "McCarthyism" every time any law enforcement agency attempted to intervene.

In the face of this mounting challenge to the stability of American society, Hoover's level of frustration peaked. One day he called me into his office and asked, "Isn't there some way we can slap some of these riot leaders in jail?" He brought his fist down on the desk. "This burning and looting is an outrage. How about the conspiracy statute?"

I shook my head sadly.

"We're keeping in close touch with the Department of Justice on all outbreaks," I said. "The protest leaders are playing it close to the chest. Publicly, they keep shouting 'nonviolence' and claim that the outbreaks are spontaneous or else provoked by local police. Privately, of course, they're agitating and provoking these youngsters to riot."

"Well, stay on top of it," he demanded. "And tell all of our special agents in charge to be alert to any possible violations within our jurisdiction."

But I hadn't told him what he wanted to hear. He was no longer satisfied with this wait-and-watch philosophy. It appeared to him— and to a majority of Americans—that the very survival of the nation was at stake. No one believed that these students and young blacks could by themselves overthrow the government. They were little more than a petulant mob. But the kind of disorder they promoted was potentially dangerous, and Hoover feared the New Left might open the door for a more purposeful revolution, one that could harness the unbridled rage.

At this point, William Sullivan came up with a plan of action, a suggestion that made him cock of the walk: use COINTELPRO— the active counter-intelligence program we used against Communists and the Klan—against the New Left. That meant infiltrating the organizations, gaining positions of authority, then gathering intelligence, promoting dissention in the ranks, and pushing self-destructive policies. And that was just for starters. Agents would recruit informants from within the organization and use them as intelligence gatherers; plant false information to mislead the organization in its development of strategy; and discredit true-believing organization officials by engineering circumstances to suggest they were disloyal to their cause and fellow members. The strategy also included using the press to embarrass the organization with hostile press releases, leaked information, and false news stories.

Bringing the full force of COINTELPRO also meant black bag work—surveilling comings and goings, bugging offices and residences, and tapping telephones lines.

If COINTELPRO sounds deliberately deceptive, an exercise in lying and mean-spiritedness, it was certainly these things, and intentionally so. Planned as a means of combatting the Communist party, those who instituted the program simply proposed that we do to the Communists what they were doing to us.

The same methods were used against the Ku Klux Klan in Mississippi. Agents became Klan members, sowed seeds of discontent, set one klansman against another, collected intelligence, and recruited informants—just as we later did to the SDS. Indeed, had it not been for COINTELPRO techniques, we might never have found the bodies of Schwerner, Chaney, and Goodman or gathered sufficient evidence to try and convict their killers.

It is difficult to assess the ultimate effectiveness of COINTELPRO against the New Left. We placed agents in their midst, recruited informants, and learned a great deal about their activities and future plans. We caused dissension within their ranks, harassed them, and built cases for indictments—some of which resulted in convictions. Eventually, the anger on campuses died down, in part because young people have a low attention span, in part because college administrations obediently transformed their philosophies and curricula to accommodate the revolutionaries, in part because of the activities of law enforcement agencies, including the FBI.

The use of COINTELPRO opened up the bureau to criticism from the Left, especially as William Sullivan's ambition got the better of him and he began to skirt closer and closer to the edge of the law, and eventually began to ignore it entirely. It wasn't the first time that COINTELPRO had been put to uses other than fighting communism. And no one ever complained that COINTELPRO had violated the civil rights of klansmen. But when it became known that the FBI was using those same tactics against the New Left in the late 1960s, the media turned on the FBI with a vengeance.

In those days, television in particular supported student revolutionaries, not only because they were protesting against the war in Vietnam, but also because they made the evening news almost as exciting as the civil rights movement had during the demonstrations of 1963 and 1964. And the press showed great sympathy for even the most militant and revolutionary black organizations, shrugging off the fact that some had engaged in robberies and murder. The Black Panthers in particular were lionized by the media; Leonard Bernstein, the idol of New York's elite, actually threw a fund-raising party for the group in his posh New York apartment, a party memorialized in Tom Wolfe's brilliant satire of the Left, *Radical Chic*. The FBI did not share in the media's enthusiasm for radicals, which brought upon it the thunder of the self-righteous media.

Still, some media critics did have a point. Increasingly Sullivan was running COINTELPRO as if it were an independent agency, without accountability to the law or even to J. Edgar Hoover. Hoover's critics blame him, and in a sense he was to blame, as was I, since these activities took place on our watch. Hoover, however, neither planned nor supervised all COINTELPRO operations. Though generally sympathetic, he was largely unaware of what was happening—the illegal break-ins to gather intelligence, the involvement of agents in undercover operations that led to violence, the intimidation of university professors and administrators.

During those days, I was assistant to the director and Sullivan's immediate supervisor, yet even I didn't know how far he'd gone. His reports were spare and conventional in tone and contained few specifics. When we got wind of his excesses, however, we asked for a complete report, after which Hoover immediately put a stop to the illegal techniques Sullivan was employing.

Sullivan almost got a second chance by skirting Hoover and going straight to the White House. In June 1970, with domestic unrest still a major problem, the Nixon White House attempted to consolidate and coordinate all intelligence initiatives to combat the forces that were destabilizing the nation—not only domestic unrest, but domestic violence. As President Nixon put it, "We must develop a plan which will enable us to curtail the illegal activities of those who are determined to destroy our society."

The chief White House figure behind the move for a comprehensive counter-intelligence program was Tom Charles Huston, who had been investigating the possibility of foreign involvement in student unrest. But the true architect of the plan that emerged was Sullivan, still in high favor with the director. And what eventuated, the so-called "Huston Plan," contained all the worst elements of COINTELPRO.

Hoover objected to the Huston Plan for at least three reasons. First, the plan codified procedures that were extralegal. The director specifically rejected intercepting mail and surreptitious entry on the grounds that they were against the law. Second, the plan was reminiscent of an earlier move to establish a super-intelligence agency, one that might invite the CIA and other federal agencies to become involved in the business of the FBI. Hoover liked things the way they were, with areas of jurisdiction strictly defined and scrupulously observed. Third, given the hostility of the press to current efforts to clamp down on the New Left, the director was afraid that if the plan leaked out—and he knew that in Washington such leaks were likely—the media would roast everybody involved over an open fire.

So Hoover killed the Huston Plan by the simple expedient of telling the president that of course he would go ahead—as soon the president gave him a written order. Nixon of course would never do that; Hoover had him checked, and he knew it. Hoover thereby stopped what might have been a major, even a criminal assault by the U.S. government on American civil liberties. Once again it was the politicians who wanted to break the law, and the supposedly power-mad Hoover who, with not a hint of moralistic grand-standing, stopped it.

This move by Hoover infuriated Sullivan and transformed him into a dedicated and dangerous enemy. Though Sullivan had not invented the Huston Plan, he had been involved in its creation; his credibility with the White House rested on its success. When the Plan was consigned to the ash heap, Sullivan's dream of succeeding Hoover seemed doomed as well. Already in his late fifties, he knew he had reached the end of his climb, still short of the peak; and the thought must have galled him beyond endurance.

Abruptly his manner toward Hoover changed. No longer did he write fawning memos, comparing the director to the great men of history. No longer did he laugh loudly at Hoover's jokes and compliment his ties. Instead, he sulked in his tent and became increasingly independent—dangerous behavior for anyone working under J. Edgar Hoover.

As for Hoover, he had changed his mind about Sullivan. Sullivan's involvement in the Huston Plan had opened the director's eyes to his subordinate's ambition and his willingness to ignore the chain of command to further his own cause. At last Hoover began to recognize Sullivan's sycophancy for what it was—an attempt to advance his own career by exploiting an old man's vanity. And when Sullivan began giving unauthorized interviews and making speeches revealing the bureau's innermost secrets, the director made his move.

Sullivan was told to take a two-week leave—to give him time to reevaluate his actions and consider his future. When he came back to work on Monday morning, he found someone else sitting at his desk. The name on the office door had been changed. So had the lock. The decision had been made: He was retiring.

Hoover's opposition to the Huston Plan notwithstanding, liberals in Congress were soon calling for an investigation of our activities. Such an investigation came in 1975, led by Senator Frank Church, who combined the self-righteousness of a spoiled preacher with the ideological zeal of an early Marxist. Predictably, the report was highly critical of our conduct during the late 1960s. Nor was that the end of the matter. During the Carter administration, Attorney General Griffin Bell—in an effort to appease the militant spirit of the times—allowed irresponsible Justice Department attorneys to indict two good men on felony charges stemming from the COIN-TELPRO activities against the New Left. On November 6, 1980, in U.S. District Court for the District of Columbia, a jury found former bureau executives Mark Felt and Ed Miller guilty of conspiring "to injure and oppress" relatives and friends of the Weathermen group, because, in the chain of command, they authorized surreptitious entry into private residences—a COINTELPRO activity used only under extreme circumstances.

It is impossible, of course, to defend all the activities of COINTEL-PRO, except in the case of an imminent threat to the survival of the nation and the lives of its citizens or the ultimate stability of the social order. Some of what went on—the black bag operations—was unambiguously illegal. And many of the other tactics, while merely skirting the edges of the law, were incompatible with the idea of a nation committed to equal protection under the law for all people, whether murderers or Ku Kluxers or raging revolutionaries.

On the other hand, no government has ever been so righteous or so foolish as to stick strictly to the letter of its laws when its very survival or the life and freedom of its citizens are at stake. Abraham Lincoln ordered newspaper presses wrecked, threw hostile editors in prison and denied them a writ of habeas corpus, illegally created a state (West Virginia), and used troops to prevent the free assembly of American citizens. Yet we have erected a monument to him in the nation's capital and he is considered one of the nation's finest heroes.

The problem is that too many people still refuse to acknowledge the dangers involved in the riots and revolutionary activities of the New Left. Like Powers, critics of the FBI want to believe that these violent and destructive mobs were simply engaged in "the American political process."

They are wrong. The FBI was willing to challenge them on their own terms to protect the larger interests of society. Bill Sullivan was the wrong man for the job. But that doesn't mean the job didn't need to be done.

13

....

Hoover, the Mob, and Joe Valachi

ON A RAIN-SOAKED NOVEMBER AFTERNOON in 1957, Sergeant Edgar D. Croswell of the New York State Police entered a motel in Apalachin, a small, unobtrusive village nestled in the mountains just a few miles from the Pennsylvania line. He was there to investigate a bad-check complaint. While he was standing at the front desk, waiting to speak to the manager, he heard the clerk on the phone.

"Joseph M. Barbara? Yes, we have the reservations in Mr. Barbara's name." And he rattled off a huge number of rooms.

Croswell was astonished at the sheer number of rooms. And the name rang a bell too. Barbara owned an enormous private estate nearby and was a suspect in connection with two unsolved murders in Pennsylvania. A rumor had also circulated that Barbara had hosted a meeting of mobsters in Binghamton, New York, only a year earlier. Croswell's curiosity was piqued.

The next day, he persuaded state trooper Vincent Vasisko and a couple of Treasury agents to accompany him on a drive out to Barbara's estate—just to look around. The Treasury agents came along because they suspected that Barbara was a bootlegger and was probably not paying federal taxes on the whiskey he sold. Although admittedly on a fishing expedition, they had alerted the state and local police to stand by.

When they arrived at the Barbara estate, they were surprised at the number of cars jammed into the huge driveway—Cadillacs, Rolls-Royces, stretch limousines. Croswell turned his patrol car into the driveway, just as a car was leaving. It made an abrupt U-turn, and raced back toward the house—obviously to warn the others that the cops had arrived.

As Croswell was telephoning his backup, men poured out of the doors like fire ants out of a damaged mound. They jumped into cars and zoomed across fields, looking desperately for escape routes. But the police set up barriers and were able to stop and identify more than sixty mobsters from various parts of the country. Included in the fleeing hoard were such well-known crime figures as Joseph Bonanno, Carlo Gambino, Vito Genovese, Joseph Profaci, Santos Trafficante, and John Scalise. Forty more slipped through the net.

Incredible as it may seem, only after this meeting was reported did the FBI have sufficient proof to say that there was such a thing as La Cosa Nostra—a national crime syndicate. And only much later did we learn the long and complicated history of organized crime in America.

On October 15, 1890, David Hennessy, the New Orleans superintendent of police, was ambushed by mob triggermen and killed. A large number of immigrants were arrested by police and questioned. Eventually, nineteen were indicted. Of those, sixteen were declared "not guilty" and the other three got a hung jury. When the nineteen were remanded to a parish prison to await the disposition of other pending charges, a lynch mob, bent on vengeance, attacked the prison. The warden, realizing he couldn't protect his prisoners, allowed them to make a run for it. Seven escaped, but the remaining twelve were shot or hanged.

The Hennessy murder and the subsequent lynchings focused public attention on the problem of crime, and rumors had it that criminals were organized into a local group quite similar to the current Cosa Nostra. A New Orleans grand jury, reporting on the lynchings, said in part: "Our research has developed the existence of the secret organization styled 'mafia.' Officers of the mafia and many of its members were not known. Among them are men born in this city of Italian origin. The large number of the Society is composed of Italians and Sicilians." The mafia was not—could not be—eliminated.

This report, drafted more than a hundred years ago, defined the organization in terms that are applicable today. Membership in La Cosa Nostra is not open to all comers. To be a full member, a candidate must be of Italian descent and be proposed by another member in good standing, and then approved by a vote.

An informant also reported that one prerequisite of membership was that the candidate commit a murder in the interest of the "family," an act referred to internally as "making his bones." This benefitted the family in three ways. First, it tested the manhood of the candidate. Second, it eliminated an enemy of the family. And third, it gave the family something to hold over the head of the new initiate should he decide to resign, or defect.

The code of La Cosa Nostra, as outlined by FBI informants, is as follows:

1. To place the organization above wife, children, country, or religion
2. To follow the orders of his captain explicitly and without question
3. To pay assessments imposed upon him by his captain, regardless of their purpose
4. To disclose nothing about the organization to outsiders
5. To respect all members, despite personal feelings; to pay all debts owed to other members; and never to steal from or make disparaging remarks about other members
6. To refrain from associating with other members' wives, sisters, or daughters except with honorable intentions.

The structure of La Cosa Nostra bears a striking resemblance to the armies of ancient Rome, with each "caporegima," or captain, responsible for a number of "soldatis," or soldiers. At the top is the boss and one or more underbosses, as well as an advisor who is called a "consigliere."

The most common criminal activities of La Cosa Nostra are labor racketeering, arson, murder, political corruption, loan sharking, gambling, narcotics, pornography, and infiltrating legitimate businesses. La Cosa Nostra families also engage in some legitimate enterprises, to turn a legitimate profit and at the same time cover up illegal operations or launder money from their illicit activities. These have included waterfront businesses, meat packing, waste disposal, vending machines, bars and liquor stores, restaurants and hotels, real estate, and administrating labor unions.

After speaking on the subject, I have sometimes been asked if it's true that the mafia is made up entirely of Italians. My answer, based on years of research, is always the same: "Not entirely, although the code does call for members to be of Italian or Sicilian extraction." And Buck Revell, an agent who speciazied in the mob, once testified: "Over the entire history of La Cosa Nostra, they have had close working relationships with Jewish mobsters, Irish mobsters, those of every ethnic stripe.... But, over a period of many years, there has been one change in membership. It used to be that you had to have Sicilian blood on your father's side... [But] the Neapolitans were able to change the rules so that you had to have Italian blood—so the Neapolitans and Calabrians could also be members of La Cosa Nostra."

Perhaps the best example that other ethnic groups were acceptable was Meyer Lansky, a non-Italian Jew, who played a key role in mob activities. Lansky was the "brains" and chief treasurer of the mafia, a man who sat at the center of a vast illicit financial empire like a clever, patient spider. Unlike many kingpins of La Cosa Nostra, he was never indicted, lived to an old age, and died in bed rather than writhing on the sidewalk, full of bullet holes. This was probably because he only served as a kind of "consultant" and was not involved in the day-to-day activities of the hoods.

But Lansky was nevertheless hounded unmercifully by the FBI

through "close surveillance" tactics that lasted for many years. Lansky used to complain bitterly that he could not "even enjoy visits from my son because of the FBI." We kept on his case because he was not only a wizard at illicit money management, but also a source of priceless information. He received a steady stream of mobster visitors, all of whom we observed, tailed, and identified. In this manner we compiled our own "Who's Who in the Mob."

There are three organized crime groups indigenous to Italy. The first, the Sicilian mafia, the largest and most powerful, emanates from the eastern region of the island of Sicily. This branch has strong connections to Palermo and is international in scope, with members in every part of the world.

The second is the Camorra, a secret society essentially from Naples, but also international in scope.

The third is the N'Drangheta, which comes from Calabria, or the "boot toe" of Italy. This last is closely allied with the Sicilian mafia, but it is largely autonomous, with strong tentacles in North America.

La Cosa Nostra was the name the "Eastern establishment" of organized crime gave itself, while the term "mafia" came from the underworld membership that originated in Sicily. The United States has become the self-identified headquarters of organized crime groups that grew from their roots in Italy and then merged.

Although La Cosa Nostra predates the 1930s, historians of crime generally credit Charles "Lucky" Luciano with establishing a "national commission" to coordinate and administer the criminal activities of the various families. After engineering the assassination of underworld boss Salvator Maranzano in September 1931, the thirty-four-year-old Luciano went on to restructure the U.S. mafia into a federation of families. He initiated plans to resolve interfamily disputes, give promotions within the ranks, and establish supervisory policies. He did precisely what the captains of industry had begun doing a few decades earlier—expanded local operations into a nationwide chain with a central board that made major policy decisions. Luciano was merely following in the footsteps of Kress and A&P—except that the "chain" he organized wasn't selling notions or groceries but illicit whisky, sex, "protection," stolen goods, and murder.

True to his name, "Lucky" was a survivor. He was never gunned down by rivals, as were so many mobsters during that era and later. He went to prison for a while in 1936, and he was finally deported in 1946. But for fifteen years he was the most successful and imaginative of La Cosa Nostra leaders, the Henry Ford of organized crime.

By the 1930s, as the result of Luciano's managerial genius, La Cosa Nostra began to assume control of whole industries of illicit operations; eventually it grew to an organization of some five thousand people in two dozen different families. Today the membership has decreased to about 1,700 identified and initiated members. Like major national and multinational corporations, it has reduced personnel and tightened its belt to survive in the leaner, meaner 1990s. Currently, there are about ten nonmembers working full-time for every legitimate member.

La Cosa Nostra has even gone international. Organized crime has grown in Canada, where two of the strongest groups are the Ruzzoto and Catroni families, the latter in control of crime in Montreal. These Canadian cousins have cooperated with La Cosa Nostra families in Buffalo and Detroit, notably the Bonannos, Patriarcas, Gambinos, and Genoveses.

Despite this now-familiar history of the mob in America, it surprises most people to learn that from the early 1930s until 1957, J. Edgar Hoover had insisted that there was no such thing as La Cosa Nostra—that is, a network of interrelated mobs that coordinated activities and maintained a kind of corporate discipline. He believed the gangs were local, and he expected local authorities to take care of the problem. Some of his critics have suggested that he refused to believe in a national syndicate because he was unwilling to undertake such a daunting challenge.

Anthony Summers, in his error-filled book, *Official and Confidential,* predictably takes a paranoid view of Hoover's early reluctance to treat the mob as a national crime syndicate. In brief, Summers says the mob found out Hoover was a homosexual and blackmailed him with photographs to keep the FBI from harassing them. Summers insists that Meyer Lansky was the mastermind of this blackmail scheme, although the FBI hounded Lansky for decades and even tapped his telephone.

The true reasons for Hoover's reluctance to target the mob were far less dramatic, though damning in their own way. His profound contempt for the criminal mind, combined with his enormous faith in the agency he had created, persuaded him that no such complex national criminal organization could exist without him knowing about it. He didn't know about it; ergo, it did not exist.

Hoover's obduracy did not mean he was unwilling to confront the mob wherever it surfaced. In fact, from the 1940s into the 1970s, Hoover launched no fewer than three separate initiatives to attack organized crime. And contrary to some historians, the FBI was quite effective, given the limitations under which the bureau labored in earlier years.

Jurisdiction was our major problem. We simply were not allowed to pursue the mob unless it clearly violated federal law. We nevertheless tried to maintain surveillance on known mobsters, looking for excuses to move in at the first indication of a federal infraction. Hoover pushed us to the limits, so much so that we occasionally stepped beyond our legal purview and were forced to back down.

Shortly after World War II ended, the FBI began its first major initiative against racketeering. Hoover called it by the code name CAPGA, and agents in all parts of the country were pressed to investigate organized crime and to gather information on all known criminals. One of the figures targeted was Bugsy Siegel.

An informant from out West had told the FBI that Siegel was coming to New York to restructure his shaky finances by negotiating a loan to build a casino in Las Vegas—the Desert Inn. The chief banker for this project, agents were told, was Frank Costello. They immediately began to surveil his activities. Every night Costello would entertain Siegel and a select group of the New York mob in the Copa Cabana, and every night agents would swarm all over the place, fitting all sorts of pieces into the giant jigsaw puzzle of organized crime.

Then, quite suddenly, the attorney general, Tom Clark, told us to discontinue our operations. Agents in the field were stunned. They were in the middle of a gold mine, picking up nuggets every hour. But the attorney general's office pointed out that we had no business investigating activities that could not be construed as violating federal law. We later heard that a complaint had been filed by Senator Pat McCarran of Nevada, claiming that our activities were designed to damage the economy of his state. As a result, we were careful in the future to find potential violations of federal law.

Of course, we had already learned a few tricks. In 1942, two desperate criminals, both involved in organized crime, broke out of Illinois State Prison. One was Roger "The Terrible" Touhy, a notorious gangster from Detroit who was doing time for the Chicago kidnapping of Jake "The Barber" Factor. The other was Basil Banghart, convicted of bank robbery. Both were serving long sentences and had little to lose.

They were armed and dangerous yet Hoover wanted to enter the case, though legally their escape only involved the state of Illinois, which had few resources for tracking down such desperate men.

Finally someone hit on the perfect solution—a clear breach of a federal statute—and the FBI swung into action. In a raid Hoover led personally, agents swarmed into the field, and Touhy and Banghart were soon recaptured. The federal law they had violated? It was the Selective Service Act, which required young men to notify their draft boards when they changed their address.

At times the bureau was able to use Labor Racketeering statutes to move into organized crime. For example, when the mob took control of some unions in the motion picture industry, they did so in violation of federal law, and we were able to enter the case.

In another famous incident, Johnny Dioguardia, a member of La Cosa Nostra, had arranged a hit on Victor Riesel, who was preparing to testify in court about mob influence in the unions. Riesel's attacker threw acid in his face and blinded him for life. Agents were able to enter the case by virtue of two federal laws: the Labor Racketeering statute and the Obstruction of Justice statute. Riesel, a man of great courage, became a national figure and, though blind, continued to write a syndicated column exposing corrupt elements in the trade union movement.

Hijacking was also a federal crime; and, since the mob often transported stolen goods in stolen trucks, agents were sometimes able to bust them on this charge. In 1947, for example, the FBI netted up to fifteen members of the Westo gang on one memorable Brooklyn night, all for hijacking.

Another major criminal the FBI brought to justice by a creative use of federal law was Larry Gallo. He and his brother, "Crazy Joe," had originally worked for the Profaci family, allegedly as hit men. According to legend, Larry was one of those who shot Albert Anastasia, right-hand man of Frank Costello, in the barber shop of the Park Sheraton Hotel in New York.

Joseph Profaci, boss of the family, was notoriously cheap, and though he made $40 million a year on his illegal lottery, he paid the Gallos in small change for the muscle they provided him. The Gallos were not the only dissatisfied family members. Almost everybody was restless and resentful, perhaps the unhappiest of all the families in organized crime.

The Gallos finally decided to break away and establish their own operation—or force Profaci to cut them in for a bigger piece of the action. So they kidnapped two of Profaci's caporegimas, then called him on the phone and asked if he wanted to deal. Profaci reluctantly agreed, and suggested a meeting place—a closed bar, after hours.

Shortly after the meeting began, an off-duty policeman sneaked in the back door of the bar to steal a beer. He entered just in time to see a couple of Profaci hoods in the process of strangling Larry Gallo. They fled and Gallo was saved. But war broke out between the two groups.

The FBI was stuck on the sidelines, until under pressure from Hoover we found a way to bust Larry Gallo. It seems that he had obtained a federally insured mortgage and, to qualify, had declared in his application that he had a substantial annual income. But on his income tax return he had listed a fraction of that figure. Our agents told him, "We've got you one way or the other, Larry. You have a choice. You can either admit you were lying on your mortgage application or else tell the IRS that you cheated on your tax return. Which will it be?" Gallo consulted with his lawyer and pled guilty to the charge of filing a fraudulent mortgage application.

Our second big push against organized crime occurred in 1957, when we established the "Top Hoodlum Intelligence Program"— some months before the police stumbled onto the Apalachin meeting. The goal of the program was to identify and track the movements of every mob leader in the United States. I am convinced that, even without Apalachin, within a year or two we would have put enough of the pieces together to prove the existence of a national crime syndicate. In the meantime, our field agents, in close cooperation with local law enforcement officers, were teletyping information to Washington daily, reporting the movements of mob members at every level.

From these reports, studied and analyzed by our intelligence experts, we began to construct the first comprehensive picture of the operations of organized crime. We began to see that one fundamental mob strategy was to use illegal means—from bribery and control of politicians and bureaucrats to threats and extortion against legitimate competitors—to promote their success in respectable business and financial dealings. We also found that the mob employed huge numbers of nonmembers—literally hundreds of thousands of petty crooks who committed more than a million crimes daily in major cities across the nation. Most people never saw the mob in action, or didn't recognize its activities when they did see them. At best they only caught a glimpse of the shark's fin.

But as our Top Hoodlum program progressed, we saw the mob break the surface of the water, and caught a glimpse of its sharp, pointed teeth. For example, we began to measure the degree to which members and associates were both murderers and the victims of murder. Mob killings were particularly gruesome—and for a reason. They were usually carried out not only as punishment for betrayal, but to warn others of the wages of disloyalty.

In the early 1960s, we began to notice sudden disappearances. When one mobster dropped out of sight, we would become curious and question local police about gangland killings. Despite the public impression that the mob tries to avoid unnecessary violence, we found that mob murder was as prevalent and brutal as portrayed by Hollywood's gangland movies. One year within a few months in Chicago alone we monitored three exceptionally brutal killings:

- Leo Foreman, ex-con, professional wrestler, and enforcer for Chicago mobster Sam De Stefano, missing for days, was finally located in the trunk of his car. He had been stabbed four times in the back, once in the chest, and once in the right forearm. He had also been shot in the left hip and right arm. Needless to say, he was dead.

- Anthony Moschiano, twenty-six-years-old and already a member of the Chicago crime syndicate, was an associate of thirty-five-year-old Thomas Durso, a Chicago police officer involved in illegal narcotics trade activities, which violated federal law. In November 1963, Moschiano and Durso had an argument in front of some of their colleagues over some heroin Durso had turned over to Moschiano. As the meeting grew more heated, Durso left the room. When he returned, he suggested that everyone come with him down to the garage. When they got there the trunk of Durso's car was open, lined heavily with newspapers, as if to protect the floor from getting soiled. Durso and his accomplices handcuffed Moschiano, stuffed rags into his mouth, and threw him into the trunk, where Durso carved him up with a hunting knife. His body was found in the Des Plaines river two months later.

- On August 31, 1964, Guy Mendolia, Jr., member of Chicago organized crime, drove his Cadillac into the garage behind his Stone Park, Illinois, home. Seconds later, five shotgun volleys rattled windows throughout the neighborhood. Then a car careened onto the street, screeched, and sped out of sight. When the first witness reached Mendolia, it was too late. He was lying on his back, mouth open, his shirt blown half off, killed instantly by several blasts, one of which

blew a hole in the back of his neck, reducing his spinal
column to jelly.

Mendolia, a notorious burglar and robber, was associated with
the notorious Paul "Peanuts" Panczko gang. In 1962, Panczko and
his gang pulled a heist that netted them jewelry valued at one and
three-quarters million dollars. In 1963, bad blood developed
between Panczko and Mendolia, and Mendolia was murdered, we
believed, by the Panczko crowd. But though police investigated the
slaying thoroughly, all involved maintained the code of silence.

A steady stream of such reports, with photographs, began to give
us a picture of life in La Cosa Nostra. First, despite their enormous
power and their reputation for revenge against transgressors of the
code, La Cosa Nostra bosses were unable to keep the system running as smoothly as before. At the lower levels, the soldiers were
often uncontrollable and either fell out with one another or
betrayed their superiors.

These "disruptions" were more numerous than most people realized. For every dead body discovered—usually intentionally, as a grisly warning—two more may have been executed leaving no trace.

As soon as Hoover heard about Apalachin, he acted. Years later he
would tell Buck Revell, "I assigned seventy-five agents to conduct a
thorough investigation of every individual present at that meeting.
They discovered that four days earlier, a national meeting of La
Cosa Nostra leaders—a gathering larger than the one at
Apalachin—had convened at the estate of Ruggiero Boiardo, a captain of the Vito Genovese family, lasting from noon until five the
following morning. As they were leaving, participants were invited
to attend the Apalachin meeting.

"At that point, it was obvious that while the largest organizations were still in New York and Chicago, a network of organized
crime extended clear across the United States and it was held
together by Cosa Nostra and mafia bosses, with roots that extended abroad, as well as into the past."

Suddenly our Top Hoodlums program had become urgent. And
it began to pay off in the most concrete way possible—in arrests

and convictions. La Cosa Nostra is run like a major corporation, with a vast staff to help its leadership. To uncover prosecutable offenses often takes months, even years of research and investigation, and even then the well-insulated bosses often evade conviction. But we began to get arrests and convictions regularly. We were also able to build files, with names and pictures of La Cosa Nostra "commission" members; the names and pictures of other "Key Cosa Nostra Leaders," identifying the area each controlled; and the organizational structure of major Cosa Nostra families, including the boss, underboss, consiglieri, and caporegimas; and a list of the legal and illegal enterprises in which they are involved.

In the 1960s we got additional help. In 1961, Congress passed antiracketeering legislation that for the first time gave the FBI federal jurisdiction over some mob activities. Our jurisdiction was further expanded with the passage of the Omnibus Crime Control and Safe Streets Act of 1968 and the Organized Crime Control Act of 1970. The first of these included a provision for conducting court-ordered electronic surveillance; the second contained the Racketeer Influenced and Corrupt Organization Statute, popularly known as "RICO." Both were clearly designed to give the FBI and other law enforcement agencies additional muscle to challenge the mob. The RICO statute was particularly useful, since it allowed us to target and destroy all their illicit activities rather than merely investigate the crimes of one individual. RICO increased criminal penalties by providing minimum twenty-year sentences and allowing the government to seize property and bring civil action to deter illegal enterprises. In all, we now had an arsenal of weapons to use against organized crime. And then we got the big break—the greatest intelligence bonanza in the history of the war against organized crime—Joe Valachi.

On June 22, 1962, a prisoner in the federal penitentiary in Atlanta seized a two-foot length of iron pipe and beat fellow inmate John Saupp to death before guards could break up the fight. The man wielding the pipe was Joseph Valachi; and he believed that the man he'd killed had been ordered by mobster and fellow prisoner Vito Genovese of the Lucchese family to kill him. Valachi knew he could never repair his ties with the mob, that he would eventually be killed. With nothing left to lose, he turned to the FBI.

We began a lengthy dialogue with him in early September of 1962. He admitted being a member for more than thirty years of one of the major families and agreed to testify publicly about the structure of organized crime in America.

But there was one major hitch. The FBI agents doing the interviews were from the Atlanta office since that's where Valachi was in prison. And the Atlanta agents had trouble understanding Valachi. He was constantly dropping names unknown to anyone unfamiliar with New York mobology and in an ethnic patois unique to New York's Italian-American hoodlums.

Eventually, the New York office asked if Valachi could be transferred to a prison somewhere in the New York area, where the Lucchese family couldn't get to him. They finally found a nice little Westchester County jail, located in White Plains. Called "the penthouse," it was as private and pleasant a canary cage as anyone could have wished.

When Valachi was safely relocated, local agents began to question him daily, and the information flowed. Everyone was delighted.

Except for one remaining problem. As with any witness, the agents weren't certain if he was leveling with them—was his memory really as prodigious as it seemed? He remembered names, faces, and events of decades past, apparently with total recall. Could he be for real?

Every evening, the agents would prepare a teletype report for the Washington office. Their supervisor would read the report before sending it. One evening, while reading away, he rose in his chair.

Valachi was telling the agents about a murder that had been committed in Valachi's own restaurant, years earlier. The victim was Vito Genovese's brother-in-law, and the hit had been ordered by Genovese himself. It seems that Genovese's wife had started frequenting her brother's bar, had met a lesbian there, and had engaged in a lengthy affair with the woman—apparently with her brother's knowledge. When Genovese found out, he couldn't kill his own wife, but he took his revenge by killing her brother, an accomplice in the betrayal.

According to Valachi's story, the brother-in-law was invited to a birthday party at the restaurant, and while Valachi went out to check the streets, the murder took place. As they were "walking" the dead man out to the car, a cop on the beat suddenly rounded the corner and headed straight for them. The policeman stopped for a moment, peered at the figure dangling between the two men, and said, "Got a real load on, ain't he?"

"Sure has," said one of the murderers, "and boy, is his wife going to be burned up!"

The cop laughed and walked on down the street.

As the supervisor read the report, it was not the gruesome humor of the story that caught his attention, but the name of the restaurant. He and his wife had eaten there often when they were first married.

She had been working in a law office, and he was just a field agent, assigned to espionage cases. The restaurant was right next to the subway stop, and after work they would meet there, have dinner, and go home. Sometimes he would arrive first and sometimes she would. Occasionally, while waiting for her, he would sit at the bar and have a drink. The owner, Joe Vega, usually sat at the other end of the bar. One night the agent and the owner struck up a conversation, and they soon became friendly.

One evening a friend of the agent's, a policeman, happened to come into the bar, saw the couple, waved, and called out, "Hey, I didn't know the FBI paid you well enough to eat in a place like this."

The agent laughed, but out of the corner of his eye he thought he saw Vega stiffen. From then on, Vega seemed as friendly as ever, but he never stopped by the table again. Then, one evening the agent saw something that explained the change. A drug dealer—one of the agent's informants—came into the restaurant, failed to spot the couple, walked up to Vega, and slipped him an envelope. It was a quick, well-executed motion, but the agent caught it.

He turned and looked at his wife sadly.

"This is a nice restaurant," he said, "but we can't come in here again—we'll have to find another place."

Sitting in the FBI's New York office thirteen years later, the supervisor yelled to the two agents questioning Valachi.

"Hey, has this guy Joe Valachi got any aliases?"

"Yeah," one said and mentioned a couple. "And, oh yeah, a long time ago he used to be called 'Joe Vega.'"

The supervisor told them the story and then came up with an idea.

"Let's make up a mug sheet with my picture on it, then show it to Valachi with a bunch of other photographs. We can see if his memory is as good as he claims it is."

They did just that. Valachi went through each picture carefully, peering at them, identifying many by name. When they came at last to the supervisor's sheet, he looked at it, and his jaw dropped.

"Holy Christ," he said, "he's one of yours."

That's when we knew that Valachi was not only leveling with us, but had a prodigious memory and a great eye for a face. From then on, we trusted his information.

Valachi gave us two things that only a mob member of his age and rank could—a history of La Cosa Nostra from its beginnings and an almost-current organizational chart of the national crime syndicate. We knew who was in charge, at what level, and how they came to power. And we also knew in detail what crimes they had committed, including murders. We knew all of this because Joe Valachi had been there, seen it all happen—and had never forgotten a single detail. (He even remembered the license tag of the getaway car he was driving in 1923 when he was first convicted of a felony.) Like most of the mafia leaders, Valachi embarked on a life of crime when he was a teenager. He ended up in Sing Sing at the age of nineteen. Five years later he was back again. While there, two important things happened: he completed seventh grade, and a member of a rival gang stabbed him with a knife. Later, talking with an old-timer, he learned why. It seems there was a bitter rivalry between the Sicilians and the Neapolitans—and he was on the wrong side. He also heard for the first time about a secret crime organization.

By 1930, he had been invited to join this organization and became a soldier in what was known as the Castellammarese War. During this period, he killed his first man and began to move up in the ranks of La Cosa Nostra. Within the next few years he rubbed elbows with such major figures in organized crime as Joe Bonanno, Dutch Schultz, Lucky Luciano, Meyer Lansky, Vito Genovese, Thomas Lucchese, Frank Costello, Albert Anastasia, and Carlo Gambino.

Valachi was involved in numerous criminal activities, including prostitution, drugs, and murder. He could sit for hours gossiping about major criminal figures—their women, their petty quarrels, their secret vices—or chronicle in bloody detail the gang wars of three decades, telling who killed whom and why. He could also diagram the interlocking network of bosses, underbosses, caporegimas, and soldati, the men who ruled every illegal activity from gambling to prostitution to labor racketeering.

And he had a knack for telling a good story, a sense of humor that he used to punctuate the brutal horror of many of his anecdotes. Some of his best tales were no more than sidebars to criminal activity—Vito Genovese's undying love for a wife who betrayed him, how he met and married his own wife, how Frank Costello punished a hotel manager for asking him not to patronize the steam bath. Others were gripping blow-by-blow accounts of a major crime in progress.

In short, Valachi put names and faces on the organizational chart we had known about and had been tracking. In many cases we had already identified the figures in the "family" hierarchy. Now we knew how they came to occupy their positions, what kind of people they were, and wherein their weaknesses lay. At that point we were ready to move into a higher gear in pursuit of the mob.

Scheduled to come before Senator McClellan's Permanent Subcommittee on Investigations, Valachi had originally intended to reveal only enough information to implicate Genovese in a number of crimes and thereby gain a limited revenge. But we assigned Special Agent James Flynn to deal with him. Flynn, a sharp and skilled interrogator, went to work, and by the time Valachi was scheduled to go before the McClellan Subcommittee, he was primed, ready, and willing to tell all. He was the greatest song bird ever to flee the cage of La Cosa Nostra.

On September 27, 1963—in the caucus room of the Old Senate Office Building in Washington—Valachi spilled his guts. He told the world almost everything he knew about La Cosa Nostra. He described in intricate detail the structure, power bases, membership requirements, codes, and identities of many members of the mob.

In a voice that sounded like a New York harbor foghorn, Valachi identified twenty-five existing active components, or "families." With minimal prodding, he described crime after crime committed by the mob, providing names, dates, and places.

Needless to say, the Valachi testimony made headlines throughout the nation, and everyone involved wanted to take credit. J. Edgar Hoover was no exception. He called me into his office one day and asked: "What do you think about calling the good work of our agents to the attention of the press? I think the FBI deserves credit for inducing Valachi to talk."

By this time I had known him long enough to understand what would please him, what he probably had in mind.

"How about a story in the *Reader's Digest* under your signature?"

"Great idea!" he shot back. "Handle it at once."

I called Special Agent Bill Gunn to my office and outlined what I had in mind. Within days he had a good first draft on the article. When Hoover, Tolson, and I had approved a final draft, the director suggested that we clear the copy with Ed Guthman, press director for Attorney General Bobby Kennedy.

"O.K.," I said. "It might cause some flak, but it would cover all bases."

The following morning I walked down the hall to see Guthman, explained the purpose of the visit, and showed him the article.

"By the way," I said, "the editors at the *Reader's Digest* have already accepted it."

Guthman, usually an easy-going man, was visibly angry.

"Oh, no you don't!" he exclaimed. "Bobby has already seen the bureau's memo on this subject. He wants a story giving the Justice Department and the attorney general the credit for this caper. In fact, Bobby has already contacted Peter Maas to write an article for the *Saturday Evening Post*."

"But Ed," I said, "Bobby and the Justice Department had

absolutely nothing to do with this matter. FBI agents made the contact with Valachi and got him to testify."

Guthman, a Kennedy loyalist, shook his head.

"Doesn't matter. We—and not the FBI—intend to take the credit. I'll be right back," he said, and stalked out of the office, a man on a mission.

Fifteen minutes later he returned with a triumphant look on his face.

"I was right. Bobby will handle this matter."

I opened my mouth to speak, then decided to drop the matter. Further protest was futile. I went back to my own office, phoned Hoover, and told him what had happened.

He was silent for a moment.

"What do you propose?" he said finally.

I already had an answer—a strategy that had worked under similar circumstances in the past.

"I suggest we leak the matter to an experienced reporter like Sandy Smith of the *Chicago Sun-Times*. That should stop them in their tracks."

"A good idea," Hoover said, "but be careful how you manage it."

Obviously he didn't want Kennedy or Guthman to find out where the leak came from—or, rather, to be able to prove we were responsible. They would know who had tipped off Smith. But that's the way you played the game in Washington. Each agency had its favorites among the press corps and cultivated their friendship by feeding them information. Sandy Smith was not in the Kennedy camp.

I called Sandy immediately, broached the subject, and explained the problem bluntly. He was not at all surprised at the reactions of the Kennedy forces and was delighted at the opportunity to break the story.

"How do we handle it?" he asked.

"Why don't you fly to Washington, check in under an assumed name, and call me. I'll bring all the facts you need to your room and you can go ahead with the story."

"Sounds good to me," Smith said.

"Please remember," I told him, "that we're walking on eggs. You can't cite the FBI. Our meeting never happened."

Then I added, "Your code number as an FBI source will be Secret Agent X-9."

Two days later, the story of how the FBI recruited Joe Valachi appeared in the *Sun-Times*. It created a furor in the press. Guthman ran down to my office so fast he was panting when he arrived, his face covered with accusations. He knew he'd been had, and he knew that someone in the bureau was responsible, and he strongly suspected me.

"How did this story get out?" he screamed, slapping the newspaper down on my desk.

I looked wide-eyed and glanced at the paper.

"You know, this fellow Smith is one hell of an investigative reporter."

Guthman demanded to know who was responsible for the leak.

"I'll check with our Chicago office and see if anyone out there leaked the story."

Guthman stared at me for a moment with undisguised hatred. He knew that I was in some way responsible and he also knew there was no way in the world he could make the charge stick. If he checked my telephone log, there would be no call. If he checked the local hotels, Smith would not be registered. If he asked Smith point-blank, he would say he couldn't betray a source. Bottom line: The *Reader's Digest* could go ahead and publish "Hoover's own account" of how the FBI persuaded Joe Valachi to tell all.

After RICO was passed in 1970, J. Edgar Hoover began to prepare for his last and greatest assault on the mob. By the end of January, he and his staff had developed a massive campaign to use the new legislation in a creative multipronged assault.

On February 8, 1971, Special Agent Oliver B. "Buck" Revell was reassigned from organized crime investigations in the field to the position of Special Agent Supervisor in the Organized Crime Section at FBI Headquarters in Washington. He'd been working in Kansas City and Philadelphia, where he had focused on the activities of the Civella and Bruno families of La Cosa Nostra. He was a

tough and dedicated investigator who knew how to get the best performance from other agents. His confidence in his own ability was
contagious. No one was surprised when Hoover brought him to
Washington to head the new effort, least of all Buck Revell. Over
the next years, Revell worked diligently with other supervisory
agents in using RICO to build criminal cases and to seize mob
assets and weaken the organization's structure generally.

This later strategy was sound. But it's difficult to say whether
Hoover, who was dead before we really learned how to use RICO,
would have gone for it. For almost fifty years he had relied on statistics—the number of criminals brought to justice—to vindicate
the FBI's role in law enforcement. He insisted that the bureau continue to have jurisdiction over such crimes as car theft because they
made us look good. Whenever anyone suggested that we follow
other priorities, he would refuse—well aware that our arrest and
conviction rate was perennially impressive because it included these
crimes, which, often enough, solve themselves.

Still, we know that the potential of RICO was not lost on
Hoover, that he saw it as a principal tool in bringing to justice the
mob's leaders and to confiscate their considerable wealth. In the
final analysis, however, I suspect that, to some degree, he would
have opted for "quantity over quality." By pursuing that strategy
in earlier times, he caught big fish as well as little, and battled organized crime with a dedication and ingenuity for which he is seldom
given credit.

14

....

Buried Alive!

WHEN I ARRIVED AT FBI HEADQUARTERS on the morning of December 17, 1968, the staff was already at work. Inspector Sterling Donahue, my assistant, was immersed in case files. Kitty Henley, my administrative assistant in the Crime Records Division, was on the phone. My secretary, Marie Robusky, was completing a lengthy memo, her fingers skipping across the keys. Another secretary, Helen Spear, was separating a pile of incoming mail into two neat stacks—one for my personal attention and one for Donahue.

At that stage of my career, I was assistant to the director, right behind Clyde Tolson in the chain of command, and in charge of all investigative activities. Four assistant directors reported to me, including Al Rosen, who was assistant director of the General Investigative Division. That morning he called me on the intercom, just as I was settling into my chair. I detected a note of urgency in his voice.

"Deke, may I see you right away?"

"Sure," I said. "What's up?"

"It may be a hoax," he replied. "If not, it could be trouble—bad trouble."

"Come on over."

He entered my office unfolding a lengthy teletype.

"We have a report from the Atlanta office that sounds bizarre as hell. So strange, I'm not sure I believe it."

He held up the sheaf of papers.

"According to this report," he said, "a girl named Barbara Jane Mackle, the twenty-year-old daughter of a prominent Florida real estate developer and part owner of the Key Biscayne Hotel, is a student at Emory University in Atlanta. She'd been cramming for midterm exams and developed a viral infection. Unable to find room in the university's small infirmary, she telephoned her mother in Coral Gables. Mrs. Mackle flew up, checked them both into a motel in nearby Decatur, put Barbara Jane to bed, and gave her some medicine."

Al jabbed the teletype with his forefinger.

"Now here's where the story gets kinky. The mother says that about 4:00 A.M. they were awakened by a knock on the door. Looking out the window, she saw a stranger who seemed to be a policeman. So she opened the door a crack and asked what he wanted. He said, 'The boy in the white automobile has been in an accident and wants you and your daughter to come right away to the hospital.'

"Half in shock, Mrs. Mackle assumed he was talking about a close friend of Barbara's—whom she mentioned by name. 'That's right,' the stranger said, 'That's the boy who's been injured.' By that point, she'd dropped her guard, and the man heaved the door open, forced his way into the motel room, and pointed a rifle at her.

"He told her to lie on the bed with her face to the wall. As soon as she'd complied, a second person ran into the room, taped her mouth, and bound her hands and feet. Mrs. Mackle was gutsy. She tried to fight back. But the men held her down and slapped a gauze compress over her nose. It contained a strong ammonia mixture, but not overpowering. She had the good sense to feign unconsciousness, and she lay there on the bed while the two men struggled with her daughter. The last thing she saw was the trailing hem of Barbara Jane's nightgown as the girl was being dragged from the room.

"Mrs. Mackle says she was strong enough to struggle to her feet, work the tape from her mouth, and scream. She knocked the telephone from its stand; but with her arms tied, she couldn't dial. When no help arrived, she hobbled outside to Barbara Jane's car, somehow got the door open, and jammed her elbow against the horn. The blaring horn brought the night clerk out of the motel office. He helped her back to her room and called the Dekalb County Sheriff's Department.

"Mrs. Mackle then phoned a friend of Barbara Jane, who raced over to the motel, where she found the poor woman hysterical. She immediately telephoned Mr. Mackle in Florida. Then somebody called the FBI."

Al slid the teletype across my desk.

"That's it. That's all we've got for now. My question: Is it for real? What do we do next?"

"We jump in with both feet," I said. "We prove that it's either a kidnapping or a hoax—but we have to assume it's the real thing."

It was certainly a bizarre story, but I was reasonably sure it was authentic—and for a very simple reason. The Mackles were known to the FBI, were friends of Hoover, in fact. He had been a guest at one of their Florida properties. It seemed absurd that the same Mrs. Mackle would make up such a story. But I also knew that over the years the FBI had been a target of some highly elaborate hoaxes and I didn't want to be victimized again.

"Get open lines to Atlanta and Miami," I went on. "Tell our agents in both offices to talk with members of the family, to report all calls or contacts concerning the matter, and to keep me continually advised. I'll tell the Old Man that we may have a major crime on our hands."

Al turned to leave.

"Let's keep a tight rein on it," I said, "and see what happens."

While investigations of kidnappings were carried out by agents in the field, they were often coordinated by senior officials in Washington, who were familiar with standard procedures and surrounded by experts who could supply advice and technical assistance. I knew I would probably be spending a good deal of extra time in the office.

Thirty minutes later, we learned that the abduction was no hoax. Someone had just phoned the Mackle house in Coral Gables. The caller had claimed that a ransom note could be found buried at a certain location on the Mackle property. An agent was immediately dispatched to the spot—a coral outcrop under a clump of pine trees. Next to the coral, in a small glass tube, he found a rolled-up, three-page message. It was photocopied and addressed to Robert Mackle.

The note stated that Barbara Jane had indeed been kidnapped, that she was safe and well, that she was being held for ransom. Proof would arrive by mail. Then, as the agent read on, his blood chilled. The message gave details of the girl's current whereabouts and condition. She was "inside a small capsule buried in a remote piece of soil" where she had enough air, water, and food to last for seven days. He read it again to make certain he understood it. They had buried her alive!

"At the end of seven days," the message said, "the life-supporting batteries will be discharged and the air supply will be cut off."

The message emphasized that the underground cell was escape-proof and was located in a spot so remote that no one would ever stumble across it accidentally. Then the following threat:

> Contemplate, if you will, the position into which this puts you. If you pay the ransom prior to the seven days, we will tell you of her whereabouts. Should you catch the messenger we send to pick up the ransom, we will simply not say anything to anyone and ergo Barbara will suffocate. The messenger knows only one of us and he will report to us via radio from the pick-up site. We will immediately know his fate.
>
> Should you catch all of us, we will never admit anything. So, this would be suicide. Again—she will die.

The ransom demand: $500,000 in recently issued $20 bills of standard configuration and with a wide variety of nonsequential serial numbers. The letter further indicated that the kidnappers would spend a minimum of eight hours administering forty-four tests to detect any kind of markings that might be applied, whether chemical or physical.

The letter demanded that the ransom money be placed in a suitcase of a specific description; and when the ransom was ready to be delivered, Robert Mackle was to place the following ad in the "Personal" section of the classified pages:

> Loved one—please come home. We will pay all expens-
> es and meet you anywhere at anytime. Your family.

When this ad was placed, the kidnappers would telephone Mackle and give him payoff instructions.

The ransom note had all the classic elements—an implied threat, an assurance of safe return, a specified amount to be paid, the promise of future contact for further instructions. But there was one additional dimension to this kidnapping—its perversity. The parents not only had to worry about the safe return of their daughter, they also had to live knowing that she was lying underground, in the nearest thing to a grave, possibly losing her sanity by the minute.

After evaluating the information and sending the letter to the FBI lab for analysis, we concluded that at the very least we were dealing with persons who'd had technical training. The wording of the ransom note, the ingeniously cruel method of secluding the victim, the specific demands of the message made one thing clear—these were not ordinary criminals, most of whom are stupid and ill educated. These were highly sophisticated adversaries. We believed our people were a match for them, but we also prayed for a little luck.

The instructions for delivery of the ransom would be crucial—as is always the case in kidnapping. At that point, someone would have to decide whether to pay, or stall for time, or try to negotiate different arrangements. As a rule, the FBI leaves this decision to the family of the victim. Although a payoff usually provides clues, agents are instructed not to recommend payoffs, since families are often disappointed. But most important is the victim: Ask any FBI

324 • Hoover's FBI

agent to name the first priority in a kidnapping, and, unlike the movie version of such cases, the answer will always be "The safety of the victim." And that means throughout. No steps are ever taken without weighing their possible effects on the victim's well-being; and the family must always agree to every step involving the ransom and payoff.

In this case, our agents in Coral Gables carefully reviewed all the demands with Mr. and Mrs. Mackle and discussed all the options, and everyone involved concluded that paying the ransom would provide additional clues, improve our chances of solving the crime, and—we hoped—lead to the quick release of Barbara Jane. But we also made it clear to the Mackles that dumping $500,000 on some lonely road in the dead of night would not guarantee the safe return of their daughter, nor the capture of the criminals, nor the recovery of the money.

The Mackles' decision was immediate and predictable. Pay the ransom. Our office in Miami supervised the preparation of the ransom money: 25,000 twenty-dollar bills. Although the serial numbers were random, in compliance with the stipulations of the ransom note, we photographed and recorded the bills for identification purposes. The ransom was locked in a standard-sized suitcase that met the specifications of the note: 31.5 inches long, 18.75 inches high, and 6.25 inches deep. The suitcase was in turn given to the Mackle family to await receipt of the payoff instructions.

On December 19, 1968, the Mackles placed the classified ad in two Miami newspapers. Now came the hard part—waiting for the kidnappers to respond. Although I was a thousand miles away in Washington, D.C., I felt the pulse of the operation every moment of the day as if I'd been in the Mackles' house.

J. Edgar Hoover called several times a day for information, as nervous as the rest of us, and doubly interested because of his personal involvement with the family. His constant concern didn't ease the tension. What could I tell him? I kept giving him the same facts and assumptions, dressing them up in new language each time he called to ask, "DeLoach, anything new down there?"

The Mackles proved a courageous family. They were worried sick and in a state of near-shock—particularly Mrs. Mackle, who had been manhandled by the kidnappers—but they held up. If the kidnappers were telling the truth (and we had no reason to believe otherwise) Barbara Jane was indeed in great danger. In the first place, she was buried alive—a terrifying situation to contemplate. Then, too, when she was abducted, she was suffering from a severe viral infection that could complicate her breathing and bodily functions, as well as weaken her resistance to the trauma.

While we were waiting for the call, we were far from idle. Atlanta agents interviewed all the employees of the Decatur motel, as well as the guests who had been there just prior to the abduction. They reviewed Barbara Jane's activities at Emory, tracing her movements during the twenty-four hours prior to her disappearance. And they investigated everyone with whom she was associated, no matter how tenuous the connection.

She was enrolled in the School of Business Administration, so one of our agents talked to the dean, who passed along some promising information.

"Her economics professor was driving to North Carolina," the dean said. "He heard about the kidnapping on the car radio, stopped at a gas station, and called me. He said two hippies had been asking questions about Barbara Jane the day before she disappeared. I have the professor's number if you'd like it."

Our agents called the professor, who provided additional details.

"The last time I saw Barbara Jane Mackle, she came to my class about three Friday afternoon. She was obviously sick, so I excused her from the exam."

"And when did you see the two strangers?" an agent asked.

"That would have been the following day, about 2:00 in the afternoon. They were in the lobby of the Rich Building—that's where the Department of Business Administration is housed. But it's usually closed on Saturday. When I saw these two, I didn't think they looked like students."

"Can you describe them?"

"One was a white male, about six feet tall, weighed over two hundred pounds—dark hair and a full beard. The other was a woman—slender, blonde, looked like the type who spent a lot of time out of doors. Even though she was petite, she looked like a tomboy. Wore a boy's shirt, brown denim slacks, and had on ragged tennis shoes."

"How did you know they were looking for Barbara Jane Mackle?"

"They were outside my office, and I heard them talking. The man told the woman there was someone there, and they opened the door and walked in. They asked me if I had a list of students. I told them I didn't. The man asked if classes would continue through December 18, and I told them classes were over, but that exams would continue through the 17th. The man turned to the woman and said, 'We can't find her in class, then.'"

"When did they mention Barbara Jane Mackle's name?" an agent asked.

"It was later that day. They left my office about two, and I saw them walk over to a car nearby—a squareback, dark blue, late model—looked like a Volkswagen. I noticed that it had a Massachusetts license plate, and I believe I remember that the number contained a zero and a two. I thought I'd seen the last of them, but they came back."

"The same day?"

"Yes. It was about 4:00 in the afternoon, maybe a little later. I was leaving my office and the bearded guy was in the hallway, using the pay telephone. That's when I heard him mention the name 'Barbara Jane Mackle.' I also heard him tell the blonde woman that Barbara Jane Mackle was staying at a motel in Decatur."

"Did you see them leave?"

"Yes," said the professor. "They trotted out of the building, jumped into the same dark blue car, and drove away."

It was an incredible performance. The professor had remembered enough details to give us a genuine lead. For the first time, we believed we might have a handle on the case. When agents checked around the campus, they found several other people who had noticed the same couple. So they were real people, they had been tied to Barbara Jane Mackle, and they knew about the motel. We even had a car description and partial ID of the license tag.

As soon as we received this information in Washington, I called the FBI office in Boston and gave them the information.

"See if you can track down the owner of the car," I said.

It was a long-shot, but Boston responded with remarkable speed. The number of license tags with a zero and a two were more numerous than the fish in the sea; but the Massachusetts Registry of Motor Vehicles, at the request of our Boston office, programmed its computer to isolate first all blue VWs, then all blue, square-backed VWs, regardless of license plate number. It was the beginning of a long and tedious process that might ultimately prove useless, but we had to try it.

Meanwhile, the Mackles waited, jumping every time the phone rang. On December 19, a letter arrived addressed to Robert Mackle. It had been posted the day before in Miami. An agent examined the exterior for a long minute, then carefully pried open the envelope. Out dropped a gold diamond ring and a snapshot of a young woman. The photographer had placed a hand-lettered sign beneath her face that bore the single word KIDNAPPED. He showed the picture to Bob Mackle, and he nodded. The girl was Barbara Jane.

Then Mackle took the ring in his hand and turned it over a couple of times.

"It's her ring," he said.

In what seemed a gratuitous display of cruelty, the kidnappers waited until early the next morning to call the Mackles. Meanwhile, the suspense and pain increased with every hour. Left to brood about the meaning of the delay, we could all come up with dark scenarios. There was a perversity about this kidnapping that set it apart from all others. With only five days until Christmas, the outlook was gloomy, and getting gloomier.

At 3:47 A.M. on December 20, the phone rang at the Mackle residence. When Mackle answered, the caller identified himself as the kidnapper and gave brusque instructions to Mackle to proceed from his house to Fair Isle Street. He was to drive along the street until he came to a wall. There a blinking light would be directed at his windshield in a series of triple flashes. He was then to place the suitcase with the ransom money inside a box attached to the light, close the lid, and leave the area.

Our agents helped Mackle with the final preparations. They placed the suitcase on the passenger seat, repeated the kidnapper's instruction one more time, and reassured him. Then he started out by himself—a frightened father on a desperate mission.

Fifty-five minutes passed. Then an hour. Nothing. At this point, we were alarmed. He'd been gone too long. Something must be wrong. Finally the phone rang again. One of Barbara's brothers snatched up the receiver. The kidnapper was angry. He hadn't made contact with Mr. Mackle, hadn't received the ransom money.

"He left over an hour ago," said the brother. "He has the money. He's probably already made the drop."

"I'll recheck," said the kidnapper abruptly, and the line went dead.

Within minutes, Mr. Mackle returned to the house, visibly shaken.

"I had trouble finding the drop-off point," he said. "When I finally reached Fair Isle Street, I drove all the way to the end and parked about thirty feet from a sea wall."

"Did you see the light?" an agent asked.

"No light, and I couldn't find the box, though I looked. Finally I dragged the suitcase out of the front seat and tossed it over the wall. Then I drove back—very slowly."

In Washington, Al Rosen and I were keeping a vigil as well. When we heard the report that Mackle had missed the contact, our hearts sank. The next report from our Miami office was even more distressing.

"About 4:00 A.M.," our agent told us, "a police officer was on routine patrol near Rickenbacker Causeway and 2900 Brickell Avenue. That's in southwest Miami. He spotted a car parked some fifty yards from the barricade at Brickell. The car was a dark blue station wagon with Massachusetts tags—number P72098. When the officer investigated, he found that the car was unoccupied but contained luggage and personal items. He radioed the license number to the police identification bureau, but got a negative response. Another patrolman joined him, and they decided to watch the station wagon from their patrol cars."

Al Rosen and I groaned. We knew what was coming.

"Forty-five minutes later," the agent continued, "they saw a guy emerge from between two houses near the car. He was lugging a large suitcase. The officers yelled for the guy to stop and identify himself. The guy dropped the suitcase and took off. The officers opened the suitcase and found it stuffed with twenty-dollar bills. They whizzed back to station in triumph, and found out what they'd done. We went down and identified the money."

"How are the Mackles?" I asked.

"Climbing the wall," the agent said.

Al and I looked at each other and shook our heads in frustration and despair. An aborted payoff! The worst possible scenario in a kidnapping. Of course, the police hadn't known what they were doing—but the kidnappers would never believe such an unlikely tale. Spooked, they might even kill the girl. Or worse—they might simply take off and leave her to suffocate when the life-support system failed.

That was day three. Everything we did took on a new sense of urgency, yet we felt as if we were running in a nightmare, legs churning, yet never moving forward. We had only four days to go until the lights went out in that underground casket.

In Washington, we mulled over the problem, trying to come up with ideas to reestablish contact with the kidnappers. Meanwhile, we sent the Massachusetts tag number to Boston, where the Massachusetts Registry of Motor Vehicles reported that the car was registered to a George Deacon of Norton. Our agents determined that Deacon was married, the father of two children, and had been employed as a research technician in the Bay State from December 1966 until May 31, 1968. At that point, he reportedly moved to Miami, leaving as a forwarding address only: Rickenbacker Causeway, Miami, Florida.

In Miami, agents were examining the station wagon inch by inch. They also obtained a search warrant to examine the luggage and other personal property. Among other things, they found the following:

- a University of Miami notebook that bore a single name—"Ruth"
- three blank pages in the notebook that had tell-tale indentations made by a typewriter (these pages had clearly been used as backup sheets; and from these indentations, our lab technicians identified the

machine as the same used in typing the ransom note)

- the Yellow Page listings from a Southern Bell telephone book, a ski mask, adhesive tape of the type used to gag Mrs. Mackle at the motel, several kinds of ammunition, and a collection of hypodermic needles
- a woman's purse that contained identification papers for one Ruth Eismann-Schier, indicating that she was a student at the University of Miami. (In the purse, agents also found plane tickets in several names, a passport application, and a Polaroid camera with seven prints—six of them presumably Deacon and Ruth, the seventh a close-up of Barbara Jane Mackle. The agents studied that photograph with growing horror. She was lying on a blanket with her eyes closed. She appeared to be dead.)

Fingerprints on some of the items were sent to our lab and quickly identified as those of Gary Steven Krist, who was on the FBI "wanted list" for unlawful flight to avoid jail. On December 20, we obtained authorization from the office of the United States Attorney to file a federal complaint charging Krist and Eismann-Schier with kidnapping. We requested a bond of $500,000 each.

Meanwhile, we investigated the background of both suspects. Krist had been born April 29, 1945, in Aberdeen, Washington. His first arrest was in 1960 for juvenile delinquency in Alaska—when he was only fifteen years old. Later he was convicted of burglary and sentenced to the Utah Industrial School for Boys in Ogden. He escaped from this institution in July 1961, stole a car, and was almost immediately caught in Idaho.

In two years he was out and managed to complete his high school education in Alaska. In August of 1963 he moved to California, where he was almost immediately charged with auto theft. The court placed him in the hands of the California Youth Authority, and he was paroled in December 1964. In March of the following year he was married in Redwood City, California, and nine months later arrested for auto theft. Committed to the Deuel Vocation Institution at Tracy, California, he once again escaped—on

November 11, 1966. This last episode gave us our authority to have him charged with "unlawful flight to avoid confinement."

We also learned something else. Krist was employed at the Massachusetts Institute of Technology in December 1966 under the assumed name of "George Deacon." (He had forged papers.) He worked at MIT until June 1968, when he moved to Florida and accepted a job with the Marine Science Institute at the University of Miami. His wife and their two children lived with him until December 13 of that year, when she took the children and returned to her parents' home in California.

We had a tougher time tracing the background of Ruth Eismann-Schier, but we succeeded. She was born November 8, 1942, in El Hatillo, Honduras. She graduated from the National University of Mexico in March 1967, receiving a degree in chemistry. From October 1967 through June 1968, she worked as a biology researcher in Washington, D.C. She then enrolled at the Marine Institute for the fall semester of 1968, where she met Krist.

We had learned a great deal in a short time. We knew the life history of both suspects, had enough evidence to indict them, and could be reasonably certain of conviction. Yet the last thing we wanted at this point was an arrest. We wanted to make certain they remained at large, so we did not release pictures or information to the press.

Our plan was to let the kidnappers know that the police intervention was an accident, that we still had the ransom money, that Bob Mackle was still eager to make a payoff. We wanted Barbara Jane back. Then we would go after the suspects with everything we'd gathered.

Our experts examined the snapshots of Krist concluded that they were taken in an efficiency apartment, probably somewhere on the Emory campus. We conducted a complete canvass of Atlanta motels, hotels, rooming houses, and similar lodgings, using the pictures to jog the memories of owners and managers.

The efforts paid off. Clerks at a hotel on Ponce de Leon Avenue in Atlanta identified the couple, saying they had checked into an apartment in mid-December. They had used the name "Mr. and Mrs. George S. Price," and they had identified their permanent residence as Jamaica Plain, Massachusetts. Mr. Price, heavily bearded, had claimed that he represented the Massachusetts Institute of Technology.

Our agents secured latent fingerprints from the hotel registration card and the apartment that were identified as those of Krist. Then they showed the Polaroid pictures to the maid.

She looked at them for only an instant.

"That's the Price couple," she said.

"Are you sure?"

She looked more carefully at the picture.

"Yes. And that's strange. Look—they've cut the cord of this venetian blind."

The agent looked at the picture again.

"You're right," he said.

We quickly confirmed that this was the cord used to bind Mrs. Mackle when she and her daughter were attacked. We were gathering more and more evidence, with new breakthroughs every hour. But our problem was still the same: to reestablish contact with the kidnappers.

We conferred at some length with the Mackles and we all agreed to publish another notice in the Miami newspapers, hoping Krist and Eismann-Schier would be monitoring the want-ads. It read:

> Father pleads to kidnappers—I had nothing to do with the action Thursday morning of the Miami police who tried to arrest you and recovered the money which I had left for you. I regret that you did not get the money because my only interest is the safety of my daughter. I pray that you have not harmed my daughter. I did everything you told me to do and I had nothing to do with the accidental appearance of the Miami police on the scene.
>
> — Robert Mackle

We only hoped the kidnappers had not been frightened away for good, that their greed would overcome their natural wariness, that they would try again. They did.

On December 21, at 10:35 P.M., the day the newspaper ad appeared, the assistant pastor of a Roman Catholic Church in Coral Gables received an unexpected call. It was from the kidnappers. They gave him specific instructions to contact the Mackles and give them information about a new drop-off site. It was described as a small side road 2.2 miles west of a trailer park on the Tamiami Trail, which cuts across the Everglades. Armed with place, time, and other necessary details, we planned a second attempt to deliver the ransom money.

By this time I had assigned a new man to take over the case in Miami. He was Inspector Rex Shroder from our Washington headquarters, an agent with the qualifications and determination to get the job done. Before he left, I told him: "Don't spare the horses, and no screw-ups!"

As the hour approached for the drop, Shroder supervised the repacking of the $500,000 in the suitcase. By this time, we could tell that Robert Mackle was mentally and emotionally drained, so Shroder offered an alternative plan.

"Why not let a substitute take your place? They aren't interested in you personally making this drop. All they want is the money. They probably won't even see who makes the delivery. That way, we'll have someone who's sufficiently detached to make clear-headed judgments."

Mackle hesitated, but finally agreed. The man selected was Billy Vessels, a former All-American football player at the University of Oklahoma and an employee of the Mackle real estate firm. We had considered using Vessels for the first drop because he somewhat resembled Mackle, so he was already well briefed.

The kidnappers had designated the Mackle's Lincoln as the car to use in the delivery, and we installed highly sensitive radio equipment that would enable Vessels to talk into a concealed dashboard mike during the drive. His voice would not only be transmitted to the Miami FBI office, but also to my office in Washington. I gave instructions that Special Agent Vincent Stacey, an old Stetson fraternity brother, should handle the Miami end of the open telephone line. Stacey was dedicated, a hard worker, and highly experienced—"a good G-man."

At 11:25 P.M. on December 21, Vessels slid behind the steering wheel of the Lincoln, the ransom-filled suitcase on the passenger seat. But we also included an extra surprise for the kidnappers—an FBI agent, Lee Kusch, crouched completely hidden behind the driver's seat—just in case.

Soon the car was speeding along the Tamiami Trail, while we all waited and prayed. We knew we'd never get another chance. After a relatively short drive, Vessels passed the trailer park, the first identification point; and in about three minutes, he arrived at the left-hand turnoff juncture, a lonely dirt road designated as "SW 132nd Street." Vessels stopped the car, opened the door, and placed the loaded suitcase in a secluded spot as directed by the kidnappers. He heard nothing and saw no one. No kidnappers stirred, and Robert Mackle had requested that there be no FBI stakeout at the site. Vessels turned around and retraced his steps. At 12:20 A.M., Vessels and Kusch returned to the Mackle residence. As soon as they hit the door, Kusch asked, "Have they called?"

The Mackles and the agents with them shook their heads. There was no phone call for the rest of the night. It was now the fourth day. Barbara Jane Mackle had lain in a living grave for more than seventy hours. And it appeared as if she would never be released. The phone was silent for most of the next day.

In addition to our anguished concern for Barbara Jane Mackle, we were increasingly angry at the perversity of the kidnappers. It appeared as if they were reneging on the bargain. Since we knew who they were, we now concentrated on finding them, though we had to be extremely careful.

In the late morning of December 22, Florida agents learned that a man named "George G. Deacon" had leased a lime-colored 1969 Ford from a car-rental agency near the Miami International Airport. At 5:00 P.M. on December 19, the man had made a cash deposit of $35, had taken the car, saying that he would return it by the same hour on December 20. He never reappeared. The clerk recalled that "Deacon" had arrived at the agency in a taxi and that his fare had been seventy cents. The clerk's description of the man fit the description of Krist. We were certain we had picked up our man's trail again.

Because of the time that had elapsed since the drop, we decided to put out an all-points bulletin on the car and on Krist. We immediately broadcast the information to all law-enforcement agencies in Florida, reasoning that if we could catch the kidnappers in time they might tell us where Barbara Jane was buried to avoid a murder charge.

As we were preparing to make an all-out push, Trisha Poindexter, a young switchboard operator at the FBI office in Atlanta, got a strange call. A man on the other end of the line said, "Listen carefully, because I have no intention of speaking to anyone else but you."

She grabbed a pencil, ready to take notes.

"I'm going to give you information about the whereabouts of Barbara Jane Mackle. And I will give these directions only once. Are you ready?"

"Yes, sir," she said.

"Go to I-85. Go to the center of town on Norcross-Tucker Road. Turn off on Buford intersection, then go 3.3 miles."

He was talking so rapidly that she could barely keep up with him, but she didn't dare interrupt the monologue.

"Come to a little road and take a left there. Across the street from where you turn left is a little house on a hill. Then go one-half mile and turn off the road to the right—and it is really not a road—and go one hundred yards up in the woods, and in the area you will find the capsule."

With that, the caller hung up.

Within minutes of the call, the Atlanta SAC (special agent in charge) called me and read what the telephone operator had written.

"Call in all available agents in the Atlanta Division and the surrounding offices. I want them all in the Norcross area as soon as possible. Tell them to keep looking until they find that capsule."

I sounded decisive, but I had two serious reservations, even as I ordered the massive search. First, we didn't know for sure whether the anonymous caller was one of the kidnappers or just some jerk with a morbid desire for attention. And second, we weren't sure that the switchboard operator had been able to record the details accurately. I called Hoover. He was pleased but cautious and told me to keep in touch.

The next call I got from the Atlanta SAC intensified my concern.

"These directions are totally inadequate," he said, "and maybe even erroneous."

His frustration was obvious, even over the phone.

"Interstate 85 does go to the Norcross-Tucker Road, which is actually Georgia Highway 141-C. And there are four directions you can travel when you get here, but not one of them is the Buford intersection."

"Is there a wooded spot anywhere near?" I asked.

"Everywhere," he said. "The whole area is wooded. It's a kidnapper's dream. Rolling hills covered with woods in every direction."

From where I sat, the task seemed almost impossible. Even if we flooded the area with agents, fanned them out in every direction, and worked day and night, we couldn't cover the kind of countryside he was describing.

As the day wore on, our best experts in cartography guided search teams along all possible routes from the intersection of Buford Highway and Tucker Road. Nowhere along these various routes did they find "a road to the left at the 3.3-mile site."

"All right," I said, "we'll have to search all roads, whether they're paved or gravel or dirt."

A little later I made yet another call.

"Nothing," he said. "We drew a blank."

Meanwhile, I was getting calls as well—from Hoover and Tolson, each glummer than the last.

"Any new development?" they would ask.

"Nothing new," I would say. "The search is continuing."

"You'll never find her alive," Hoover said with a note of finality.

During the next call, Tolson cut off my report with a curt comment: "You're on a wild goose chase, DeLoach. You won't find that girl alive."

I hung up the phone and cursed. But that was Tolson—never a fount of inspiration, even in the most successful cases.

By then a team was moving along Berkeley Road, also known as McGhee Road, a little more than three miles north of the Buford Highway and the Norcross-Tucker Road junction. There was no hill at the junction, but agents did see a small shack perched on a mound of dirt at the northwest corner, and the road was identified by a large sign pointing to Lake Berkeley. Half a mile down McGhee road, they found a pathway on the right, leading into a wooded dumping area. After a hundred feet or so, the pathway came to an end.

They weren't the first team to scout McGhee Road, but earlier searchers were looking for something more conspicuous than a narrow pathway. This team parked near the dump site, and two agents began to go over the terrain with greater care, one covering the vicinity of the dump, the other moving back into the woods. As the second agent went farther and farther into the trees and bushes, he began to wonder if he had gone beyond the designated search pattern.

Then, as he was about to turn around, he glanced down and saw what looked like red clay showing beneath the underbrush. The earth appeared to be freshly disturbed.

"Hey!" he yelled. "Come here!"

The other agent joined him, and together they began to remove leaves and branches from a space about four by ten feet. As they did, they heard a chugging, as if the earth under their feet had a pulse of its own. The pump!

One of them yelled, "Barbara! Barbara Mackle! This is the FBI!"

Then they heard a frantic beating beneath the earth.

Back in Washington I got the call: "We've found it! We've found it!"

"Anything on the girl's condition?"

"At this point—negative."

I immediately called Hoover. He echoed Tolson's perpetual gloom.

"You'll never find her alive. She's been in that coffin too long. But keep me posted."

At the site, the agents had listened to the sounds beneath the earth and located precisely where the capsule was located. One agent had begun to dig frantically, furiously with his hands and a stick, while the other had raced to the car radio to call for help. Back at Atlanta headquarters, the SAC looked at his watch. It was 4:13 P.M.—just three hours and eighteen minutes after Trisha Poindexter had taken the phone call.

In the woods, all agents were converging on the scene to help in the rescue. Inexplicably, no one had thought to bring shovels, so they dug with boards, sticks, and tire irons. Some dug with bare hands until their fingers were bloody. After digging about ten minutes, they uncovered the top of a bluish gray box whose lid was tightly secured by screws. Some were removed with pen knives, others simply ripped off with car tools.

As they removed a section of the top, they first saw a gold-colored blanket, then the ashen face of Barbara Jane Mackle. She was sobbing, tears of joy and relief running down her face.

In a voice barely audible she told the agents, "I knew you'd find me. I knew it."

She was too weak to climb out on her own, so the agents lifted her very carefully, placed her on a makeshift stretcher, and carried her out of the woods. At that point, the SAC, who had been monitoring the whole operation on a two-way radio, called me.

I immediately contacted Hoover, and in a voiced choked with emotion, I said, "We've got her, and she's alive."

"Thank God!" he said. Then, in a more official tone, "I'll call the parents personally. Give me the number."

After I'd hung up, an agent standing next to me couldn't resist saying, "My, the Old Man is going overboard to help, isn't he?"

I grinned.

"I don't blame him," I said. "If I were director, I'd do the same thing."

"I wonder what he'd have done," the agent asked, "if the news had been grim?"

Barbara Jane was first taken to the nearby home of an FBI agent, where a physician examined her. She didn't seem to be in shock and was recovering rapidly. She was taken to join her father, who had flown up from Miami and checked into an Atlanta hotel.

After she'd recovered sufficiently, we questioned her about her kidnappers and she gave us some valuable information. She told us that after her mother had been bound and gagged in the Decatur motel, the two had forced her at rifle point into the rear seat of a small station wagon. Then she realized to her astonishment that the smaller of the two kidnappers was not a young man but a woman.

They drove for a long time—she wasn't sure just how long. Then the car stopped, and she was hauled out. They spread a blanket and told her to lie down on it. The woman took out a hypodermic needle and knelt down beside her.

"This is a tranquilizer," she said matter-of-factly.

They gave her a black sweatshirt to put on, then told her to lie down again on the blanket, face up. The man aimed a Polaroid camera down at her. Just before he snapped the picture, she closed her eyes.

"Where are you taking me?" she asked. She was shocked and terrified at the man's answer.

"We're going to bury you in a capsule underground. Don't worry. You'll be O.K. I've already tested the whole system myself. But you won't be able to escape. You'll have air, water, and food."

Seeing she was near hysteria, he reassured her by describing how the fan, pump, and lamp worked together to maintain the flow of air and a certain amount of light. Then he showed her how to use the switches.

"The battery will last for seven days," he told her, "but you have to use the light as little as possible. It runs down the battery."

He told her she would be returned to her family "just fine," as long as her father paid the ransom within that amount of time.

"If he doesn't pay," the man said, "well, we'll let you out anyway."

An FBI agent showed her the photographs left in the station wagon.

"Are these the people who kidnapped you?"

"Yes," she said.

"Are you absolutely sure?"

"Yes. No question about it."

Following my instructions, the Atlanta office shipped the capsule and its contents to our laboratory in Washington. When it arrived,

I went in to look at it. It was the nearest thing to a coffin this side of a cemetery—only eight feet long and two by two in width and depth. As I stared at it, panic seized me. It would be a nightmare to be trapped in such a tiny space, even for thirty minutes, and she'd been in there for eighty-three hours.

The capsule was built of three-quarter-inch plywood; and exclusive of bedding and equipment, it weighed 240 pounds. Even this tiny space was broken into three compartments, with spaces allocated respectively for the battery and the ventilation equipment. The interior was lined with fiberglass—similar to the product installed in a work trailer used by Krist at the University of Miami Institute of Marine Sciences. Portions of the same plywood were also found in the trailer. Luckily, a piece of the plywood in the capsule bore Krist's "latent" palm print—a print invisible to the naked eye that can be "lifted" with the proper equipment. The print was one more piece of evidence that linked him to the crime.

The capsule had been designed with electrical wiring, circuitry, and switches as a highly efficient though rudimentary life-support system. The components consisted of a 12-volt automotive battery, a home-built ventilating fan, a small plastic water pump, a standard light socket with a low-wattage bulb, terminal strips for wiring connections, and switches for the fan, pump, and light. Every item used could have been purchased at a neighborhood hardware store. As a life support system it was dangerously marginal. We estimated that if the pump had run nonstop, it would have drained the battery in approximately two hours. And there was also the risk of a short circuit or other failure in the electrical system. One malfunction, and the capsule would have become a real and permanent coffin. When we asked Barbara Jane how she kept her sanity she said, "I sang songs, went over homework in my mind, recited passages from the Bible—and prayed."

The night we found Barbara Jane Mackle, we placed Gary Steven Krist on the FBI's list of "Ten Most Wanted Fugitives." His picture, physical description, and fingerprints were flashed to all law enforcement agencies in the United States and later to numerous cooperative agencies throughout the Free World. We did omit one piece of information about his physical condition, because we didn't know precisely how to word it. Krist had received emergency treatment by a surgeon on the night of the aborted ransom payment. When challenged by Miami police, he had dropped the suitcase, dashed into the darkness, and vaulted a barbed wire fence. His testicles snagged on a steel barb, ripping a gash that required several stitches in his scrotum.

Needless to say, we were not sympathetic.

Our "Ten Most Wanted" program was specifically designed to focus the public spotlight on the most desperate criminals still at large. We wanted these fugitives to feel the heat, to fear that everyone who passed them on the street had seen their picture in the newspapers or on television or on some bulletin board—that the American people were ganging up on them. It worked. As one badly wanted bank robber complained after his capture, "I got damned tired of seeing my picture on television. Hell, I didn't want to get shot, so I gave myself up." Now Krist had joined the list.

With Barbara Jane safe, the search for the kidnappers moved into high gear. Within hours of the rescue, agents in West Palm Beach, Florida, reported that on the morning of December 22, a marine supply company sold a motor boat to a man fitting Krist's description. According to the salesman, "the guy was driving a late-model, metallic-green Ford. We talked about boats in general for a while. Then we got down to business. He said he was looking for a motor powerful enough to hit forty miles per hour with ease. I told him he needed an 85-horsepower outboard. He looked at what we had. Knew what he wanted. Paid $2,239 to close the deal."

"Did he take the boat with him?" the agents asked.

"He went somewhere first. Said he'd be back in three hours, wanted the craft to be ready by then."

"Did he haul the boat with him on a trailer?"

"Not at all. Somebody must have dropped him off, because he had no car. He took the boat out for a test run. Came back, happy as a clam. Then he said he was going to Fort Lauderdale and asked for directions to the nearest inlet. We told him how to get to the Palm Beach inlet. Last time we saw him he was headed north."

"What time was that?" the agent asked.

"Must have been around two o'clock."

"What name did he give you?"

"Horowitz."

An agent pulled out a copy of the snapshot.

"That him?"

"That's the guy. No question about it."

He'd identified Krist.

The agents checked the cash used to pay for the boat. Sure enough, the twenties were part of the ransom money, as indicated by their serial numbers. So we knew that he might be planning to escape over water, or else hide out in the Everglades until the heat was off. Almost immediately we seconded a number of additional agents to the Miami office.

We were now into the weekend, but few headquarters personnel were doing last minute shopping or watching Christmas specials. My office resembled a military outpost, as individual agents and teams of two and three came barreling in to report new developments, check for information, and receive follow-up instructions.

At 3:00 P.M. we got a call from Fred Frohbose, special agent in charge, Miami.

"We've been checking hotels and motels in the West Palm Beach area, and we struck oil. On December 22, an 'Art Horowitz' registered at a hotel on North Dixie Highway. I showed Krist's pictures to employees and we got a positive ID. What's more, the guy was seen hauling a large, light-blue suitcase from the trunk of a 1969 Ford. A bellboy said he noticed it because it weighed about eighty pounds. When the bell boy made a comment, Horowitz said it was filled with electronic equipment."

"Is he still there?" I asked.

"No. The guy was in the hotel for about thirty minutes. Then he came out, lugging the same suitcase, and headed for the parking lot."

We were getting lots of information, lots of evidence, but wherever we went, Krist had already come and gone. It was frustrating, and as Mark Felt stressed, it was essential that we catch our man early, before he had a chance to lose himself in the vast anonymity of urban America—or the swamps of Florida.

Of course, we hadn't forgotten about Ruth Eismann-Schier. It was increasingly obvious that she and Krist had split up, knowing they were less likely to be spotted traveling alone than as a pair. We reasoned that she was holed up somewhere and would be harder to locate. We were looking in the same places, showing her photograph as well as his, but so far no one had spotted her.

Evidence suggested that Krist was the leader. He had planned the kidnapping, designed and constructed the high-tech coffin, and masterminded the sudden abduction. And he was on the move. Since he was the one more likely to reveal himself, we devoted more time and effort to his capture.

Miami agents next found Krist's Ford in a parking lot, where he had stored it for ten days. A parking lot attendant said he'd seen the suspect leave the car and walk south on Narcissus Street, carrying a bulky duffel that looked like army surplus. He was also carrying a smaller canvas handbag. The attendant identified Krist from the snapshot the agents showed him. Again, we'd just missed him.

Since we knew he'd bought a boat, we put out flyers at boat stops all over South Florida. Soon we began getting calls from operators of marinas and locks on the Florida Cross State Canal, which runs from the Atlantic coast westward through Lake Okeechobee to the Gulf Coast. They had seen Krist. He had moved inland. At that point, we took to the air, placing FBI agents aboard Coast Guard planes.

Then the trail cooled again. We needed a break—and we soon got one. On December 23, shortly after 9:00 A.M., two of our agents flying with the Coast Guard spotted Krist in a small craft in the Gulf of Mexico, south of Fort Myers. Joe Santoiana, special agent in charge of our Tampa office, called to give me the report.

"Alert Rex Shroder," I told him. "Round up as many agents as you can and converge on the Fort Myers area. And remember, every minute counts."

In less than an hour, Santoiana and three Tampa agents were aboard a Coast Guard helicopter headed for the target zone. As they flew south, other agents joined the growing task force—some by automobile, others in privately owned aircraft, still others in boats—all moving from different directions toward Fort Myers to intercept Krist before he could find a hiding place in the thick marshlands.

The next time agents spotted him, he was cruising at high speed along Cayo Las Costa Island, through the Boca Grande pass, and then into Charlotte Harbor, heading toward Punta Gorda. Just as Santoiana's team aboard the helicopter spotted Krist, the fugitive realized he was being tracked. He panicked, spun his boat around sharply, and rammed the bow into a mud bank, about two hundred yards from a mangrove swamp. From high above, our agents used their maps to identify the site as Hog Island.

The helicopter swung low over the swamp, just as Krist, clutching the suitcase, dashed from the water's edge across a narrow strip of muddy sand and into dense underbrush. Given the boggy ground underfoot, he could not avoid leaving a telltale set of footprints from the boat, whose motor was still running, churning up a fountain of mud and seaweed. He crouched under the sprawling branches of tropical trees, trying to hide, as the copter's blades whipped the air into a frenzy all around him.

Yet ironically, though agents knew precisely where he was and were within shouting distance, he was safe for the moment. The chopper pilot couldn't risk a landing in such a treacherous area. The best he could do was to withdraw and hover about twelve feet above the shallows, some fifty yards offshore.

I was following the chase by phone, fully aware of the frustration of the agents in the helicopter. Shroder described their exact location and the problems they faced. "O.K.," I told him, "you and Santoiana and the two Tampa agents look for a safe place to drop. Find solid ground, and jump down to the ground. But for God's sake don't do anything dangerous. That bastard may try to ambush you, and he's probably armed."

Leaving one agent in the plane as a spotter, the four of them jumped onto what appeared to be solid ground and immediately sank up to their knees. But they were on the ground and close to their quarry. They fanned out like Marine raiders and moved through the shallows, keeping one eye out for Krist and the other for snakes and alligators.

As they moved through the slush and heavy underbrush, Krist would have to hear them coming, and I only hoped he wouldn't panic and start firing. When they started out, they kept their eyes on the spot where the fugitive had last been sighted, but as they moved slowly in widening circles, trying to keep each other in view, they met up with trees, bushes, and vines. In the background, they heard the steady grind of the boat motor. By the time they had scouted several hundred yards in all directions, they converged— without their quarry. Krist had somehow slipped through their grasp.

While they were engaged in this fruitless search, a second team of agents gathered at a hump-backed bridge near the small fishing village of El Jobean. They were only a few hundred yards away from the action, and from the bridge they could spot the spray of mud and water from the still-churning motor. One of the agents was agile enough to lower himself to shore and begin slogging through the treacherous mud. After a tiring trek, he reached the boat and cut the motor.

For his trouble, there was a reward, a remarkable find: the olive-drab duffel bag that Krist had been carrying. He checked inside and gasped. It was stuffed with twenty-dollar bills. A final count revealed the total figure as $479,000.

Sitting back in Washington, unable to visualize the terrain, I couldn't understand why they hadn't captured Krist almost immediately. We had to be closing in on him—or were we? It was an island, wasn't it? How could a man escape two search parties on an island? I hadn't reckoned on the density of the undergrowth and Krist's almost animal-like determination to avoid capture. Somewhere in that swamp he was crouched and terrified—everything he'd gained irrevocably lost, his free life measured now in minutes rather than years. A man in those circumstances can be extraordinarily cunning.

He might have despaired had he realized that a third team of agents from as far away as Savannah was at that moment making its way onto the narrow strip of beach that surrounded Hog Island, accompanied by local law enforcement officers, who had answered our call for help and volunteered for the manhunt. Shroder positioned these newcomers in a long line in the shallows where Krist had last been seen. At Shroder's signal, they began a systematic sweep across the island, poking into every clump and hollow that could be used as a hiding place. Although they were moving along together—with orders to keep visual contact at all times—they often lost sight of each other in the tangle of trees, vines, and bushes.

First, the team worked its way across the width of the island. Not infrequently searchers found themselves neck-deep in the black waters, and a few of them had to be pulled out of mud pits that sucked like quicksand. After completing the sweep across the island, the team proceeded north and then south, covering areas previously unsearched.

No Krist.

Agents aboard small boats, swamp buggies, anything that could float patrolled the numerous inlets and streams that ran from the Myakka River through portions of Hog Island. Though swamp buggies were built to go almost anywhere, frequently they had to be pulled through the bogs and mires. As the teams searched, the shadows deepened and the tide came in. Soon the sun had set and the entire island was a foot below the surface of the Gulf of Mexico.

At this point, Shroder decided to move some of the searchers to the mainland for supplies and to talk strategy. A select few—those most familiar with the local landscape—remained behind to seal off all possible routes of escape. Everyone was convinced that Krist was still on the island—but where?

As darkness fell, water craft began ferrying agents and officers between Hog Island and the small fishing village of El Jobean. Krist's runabout was also secured as evidence. And agents on the island continued to probe the brush and hollows, though with less and less hope of spotting Krist. It was now after midnight.

Suddenly, there was a splash in the water—something obviously larger than a trout or a red fish. Flashlight beams turned in the direction of the sound, crisscrossing each other in the night. Then, across the dark water, a shout echoed.

"We've got him! We've got him!"

Krist, secure in his hiding place for the entire day, had decided to make a last, desperate, hopeless run for freedom and had run right into two Charlotte County sheriff's deputies. As searchlights played along the edge of the swamp, the three men emerged, two grinning law officers with an exhausted, bedraggled Gary Steven Krist sagging like a drowned rat between them.

In the early morning hours of December 24, after I'd told Hoover about the capture of Krist, the Old Man had decided to phone Robert Mackle to tell him the good news. But before he made the call, he wanted to make certain that the captive was in fact the kidnapper.

With the help of a radio dispatcher, a message was patched through to Shroder, who was, at that very moment, on the highway escorting the handcuffed and half-drowned Krist to Fort Myers. He answered the call and heard a crackling message over the radio.

"The director wants to know if you have positive identification on Krist."

Totally exhausted and soaking wet, Shroder exploded.

"How in hell am I supposed to do that? I don't have any fingerprint equipment with me."

Then he thought about it for a moment.

"Oh, yeah. Wait a minute!"

Shroder shook Krist, who was only half conscious after his fourteen-hour flight through the mangrove swamp.

"Just relax," Shroder said. "We have to check something."

With the help of a fellow agent in the car, Shroder yanked down Krist's pants and undershorts. By then the suspect was wide awake and terrified. A flashlight beam exposed the proof: the barbed wire gash and surgical stitches in Krist's scrotum.

Shroder grabbed the mike.

"Tell the director we have a positive ID!"

Our operation was two-thirds over. The victim had been rescued and the principal subject captured. But where was Ruth Eismann-Schier? We had no clues.

Again, we turned to one of our most productive strategies—the "Top Ten Fugitive" program. On December 28, 1968, we placed Eismann-Schier on our "Top Ten" release, charging her with kidnapping, extortion, and aiding and abetting in the commission of federal offenses. It was a historic occasion: she was the first female to make this list. Her picture appeared in newspapers, on television screens, and on post office bulletin boards. We even distributed posters to the authorities in Honduras, where she was born, and in Mexico, where she once lived. She was described as twenty-six years old, five feet three inches, 110 pounds, athletic build, with green eyes and blonde hair. We warned that she had abducted her victim at gunpoint and was presumed armed and dangerous. There was no response.

Weeks passed, then months. Finally, on March 5, 1969, routine FBI work paid off.

The chief of the Oklahoma Bureau of Investigation gave the local FBI office a copy of the fingerprints of one "Donna Wills," who resembled the sole female on the "Ten Most Wanted" flyer. Ms. Wills had been fingerprinted on February 27 when she applied for a nursing position at a hospital in Norman, Oklahoma. The fingerprint card had been routinely sent to the State Bureau of Identification for comparison with prints on file. There a technician made a match—with Ruth Eismann-Schier's prints.

We found out that when "Donna" had come to the hospital to apply for the job, she'd been accompanied by a male student at the University of Oklahoma. Our agents contacted the young man.

"I haven't seen her since the day I drove her to the hospital to apply for the job," he said.

"Where did you meet her?" an agent asked.

"At a drive-in restaurant."

"Is she still working there?"

"I guess so," he said, "unless she got the hospital job."

He agreed to accompany agents to the restaurant to make an identification. When they arrived, she was carrying a tray of food out to a car, and the agents stepped forward and arrested her without incident.

The trial of Gary Steven Krist opened on March 7, two days after Ruth Eismann-Schier was captured in Oklahoma. It was a state, not a federal trial, because Barbara Jane Mackle had never been transported across the Georgia state line. On advice of counsel he entered a plea of "not guilty by reason of insanity." Given the overwhelming evidence we'd gathered, he could hardly argue he hadn't committed the crime. The prosecution produced seventy-four witnesses—including thirty-five FBI agents, lab experts, and fingerprint technicians—and 207 exhibits, 179 of which were admitted into evidence. Krist and his lawyer examined the case against him, conferred, and changed the plea to "guilty."

On March 21 at Superior Court in Dekalb County, Georgia, Ruth Eismann-Schier entered a plea of "not guilty" to the charge of kidnapping for ransom. Like Krist, she changed her plea to "guilty"—in her case, in exchange for a reduced charge of "kidnapping." She received a sentence of seven years.

On May 26, Gary Steven Krist came to court for sentencing. Under Georgia law, he faced the possibility of death in the electric chair. Even though he had not killed the victim, I found it difficult to imagine a case in which the maximum sentence for kidnapping was more deserved, given the manner of the crime—burying a victim alive. It cried out for the most severe sentence available.

Yet neither the story of Barbara Jane Mackle's eighty-three-hour ordeal, nor the anguish and grief of her parents, seemed to outrage the jury. In the end, they felt sorry for Krist and recommended mercy. The judge sentenced the convicted criminal to life in prison. He would be eligible for parole in just ten years. He was out in eleven.

15

....

Congress

MEMBERS OF CONGRESS could be as imperious in their demands as the president of the United States. Stalking about on Capitol Hill like royalty, they were the nearest thing to an aristocracy this country had ever seen. In most cases, they were in office for life, or until they decided to call it quits. They exempted themselves from many of the laws they passed, had fringe benefits worth many times their salaries, and staff to do most of their work. And they were wined and dined by lobbyists eager to win their votes.

When they came to the FBI for favors—sometimes demanding instant service—we usually helped them. Occasionally we told them to go to hell. Of course, we were careful about it. We needed friends in Congress, and we made a good many by helping them with a smile. But when members of Congress tried to treat us like dogs, we could sink our teeth deep.

Senator Joseph McCarthy was no personal friend of J. Edgar Hoover, although both men were fiercely anticommunist. McCarthy, head of the powerful Senate Internal Security Subcommittee, took advantage of Cold War tensions to further his political career. One day the Wisconsin Republican was a faceless name on the Senate's roster. The next he was a roaring lion, waving lists of alleged traitors in government, calling for heads to roll.

Hoover didn't like him, in part because of his failure to speak authoritatively on the threat to internal security, in part because McCarthy had supplanted the FBI director as the nation's chief enemy of communism. The director couldn't ignore McCarthy, but he kept him at arms length. When the senator's efforts finally began to involve the FBI, Hoover set the man straight. Ironically, it was the FBI that saved his hide when he was the victim of the same kind of irresponsible charges he habitually made.

Over the years McCarthy had received threatening letters which he routinely turned over to the FBI. Many of them were the product of blind rage over his attacks on the Truman administration. Virtually all were anonymous or else signed with obvious pseudonyms. Some accused him of sex crimes, including homosexual acts. These letters were explicit, with dates and locations of gay sex parties. McCarthy was outraged by these letters, but not cowed. He wanted us to take action. We had better things to do.

Then Senator William B. Benton of Connecticut received a letter, laced with obscenities, that accused McCarthy of sodomizing several American servicemen. One act was alleged to have taken place in New York City, and others at the old Wardman Park Hotel in Washington. The signature on the letter appeared to be deliberately disguised. Benton gave the letter to McCarthy, who sent it along to us.

McCarthy subsequently learned that copies of that letter had been circulated to high-ranking officers in the U.S. army—at the very time he was carrying on his famous feud with the army. He immediately called Hoover and demanded an investigation. He was afraid the army would leak the details to the Washington press corps, and that some reporters would publish them without bothering to check the facts just to embarrass him.

Hoover called me in to discuss the matter.

"We don't have any clear jurisdiction," he said, "but I suppose we could regard it as an implied threat or attempted extortion."

"Run this down," Hoover decided, "but make damn sure you keep it out of the press."

I was an inspector at the time, so Hoover assigned another inspector, Gerald C. Gearty, to help me on the case. We carefully examined all the letters in the file. Several of the "homosexual" letters seem to have been written by the same hand. One contained a return address in New York City.

We contacted our New York office and asked agents to check the address. One of the agents called back to tell us that the occupant of that particular apartment was an Eastern Airlines flight attendant—a gay out of the closet. This sounded like our man, so Gerry and I headed for New York; I would report to Hoover every evening between eight and nine o'clock.

We located the suspect in midtown Manhattan, in his basement apartment. The flight attendant draped himself on the sofa and answered our questions. He denied having attended the Washington parties mentioned and said he had no knowledge of the letter. We asked for a sample of his handwriting, and he gave us one on a piece of his stationery, though a little reluctantly, I thought.
After we'd left, I told Gerry, "He's a pathological liar."

Gerry nodded his agreement.

The FBI laboratory noted numerous peculiarities of the suspect's handwriting that were identical with the writing on the McCarthy letter. And the piece of stationery was from the same lot as the flight attendant's. Since we had no intention of pressing charges against him, we had all the proof we needed. We caught another flight to New York and rang the suspect's doorbell.

He opend the door and we sat down and quietly laid out the case against him. And he confessed. He was trying, he said, to smear other people as well as McCarthy, including two society leaders in New York. He admitted that the charges were untrue. He had attacked McCarthy, he said, because, "McCarthy has tried to expose commies and homosexuals in government, and I hate him."

Taking it from there, we talked vaguely about possible charges and eventually extracted a promise that he would never write another slanderous letter. When we returned to Washington, we briefed Senators Benton and McCarthy, and the matter was resolved without a public airing in gossip columns and the Sunday supplements. Estes Kefauver, the Tennessee Democrat, was another prominent senator with whom we had dealings. The director didn't like him either, in part because Kefauver threatened to become the nation's leading crusader against the mob. Kefauver gained a nationwide reputation when he chaired the Senate Special Committee to Investigate Organized Crime in Interstate Commerce. The committee held hearings that were shown on network television, and as a consequence, Senator Kefauver became a national celebrity and a potential candidate for the presidency.

Kefauver, a large man, was often photographed in a coonskin cap, a trademark from a past political struggle, but it suited his public role as a simple and courageous backwoods primitive, a country boy come to Washington to clean out the crooks and bullies.

That was his public persona. Among Washington insiders he was known to lead a slovenly life. Among other things, he was a heavy drinker and a chronic adulterer. Yet I had no reason to question his physical or moral courage—his bread-and-butter as a politician.

Then, on September 2, 1959, he called me with a personal problem. As usual, an assistant placed the call, and as I sat there waiting, like the dog in the old Victrola ad, the senator finally came on the line.

"My brother-in-law, Paul McQuiddy, received a phone call from a man who didn't identify himself. He told Paul—and this is an exact quote—'When Estes comes back to Tennessee, there'll be sticks of dynamite under his house—that's for sure.' Now, I'd like to go home at the end of the session, but only if you people can make sure that I don't get bombed."

He delivered this speech in an accusatory tone, as if the FBI had been responsible for the call. He wasn't asking for advice. He was demanding that we make the world safe for Estes Kefauver.

In the first place, this was obviously the first death threat he had received, and I was surprised. Most politicians get calls like this at various points in their careers. They learn to live with the danger, particularly when they consider how few threats of this sort have ever been carried out.

In the second place, the threat was obviously frivolous, otherwise

the would-be assassin wouldn't have told the brother-in-law precisely how the assassination would be carried out. A serious killer
would almost never have made the call in the first place; he would
simply have stepped out of the night with a shotgun, blown the
unsuspecting senator away, and driven off in his pickup truck under
cover of darkness. The great crime-buster should have figured this
out all by himself. Instead, he came to us for help.

"I know you must be distressed, senator," I told him, "but unfortunately, the FBI doesn't have any jurisdiction in such cases."

"You don't have jurisdiction? Man, I'm a United States senator!
Are you telling me that the Federal Bureau of Investigation has no
jurisdiction over a threat to my life?"

I went through the usual drill about the mission of the bureau.
Kefauver was deeply disappointed. He'd been counting on us to
assign a whole legion of agents to guard him.

"But what am I going to do?" Suddenly he sounded like a small
scared boy.

"Senator, we'll notify the local police chief and ask him to search
under the house and post a guard until you arrive."

The man who had stood down the mob was by no means reassured. Like so many people in Washington, he had assumed the
FBI could protect him from all enemies. When he finally hung up,
I could tell from his voice just how he felt: The scourge of the
criminal class, the fearless senator was absolutely terrified by one
prank phone call. When I heard later that he'd died of a heart
attack, I wondered if someone had sneaked up behind him and
said "Boo!"

Sometimes lawmakers came to us with problems that, though outside our jurisdiction strictly speaking, we were able to help resolve.
One day Senator Thomas Kuchel, a Republican from California,
came into my office with a troubled look on his face.

"I have a problem, and I think you people are the ones to solve it."

"What can we do for you, senator?" I asked.

"I've heard from a very reliable source that one of my staff members is running a bookmaking operation right out of my Los Angeles office."

"That's a new one on me," I said with a grin. The story was so outrageous it was funny. Senator Kuchel, however, was not amused.

"I don't have to tell you what something like this could do to me politically."

"Do you know who's involved?" I asked.

He shook his head, and practically moaned, "What should I do?"

I said, genuinely sympathetic, "Let me do some quick checking, and I'll get back to you."

I called William Simon, the special agent in charge for Los Angeles, and asked him if he knew anything about the matter.

"No," he said, "but it seems unlikely. I'll check out the story and get back to you."

A couple of days later he called.

"As preposterous as it may seem," he said, "the senator was right. Some guy is taking bets out of Kuchel's L.A. office."

"You have his name?"

He gave it to me, and I called Senator Kuchel and gave him the information.

"What do you suggest I do?" he said.

"Simple. Fire the guy, and let him play the ponies on his own time."

"What about the law?"

"We don't have absolute proof that he's a bookie. Just that he's placing bets. Get rid of him before anyone finds out for sure."

Kuchel fired the man, and that was the end of his problem.

Some very simple problems we chose not to solve for the lawmakers. We had to draw the line someplace. One morning I got a phone call from the office of Congressman Adam Clayton Powell of New York City. Powell, a Baptist preacher from Harlem, was well known in Congress for his high living and poor attendance record. Powell of course did not make the call himself, but an assistant.

"The congressman would like to see you in his office, if possible, about an important matter."

"Do you know what it's about?" I asked.

"Something he'd like the FBI to do."

I made an appointment to see him that afternoon and showed up at the exact time.

"He'll be with you in a minute," the receptionist said. Forty-five minutes later, I was ushered into the office, where Powell sat behind a huge desk. He motioned me to sit down.

"What can I do for you, congressman?" I asked.

"My television set's broken," he said. "I don't know what's wrong with it. Maybe no more than a burned-out tube. I'd like you to fix it for me."

We sat in silence for a moment.

"I don't understand," I said finally. "I'm from the FBI."

He seemed annoyed by my reaction.

"I know that," he said. "I don't want you to fix it, I want the FBI laboratory to fix it."

"Congressman," I said, "the FBI is not in the television repair business."

"Look," he said, "this is a matter of national security. You are concerned with guarding the national security, aren't you?"

I said we were.

"A number of sensitive issues are discussed in this office. Suppose someone bugged my television set when they repaired it and then brought it back into the office! That's why I want the FBI laboratory to repair it. That way I'll be sure."

I had the distinct feeling he was testing me to see if he could work the system for one more perk—free TV repair. I returned his smile and shook my head.

"Sorry, congressman. We just aren't in that business."

He didn't take my refusal well, and I got out of his office as quickly as possible. Driving back to the bureau, I realized that had I said yes, the FBI might soon have been repairing radios, toasters, automobiles, vacuum cleaners, and coffee pots—all in the interest of national security.

Sometimes congressmen would call when they'd had too much to drink, and I never knew whether they would be sentimental about the FBI or belligerent. Representative Carroll Kearns, a Republican from Pennsylvania, called me late one spring afternoon, and I knew at once he'd been drinking. He wanted to tell me a story.

"I was playing bridge at a friend's. I was dummy. Went out on the porch for a breath of fresh air. Four men and four women piled out of two separate cars. Ran up on the porch. Began to slap me around."

"Congressman!" It was Kearns's secretary on the extension, trying to get him off the line.

"Shu' up," he told her. "I'm talking to the attorney general."

She hung up, and he went on with his story.

"Like I said, they got out of cars, and I recognized all ten of them. Know who they were?"

I said I couldn't guess.

"They were Jimmy Hoffa's people."

"Congressman," I said, "you did a great job holding off that many people, but unfortunately this is not a matter in which the FBI has jurisdiction. Maybe you should be talking to the local police."

I suspected somebody was there in the office, trying to get him to hang up the phone.

"Yes! Yes!" he said. "Thank you for your help." Suddenly there was a click on the other end of the line, and I was off the hook.

Like presidents, some congressmen wanted to play politics and wanted us on their team. James Eastland was one of the most powerful men in the Senate, and one of the most competent. He headed the Senate Judiciary Committee, which had legislative jurisdiction over the Justice Department—and thus the FBI; but he was careful never to interfere in our operations nor to tolerate undue pressure by others. I never knew him to drink while the Senate was in session; but many times when I needed to see him, he would suggest that I wait until Congress had adjourned for the day. Then I would ride with him on the underground railroad to his office in the New Senate Office Building. Once we got there, he would instruct Jean Allen, his secretary, to hold all calls.

"It's been a long day," he would say. "How about a little sip of Scotch?"

All FBI agents were aware that Hoover would can our butts for drinking on duty, even if the work day was over. But I also knew the Old Man would give me a tongue-lashing if he found out I was stupid enough to refuse a drink from the chairman of the Senate Judiciary Committee. Besides, it was a rare honor, since everyone knew he only drank with friends.

In March 1970, Courtney Pace, Eastland's administrative assistant, called to say that Jim wanted to rebut statements that Senator Paul Douglas of Illinois had made that morning on the floor of the Senate. Douglas, a liberal Democrat, had said that "there is less crime among members of the Negro race in the city of Chicago than there is in Southern cities among members of the same race."

"What he's trying to prove," Pace said, "is that Negroes commit more crimes in areas where they aren't considered equals. We doubt that the statement is true. What we want is a breakdown of crimes by race from eighteen major cities throughout the South, including some in Mississippi."

You didn't need to be a CBS reporter to know that this request was a hot—a very hot—potato. In addition, if we had acceded, we would have violated our commitment of confidentiality to the local police who had furnished the information. I told Pace we couldn't give him what he wanted.

Pace hadn't been off the phone for a full minute when Jim Eastland rang. I told him the same thing. He was furious.

When I sent a memo to the director, reporting the incident, he blue-inked a predictable message: "We must not allow ourselves to be used in what is purely a political quarrel."

In mid-November 1961, I got a call from the "Wizard of Ooze" himself—Senator Everett Dirksen of Illinois, one of the great orators in the Senate and a Republican stalwart in Congress. Dirksen was still smarting over John F. Kennedy's defeat of Richard Nixon in 1960, and wanted to talk about the election.

"Are you aware," he said, "of the steam and smoke rising as the result of voter fraud in Illinois?"

"Well, Senator, I've..."

"In which case let me give you the whole story."

He went into elaborate detail about the way Mayor Richard

Daley had held out key boxes in Chicago until the rest of the state had reported, then made certain that his precincts reported a Democratic margin large enough to carry Illinois for Kennedy.

"I know damn well Nixon won Illinois," he roared. "He was cheated out of his victory by fraud."

Indeed, the whole country was talking about possible election fraud that year. (One Republican leader in the state was quoted as saying that she wanted to be buried in Chicago when she died so she could remain active in politics.) Personally, I believed the charges warranted investigation, but I had to sidestep the issue.

"Senator," I said, "I can't help you. But there is a way to get us involved."

"Great," he said. "Tell me what it is."

"All you have to do is talk to the attorney general and get his O.K. for an investigation."

"Thanks a hell of a lot," he said, and hung up.

The current attorney general was Robert F. Kennedy.

"Whistle blowers" are very much in vogue these days, as are "watchdog" groups. It's all part of the antigovernment mood. But to the FBI, watchdogs and whistle blowers were mostly a pain in the ass; they were forever calling on us to conduct investigations based on little more than vague suspicion.

Congressman H. R. Gross, a Republican from Iowa, was a well-known watchdog of federal funds and was continually calling our attention to what he considered serious violations of the taxpayer's trust. In January 1962 he demanded a hearing with the director, and Hoover called me in.

"I want you to sit in, DeLoach," he said. "We'll make it as brief as we can. After about thirty minutes, we'll tell him we have other appointments waiting."

That afternoon, Congressman Gross barreled into bureau headquarters, and—in a heated session—protested the use of an Air Force 707 jet to transport the Sargent Shriver family on a vacation trip.

"What's more," he said, "When I asked the air force for details, they wouldn't tell me a thing! Obviously they're covering for Shriver because he's the president's brother-in-law. That Peace Corps he's running is full of nothing but a bunch of halfwits and radicals."

He went on and on with his denunciation until Hoover looked at his watch. The half hour was up.

"We understand how you feel," Hoover broke in, "but you've come to the wrong place for help. The FBI has no jurisdiction in such matters."

The congressman leaned over Hoover's desk.

"Then I'm going to sponsor legislation making you director of the CIA as well as the FBI. That way you can investigate any damn body you want to!"

"Don't do that!" Hoover and I both cried at once. The idea terrified us. We had enough work to do. Any legislation that proposed to combine the two agencies under Hoover's direction was bound to make serious trouble for the FBI.

"I'm going to do it!" he insisted. "I'm going to get my staff to draw up the legislation first thing Monday morning."

After trying our best to get rid of the congressman, suddenly we found ourselves urging him to sit down and listen. He thought Hoover was being too modest. We argued and begged, we pushed him back into his chair every time he started to leave. Finally, reluctantly, he dropped the idea and, with a sigh, we saw him to the door.

Sometimes legislators' Machiavelian maneuvers backfired. In May 1962, I got a call from Old Flourmouth, Senator Ralph Yarborough, a liberal Democrat from Texas. He wanted me to come to his office and personally interview him on the Billy Sol Estes matter. Estes, a Pecos, Texas, country slicker, had made millions of dollars by renting nonexistent grain storage facilities and was linked to kickbacks involving high government officials. Old Flourmouth was anxious to let the people of Texas know that he wasn't a party to any of this shady dealing. As he put it, "I want to put all my cards on the table."

Yarborough was an enemy of then-Vice President Lyndon Johnson. We figured he had a political axe to grind and he wanted to use us in some way to achieve his purpose.

"Be careful," Hoover said. "He's devious and vindictive. Don't let him involve us in his wars."

I went to his office and, sure enough, as soon as I sat down we were co-conspirators.

"I want you to be damned sure," he said, "that Lyndon Johnson doesn't hear a single detail of what I'm about to tell you."

I assured him that I was discreet.

"Johnson's backing John Connally for governor back in Texas," the senator went on, "and his chief opponent is a man named Yarbrough. No kin to me. Doesn't even spell his name the same. But they're telling some lies about him, and I'm afraid people will get mixed up and think it's me. That's why I want you to interview me about Billy Sol Estes."

I saw a way out for us—a way that he might just fall for.

"Senator," I said, when he'd finished, "if we conduct an interview with you, we'll have to report it to the attorney general. And there's no way Bobby Kennedy won't tell the vice president."

"Hmmm," said Yarborough, "I was afraid of that. Trouble is, Lyndon has already leaked stuff about Billy Sol Estes and this Yarbrough to the press. False rumors. I want them stopped."

"And you think that if you're interviewed by the FBI, it will stop the press reports about this other Yarbrough?"

"That's right," he said.

I tried to figure out his reasoning, but couldn't. I was convinced that he had an ulterior motive.

"All right, senator," I said. "I'll send someone over to take your statement."

I assigned two men to interview Senator Yarborough, with me sitting in. He spoke in generalities and circumlocutions—the sort of answers guilty men often give. Most of the questions dealt with campaign expenditures and were designed to solicit facts that would lead to charges of criminal violations. Yarborough gave the agents a list of campaign contributions totaling $7,000 from Billy Sol Estes and other members of the Estes family between the years 1954 and 1960.

"I also received crates of cantaloupes, grapefruits, and other similar gifts," he said expansively.

At this point his eyes suddenly widened. He realized what he had said. Cold sweat broke out on his brow.

"Gentleman," he said, rising unsteadily, forefinger pointed skyward, "I have to call this little meeting to a halt. I have important business on the floor of the Senate."

He fled from his office like a thief with the family silver in tow. Then he stopped and beckoned me to the hall.

"I want your promise, now, that this information won't fall into the hands of the vice president."

"Senator," I said, "I told you earlier I couldn't make such a promise, that the attorney general would probably pass the information along."

"Oh, my God," Yarborough wailed, rushing down the hallway, "Oh, my God!"

I still don't know what he had in mind. I can only speculate that he wanted word to reach Lyndon Johnson that he had spoken with the FBI. It was a game the two of them understood better than I did.

As things developed, it was a deadly game. The feud between Johnson and Yarborough became so serious that it began to threaten the ability of Kennedy to carry Texas in 1964. To end the quarreling and unite the Texas Democratic party, Kennedy made a trip to Texas in November 1963—a trip that cost him his life.

Few members of Congress were unaware of Martin Luther King's extravagant sexual exploits, as well as his associations with purported members of the Communist party, USA. In fact, they frequently came to us with new information about King.

But they also tried to get information from us that might be damaging to King. Indeed, many critics of the FBI have maintained that the bureau leaked tidbits about King to conservative members of Congress and to the press in a deliberate attempt to smear King's name and frustrate his attempts to desegregate the nation. That was never the case—as I can testify.

Hoover's quarrel with King had nothing to do with desegregation. King had impugned the objectivity and integrity of the FBI—and, by implication, the character of its director. The conflict between Hoover and King was entirely personal. The Old Man was not out to undermine King's civil rights campaign.

Congressman Edwin Willis, chairman of the House Un-American Activities Committee, wanted to know far more about King than the gossip currently making the rounds. A Democrat from Louisiana, Willis contacted me in mid-March 1964 and said he wanted to expose some of King's conduct, but feared his revelations might damage the Democratic party. Twice in one evening he called me at home to urge that I see Congressman Howard Smith and discuss with him the propriety of making information about King public.

"He's one of the most powerful men on the Hill," he told me. "He'll know what to do—and how to do it."

As usual, this was a political problem—his, not mine. On the other hand, he was a congressman and apparently he had no one else he could trust, so the next day I called Judge Smith's office for an appointment.

I met with Judge Smith at 3:15 that afternoon. Smith had been in Congress so long and was so powerful that he could do whatever he wished—including challenge the reputation of high-flying Martin Luther King. When I was seated in his office, he explained why he had become interested in King.

"Mr. Hoover's off-the-record answers to questions we asked in the Appropriations Subcommittee got me to thinking. Here is a man who is lionized by the press and regarded by many Americans as a saint. Yet the federal government has information about him— very damaging information—denied to the general public. Apparently no one in Congress has the courage to go public with this information—except maybe me."

He paused, waiting for my reaction.

"I had no idea Mr. Hoover had discussed this matter before the subcommittee," I said. A true statement.

"Oh, yes. And I'm sure you know more about King than Hoover told us."

I was swimming in deep waters. I wasn't sure what Hoover had said, if anything; and I certainly wasn't going to supply Congressman Smith with additional information on King, if indeed I had any.

"I'm sorry, Judge Smith," I said, "but I'm really not at liberty to discuss this matter."

"Well, the question is: Should I discuss this in public? Now I know the liberals will charge that I'm just bringing all this up to defeat civil rights legislation. But that's not true. I just think it's morally wrong for the man who's supposed to be the spiritual leader of 10 million blacks to have communists on his staff and to engage in illicit sex without his followers knowing the full story. But I'm going to need specifics. I was hoping you might be able to supply them."

I remained firm.

"Would you pass along my request to Mr. Hoover?" he said.

"I'll be happy to, Senator," I said, "and if he tells me to make this material available, I'll personally bring it to your office."

I wrote up a report and passed it along to the director. It came back to me with a message written in familiar blue ink: "Someone on Rooney's subcommittee has violated the secrecy of the 'off-the-record' testimony I gave re King. I do not want anything on King given to Smith or anyone else at this time."

Here was a perfect opportunity for Hoover to unload on King, to put damaging information about him into the hands of a Capitol Hill colossus who was fully capable of discrediting King. Smith, moreover, as Chairman of the powerful Rules Committee, could have hurt us badly on the Hill. But Hoover maintained the highest ethical standards where information on Martin Luther King was concerned, something for which he is seldom given credit.

Even in the heyday of the FBI, when Hoover could walk on water, the bureau had its enemies on Capitol Hill. One of these was Congressman Donald Edwards, a Democrat from San Jose, California. He could always be counted on to speak against any increase in our appropriations or to question any investigation that drew public controversy. His opposition was not ideological. It was believed to be purely personal.

Edwards had been an FBI agent himself, though only for a few months; and when politically expedient, he would boast it. His bitterness apparently stemmed from a miscalculation on his part. In late 1940, he joined the FBI in the belief that special agents would be exempt from military service. Then, after carefully gauging the political winds, he decided that the United States would not enter the European war after all, so he resigned.

By late 1941, the winds had shifted and Edwards scrambled to be reinstated, but the director turned his application down. From that day forward he was an implacable enemy of the bureau.

When on the Hill I made a practice of avoiding him. But in November 1964, Edwards wrote me a personal letter, implying that the FBI had leaked information from his meager personnel file to a political opponent. The charge was untrue, and I wrote and said that if he had proof of such an accusation he should make it public, and if he didn't, he should refrain from making irresponsible charges. I also suggested that he had an inflated opinion of his own importance if he thought the FBI had taken the slightest notice of his political adventures.

Still, we couldn't ignore him completely. He was a member of several House committees that could harm the FBI. He was not powerful enough to screw up the works; but he could help make our lives easier.

I ran into him again in 1965, this time in Mississippi. I was there to aid the FBI in investigating civil rights violations; and, as best I could tell, Congressman Edwards was there to fish in troubled waters for publicity. He called press conferences and made sweeping generalizations about the problems of blacks and the ongoing investigation, focusing his criticism on the bureau. Among other things, he said, "Students promoting civil rights down here have little faith in the FBI." I made a mental note of it.

Later that month, when I attended a reception in the Caucus Room of the Cannon House Office Building, I cornered him and asked what he meant by his remark. Taken aback, he resorted to the usual congressional dodge: "I didn't exactly say that," he said. "I was misquoted."

"But you did criticize the FBI's investigations, didn't you?"

"Yes," he said a little sheepishly. "And I wish I hadn't. I've been taken to task at least a hundred times by friends of the FBI because of that quote. I'm getting to be known as 'the congressman who hates the FBI.'"

I shrugged my shoulders, clearly implying that he'd earned the reputation.

"But it isn't true," he said, grabbing my sleeve. "I have the highest respect for the FBI. I was an FBI agent myself. Did you know that?"

I told him we were well aware of his record, and he excused himself as quickly as possible.

Later in the evening, he was one of the speakers; and he took the opportunity to praise the bureau and its great leader, J. Edgar Hoover. I left the reception that night with a sense of satisfaction. Congressman Edwards had been reprimanded. He had learned his lesson.

The next thing I knew, Edwards was launching a tirade against the FBI in a committee meeting, and from that day forward he was unremitting in his criticism and obstructionism. It confirmed what I'd often thought about overnight conversions. Nothing changes.

Most spokesmen for government agencies were routinely raked over the coals by one or more members of a congressional committee, if only to allow them to flex their egos. But during my twenty-eight-and-a-half years of service, no representative of the FBI was treated in such a manner, for at least two reasons.

In the first place, during those years, the bureau enjoyed widespread support from the general public. It was only toward the end of the 1960s that the Left began to undermine that support. In addition, we did our homework and behaved in a professional manner. We were efficient and courteous, regardless of party affiliation or ideological bent; and we went out of our way to anticipate questions and to head off confrontations.

We almost ran into real trouble in May 1966. Senator Eugene McCarthy of Minnesota—presidential aspirant, and guru of the Democratic Left—proposed to establish a Senate subcommittee to oversee the activities of the Central Intelligence Agency. The bureau could have lived with that, but then McCarthy added a paragraph that would have given the oversight subcommittee jurisdiction over "the intelligence community," that is, control over the FBI.

When a "test vote" was taken on May 10, eleven committeemen voted in favor of McCarthy's resolution, and six against it. One member abstained, and another walked out of the meeting before a second vote could be taken, thus stalling final action by ensuring the lack of a quorum.

McCarthy's antics put Hoover into a funk. If such legislation passed, it would mean one more committee to which he would have to report. He particularly dreaded the thought of having to appear before a panel that included William Fulbright of Arkansas, Gale McGee of Wyoming, Albert Gore of Tennessee, Frank Church of Idaho, and Wayne Morse of Oregon—all liberal Democrats.

Hoover called me in and laid it on the line. If this bill passed, I could see myself conducting FBI tours. I told him I understood perfectly and went back to my office to hatch some sort of strategy.

I started my campaign by meeting with Senator Thomas Dodd, a Democrat from Connecticut, who had submitted his proxy in favor of the legislation. After hearing my arguments, he contacted McCarthy and withdrew his proxy.

I next saw Karl Mundt, a Republican Senator from South Dakota and a longtime friend. He was characteristically blunt in his evaluation of the situation.

"The group pushing this resolution is the same old bunch that is anti-Vietnam, anti-CIA, anti-FBI, anti-everything that smacks of sound security."

I agreed, then put him on the spot.

"Would you be willing to go before the committee on May 17 and argue that the FBI should be excluded from the legislation?"

"Sure," he said. "What should our main argument be?"

"That the FBI has no foreign intelligence jurisdiction and therefore doesn't belong in the same category as the CIA."

Mundt agreed. Then I went to see Senator Bourke Hickenlooper of Iowa. He was out of town, but his administrative assistant, Dan O'Brien, assured me that Hickenlooper would be supportive.

"By the way," O'Brien said, "you should talk to Dick Russell about this matter. This proposed legislation would require Russell to appoint three members of his own Foreign Relations Committee to serve on the 'watchdog committee.' He's hopping mad."

I thanked him for the tip and jogged over to Senator Russell's office. From the moment I hit the door he began to denounce Fulbright.

"The man's a sieve. He leaks everything that comes to him. He can't keep a secret for as long as it takes him to get from the conference room to the men's room. He'll stop, dancing on one foot and then the other, just to tell somebody what he's learned five minutes earlier. You might as well make the editorial board of the *Washington Post* ex officio members of any committee he sits on."

He got up and paced the floor.

"Besides, this resolution is an insult to me personally—a deliberate insult by Gene McCarthy. I'll fight it in committee, and if it gets on the floor, I'll fight it there as well"

At the time, I was chairman of the American Legion's Public Relations Committee, so, with Legion approval, I was able to send the following telegram to members of the Senate Foreign Relations Committee:

> Reference resolution by Senator Eugene McCarthy to Foreign Relations Committee re overseer group on foreign intelligence. The American Legion strongly feels the FBI, which has no foreign intelligence responsibilities whatsoever, should be excluded from this resolution. Current checks and balances on FBI are more than sufficient. Its operations are fully accounted for at all times to responsible members of appropriations committees of Congress. Signed, Eldon James, National Commander.

The Legion followed up with personal contact and reached Senator John Sparkman of Alabama at his home. Sparkman agreed to go along. We were making definite progress.

But I didn't stop there. I phoned Senator Frank Lausche, Democrat from Ohio, who agreed to support our position, or else be absent for the vote. I also called the White House and talked to Marvin Watson, one of Lyndon Johnson's top aides, and asked him to request that the president talk to Mike Mansfield, the Montana Democrat. Johnson, who distrusted McCarthy, complied, and Mansfield, who believed the resolution should be tabled, agreed to miss the meeting of the Senate Foreign Relations Committee where the matter would be discussed.

At that point, we had six solid votes, had added a couple more, and had reduced the number supporting McCarthy by several. But as insurance, I contacted seven members of the Senate Rules Committee, a majority sufficient to block the resolution if it should pass the Foreign Relations Committee. I reported all this to Hoover, who was characteristically skeptical. We both knew that political alliances can fall apart in the heat of battle, and that on Capitol Hill, promises are as brief and fragile as morning glories. So I sat by the phone and chewed my nails until the call came. We'd won! The FBI was excluded from the resolution.

When I retired from the FBI, Mike Mansfield took the floor of the Senate to praise my work in the bureau and to express regrets that I was leaving government service. A eulogy of this sort is an honor few public servants receive, and I appreciated it, not so much because it was from the majority leader but because it was from Mike Mansfield, a man whose wisdom and integrity were respected by colleagues on both sides of the aisle.

Working with members of Congress was not an easy job, and much of what I did fell into the category of "bureaucratic trivia"— salving bruised egos, performing menial tasks, shepherding special bills through the legislative process, talking to drunks late at night, reassuring people they weren't being shadowed or bugged, and promoting the interests of one federal agency in the halls of another. I found that most congressman were ordinary men with ordinary virtues and vices. A few were monsters. An even smaller number were great statesmen. I was fortunate to have known them, and even more fortunate to end my service with many friends on Capitol Hill and without a single significant or powerful enemy. Such could not been said of any president during my lifetime.

16

....

LBJ

I WAS SITTING IN THE OFFICE of J. Edgar Hoover when Helen Gandy, his secretary, buzzed me and told me to pick up the telephone that sat on the director's desk, right next to his Bible. When I did, I heard a familiar drawl.

"Deke, I understand you're in there with old Edgar. Can you talk?"

"Uh, yes, sir," I replied. I couldn't think of an instance when you couldn't talk to the president of the United States.

"Walter Jenkins tells me you feel a little uncomfortable about my contacting you rather than talking to Edgar," said Lyndon Johnson. "Is that true?"

I glanced at the director, who was engrossed in a document and paying little attention to my conversation. Still, I offered a guarded reply.

"You're the boss," I said. "Either way will be fine, but I feel Walter raised a valid point that you might want to consider from time to time."

"All right. I know what you're driving at, and I'll try to remember. But Edgar talks so damned fast it's hard to understand him. Besides, he's long-winded. He wears me out."

"Yes, sir," I said. "I understand perfectly."

"Deke, call me when you get back to your office."

"Yes, sir, I'll do that."

He'd given with one hand and taken back with the other. He was going to be more understanding in the future, he had said, but he had called me in the director's office and asked me to get back to him as soon as I had left Hoover's office. I remembered the old biblical warning about serving two masters. Both Lyndon Baines Johnson and John Edgar Hoover were masters in every modern sense of the word. Strong-willed and opinionated, they both expected to be obeyed; pleasing them simultaneously required every bit of diplomacy I could muster.

Barely two days after the assassination of John F. Kennedy, the new president called the director and requested that I be appointed as the FBI's liaison representative with the president and his staff. At that time, my only experience inside the White House had been as a guest when President Kennedy had entertained the judiciary on the Tuesday evening prior to his fateful trip to Dallas. Now I would be making regular trips there.

The thought excited me and boosted my ego. I would frequently be in the presence of the president himself, the most powerful man in the world. I would be assisting him in making important decisions concerning internal security. I would have a small role to play in shaping history. It never occurred to me the position would be politically dangerous, or that it would mean years of walking a very fine line between upholding the Constitution and obeying the demands of one of the most imperious men ever to occupy the White House.

My friendship with President Johnson had started in 1958, during his reign as majority leader of the Senate. I'd been asked by Clyde Tolson, number two man in the FBI hierarchy, to drop by the office for a "strategy session."

"Deke," Clyde said when I was seated, "don't you think it would be a good thing if Congress would award the boss his salary for life?"

The question had only one possible answer.

"Absolutely," I said. "But we'll have to wait until the next session of Congress. They're about to adjourn."

"No," said Tolson—somewhat imperiously, I thought—"the boss wants it done now. So whom should we contact?"

"Among the Republicans, I'd say Styles Bridges of New Hampshire."

"Good suggestion," said Tolson.

"And let's try Lyndon Johnson on the Democratic side," I said. "He runs the Senate. We'll worry about the House later."

One of Hoover's oddities was that, despite his enormous success and what seemed to everyone the immense security of his position, he was perpetually worried about the future, and this sudden campaign was probably the result of several sleepless nights during which he saw himself in his sunset years deprived of all the perks he now enjoyed. I left Tolson's office, went back to my own, and made an appointment to see Lyndon Johnson.

Once in his office, I apologized for the lateness of the request, but he waved my remarks aside.

"I don't see any reason why we can't do this," he said, "even at this late hour of the session. If you can get Styles to join me, then we have a good chance. Go and see my administrative assistant, Walter Jenkins. Get him to work out the wording for the bill."

Jenkins was less optimistic.

"I'm not sure we can get the bill ready in time. But I'll try."

As we talked over the possibilities and pitfalls of the legislative process, I found Jenkins to be friendly and intelligent. I also realized that he was loyal to the man for whom he worked and made it his first order of business to protect Johnson's flanks.

"Let me see what I can do," he said. "Meanwhile, why don't you go ahead and talk to Senator Bridges."

I was reasonably certain Bridges would come aboard. He'd been a longtime supporter of Hoover and was an old friend of Dick Auerbach, the special agent in charge of the FBI's Seattle office. As I suspected, the senator was very receptive to our proposal.

Within a week, we had a bill, were lining up support, and approval seemed imminent. Two days before Congress adjourned, Bridges introduced the resolution in the Senate, backed by Lyndon Johnson. In the House, Judge James C. Davis, a leading Georgia Democrat, was primed and ready to move as soon as the Senate acted.

Unfortunately, minor objections at the time of introduction postponed the vote until the final day. I was growing increasingly nervous, because I had an important speech scheduled in Cincinnati, and I knew that Tolson would have me keelhauled if I left town and the resolution died.

"Don't worry," Walter Jenkins kept assuring me. "It's in the bag. Go to Cincinnati and give your speech."

I did go, but I worried every minute. I made my speech—to a convention of several hundred law enforcement officers—and then rushed to the telephone to check the status of the legislation. I couldn't locate Styles Bridges, who was in New Hampshire and wasn't expected back in Washington until 2:00 P.M.

When I reached Jenkins, my blood ran cold.

"I'm not sure it went through," he said, obviously preoccupied with other matters.

I tried Judge Davis, who seemed calm and equally unconcerned.

"I'll stand by on the floor of the House. When it comes over from the Senate, I'll introduce it. Assuming, of course, it does come over."

At that point, I was panicking. My mother-in-law lived in Cincinnati, so I caught a cab, went to her house, and started making phone calls. By the end of the afternoon I'd talked to thirty-seven people, none of whom could give me a straight answer. I also made arrangements to have two of our agents at Washington National Airport waiting in an FBI car to rush Senator Bridges to Capitol Hill. I was talking to one of them when the Senate passed the resolution by voice vote.

I immediately called Judge Davis, who said, "Good. Anything the Senate can do, the House can do better."

Riding the wave of conviviality as the members prepared to adjourn, the judge made a short, impassioned sales pitch that offered the members little choice—vote for the bill or find themselves on the side of criminals, communists, and all the other enemies of God and country. With a resounding voice vote, the House also passed the resolution.

Out in Cincinnati I was still unaware of the outcome; but I went out for dinner and drinks with two old friends, Ed Mason, our Cincinnati SAC, and Boris Litwin, a local jeweler and civic leader. I had given the restaurant's phone number to the FBI switchboard, with emphatic instructions: "Forward any calls from Capitol Hill." At 7:00 P.M., Styles Bridges called.

"Deke," he said, "you've got your resolution. It passed both houses—almost unanimously."

I thanked him profusely, went back to the table, and ordered a hefty meal. At 7:15, I lost my appetite. Walter Jenkins called, very apologetic.

"Sorry, Deke," he said. "It was too late. Maybe we'll get it through next year."

For a moment I was speechless. I began to think about alternative job opportunities.

"But Walter," I protested, "Senator Bridges just told me the bill passed both houses with hardly any opposition at all."

"Well, I'll be damned," he said. "Wait'll I tell Mr. Johnson."

Later, after a cautious meal, I called Clyde Tolson to give him the good news. But before I could say a word, he lit into me.

"There was no need to call, DeLoach. We know you failed to pull it off."

Did he know something I didn't? I quickly concluded that he'd talked to Jenkins and accepted his word without checking further. For this single moment I was in the catbird seat.

"On the contrary," I said evenly, "the resolution passed in both houses."

There was a long pause. I could picture him—his mouth turned down, his large nose spread across his face—as he regrouped his thoughts.

"O.K.," he said. "Thanks for the good job."

That five-word compliment, doled out like a miser spending his last penny, was the only thanks I got. I wasn't even reimbursed for my thirty-seven telephone calls. When I returned to Washington, I drafted personal letters of appreciation to Johnson, Bridges, and Davis for J. Edgar Hoover's signature.

On the bright side, in the process, I did get to know Lyndon

Johnson and Walter Jenkins, and their friendship was worth the hassle in Cincinnati. Over the next few years, I had hundreds of contacts with Johnson and his staff. Sometimes I spent only a few minutes in his office, sometimes for many hours. Occasionally the Johnson people were doing the FBI routine favors, but most of the time we were helping them with requests from their constituents. Once in a while, we worked together on "extraordinary" problems.

Shortly after Johnson became vice president, he was pushing one of his close friends for a top job in the new Kennedy administration, and having very little luck. The Kennedy White House, which despised Johnson, had quietly but firmly expressed its opposition. Meanwhile, Johnson's candidate was undergoing the required routine background check by the FBI.

In the midst of this quiet struggle of opposing wills, Walter Jenkins called me. After explaining the situation, he said, "The vice president would like you to interview him on this candidate's qualifications so his opinion will be a matter of public record."

"I'll do it whenever he's ready," I said.

After conducting the routine interview in the Old Executive Office Building, I started to leave.

"Thanks, Deke," Johnson said. "I appreciate your help, though it's not likely to do any good. Somebody over in Presidential Personnel doesn't like this guy, and they're going to blow him out of the water."

"Do you know who it is?" I asked.

"No, though I have my suspicions."

"Then why don't we interview them as well? Get their negative comments on the record?"

Johnson shook his head.

"They'll never talk for the record. They're afraid of the political fallout. My man has clout."

"All well and good," I said.

Johnson's eyes lit up, and he slapped his knee.

"That's a hell of an idea, Deke."

So we interviewed members of the Kennedy staff. Johnson was dead right. They said only positive things. At that point, the record contained nothing but glowing accounts of the candidate, including a number from Kennedy's own staff. Johnson's man got the job, and the vice president owed me one.

From then on, he called on me ever more frequently for favors. During the Kennedy administration, Billy Sol Estes—one of the greatest wheeler-dealers ever to farm the government—was on the front page of every newspaper in the country. A Texan, he was accused of running a giant scam involving grain elevators and was under an investigation that eventually led to his imprisonment.

Just when Estes' boyish face was appearing nightly on network news, a rumor surfaced that he had paid for Lyndon Johnson's private plane. The Democratic party was concerned, and the Johnson people were panicked. The vice president and his staff made calls to Texas and finally discovered the man who was the original source of the rumor. Then Jenkins called me.

"This man is ready to make a statement to the FBI about his charges. Will you personally take the statement if I bring him over to FBI headquarters?"

"Sure," I said.

"We want this man to tell the truth, if you understand what I mean," Walter said.

"I'll try to get it out of him," I said.

Walter thanked me in advance. I could tell he was worried. The Kennedy crowd would have loved to get something on Lyndon Johnson, enough to force his resignation or keep him off the ticket in 1964. And Billy Sol Estes would be a 240-pound albatross around Johnson's neck.

Walter brought the man over, and I took the statement. At first he stuck to his guns, but it was clear from his hangdog look and the vagueness of his statement that the whole story had been no more than a malicious speculation.

I began to question him in detail, asking for clarification, pointing out contradictions. Then I enumerated the penalties for lying to a federal agent while under oath. I saw him mentally tabulating the years he'd spend in prison, and I knew I had him. Eventually he admitted that he had a creative imagination and no factual evidence whatsoever. He signed a statement to that effect.

After we'd finished and Johnson's staff had funneled the statement to the press, the controversy died—one of the few instances in which truth overtook fiction before any great harm was done. But, again, Johnson was in my debt. Indeed, he began to believe that I was rather extraordinary; it didn't seem to occur to him that any FBI agent could have frightened a petty liar into recanting. But when Johnson suddenly became president of the United States, he wanted me to be his bureau liaison. And that's when the White House phone calls started.

It was on a Saturday morning—before astronauts had walked on the moon, before satellite communications, before call-waiting—and my daughter Barbie was on the telephone with a school friend. We had a three-minute limit on calls at our house, but she had chattered on and on. When she finally hung up, the phone rang immediately.

"Daddy, telephone!" Barbie yelled.

When I picked up the receiver, a female voice said, "Hold, please, for President Johnson."

In a second he was on the line.

"Deke," he said, "you've got some real talkers at your house. We've got to do something about that."

I told him about the three-minute rule but that it was sometimes violated, and we moved on to why he'd called. The conversation was brief. After I hung up, I went looking for Barbie.

The next morning, Barbara had all the children decked out for Sunday Mass at St. Mary's, but just as we were all piling into the old Buick, two men drove up, parked in front of our house, and got out. One carried a tool chest and the other a metal box.

"Is this the DeLoach residence?" one asked.

Seated in the driver's seat and just about to close the door, I nodded, puzzled that a repairman would be coming around on Sunday morning—particularly when nothing was broken.

"Good," he said. "We have instructions from the White House to run a direct telephone line into your house."

"Are you sure?" I asked.

"Positive."

I got out of the car, walked back to the kitchen door, and let them in.

"O.K.," I said, "you can put it right over there, beside the other phone."

"Sorry," said the man with the tool box. "We've got orders to locate it in your bedroom."

I shrugged my shoulders and led them upstairs. No point in arguing with the president. Besides, at that moment my ego suddenly swelled to twice its size. A direct line to the White House! I was flattered to be singled out for such an honor, but I realized as well that it would make me perpetually accessible.

In addition, I had to worry about the impact of the White House telephone on the Old Man. Hoover was delighted to see Lyndon Johnson become the thirty-sixth president. Instead of having to endure the whims and maneuverings of the Kennedy clan—especially Bobby—the director was now dealing with an old across-the-street neighbor from 30th Place, N.W., where the Johnsons had lived for nineteen years and where, as little girls, Lynda Bird and Luci Baines had slipped across the street to steal his roses. But now that I was liaison to the White House, I didn't want the Old Man to think I was cutting him off from his old neighbor.

So my job was getting tougher with each passing day. I had to keep the president happy with the FBI and supportive of its activities, yet avoid allowing the director to feel he was being slighted or bypassed. The two men were natural allies, if only because of their mutual animosity toward Bobby Kennedy. But their relationship required nurturing. Both were headstrong, used to exercising power, and determined to get their way. Sooner or later, I knew they were bound to collide—like two hurtling planets with intersecting orbits.

Early in our relationship, I discovered that the president was an unapologetic horse trader, even with someone as insignificant as I. Only weeks after he'd been sworn in, he called me into the Oval Office and asked me to sit down, a benevolent smile on his face.

"How are things over at the FBI?"

I told him we were doing just fine. He nodded approvingly.

"Well, if there's anything I can do for you, just let me know."
I expressed my appreciation.
Then he got down to the business at hand.
"Deke," he said, "I didn't know you were a big dog in the American Legion."
I admitted that I had been national vice commander and was now chairman of the Legion's Public Relations Commission.
"You know, with all of this antiwar sentiment building up, it would be a big help to me to have a show of public support. I know most legionnaires support what we're doing around the world. Wouldn't you say they did?"
I told him the truth—that I thought he was right.
"It would be a big help to this administration—and to me personally—if we could get some letters and telegrams into the White House supporting our handling of the war in Vietnam."
"I think that might be arranged," I said.
"Good," he said. "Good. I would be very grateful."
He gave me a long, soulful stare, and I told him I would get on it. When I returned to the office, I made a call to William F. Hauck, the American Legion's national adjutant. Sure enough, a spontaneous wave of enthusiasm for the president's Vietnam policy swept through the Legion ranks and hundreds of supporting letters and telegrams flooded the Oval Office.
As always with Lyndon Johnson, there was a payback. The president allowed the Legion's Public Relations Commission to hold its convention session in the Cabinet Room of the White House—an unprecedented honor that was not lost on Legion members.
On January 21, 1964, Walter Jenkins called me to say that the president wanted the FBI to produce a recording instrument that he could "use to tape his conversations with business executives, civil rights organizations, and other groups."
"He wants what?" I asked.
"Just an unobtrusive little instrument that would record conversations—you know, when he paces back and forth the way he does, something he could use in the Oval Office, the Cabinet Room, or the 'Fish Room.' He thinks his extemporaneous remarks are better than some of his written speeches. He wants to preserve them to use

again."

It sounded to me as if the president wanted to bug his visitors and aides, but I didn't use that word in talking to Walter.

"I'll see what our lab can do," I said.

I went up to the seventh floor to see Ivan Conrad, assistant director in charge of the laboratory. Two weeks later I reported in a memo to the director that Conrad and Special Agent John Matter had perfected a prototypal instrument for the president—a specially modified Uher Report one-quarter-inch tape recorder. I told him that the prototype worked quite well and that the president should be pleased with it.

Later I found out that Hoover was scheduled to have lunch with Johnson, and I sent him another memo, suggesting that he might want to see a demonstration of the recorder before he went over there. He fired a memo back saying, "Not necessary for me to see it. When will it be delivered to the White House?"

I said I'd deliver the recorder to Jenkins the day before Hoover's luncheon. Hoover never replied. Clearly he had his own suspicions about Johnson's reasons for wanting the machine. He had approved the request because he had no choice but, as he often did on ethically questionable matters, he was now distancing himself from the project.

When I delivered the Uher machine at the appointed time, Jenkins and his assistant, Dick Nelson, were impressed with the compactness of the unit and praised the high quality of the completed tapes. Then I showed them how to work the machine and left it in their hands. That was the last time I saw the Uher, and no one ever mentioned it again. But when Richard Nixon got into trouble for result of using a similar device and the Democrats were expressing shock over the secret taping of White House conversations, I remembered the Uher.

President Johnson also enlisted me in his war to keep Bobby Kennedy from spoiling his reelection campaign. Why did the third-ranking officer in the FBI get involved in what was essentially a political campaign? Because when the president invites you to be of assistance, you say, "Yes, sir"—that is, if you want to continue working in the executive branch. Besides, Johnson usually gave me, and himself, a figleaf to hide behind, usually national security. The president defines some tactic as a matter of national security, and it just conceivably is a matter of national security. The matter of Bobby Kennedy, the first such request asked, had nothing to do with national security, but then it wasn't a big deal either—except that the first time always leads to a second.

The controversy began with a movement to put Bobby Kennedy on the 1964 ticket as Lyndon Johnson's vice presidential nominee. The very idea drove the president's staff into a wild tarantella. When John Kennedy was president, Lyndon Johnson was persona non grata in the inner circle of the White House. The Kennedy crowd either ignored him or spoke of him with scorn and derision. And since John Kennedy's death, Johnson's people had swallowed more than their fill of Bobby, the keeper of the keys of Camelot.

Johnson nonetheless weighed carefully the pros and cons of sharing the ticket with Bobby. He wanted to win, and he wanted to be able to govern; and if he concluded that Bobby could help him do both, then he was willing to consider the unlikely pairing, despite the warning of Clark Clifford, who told him: "You two are very unalike, and even under the best of circumstances, you could not perfect a friendly working relationship."

Clifford, friendly to both men, knew that Bobby resented Johnson and looked on him with barely concealed contempt. After having dreamed dynastic dreams and seen them dashed in a few seconds in Dallas, Bobby could not bear the sight of the man who had been the beneficiary of such a tragedy. If he did not like Johnson as a man, he loathed him as a chief executive and boss. Like Johnson, however, he was willing to consider the alliance in order to reestablish the Kennedy claim in the White House at some later date.

President Johnson turned the problem over and over, then made his decision. In a carefully worded press release, he announced, among other things, that none of his cabinet members would be selected as his running mate. That meant Attorney General Robert Kennedy, the only cabinet member really in the running. Later in the day, even as the news media were beginning to report the decision, Walter Jenkins came up to me at the Sheraton Hotel, where I had just finished making a speech, and told me what had happened.

"The president saw Bobby early this afternoon," Jenkins said. "He gave it to him point-blank and straight: no vice presidential post."

"How did Bobby take it?" I asked.

"Like a spoiled child. Couldn't conceal his disappointment. When he left the Oval Office, he stopped at the doorway and said, 'We would have made a great team.'"

I stood and waited. I knew he'd driven down to the hotel for a reason.

"The president wants you to come to the White House and look at the seventy-two telegrams that have arrived since the public announcement this morning. He wants to know if you think they're the real thing, or just something Bobby's people cooked up."

"Why me?" I asked. "You have plenty of people who know more about politics than I do."

"Because you're objective and you're used to evaluating documents."

I knew this was unprecedented—to ask an FBI official to analyze White House mail for political reasons. But I went because I had no choice. When I arrived, I was handed the box of telegrams and given the desk of Mildred Stegall, a close friend of the Johnson family and one of the president's top administrative assistants. Like Walter Jenkins, she was extremely loyal to LBJ.

"Look through them," said Jenkins, "then come into the Oval Office and tell the president what you think."

I examined the telegrams, made some notes, then told Mildred I was ready to see the president. He was seated at his desk and gestured for me to sit down too.

"Well, Deke, what do you say?"

"I don't think you have too much to worry about, Mr. President. Twenty of the telegrams came from the Boston area. Forty are signed with names that are Irish or some other ethnic group likely to be Catholic. Twelve are from Catholic clergy. Not a single wire comes from a significant political figure. You can be pretty sure this is a campaign orchestrated by some of Bobby's old supporters. I don't see a groundswell."

He grinned and thanked me for my expert opinion. I had told

him what he'd wanted to hear—that his dumping of Bobby Kennedy hadn't cost him significant support in the Democratic party. I left him a contented man, which is the way you want to leave a sitting president.

As the months rolled by, the campaign went well for the Democrats. Barry Goldwater started out as a decided underdog; and he did little to improve his position, attacking Social Security in Florida and TVA in Tennessee. The Democrats depicted Goldwater as the man most likely to start World War III, and by October a Johnson landslide was clearly in the making. But politics is never that easy. Eventually a disaster struck.

I first heard the news early one morning when I got a call from Les Trotter, assistant director in charge of the Identification Division. "I thought you'd like to know that a friend of yours was arrested last night."

I was sure it was the beginning of a joke.

"Who?" I asked, and waited for the punch line.

"Walter Jenkins," he said.

"On what charge?"

"He was caught in a homosexual act with a man from the Old Soldier's Home in the restroom of the YMCA."

I was stunned. Walter was a family man, and I had never heard a breath of scandal about his private life. We'd run a name check on him at the beginning of the Johnson administration and had come up with absolutely nothing. The story was preposterous.

"There's some mistake," I said. "Another Walter Jenkins."

"No," said Les, "it's the same guy. The Metropolitan Police sent over his fingerprints, and I've already verified them."

"Are you sure there isn't some misunderstanding—I mean, about what occurred?"

"Afraid not," Les said. "The case seems open and shut."

After I hung up, I sat at my desk in a dazed silence. My first reaction was sorrow. I liked and admired Walter. He was one of the better people I'd met in government, and I knew it would all be a matter of public discussion in a matter of hours. His life would be wrecked.

Then I thought of the president. Soon—any minute—he would

be calling me, asking me what had really happened, what I'd done. At the moment I had no answers to such questions, so I immediately assigned two agents to meet with the Metropolitan Police to determine precisely what Jenkins had done and what charges would be filed.

When they came back and reported to me, I knew the story was true. It was no mistake, and certainly no frame. At first, the Metropolitan Police didn't even know whom they'd caught in their net. I was now prepared to talk to the president, who was campaigning in New York, the home state of Goldwater's running mate.

I waited at my office all afternoon and into early evening, but there was no word from the president. Then, a little after 7:00 P.M. he called.

"How are you, Mr. President," I asked.

"I feel like hell," he said. "I have a bad cold, and in a minute I have to go down and make a speech."

He paused, then asked me.

"Is it true?"

"Yes, sir," I said. "I'm afraid it is."

"How do you know?" he asked belligerently.

"Because we checked the fingerprints the Metropolitan Police took and because two agents verified the details with the arresting officer."

I heard him take a deep breath.

"It's a frame," he said. "Somehow the Republicans have engineered this because we're whipping their butts."

"No, sir," I said. "I only wish that were true. But I'm afraid it's not. Walter did what they said he did."

He cursed under his breath.

"O.K.," he said. "Then I'll fire him immediately—tonight. That'll end the matter."

"I wouldn't do that," I said. "It would look like you were throwing him to the dogs for political purposes."

"Then what do you suggest I do?"

He'd listened to my advice before. I only hoped he would listen this time.

"Announce that you're going to look into the charges, that you want to investigate the matter before you do anything publicly.

Then, give Walter an opportunity to resign."

"O.K.," he said. "That's probably good advice. Where's Walter now?"

"He's in George Washington University Hospital," I said. "Under a doctor's care."

"Good! Then here's what I want you to do. You and Lady Bird go to see Walter at the hospital tonight—right now. Talk to him. Find out what the hell he's got to say for himself. Then report back to me."

I immediately hopped a cab over to the White House and found Mrs. Johnson huddled with Clark Clifford and Abe Fortas in Walter's office. They hadn't talked to the president since I had.

"He says he wants Mrs. Johnson and me to see Walter at the hospital tonight."

Both Fortas and Clifford questioned this move.

"The place will be crawling with reporters," said Fortas. "If you step through the door, they'll be all over you."

Clifford said he agreed, and I was put in an awkward position. I had my orders. They were, in effect, countermanding them. I knew that Johnson would be furious if I didn't do just as he'd said. I turned to Mrs. Johnson, who came to my rescue.

"If Lyndon wants us to go over there," she said, "then I think we'd better do it."

I nodded in agreement.

"First," I said, "let me call and see if Walter's still there."

I called the hospital and was told that no one could see Mr. Jenkins, but I managed to talk to his doctor.

"He is under heavy sedation now," he said. "There's no way anyone can speak with him until tomorrow morning."

He told me to come by Walter's room around 9:00 A.M. We all agreed, but we changed the plan. Mrs. Johnson wasn't available; and I decided I should not interview him myself, not with notepad and pencil in hand. We'd been good friends. My objectivity would be questioned. And besides, I wasn't sure I was up to it. So I took two agents with me, spoke to Walter briefly, and introduced the agents. Then I stood back and let the agents do their job.

Walter told them the charges were true, that he'd been working day and night for months and months, that he'd attended the opening of the new *Newsweek* office and had a few drinks, and that in a weakened state an old urge long suppressed had suddenly, inexplicably overwhelmed him. Abe Fortas later told me in confidence that poor Jenkins had done the same thing under similar circumstances years before—in Mexico. That's why we'd missed it in our security check.

Later Walter would repudiate his statement and say that he'd been falsely accused, perhaps for the sake of his public reputation, perhaps for his family. But he had, in fact, freely admitted the solicitation.

He immediately packed up, left Washington, and returned to Texas to rebuild his life—a genuine casualty of the political wars. Lyndon Johnson had literally worked him beyond his limit. Lady Bird, I believe, recognized that more than anyone at the White House.

Most of the rest were too worried about the political fallout to think about Walter. There was none. Even at a time when homosexuality was universally condemned, the American people recognized a personal tragedy when they saw one and refused to let the incident affect their choice for president. The Goldwater team behaved admirably, refusing to make an issue of a sad revelation that occurred in the waning hours of a one-sided campaign. The only losers were Walter, his family, and the many people like me who were his friends.

Early in 1965, trouble erupted in the Dominican Republic. The president had hoped to see politicians favorable to the United States remain in power in that island country, but word came from Santa Domingo that a communist coup was imminent. The papers were full of the story the day the president called me on the phone.

"Deke, I want you to send twenty-five men to the Dominican Republic and I want it done immediately. I want them to worm their way into influential circles, find out what's going on, and send the intelligence back to Washington so I can make the right decision at the right time. I plan to send the Marines in there to put down the disturbance, I'm going to say that it's to protect American lives and interests, and I want the FBI to tell me when to move and to gather evidence to justify what I do after the fact."

"But, Mr. President..."

"I want them down there in three days."

"...this is the responsibility of the CIA and the Department of State."

"I don't give a damn whose responsibility it is," he barked. "I want somebody in there I can depend on, somebody who'll give me straight information. Hell, I can't depend on the CIA. Or those striped-pants boys at State. I have the power to get this done right, and I'm exercising it. Call me back if you have any problem with Edgar."

It wasn't Hoover alone that concerned me. It was also the CIA, the Dominican Republic, and the U.S. press. Not only were we engaging in intelligence gathering more properly assigned to another, extremely jealous agency, we were also "invading" a foreign nation to collect military information. Some people call that kind of activity "espionage." I didn't like the idea of our agents being picked up and tried as spies. Yet the operation had been decreed from on high. It would have to be carried out.

"All right, Mr. President," I said. "We'll do the best we can."

I called Hoover and said, "Once more, the president just called and wants us to do the impossible."

"What now?"

When I outlined the president's orders, he grumbled for longer than usual.

"O.K.," he said finally. "Go ahead. Get John Mohr [an assistant to the director for Administration] to help you."

Then he gave a long sigh.

"I don't know how we'll ever explain this if word leaks out."

I went to John Mohr and told him what we were facing. He came up with a sound idea.

"Let's see if we can find men who've not only been down there and speak Spanish, but who also have graduated from the FBI National Police Academy, or who have contacts on the Dominican Republic police force."

I liked this suggestion. The ability to speak Spanish would prove essential; and graduates of the academy were an elite group who had additional training in a number of specialized areas. Moreover, since foreign police officers were also trained at the academy, bureau graduates invariably made valuable contacts with law enforcement officers of other nations.

By that afternoon, we had isolated thirty candidates, scattered all over the United States, and sent them carefully phrased telegrams, ordering them to report to my office in Washington by noon the following day. After they'd assembled, we culled out five who either couldn't be away from home for an extended period or whose qualifications weren't quite so strong as those of the others. No one wanted to beg off. They all liked the idea of a change of scenery and high adventure.

When I briefed the men, they were wide-eyed at the assignment. They knew as well as I what the FBI could and couldn't do, and as soon as I opened the floor for questions, they began to fire them.

"How long will we be on foreign soil?"

"Will we be carrying sidearms or concealed weapons?"

"Will we be using FBI credentials or will we work undercover?"

"What kinds of risks will we be running beyond the ordinary when we work in the field?"

I told them the stay was indefinite, that they would be leaving in two days, that they would be required to turn in their badges and credentials before they left.

"Your every move," I said, "must be discreet and your identities secret. You'll make contact with previously established sources, arrange for your own accommodations, and quickly establish a concealed office that can be used as a coordinating point."

I added that we hoped to install a teletype that would transmit coded messages daily to headquarters in Washington. These messages would be decoded and delivered to the White House every day. Clark Anderson, an experienced former legal attaché, would be the agent in charge.

After the selection was complete, our liaisons with the State Department and the Central Intelligence Agency passed along a simple, one-sentence statement: "Twenty-five FBI agents will be in the Dominican Republic for an indefinite period of time, working under White House jurisdiction." I shouldn't have been surprised had State and the CIA already heard the news. No operation that large is leak-proof—at least, not in Washington.

That evening the president called and asked if arrangements had been made.

"Yes, sir," I told him. "The agents will all be in place within your three-day limit."

"Excellent!" he said. "Now here's the way I want you to handle the matter. Every morning at seven o'clock sharp, I want you to meet Abe Fortas in the Situation Room of the White House. After you and Abe study all the input from State, the CIA, the military, and your own people, you're to dictate a confidential memo telling me what you think I should do. Have this on my desk by nine each morning."

At this point, Fortas was still working in the Washington law firm of Arnold, Fortas, and Porter—three months before Johnson appointed him to the Supreme Court late in July.

Abe Fortas and I encountered no particular difficulty in assimilating all of the details, evaluating them, and summarizing the information. We usually had the president's report on his desk by 8:30. But we never made any recommendations. Abe had convinced me: "The president will make up his own mind anyway. We'll just submit our two-page summary to him every morning."

The president was true to his word. On April 28, 1965, days after our agents had gone in, he ordered twenty thousand Marines to the Dominican Republic "to protect American citizens." Weeks later, after the turbulence had died down, I asked the president if we could withdraw our FBI personnel.

There was silence on the other end of the line, and I was afraid for a moment he was going to make the Dominican Republic a permanent FBI field office.

"O.K.," he said finally. "But keep an office for a while longer. Just in case."

I immediately called Clark Anderson in Santo Domingo.

"The president says you can come home," I said, "so pack up and get the hell out of there."

As we were working out details the line suddenly went dead. I tried to call back, but couldn't get through. About twenty minutes later, Clark called back.

"Sorry about that," he said. "A stray bullet cut the telephone line just outside our office."

I weighed the wisdom of reporting that incident to the director and the president—and decided against it. I wanted the men out as soon as possible. As it turned out, Johnson kept the Marines in the tiny republic for several months, until an "inter-American peace force" from the Organization of American States took over peace-keeping operations.

I doubt that the presence of the FBI in the Dominican Republic contributed significantly to U.S. operations there. Intelligence wasn't hard to come by, and the CIA, the State Department, and the military probably provided enough information to satisfy the president. We were merely his security blanket, people in whom he had complete confidence. If we corroborated what everyone else was telling him, then he felt certain he was getting the truth. And perhaps that was reason enough for our brief and very illegal presence.

Lyndon Johnson was obviously upset when he called me late one afternoon.

"Have you seen the front-page story in the *Washington Post?*" he asked.

I knew which story he meant, and I told him I'd seen it—the confessions of a call girl who said she'd been to bed with numerous members of the White House staff, leading members of Congress, and had engaged in fairly exotic practices with some. Needless to say, the entire city was talking of little else.

"I want to find out if that bitch is telling the truth," he said. "Send some experienced agents over there and pin her down, make her give details, tell her to put up or shut up! If she's telling the truth and she can prove it, then get the names of the men she's been to bed with."

I agreed, reluctantly. It was a sordid mess, and the chances of any security violations were slim. But there was always the possibility, so I told the president we'd find out everything we could.

I called the Washington field office and asked the special agent in charge to send me two of his best men. When they arrived, I briefed them, then sent them over to the woman's address. Three hours later, one of the agents called.

"Every time we try to pin this broad down about a specific episode, she jumps to another name and a different story. She claims she's had sex with several White House staffers and senators. In fact, she brags about her activities. But she won't give us any names. We're getting nowhere."

That wouldn't satisfy the president. I thought for a moment. Then an idea hit me.

"Ask her if she's ever been to bed with Senator Carl Hayden," I said.

"Great idea," he said. "We'll try it and get back to you."

Twenty minutes later he called back.

"It worked," he said. "When I asked her if she'd been in the sack with Hayden, she said, 'Many, many times.' We gave her a stern lecture about lying, warned her she could be sued for slander, and left her with tears in her eyes. She got the point when I told her how old Hayden was."

"Good work," I said. "Let's call it a day."

Carl Hayden, the distinguished senator from Arizona, was ninety years old at the time. Later, the director asked me to pay a personal call on the senator and present him with a pair of cuff links fashioned from Hayden's own fingerprints, which had been taken when he was a deputy sheriff, before Arizona had become a state. While I was there, I told the senator how we had broken the call girl's story.

He smiled broadly.

"Is that so? Now where did you say this girl lived, Deke?"

The president laughed at the story and then asked, "Are you sure she didn't mention my name?"

Like most career politicians in Washington, Lyndon Johnson was a very busy man, but he still found time to be protective of his daughters, Lynda Bird and Luci Baines. He was a family man, and I liked that in him.

When Lynda Bird became involved with actor George Hamilton, Johnson became an anxious father. To him, Hamilton seemed no more than a slick opportunist, an upstart taking advantage of his movie fame to charm the daughter of a rich and powerful man. Washington was alive with stories about the couple, and the president knew he had a problem—and one of the ways he solved problems was to call in the FBI.

He rang me on the phone one day and gave me my marching orders.

"I want you to go up and see Abe Fortas. I want the two of you to come up with a way to stop George Hamilton from seeing Lynda Bird. I can't have her marrying that damn actor. I think he's nothing but a flake. Also, I want a complete rundown on him."

I couldn't believe what I'd just heard. At the time, Abe Fortas was an associate justice of the Supreme Court, a lofty perch to which Johnson had appointed him in 1965. But as far as the president was concerned, Fortas's seat on the Supreme Court didn't preclude him from doing a little moonlighting for the president. So I went over to see Fortas; and after we'd had a good laugh, the two of us worked out a vague strategy.

We would begin by having the FBI run a very discreet check on Hamilton to see if anything turned up. It was a fishing expedition, but we hoped we might uncover something in his past that would discredit him in the eyes of the president's elder daughter. No shocking reports came back to headquarters. Hamilton didn't have a wife stashed away in some dark corner of the country. He had no felony convictions for murder, rape, or armed robbery. He was not a dope fiend. A few of the folks in his home town said he was a spoiled brat as a child and hadn't changed much since—but that was about all we could find.

Every few days I would hustle over to Abe's office in the Supreme Court building. He would sweep in, his robes fluttering, and the two of us would pore over the gossip columns and try to think of ways to break up a young couple in love. We were both unqualified for the job, and we knew it. And each day we expected the president to call and chew us out.

Fortunately, before the president lost his patience, the ardor between Lynda and George cooled of its own accord. They stopped seeing each other for one of the many reasons romances go awry. I doubt the president's daughter ever knew of her father's efforts to intervene in this affair. Justice Fortas and I were relieved that our services were no longer required. He was soon involved in troubles of his own, and I went back to acting as peacemaker between Johnson and Hoover—a full-time job in those days.

17

....

The Lion in Winter

ON MARCH 31, 1968, Lyndon Johnson, in a broadcast to the nation, announced that he would not seek his party's nomination for reelection. The morning after he made the announcement, I dictated the following memo to J. Edgar Hoover:

> I have talked on a confidential basis at some great
> length this morning with both Mrs. Stegall and, on the
> direct line to the LBJ Ranch, with Walter Jenkins. Both
> are well informed about the president's activities.
> The president's decision not to seek the Democratic
> nomination... was not made because of any opinion on
> the part of the president that he would have difficulty
> in defeating Robert Kennedy.... He made the decision
> because he is extremely tired, very sick of all the criti-
> cism being heaped upon him, and because of the deteri-
> orating Vietnam situation about which he heard first-
> hand after conferences all week long with the military,
> particularly General Adams who will succeed West-

> moreland. The president frankly feels he could not con-
> tinue physically the schedule he has been keeping for
> the past several months.

I went on to say that Johnson had fully intended to run again—
almost until the moment he made the decision on March 30. In fact,
he'd selected a staff member to handle his campaign and had
briefed no fewer than twenty-five Democrats who were to fan out
and talk to delegates in the various states. I concluded by saying
that Johnson felt Hubert Humphrey would get the nomination, and
that if Bobby Kennedy were the Democratic nominee, Richard
Nixon would be the winner.

For personal rather than political reasons I was sorry to see Lyndon Johnson choose to leave the White House. I got along extremely well with his staff. And whether or not I agreed with his political decisions—and I didn't all the time—I liked Lyndon Johnson
personally. Yet he was a difficult man to work with. He could be
demanding, dictatorial, outrageous—and dangerous. His refusal to
accept that the FBI was not his personal political boy was dangerous to us. And in the waning days of his presidency, when he still
wanted to use us but would soon have no power to protect us, he
was more dangerous still.

Late in October 1968, I got a call from Bromley Smith, assistant to
McGeorge Bundy, security adviser to the president. The campaign
was in full swing, with election day looming on November 5. Lyndon Johnson was not seeking reelection, but Vice President Hubert
Humphrey was leading the Democratic ticket. Humphrey, having
inherited the burden of the president's Vietnam policy, was running
behind Richard Nixon. But it never occurred to me that Smith
wanted to talk politics.

As soon as I answered he said, "Call me back on the green line."

The green line was a scrambler phone; when I dialed back, he
sounded like TV's Maxwell Smart.

"I'm phoning on behalf of the president and the secretary of the
National Security Council," he said. "I want to discuss a very sensitive matter in very general terms. Someone will fill in the details later."

"Go ahead," I said.

"We need immediate action," he said. "I'll be glad to have someone confirm my authority if necessary."

I wondered if he wanted me to launch a nuclear attack on the Soviet Union.

"What do you want me to do?"

"We urgently need to know the identity of every individual who enters the South Vietnamese Embassy in Washington for at least the next three days. In addition, we want an accounting of every phone conversation—an English translation, both incoming and outgoing calls. Call the attorney general if you need wiretap approval. Also, place a wiretap on Mrs. Claire Chennault at the Watergate Apartments. Follow her wherever she goes."

"On the telephone tap, we will need the attorney general's approval," I told him.

After he hung up, I called Clyde Tolson, then J. Edgar Hoover. After making some of the arrangements, I called Smith back—on the green line.

"A wiretap surveillance will start today on the Vietnamese and Mrs. Chennault. In addition, we will put a close physical surveillance on her. We don't currently have a wiretap on the embassy or Mrs. Chennault, but we'll activate them as soon as we get permission from the attorney general."

"Good," he said. "I'll call the AG immediately."

After he'd hung up, I instructed the FBI's Domestic Intelligence Division to start the physical surveillance and to put in a written request to Ramsey Clark for approval of the wiretap. In this case, I wasn't content with verbal approval. I wanted a written record.

Bromley Smith called me again at 10:45 A.M., this time agitated.

"I talked to the AG," he said. "He questioned the propriety of my calling him on a direct line. Wanted me to come over to his office. I told him we didn't have time, and he said Dick Helms of the CIA always came over in person—but never mind that. When I told him we needed an immediate wiretap on the South Vietnamese Embassy and Mrs. Chennault, he claimed one had been hooked up on the embassy last week. When I told him the FBI had said otherwise, he said 'O.K., but this is a very unusual way to handle the problem.'"

"Don't worry about it," I told him. "We've just sent a memorandum to Clark requesting the taps. He's a born bureaucrat, and he's used to getting requests this way. He'll sign."

Smith expressed his relief and gratitude.

"There's only one problem," I said. "We don't have a Vietnamese interpreter at the FBI, but we'll borrow one from the State Department."

"Oh, no!" Smith croaked. "Please don't contact State. This matter is much too sensitive. The White House will contact Secretary Rusk or Undersecretary Katzenbach. Then State will call you."

Within the hour, Ramsey Clark approved the request for the wiretaps, and the operation was given the code name WF 1525 S. Most of what we picked up over the wiretaps was garbage—routine calls from tradesman and businesses, many calls in Vietnamese. Then, at 7:30 A.M. on October 30, 1968, a curious conversation was recorded.

A woman called South Vietnamese Ambassador Bui Dhien and the two of them spoke in English. The woman told the ambassador she was sorry she hadn't talked to him the day before "inasmuch as there were so many people around." She paused, then added, "I thought you might have some information this morning. What is the situation?"

"Just among us," said the ambassador, "something is cooking."

"Is Thailand going to be representative of both South Vietnam and the Viet Cong?"

"No, nothing of this sort yet," said Bui Dhien. "If you have time today, you should drop by and talk to me. Time is running short."

"I'll see you right after the luncheon for Mrs. Agnew."

After we listened to the conversation, suddenly it all made sense. The White House had earlier told us that Anna Chennault, widow of General Claire Chennault of the Flying Tigers, had been meddling in U.S. foreign affairs and that she was in contact with the South Vietnam Embassy. The presidential staff was worried because she was known as a "strong Republican."

That particular conversation simply hinted at further exchanges and intrigue. But on November 4, at 2:25 P.M., less than 24 hours before the election, Bromley Smith called me.

"The president has instructed that all copies of messages being routed from the FBI to the White House that concern the South Vietnamese Embassy and Mrs. Chennault be treated in the strictest confidence. All precautions must be taken to protect these communications. After all, this situation may very well blow the roof off the political race."

At this point, I was beginning to suspect that this surveillance had less to do with national security than with partisan politics.

"We treat all FBI communications with great secrecy," I told him.

"The story is leaking out in Saigon," he said, obviously concerned.

Of course, I didn't know precisely what story he was talking about, nor could I guess. I knew little about the inner workings of the political regime in South Vietnam, though the war itself had been front-page news for years. No "story," however, broke in time to affect the election.

On November 7, two days after the election, Smith called again.

"I've discussed this overall matter with the president," he said. "He wants the FBI to abandon its physical surveillance of both Mrs. Chennault and the South Vietnamese Embassy. However, he wants you to continue to keep the wiretaps in operation. The president is of the opinion that the intelligence obtained has been of the highest order. The facts furnished by the FBI have been exactly what was needed by the White House. The president and I are very grateful."

I was still puzzled, and more than a little annoyed. We were in the middle of something political—or so I suspected. I called the Domestic Intelligence Division and ordered the physical surveillance canceled. I also said the wiretaps should be continued.

At 6:30 P.M., November 8, three days after the election, I received a White House call from Jim Jones, then special assistant to the president, later a Democratic congressman and chairman of the House Appropriations Committee, and currently U.S. ambassador to Mexico.

"Deke," he asked, "do you know about the Albuquerque thing?"

"Albuquerque thing?"

"O.K. In brief, here's what happened. Apparently Richard Nixon phoned Mrs. Chennault from Albuquerque, New Mexico, on November 2. This call, as best we can tell, was in connection with a previous conversation between Mrs. Chennault and Ambassador Dhien, asking the South Vietnamese to honor a request to delay participation in the Paris Peace Talks. The ambassador sent a coded cablegram to the government in Saigon."

I was aghast at the implications of what he'd told me. It seemed unthinkable that an American of Nixon's stature would do such a thing, even to ensure an election victory that already seemed well within his grasp. But polls in the last days had shown the race was tightening. Humphrey had improved his position dramatically over the past two weeks. Perhaps the Republicans had been worried enough to try such a strategy, even though Nixon finally picked up 302 electoral votes and Humphrey only got 191. (Governor George Wallace took forty-five as a third-party candidate.)

"The president is very upset," Jones said. "He feels it represents a grave national security problem. The president wants additional information about this matter—tonight!"

"What additional information?" I knew I wasn't going to like the reply.

"Specifically, he wants to know what time Nixon's plane landed in Albuquerque, the length of each phone call, and what time Nixon's plane departed from Albuquerque. He also wants to know—tonight—if Nixon placed a call to the secretary of state [Dean Rusk] or any other member of the cabinet in connection with this matter. He wants to know also whether any individuals in Nixon's party placed calls to any government officials in Washington; and if so, what persons were called and the length of each call."

I thought I'd better say something before he went any further.

"You're demanding the impossible," I said. "The Albuquerque telephone company will be closed by the time our agents get to it. And since Monday is a holiday, we couldn't possibly get any information from the telephone company until Tuesday morning, November 12."

"The president insists he wants this information tonight," Jones said. "You'll just have to reach telephone officials at home."

"That sounds reasonable on the surface," I said, "but if the president forces the FBI to contact these people and have them open up their files during the night hours or on a holiday, people will be squawking on all three networks and on the front pages of every newspaper in the country."

There was a long pause while what I'd told him sank in. The president wanted quick answers. But how could a few days wait matter now with Nixon already President-elect? Johnson was not a good loser, of course, and as far as I could see the only thing he could possibly accomplish was to critically wound an incoming president. Even so, Johnson was playing with fire. A story about how the Democrats used the FBI to pry into Nixon's campaign activities could cut both ways. Indeed, with Lyndon Johnson's reputation for political hardball, it would probably end up helping the incoming Republican president, who, at that moment, didn't seem to need any help.

Jones backed off slightly.

"I'll tell the president the FBI is reluctant to handle this for fear it will become known. Is that what you recommend?"

"Absolutely," I said. "But equally important, the president should know that he's asking us to perform a task that's virtually impossible."

"I'll get back to the president with this," he said, "but if he wants the information tonight, I'll call you right back."

As soon as Jones hung up, I called Hoover, who listened, then said curtly, "Lyndon Johnson is always asking for the impossible."

I was happy that he didn't add (as he often did), "But give the president what he wants."

Jones called back in about an hour.

"The president agrees with you that we shouldn't contact telephone officials at night. However, the president insists that this information be obtained first thing Tuesday morning. He wants absolute secrecy concerning this matter—but wants the information regardless of the consequences."

Johnson had never had much respect for the limits of our jurisdiction. He and his staff took it for granted that we would perform all tasks, using us as aides, political henchmen, and messenger boys. The director, though he may have resented such misuse, had been reluctant to challenge the president. Would Hoover continue to acquiesce, even as Johnson's power waved?

On Saturday afternoon, November 9, I sent a locked pouch to Hoover at home, in which I enclosed a memorandum suggesting a cursory investigation—enough to get LBJ off our backs but not get us into trouble. For instance, I recommended against turning to the phone company for records. But if I was trying to find some cover, Hoover completely outdid me.

The Old Man—who had enjoyed a longtime friendship with the Republican candidate—called Richard Nixon on Sunday, November 10, and tipped him off that Johnson had put us on his tail.

When my memorandum was returned by Hoover, he'd scrawled in the margin: "We are not going to make any move along the lines suggested by the president. The president-elect did not stop in New Mexico, so no calls such as the president suspects could have been made."

That was Monday morning. On Tuesday morning, Clyde Tolson called me into his office and said, "The boss feels that you should discreetly carry out the president's instructions, but don't cause any embarrassment."

Talk about covering your tail! I had written instructions from the director to decline the White House's request and verbal instructions from his second-in-command to do just the opposite. The Old Man had gone on record in case the bureau's role was ever made public.

I understood that at this point whatever we did for Johnson would be minimal—appeasing a lame duck president whose party had lost the election and in two months would pack its bags and leave office. What he was asking us to do was in any case beyond the purview of the FBI and maybe illegal under the Hatch Act, which at the time forbade federal employees from engaging in partisan politics, all because he was angry at the Republicans and wanted to get even. He had an enormous capacity for vengeance. It was part of his creed to pay your political debts—on both sides of the ledger. Just as he believed in rewarding an old friend like Abe Fortas with a seat on the Supreme Court, so too he believed in rewarding an old enemy like Richard Nixon with an embarrassing and perhaps politically fatal charge of risking the lives of U.S. servicemen in Vietnam to win advantage in an election.

As it turned out, Hoover was correct. Nixon had not been in Albuquerque. But Vice President Spiro Agnew had. We learned that he had arrived at 11:15 A.M., November 2, by private plane. He'd made a speech at a local high school, lunched, and boarded his plane in the early afternoon, headed for Harlingen, Texas.

Armed with this information, I called Jim Jones.

"Jim," I said, "Nixon never made a stop in Albuquerque, couldn't have phoned Anna Chennault from there. Agnew was there for a short time, but not Nixon."

"That's hard to believe," he said.

"It's true."

"Then who could have made the call to Mrs. Chennault?"

I told him I didn't know.

"Send us what you have on Agnew. The president will want Mrs. Chennault's phone calls checked carefully for any clues leading to the identity of the person who called her on November 2."

"Jim," I said, "it'll be tough without tipping our hand."

"You've got to do it," he said, "and without getting caught. The president is adamant."

"Why don't you just ask us to take all the salt out of the ocean?"

"Do it," he said.

I reported this conversation to Hoover and he shook his head.

"Don't take any further action on this matter," he said. "I'm seeing the president for lunch on the 13th. If he brings it up, I'll explain the problems to him."

For Hoover that was the end of the matter, but not for me. Jim Jones called me again on the 13th. They now blamed Agnew for the call.

"The president is most anxious to receive details on whether Spiro Agnew or a member of his party actually called Mrs. Chennault from Albuquerque. In fact, the president is becoming exasperated."

"Jim," I said, "we have already given the White House a report on Agnew's movements. Furthermore, the president told the director at lunch today that he felt virtually certain he knew the identity of the person making the call."

"No, Deke," he said, "the president wants specifics. He isn't satisfied with what you've gotten so far."

"I'm not sure we can get anything else, Jim," I told him.

He suspected it was untrue and hung up abruptly. He was on the griddle too.

Minutes later my telephone rang again. I could feel the heat as I picked up the receiver. Sure enough, it was Lyndon Baines Johnson, shouting at the top of his lungs.

"Why in hell haven't you obtained the information I want?"

"But Mr. President," I said, "we sent you the material on Agnew, and..."

"Those aren't the facts I want!" he screamed. Then his voice settled down to a low growl. "I cannot understand why good friends, for whom I have done so much, can't handle a little assignment like this."

He paused for a moment, and I heard breathing on the other end of the line.

"I don't plan to leak this information to the press," he said. "I need it for national security purposes."

He knew that we were dragging our feet—and he knew precisely why. But he also realized that once he had spiked the magic words we would have to heed the appeal to national security. He was telling us—in terms we were hardly in a position to deny—that this was not a partisan political matter, as we suspected, but something related to the war effort. I didn't believe a word he said, but I couldn't challenge his statement.

When I said nothing, he exploded.

"Do you know who your commander-in-chief is?"

"Yes, sir," I responded quickly. "There is no doubt in my mind."

"All right, then. Get me the information and make it damn fast."

People who live in the real world (rather than in Washington) and never deal with the president of the United States don't understand the enormous impact of the office itself. Lyndon Johnson as a man was impressive, but hardly intimidating. I could have calmly told that man to go to hell. But President Lyndon Johnson was another matter. The office confers a special power that adds several feet to the stature of anyone who holds it. Somehow when you're in the presence of the president (or even talking to him on the telephone) you feel the strength of millions of Americans in his eyes and voice and movements. You're not frightened of him, but it's difficult not to be intimidated by the millions of people whose will he embodies. I had come to where I felt comfortable in the presence of Lyndon Johnson, but it was the comfort you feel in the presence of a tamed lion. Now the lion was angry, and roaring.

I called the director and reported my conversation. He wasn't any happier than I was. Richard Nixon's transition team was already hard at work in Washington. Lyndon Johnson was fading daily like the Cheshire Cat. We were looking to the future, and Johnson was the past—almost. He was still the president of the United States.

"In view of his attitude," I told Hoover, "we have no choice but to proceed with the inquiry as ordered."

Hoover didn't disagree. So I phoned Tom Jordan, our SAC at the Albuquerque office, and instructed him to check toll calls made on November 2 by Agnew or any of his party.

"Don't make any requests during nonbusiness hours. Make this look as routine as possible."

Jordan called me back with the information the White House wanted.

"Three calls were made from the plane as it rolled to a stop. Agnew had a call waiting for him when he arrived at Albuquerque. He or his aides made five calls while he was there. One was to Secretary of State Dean Rusk, which lasted for three minutes. We don't know who made that call. The second was made by Kent Crane, an Agnew staff member, to one Cal Purdy in Harlingen, Texas. That one lasted for three minutes and ten seconds. Crane then made two calls to New York City, the first to an unidentified person. He was on that one for just under ten minutes. The second Crane call was to one Jim Miller, lasting two minutes and twenty-two seconds. The fifth and last call was also made by Crane—to a

Mr. Hitt of the Nixon/Agnew Campaign Committee in Washington, D.C."

I was taking notes. Three phones were involved. No calls to the South Vietnam Embassy. None to Anna Chennault. I thanked Jordan for a prompt and thorough report, then called the White House. We also followed up the call with a written brief. Neither Jim Jones nor Lyndon Johnson asked for more information, and we dropped the surveillance of Mrs. Chennault and the South Vietnamese Embassy, though for a while we left a wiretap on the embassy.

On October 29, 1969—almost a year after the incident— J. Edgar Hoover had an appointment with Anna Chennault. As was the case when he met with anyone he didn't know, we briefed him on her background and accomplishments. This briefing included information gleaned from the physical surveillance conducted between October 30 and November 9, 1968, including her contacts with the South Vietnamese Embassy.

Among the materials we passed along to Hoover was a passage in *The Making of the President*, by Theodore H. White, in which Anna Chennault denied trying to generate resistance to the Peace Talks on behalf of the Nixon campaign. In fact, she branded the allegation "an insult," asserting that "someday, when the right time comes, all the facts will be made known." Hoover never told me the outcome of their conversation that day. Neither did he dictate a memorandum for the files. And I soon forgot about the matter.

In retrospect, I still believe—as I believed then—that, despite assurances we were acting in behalf of national security when we were ordered to tap Mrs. Chennault's phone, we were in fact on a political mission for the Democratic party. There's no doubt in my mind that any damaging evidence uncovered in our investigation would have been promptly leaked to the nation's press to embarrass the Republicans. But we had been given specific orders. We'd been told we were involved in a security matter. We had no alternative.

For a while after the election I remained the FBI's liaison with the White House—but in name only, with none of the closeness I had enjoyed with President Johnson. Indeed, the fact that I had been

"Johnson's man" made members of the new administration cautious in their dealings with me. Barely a month after Nixon took the oath of office, the White House line was removed from my bedroom.

One of the Republican suspicions was planted by Hoover, who—though he profited from it—resented my close relationship with Lyndon Johnson. In fact, I discovered that Hoover—embellishing the Chennault episode—had told President Nixon that I had once planted a bug on his campaign plane.

Eventually this story would find its way into FBI folklore. Indeed, from time to time I still run across it in accounts of the Johnson years. I'm always surprised that anyone could believe such a tale, because the bugging of a campaign plane would have to be categorized as "Mission: Impossible." No one could have approached such an aircraft without being apprehended and questioned by the Secret Service. You might as well try to put a bomb aboard.

Besides, anyone who understood how the FBI operated should have known that had I ordered electronic surveillance, it would have been known throughout the organization and gotten back to the director. Such an operation would definitely have to have been approved by J. Edgar Hoover. Had I ordered a telephone tap—and the intelligence in question was transmitted via telephone—I would also have needed authorization from the attorney general. I wondered at the time if Nixon could really have believed such a charge, given his familiarity with the bureau.

Whatever Nixon's reaction, henceforth I talked only to staffers about routine matters such as screening candidates for positions in the executive branch and—occasionally—about Vietnam protest groups. It wasn't so exciting, but in some ways I felt more comfortable. The Nixon years brought me blander days and sleep-filled nights. Years later, incidentally, I learned from Bob Haldeman, Nixon's chief of staff, that the president had known the bugging charges were false.

But the director was in his glory. Richard Nixon was "his man." Hoover had been an admirer of the president-elect since the prosecution of Alger Hiss, when Nixon became, for a time, the chief spokesman for anticommunism in America. Nixon was also a friend of Hoover's friends, Clint Murchison and Sid Richardson. Years earlier, the director and the new president had partied together at the San Diego hotel owned by the two Texans, and Hoover had established a personal relationship with "Dick."

As soon as Nixon entered the White House, Hoover was a regular for lunches and dinners and private conversations in the Oval Office. Back at FBI headquarters, we began to hear him saying, "Dick said this... Dick did that." This went on until—as was always the case with Hoover and other men of strong will—the two had a falling out. I don't know precisely what triggered the split, but soon enough the grumbling and growling began again.

To those who ask me if other administrations have used the FBI for purposes as shamelessly political as those of the Johnson administration, I simply reply, "Is water wet?" From Franklin Roosevelt to Richard Nixon, all the presidents under whom I served used the FBI in this fashion. Roosevelt ordered us to spy on his wife as well as his political enemies. Richard Nixon, through Henry Kissinger, ordered wiretaps on several journalists and on his own staff members to plug leaks that were said to involve classified material. But his reasons were selfish rather than patriotic; he wanted to avoid political embarrassment.

In 1975, I was subpoenaed to testify on this and many other subjects before the Senate Intelligence Committee, headed by former Senator Frank Church. During an appearance on December 3, 1975, the members of the committee questioned me at some length about the Chennault matter and other such cases. After I'd finished one such anecdote, the late Philip Hart, senator from Michigan, asked me, "Why didn't the FBI say 'No!' to the White House?"

"Because we were investigators, not politicians, and therefore we shouldn't be held accountable for orders issued by the president of the United States."

"Perhaps we need a politician in the FBI to analyze such White House requests," mused Senator Hart.

I bit my tongue to keep from arguing with him, because I would have revealed my feelings about politicians in general. I had dealt with them over the years—members of Congress, presidents, cabinet members, and their staffs—and few of them ever bothered to learn the true mission of the FBI or allow the bureau to perform only its limited duties. Nor did they have many scruples about asking us to go beyond our proper purview as defined by law and federal regulations.

Whether liberal or conservative, Democrat or Republican, virtually all of them were willing to see the FBI used in the most illicit and unacceptable way to serve their own agenda. Yet these same politicians would invariably recoil in horror at the thought that their enemies would do the very same thing. And I don't think their outrage was feigned. I believe the double standard they adopted was something they could justify in ideological terms to themselves and to others: the end justifies the means. For this reason alone, the FBI should always be in the hands of law enforcement professionals rather than politicians with a party to serve and an agenda to promote.

With the advent of the new administration, I lost touch with Lyndon Johnson, who returned to the LBJ Ranch in Texas. But I was destined to have one more conversation with him. I was having a quiet dinner with my family in Connecticut when the phone rang. Our youngest son, Mark, answered and came running back into the dining room.

"Dad, it's President Johnson."

"Deke," he said, "I received a call from the *Washington Evening Star* this afternoon. A reporter says he's writing an article on Mrs. Claire Chennault, and he claims I ordered the FBI to place a surveillance on her because of some request she supposedly made to the South Vietnamese ambassador. I never did a thing like that, did I?"

Did he want me to let him off the hook, to say I would back him up in his emphatic denial? Or had he actually forgotten the incident? I wasn't sure. But I knew he appreciated straight answers, so I gave him one.

"Yes, you did, Mr. President. I vividly recall the matter."

He gave a long, audible sigh.

"Well, if you say I did, there must be something to it. But if they try to give me any trouble, I'll pull out that cable from my files and turn the tables on them."

He ended the conversation graciously.

"Tell your family I love you and them."

A few days later, Lyndon Baines Johnson was dead.

18

·······················

A G-Man's Goodbye

ON OCTOBER 22, 1971, G. Gordon Liddy wrote a memo on White House stationery that instantly became a model for all future memos written by Nixon staff members. It was brilliant. It was detailed. It was comprehensive. It gave the history of the question, recommended a course of action, and outlined both the negative and positive consequences should the president act on the recommendation. The subject of the memo: the directorship of the FBI. The course of action recommended: that the president fire J. Edgar Hoover immediately.

Shortly after Liddy's submitted memo had made its way to John Mitchell, attorney general of the United States, Mitchell called me. By then I had left the bureau and was already a vice president of Pepsico, living in New York; so I was a little surprised to hear from him.

"Deke," Mitchell said, "I wonder if you could fly down to Washington and see me on an important matter."

"Sure," I said. "When do you want to see me?"

"How about tomorrow?"

I made arrangements to fly down in our corporate jet and took a cab to the Justice Department, where Mitchell met me, a worried look on his face, and ushered me into a small room behind the attorney general's formal office. After I sat down, he continued to pace the floor. Then, without prologue, he turned to me and said, "How can we get J. Edgar Hoover to leave office without him kicking over the traces?"

I was stunned, in part by his abruptness, in part at the very thought that Hoover was about to be removed—because I could tell from the cold glint in Mitchell's eye that he meant business.

"Is it really necessary?" I asked, trying to avoid the question.

"Absolutely," said Mitchell. "It has to be done—and done quickly."

I nodded and sat in silence for a moment. My immediate reaction was sympathy for the Old Man. Even though we'd had our differences, particularly toward the end, I still regarded him with the highest affection; and the thought of the humiliation he would suffer was painful to me. But I realized the time had at last arrived; and I knew that I could best serve him by making his departure as dignified as possible.

"Here's how I would do it," I said. "Offer him the post of "director emeritus." Give him an office at the bureau—a big office. Let him keep Helen Gandy as his secretary. Let him keep his bulletproof limousine. Pay him the same salary. And tell him he will consult directly with the president on such important matters as national security and organized crime."

Mitchell sat down, broke into a broad grin, and slapped his desk.

"That's a great idea!" he said. "We'll do it just the way you said. I'll tell Dick immediately."

"And one more thing," I said. "This can't come from you. It has to come from the president himself."

Mitchell nodded in agreement.

Flying back to New York I had to convince myself that I hadn't betrayed Hoover, that I'd bargained with his enemies for the best possible deal. After reviewing all the options, I finally concluded that I'd done the right thing. For a couple of weeks I watched the nightly news, expecting to see Hoover's bulldog face on the screen and hear of his new appointment. But nothing happened.

Then I got a second call from Mitchell. Could I fly down again? I went the next day and was once again ushered into the small office. After we were both seated, Mitchell looked at me with sad eyes.

"Deke," he said, "The president met with the director yesterday at breakfast. He told Hoover everything you said, but it didn't work."

"Didn't work?"

"Hoover didn't even listen to what Dick was saying. He just kept right on talking as if the words had never been uttered."

He paused, then shook his head.

"Dick didn't have the guts to interrupt him."

I didn't say anything. I couldn't imagine a president of the United States being so intimidated by a subordinate. Lyndon Johnson would have been more than equal to the task. After hearing what Mitchell had to say, I was in a better position than most Americans to understand Nixon's later problems with Watergate.

But Mitchell hadn't called me down to Washington just to tell me Nixon had lost his nerve. What did he want? I soon found out.

"We want you to tell him," he said.

I shook my head.

"Oh, no. No. Absolutely not. To him, I'm just a former subordinate. It would be an insult for me to tell him such a thing—and he wouldn't accept it. I won't do it—can't do it."

Mitchell thought for a moment, then nodded, perhaps more in acceptance than agreement.

"All right," he sighed. "I guess I'll have to tell him myself."

Months later, only a week before Hoover died, I had lunch with him and Tolson at the Waldorf Astoria. We talked pleasantly about old times, and the director also talked cheerfully about his future plans for the bureau. He made no mention of retirement or a new position as director emeritus. I smiled to myself. John Mitchell hadn't had the guts to tell him either.

On May 2, 1972, Tom Moton, Hoover's chauffeur, was in the kitchen of Hoover's home; he had been there since 7:30 A.M., waiting for Hoover to call for him to go upstairs and carry down the director's briefcases, which he brought home with him every night. Over the years, it had been the same routine. Moton would escort Hoover to the car. They would drive to Tolson's home at the Dorchester apartments and pick him up. Then they would go on to the office. An observer could stand on any street corner and set his watch as they passed by. That is, until the last years—when Tolson had been ill, and Hoover had begun to slow down.

This morning the old man was even later. Annie, the housekeeper, was a little worried. She remarked that she hadn't even heard the shower water.

At 8:45, the fifth floor at FBI headquarters was relatively quiet. Hoover hadn't yet arrived. Assistant Director Tom Bishop, head of the Crime Records Division, was briefing his staff on the director's appointments. Two people were scheduled to meet with Hoover that morning. One was Lynda Bird Robb, older daughter of President Lyndon Johnson and at that time a reporter, who was flying up from Charlottesville, Virginia, to write a magazine article on Hoover's two Cairn terriers. She was scheduled for 10:30. It would be an easy interview. Hoover had known Lynda since she was a child, and the conversation would be restricted to dogs. No need for a briefing.

Shortly before 9:00, Bishop's phone rang. It was Helen Gandy.

"Mr. Bishop," she said, "cancel all of the director's appointments. He won't be in."

"But, Miss Gandy," he protested, "Lynda Robb has an appointment a little more than an hour from now. She's on her way. Do you want me to cancel that one?"

"Wait a minute," she said. Bishop could hear her talking to a man nearby. "Yes," she said, "cancel that one too."

Bishop slammed down the phone.

"What's the matter with the director?" he said to the four aides in the room. "I think he's in the office, because I heard Miss Gandy talking to someone. What in God's name can I say to Lynda Robb? She flies all the way up here and we tell her to forget it!"

At that moment John Mohr stepped into Bishop's office and closed the door. Bishop started to complain about the call he'd just received, but one look at Mohr's face stopped him cold.

"What I'm going to tell you is not to leave this room."

Five heads nodded.

"He died last night," said Mohr, visibly fighting to control his voice.

"Who died last night?" Bishop asked.

"The director."

"Holy shit!" said one of the aides.

"The gag rule is on," Mohr said, "because the White House wants to make the announcement later on this morning."

After the first shock, Bishop's mind immediately turned to practical matters.

"Lynda Robb will hit the door shortly. What do I say?"

"Put her in an adjoining room," said Mohr. "Don't tell her anything. Play for time. Say the director's been delayed."

I was in Indianapolis on business for Pepsico, the company I'd joined after leaving the bureau almost two years earlier. At 9:30 that morning, the attorney general, Richard G. Kleindienst, called me in Indiana, after getting my number from our corporate headquarters in New York.

"Deke," he said, "the director died last night, apparently of a coronary. His body wasn't found until this morning."

J. Edgar Hoover dead?

I couldn't believe it. He was a permanent and indestructible institution of the American government. I never thought that he would ever really die.

"Nobody knows about this except Hoover's household staff, a few top FBI people, and me. Please don't say anything until we issue a press release at noon."

"Of course not," I said hoarsely.

"Deke, I'm going to recommend to President Nixon that you be appointed interim director."

I started to speak, but he interrupted me.

"I know you don't want to return permanently, but please consider coming back as acting director. It's important that we have somebody of your experience and stature."

I heaved a sigh. All sorts of problems came to mind, not the least of which was what Barbara would think about making another move. At this stage, she was uppermost in my mind.

"In the meantime," Kleindienst said, "whom would you recommend to hold the organization together?"

"John Mohr," I said instantly. "You couldn't find a better man."

"A good choice," he said. "I'll get right on it. Could you call me back shortly after noon? By then the news will be public and I'll know a little more about the president's frame of mind."

At 12:15 I called the attorney general back. He was apologetic. He had discussed my possible assignment with President Nixon, who had another candidate in mind as acting director. Kleindienst, a good friend, promised to give me the details later.

"Let me know if there's anything I can do," I said.

"I think it might help if you could fly to Washington. If you were on the scene, it might be easier to get you named director. Maybe we can get him to change his mind."

I hesitated.

"I'm grateful for your support," I said, "but I'm not sure I want to be in the running. Frankly, I'm not sure I could take the salary cut."

He told me that he understood. I found out later that Kleindienst had strongly recommended to President Nixon that I be appointed and installed immediately as director of the FBI. A short time later, John Mitchell—Nixon's former campaign manager and then-attorney general—called and asked me to meet him for lunch at the Wall Street Club in New York City. There he told me that the president wanted me to become director. Two days later we met again at the same place, and I told him that I declined. Patrick Gray, from the Department of Justice, was named acting director shortly thereafter.

Back at FBI headquarters the phones were beginning to ring. The neighbors had tipped off the press that something strange had happened at the director's house. Reporters began to ask if anything had happened to Mr. Hoover. The people in Crime Records offered vague and unsatisfying answers.

Meanwhile, Lynda Robb had arrived and was waiting in an office, increasingly puzzled by the postponement of her interview. John Mohr considered the risks involved and finally decided she should be told. The agent who had met her and welcomed her to the FBI went back and apologized for the delay.

"Can you keep a secret?" he asked.

"Yes," she said, a little puzzled.

"We have some bad news. Mr. Hoover is dead."

She gasped, then murmured, "Oh, I'm so sorry."

After a minute of awkward conversation, she left FBI headquarters. Once outside, she headed for the nearest public telephone and put in a call to Johnson City, Texas. It wasn't exactly breaking her promise to tell the former president of the United States what she'd just heard.

Shortly before noon, the White House made its announcement; and FBI headquarters became bedlam. Reporters, camera crews, TV anchors stormed up to the fifth floor, which soon looked like the New York Stock Exchange on Black Friday. People were weeping, cursing, and shoving each other. The press accused staff of withholding information, when in fact the bureau knew very little of the details surrounding the death.

To avoid undue attention, Hoover's body had been wrapped in a blanket, carried to the car, and transported to Gawler's Funeral Home on Wisconsin Avenue. That afternoon, John Mohr asked that all who wished to pay their final respects and view the remains go to Gawler's that evening. He knew that, at the insistence of the White House and members of Congress, the body would soon be transferred to the Capitol Rotunda, where Hoover would lie in state, just as had John Kennedy and previous presidents throughout the nation's history.

Those who went to the funeral home were shocked at what they found. The body, lying in a magnificent bronze casket, had been placed in a second-story chapel—softly lit and banked with flowers. Hoover was dressed in a dark suit, wearing his Legion of Honor medal and his favorite sapphire ring. Yet his body seemed frail and spent, as if he had shrunk to gnomic size in death. The usual black coloring had been flushed from his thinning gray hair, and his customary ruddy face was now an ashen mask, cheeks and neck swollen. Several staff members visited Helen Gandy that night and suggested that the casket be closed.

Time had dropped its final veil over the face of this mysterious man who had been loved and hated, respected and feared, honored and condemned. In life he had moved among the great figures of his day, the protectors of the public good as well as society's most destructive enemies. But in the end, like all of us, he had died alone.

J. Edgar Hoover was a rare individual. He had a nobility of purpose. His early vision and acquired prestige drove the FBI into becoming the world's foremost law enforcement agency. The new innovations introduced under his watch—the centralization of fingerprints for use by all authorized police organizations; the famed FBI Laboratory also used by such organizations; the solution of crimes through scientific analysis; the intense and constant training of agents and police in new methods; the National Crime Information Center—not only brought higher standards to his profession, but forever branded him as the Father of modern day law enforcement.

Part of his success was due to the era in which he came to prominence. He then capitalized on this foundation. He was the right man at the right time. Monastic in being, the FBI was largely his life.

Hoover always wanted strong and forceful men around him and he was quick to grasp and implement their new ideas. Still, his men usually kept their distance in a formal, disciplined atmosphere. Relationships with him were not balanced; those around him had to earn their position through hard work and sacrifice. The rules were always his.

America fortunately has had many such great men. Their human frailties, egos, and sometimes greed, while obvious to those around them, are outweighed by the tremendous assets given to the institution they served and their profession as a whole.

History will judge them accordingly.

Bibliographical Note

PERHAPS BECAUSE OF MY FBI TRAINING, I have been blessed with a pretty good memory. I am able to recall with some degree of accuracy names, dates, and the specific details of cases that were closed 40 to 50 years ago. However, even when I was younger, I kept detailed notes during conversations and immediately translated them into memos that were placed in FBI files. So when I decided to write this book, I sent a request to the bureau under the Freedom of Information Act, asking for every bit of correspondence in which I was involved heavily. I waited for weeks; and when the material came, I understood why the fulfillment of my request had taken so long: They sent me more than 6,000 separate items, many of them irrelevant, some of them invaluable as primary sources for this narrative.

Much of what I have written is based on these detailed notes and memoranda, amplified by my own recollection of many of the events. Indeed, few memoirs are based on such a specific and detailed record of the past, because most people haven't been required to keep meticulous notes on every day's important activities (since most people didn't work for J. Edgar Hoover). At the time, the note-taking and memo-writing seemed dull and time-consuming tasks. But when I began this book, I was grateful for all those countless hours spent decades ago.

As I began research on the project, I decided not to confine my narrative to what I had experienced myself, particularly since others had dealt with a wide range of questions concerning Mr. Hoover that didn't always involve me directly—his private life, his relationship with Clyde Tolson, his childhood. As a consequence, I have read almost all of the biographical materials—magazine articles as well as books. I did not find them uniformly valuable so I have been selective in my use of them—probably focusing on the best and the worst.

I hope I've given credit within the text to writers to whom I am indebted for specific details and quotations. If I have overlooked anyone, I apologize. In some cases I have included a reference within the text itself.

Chapter Two contains some anecdotes concerning Mrs. Roosevelt and John F. Kennedy that were recorded at a reunion of respected and experienced retired FBI agents in Purchase, New York. I was the host; and after lunch, with everyone in agreement, we turned on the tape and started talking. I have changed only a few words here and there to make the narrative flow, but the flavor and meaning of the original yarns remain intact—a genuine example of oral history.

In Chapter Five, I have used quotations and information from a well-researched article by Ovid Demaris ("The Private Life of J. Edgar Hoover," *Esquire,* September, 1974, 71-78, 161-165). Demaris' interviews with Hoover's nieces and other unlikely sources added an important dimension to my understanding of Hoover.

In Chapter Six, many of the details and quotations come from my old friend Jim Bishop's excellent book, *The Day Kennedy Was Shot* (New York, 1968). I make no apology for drawing so heavily on Jim's work because I originally supplied him with much of the raw material from which he fashioned his own best-selling narrative. In addition, I used the Warren Commission report—"The

Assassination of President Kennedy" (New York Times Edition, 1964).

In Chapter Eight, I have relied on an old friend, Don Whitehead, whose *Attack on Terror: The FBI Against the Ku Klux Klan in Mississippi* (New York, 1970) provided me with a substantial source for my own narrative. In the flyleaf of my copy of his book, Whitehead wrote: "To Deke—who, more than anyone else, made this book possible in the last months of a distinguished FBI career."

Chapter 12 is based in large part on FBI reports and internal memos. However, I did make use of essays from an excellent but little-known collection on student unrest, *Seeds of Anarchy: A Study of Campus Revolution,* edited by Frederick Wilhelmsen (Argus Academic Press, Dallas, 1969). Particularly helpful were essays by John Meyer, Jeffrey Hart, and then-Governor Ronald Reagan of California. I also derived information from *Secrecy and Power,* by Richard Gid Powers (New York, 1987).

In Chapter 13 I have relied, for the most part, on FBI reports, which are extensive and detailed. However, I did gain information from *The Valachi Papers* by Peter Maas (New York, 1969) and from *The FBI Story* by Don Whitehead (New York, 1956). Also, as the narrative suggests, I drew heavily on conversations with former agents who were involved in the investigation of organized crime.

Finally, I am indebted to a host of ex-agents, including those already mentioned above, for information and helpful suggestions. As they read this book, they will recognize their own contributions, which are too numerous for me to acknowledge individually. I hope they will all write memoirs of their own.

Index

role in King assassination investigation, 225-226
safety concerns regarding Democratic Convention of 1964, 3-9
taping of White House conversations, 380-381
use of FBI, 376-394, 404-405, 409
and Vietnam War, 216-217, 380, 395-396
waiving of mandatory retirement age for Hoover, 14, 110-112
Yarborough-Johnson feud, 361-363
Johnson, Paul, 182-183, 197
Johnson, Tom, story on Oswald threats against Hosty, 158-160
Jones, Jim, role in surveillance of Chennault and South Vietnamese Embassy, 399-401, 403-404
Jones, Milton A., Liddy's practical joke on, 96
Jones, Wilmer Faye, 179-180
Jonsson, Eric, role in investigation of J. F. Kennedy assassination, 151-152
Jordan, James, involvement in slaying of civil rights workers, 196-197
Jordan, Tom, 405
Journal of the American Medical Association, review of J. F. Kennedy autopsy findings, 156

K
Karpis, Alvin, 93-94
Katzenbach, Nicholas, 55-57, 398
Kearns, Carroll, 357-358
Kefauver, Estes
dealings with the FBI, 354-355
Hoover's opinion of, 354
relationship with Hoover's FBI, 17
Kellerman, Roy, role in investigation of J. F. Kennedy assassination, 130
Kelley, Clarence
hears story on Oswald threats against Hosty, 158
named FBI director, 416
Kennedy, Devereaux, role in student movement, 280-281
Kennedy, Jacqueline, 114, 115
Kennedy, John F.
assassination of, 4, 5, 18, 113-141, 149-153
conspiracy theories on assassination, 153-161

FBI files on, 30, 37-39
relationship with Hoover, 379
relationship with Johnson, 376-377, 382
Ruby's reaction to assassination of, 143-148, 149
warns King of links to Communist party, 214
Warren Commission report on assassination, 148-149
Yarborough-Johnson feud and, 363
Kennedy, Robert
authorization of wiretapping of King, 213, 214-215
demands to lower bureau admission standards, 91
funeral of, 250
introduces DeLoach to President Kennedy, 118
Maas' relationship with, 78
presidential election of 1968, 396
receives notification of brother's assassination, 116
relationship with congressmen, 360, 362
relationship with Hoover, 379
relationship with Hoover's FBI, 11, 25, 47-59
relationship with Johnson, 379, 381-384
role in civil rights movement, 164, 175
role in Drummond spy case, 268-269
role in fighting organized crime, 314-316
The Kennedy Assassination Tapes— A Rebuttal to the Acoustical Evidence, 158
Kessler, Ronald
on FBI files, 27
on Hoover's relationship with Congress, 34-35
Kidnappings
FBI jurisdiction over, 18, 19
FBI procedures, 323-324
Lindbergh baby kidnapping, 19
Mackle kidnapping investigation, 319-349
King, Coretta
Clark's condolences to, 229
receives FBI tape, 211
King, Martin Luther, Jr.

American Left's perception of
Hoover's feud with, 91
assassination investigation, 223- 257
assassination of, 219-220, 223
civil rights goals, 163, 199-200, 201-
202, 214-216, 218-219
Communist party links, 202, 213-
215, 217-218, 284
Congress and, 363-365
criticism of FBI, 177, 198, 200-201,
208
FBI tape of, 211-213
March on Washington, 200
meeting with Hoover, 207-211
Memphis labor march, 218-219
New Left and, 229, 240, 280
praise of FBI, 198, 208-209
promiscuity of, 202-203, 211-213
public perception of Hoover's feud
with, 52
relationship with Hoover, 199-220,
256-257, 363-364, 365
relationship with Hoover's FBI, 17
Vietnam War views, 216-217
Kirkland, Ernest, 168, 169
Kissinger, Henry, 408
Kleindienst, Richard G., 415-416
Klein's Sporting Goods, Inc., 131
Krist, Gary Steven
conviction and sentencing, 348- 349
involvement in Mackle kidnapping,
330-333, 334-335, 339, 340-347
Ku Klux Klan
civil rights movement and, 163, 164-
165, 176-178, 215
COINTELPRO tactics against, 176-
177, 292
involvement in slaying of civil rights
workers, 167, 175, 176-
178, 191-193, 196-197, 198, 209
treatment of Wilmer Faye Jones, 179-
180
Kuchel, Thomas, dealings with the FBI,
355-356
Kusch, Lee, role in Mackle kidnapping
investigation, 334

L
Lacey, Robert, on Hoover-Tolson
relationship, 79-81
Lansky, Meyer
blackmail activities, 77, 78-81, 302-
303
FBI surveillance of, 300-301, 303
organized crime role, 300-301, 313
Lash, Joseph P., relationship with E.
Roosevelt, 43-44
Lausche, Frank, dealings with the
FBI, 369
Lawson, James, 166
Lawson, Winston, role in investiga-
tion of J. F. Kennedy assassination,
138, 140, 141
Lee, Robert E. (Inspector), DeLoach
interview with, 84
Lennon, John, 285
Levison, Stanley, Communist influence
on King, 213-215, 217, 218, 219,
284
Liddy, G. Gordon
on Hoover's relationship with
Congress, 36-37
imitation of Hoover's signature, 96-
97
memo suggesting firing of Hoover,
411
Light, Harold, escort of James Earl
Ray, 253, 254
Lincoln, Abraham, 296
Lindbergh baby kidnapping, 19
*Little Man: Meyer Lansky and the
Gangster Life,* 79-81
Look magazine, King's call for
demonstrations, 219
Loraine Hotel, 223, 224
Lowmyer, Harvey. *See* Ray, James Earl
Lucas, Jim, 181
Lucchese, Thomas, 313
Lucchese crime family, 309, 310
Luciano, Charles "Lucky," 301-302,
313
Ludlum, Robert, description of Tolson,
69, 71
Lundberg, George D., comments on
J. F. Kennedy autopsy, 156

M
Maas, Peter, 78-81, 314
Mackle, Barbara Jane, kidnapping

Acknowledgements

I WOULD BE SAILING under false colors if credit for this book were not given where due.

My deepest appreciation is expressed to a number of friends and acquaintances who have given generously of their time to be of considerable assistance in writing this book:

Al Regnery, Publisher, who showed great faith in my original manuscript and who lent constant encouragement; Jeff Carneal, President of Eagle Publishing and Richard Vigilante, Executive Editor, whose constant belief in the book, and whose great assistance and ability was most helpful.

Tom Landess, a former college professor and writer, whose help in research, advice, and "polishing" my efforts greatly "pushed" me onward.

Former Special Agents and FBI Executives Fern Stukenbroeker, Larry Heim, Donald G. Hanning, Buck Revell, William G. Simon, Ben "Reverend" Fulton, Bob Gemberling, Barry Hoffman, Thomas B. Coll, Marlin Johnson, Sam DeVine, Administrative Assistant Marie Newsome, and Attorney Richard Woods.

Former Federal Judge and FBI Director William Webster. The many current FBI Agents and clerical personnel who, under the Freedom of Information Act, furnished hundreds of memoranda from FBI files.

And to Ambassador Faith Whittlesey goes my highest appreciation.